A

GOOD PROVIDER

IS ONE

WHO LEAVES

ALSO BY JASON DEPARLE

*American Dream: Three Women, Ten Kids,
and a Nation's Drive to End Welfare*

A

GOOD PROVIDER

IS ONE

WHO LEAVES

ONE FAMILY AND MIGRATION
IN THE 21ST CENTURY

Jason DeParle

VIKING

VIKING
An imprint of Penguin Random House LLC
penguinrandomhouse.com

Library of Congress Cataloging-in-Publication Data

Names: DeParle, Jason, author.
Title: A good provider is one who leaves : one family and
migration in the 21st century / Jason DeParle.
Description: [New York, N.Y.] : Viking, [2019] |
Includes bibliographical references and index. |
Identifiers: LCCN 2019011071 (print) | LCCN 2019017314 (ebook) |
ISBN 9781984877758 (ebook) | ISBN 9780670785926 (hardcover)
Subjects: LCSH: Comodas, Rosalie. | Comodas, Rosalie—Family. |
Filipinos—United States—Biography. | Immigrants—United States—
Biography. | Filipinos—Employment—Foreign countries. | Foreign workers,
Filipino—United States. | United States—Emigration and immigration—
History—21st century. | Emigration and immigration—History—21st century.
Classification: LCC E184.F4 (ebook) | LCC E184.F4 D47 2019 (print) |
DDC 305.899/21—dc23
LC record available at https://lccn.loc.gov/2019011071

Printed in the United States of America
1   3   5   7   9   10   8   6   4   2

DESIGNED BY MEIGHAN CAVANAUGH

For my parents,

James and Joan DeParle

Home has its charms, and native land has its charms, but hunger, oppression and destitution will dissolve these charms and send men in search of new countries and new homes.

—Frederick Douglass, 1869

A good provider is one who leaves.

—Peachy Portagana Salazar, 2006

CONTENTS

PART II

HERE

THE PORTAGANA FAMILY

VENANCIO PORTAGANA — **ASUNCION YAYA PORTAGANA**

TITA (b. 1946)

Husband, Emet Comodas, worked in Saudi Arabia

5 of 5 children worked abroad in Saudi Arabia, the United Arab Emirates, Singapore, Qatar, and the United States

ROSALIE COMODAS VILLANUEVA (b. 1971)

Worked in Saudi Arabia, the United Arab Emirates, and is now a nurse in Texas

Husband, Chris Villanueva (b. 1975), worked in Saudi Arabia, the United Arab Emirates, and the United States

3 children:
Kristine (b. 2003)
Lara (b. 2005)
Dominique (b. 2006)

MIGUEL

Did not work abroad

0 of 4 children worked abroad

GLORIA

Did not work abroad

3 of 3 children worked abroad in Singapore, the United Arab Emirates, and Taiwan

TESS ALISCAD (b. 1972)

"The Facebook Mom"

FORTZ

Worked in Saudi Arabia and Oman

4 of 4 children worked abroad in Oman, the United Arab Emirates, and on a cruise ship

VIRGINIA

Worked in Saudi Arabia

Immigrated to Canada

3 of 3 children worked abroad; 2 moved to Winnipeg, 1 worked on a cargo ship

FERING	BANDOY	PEACHY	PABLITO	ENYANG	CHANG IDHAY
Worked in Saudi Arabia	Worked in Saudi Arabia	Husband, Weny Salazar, worked in Saudi Arabia	Worked in Saudi Arabia	Husband, Bobby Avilas, worked in Saudi Arabia	Worked in the United Arab Emirates
	Wife, Aurora, worked in Saudi Arabia				Husband, Ray Alcantara, worked in Saudi Arabia
2 of 7 children worked abroad in the United Arab Emirates	2 of 4 children worked abroad in Saudi Arabia and Oman	2 of 3 children worked abroad in the United Arab Emirates and on cruise ships	1 of 3 children worked abroad in Saudi Arabia	1 of 3 children worked abroad in the United Arab Emirates	1 of 2 children worked abroad in the United Arab Emirates

ARIANE SALAZAR-NAVARETTE (b. 1982)

and husband

MANU NAVARETTE (b. 1980)

Worked abroad as cruise ship workers

MAIN CHARACTERS:
Tita Portagana Comodas and Emet Comodas
Rosalie Comodas Villanueva, Chris Villanueva, and their children
    Kristine, Lara, and Dominique
Tess Aliscad
Ariane Salazar-Navarette and Manu Navarette

FIRST GENERATION: 9 of 11 Portagana siblings worked abroad—or had a spouse who did—in Saudi Arabia, the United Arab Emirates, Oman, and Canada

SECOND GENERATION: 24 of 41 cousins worked abroad in Saudi Arabia, the United Arab Emirates, Oman, Qatar, Singapore, Taiwan, Canada, the United States, and on cruise ships

A

GOOD PROVIDER

IS ONE

WHO LEAVES

Finding Jesus in the Slums

Thirty years ago, I was a young reporter in Manila with an interest in shantytowns, the warrens of scrap-wood shacks that covered a third of the city and much of the developing world. I called the Philippines's most famous nun, who lived in a slum called Leveriza. Though I didn't say so, I was hoping she would help me move in.

Sister Christine Tan was a friend of the new president, Cory Aquino, and busy on a commission rewriting the constitution.

"Call me back in a few months," she snapped.

Hoping for a quicker audience, I explained that I worked with another nun in her order. Apparently, they weren't friends. "That's a mistake!" she said. "Meet me tomorrow morning, outside the Manila Zoo."

Raised in affluence, educated in the United States, Sister Christine had gained her renown as a critic of Ferdinand Marcos, the American-backed dictator who had proclaimed martial law in 1972 and plundered the country with the help of his shoe-happy wife, Imelda. "I hate their deceitfulness, their sham, their greed, their avarice, their lies, the deliberate trouncing of our rights and the burying of our souls," she once said. The Vatican had told her to tone things down. The police had threatened arrest. Sister Christine had defied them all and gone off to find Jesus in the slums. At fifty-six, she had a smooth, grandmotherly face, which made her look gentle, though she wasn't.

"Are you CIA? . . . You wouldn't tell me if you were, would you?" she began. When she called herself "anti-imperialist," it sounded like an accusation.

"The poor are magnificent people, unlike the rich," she said, but boarding in Leveriza wouldn't work. Most of the shanties lacked toilets, and Americans can't live without them. A host would feel obligated to serve pricey food. I'd be a burden. She denounced the United States for keeping military bases in the Philippines, then suddenly waved a hand above her head. "That's all up here," meaning her views of American policy. "Somehow, we have to build links between the First World and the Third World." If I returned in a few days, she'd see what she could do.

Sunk into a mudflat near Manila Bay, Leveriza held fifteen thousand people in a labyrinth of alleys behind the whitewashed walls of one of Imelda's old beautification campaigns. Children played beside listing shacks. Women squatted over tubs of laundry. Roosters crowed. Sanitation mostly meant "flying saucers," bundles of waste wrapped in newspaper and flung in the surrounding canals.

I figured that Sister Christine would use the time before my return to approach a potential host or two. Instead, she led me into the maze and auctioned me off on the spot. I knew just enough Tagalog to realize our first prospect was aghast. "*Hindi pwede*, Sister!" *It's not possible.* The second candidate smiled more but ducked as rapidly. The third was too astonished to respond. Tita Comodas was forty years old and sitting at her window in an old housedress, selling sugar and eggs. A scruffy American looking to rent floor space had the appeal of a biblical plague.

Her thin patience exhausted, Sister Christine left. "If you don't want him, pass him on to someone else. And don't cook him anything special—if he gets sick, too bad!"

I don't know who was more frightened, Tita or me. Neighborhood entertainment was scarce; we drew a crowd.

"Ask him if he eats rice!"

"Ask him if he knows how to use a spoon!"

"Ask him if he wants to marry a Filipina!"

Tita had a boisterous neighbor who fed her questions and whooped at the answers. But Tita struggled to see the humor—after all, it was her house. The reasons to decline were many. Her husband was working in Saudi Arabia . . . she was busy raising five kids . . . she already had two relatives sleeping on the floor . . . her English was limited and my Tagalog was worse . . . Who knew what problems a strange foreigner might cause? Then she surrendered to what she took as Sister Christine's request and said I could move in. I stayed on and off for eight months and made a lifelong friend.

The eldest of eleven children raised in a farm family, she had quit school after sixth grade and moved to Manila as a teenager to work in a factory. Marriage and children followed, with home a series of Leveriza hovels, each as forlorn as the last. Her husband, Emet, had hustled a job cleaning the pool at a government sports complex and held it for nearly two decades. On the spectrum of Filipino poverty, that alone marked him as a man of modest fortune. But a monthly salary of $50 wasn't enough to keep his family fed. Their eldest daughter had a congenital heart defect that turned her lips blue and fingernails black and who needed care that he couldn't afford. After years of worrying over her frail physique, Emet had dropped to his knees and asked God for a decision: take her or let him have her. God had answered in a mysterious way. Soon after, Emet got an offer to clean pools in Saudi Arabia. He would make ten times his Manila wage but live five thousand miles away in an Islamic autocracy when stories of abused laborers were rife. He accepted on the spot. By the time I arrived, years later, his daughter had more medicine and the shanty had a toilet.

Up before dawn to cook the breakfast rice, Tita was a weary

homemaker, trudging to the market every day and scrubbing her hands raw over laundry. But she was also a lieutenant in Sister Christine's slum improvement group, a small army of housecoat revolutionaries that ran Bible studies, sold subsidized rice, joined political protests, and found strength in the nun's message, counterintuitive amid the squalor, that Jesus had a special love for the poor. Tita's life revolved around eggs: she bought two thousand a week to sell in the group's co-op stores and stacked them under a kitchen light in an attempt, only partly successful, to protect them from the rats. The enterprise was metaphoric: in the post-Marcos Philippines, her hopes and the country's were equally fragile. Despite a limited education, or perhaps because of it, Tita was full of questions. She read English newspapers with a Tagalog dictionary and asked me about the news. *"Ano ang imperyalismo?"* she asked me. "I'm always hearing, 'No to imperialism!' but I don't know what means 'imperialism.'"

Tita's oldest child was an indifferent student of modest ambition who spent his spare time on the family farm. The second was sick. The two youngest boys were spindle-legged scamps, busy chasing roosters through the alleys. That left Tita's middle child, Rosalie, her confidence keeper and chief helpmate.

A slight, shy, doe-eyed girl, mature beyond her fifteen years, Rosalie was easy to overlook. Her religiosity cloaked her ambition. In addition to school and chores, she was a stalwart of Sister Christine's youth group; when it staged plays, Rosalie played the nun. Noting Rosalie's strength and faith, Sister Christine saw the makings of a real nun, but Rosalie had another idea. There was a nursing school near Leveriza, and the students looked smart and clean in their starched white dresses. Filipino nurses went far in life. Some went as far as the United States.

IN 1965 (six years before Rosalie was born), Lyndon Johnson sat beside the Statue of Liberty and signed an immigration law he both celebrated

as a civil rights landmark and dismissed as a measure of little consequence. Johnson said he was ending a "cruel and enduring wrong" by
abolishing quotas from the 1920s that banned most nonwhite immigrants. Passed in an age of peak immigration, aimed at southern and
eastern Europeans—the nonwhites of the day—the quotas had kept immigration to a trickle for four decades. Johnson praised the new law for
ending discrimination but insisted it wouldn't attract more people or
change America's ethnic composition. "This bill that we sign today is
not a revolutionary bill. It does not affect the lives of millions. It will
not reshape the structure of our daily lives, or really add importantly to
either our wealth or our power." He added, "The days of unlimited immigration are past."

Johnson was spectacularly wrong. In the decades that followed, the
foreign-born share of the population soared to near-record highs, and
immigration set the United States on course to become a majority-
minority nation. The United States counts more than forty-four million
immigrants, nearly five times as many as in 1965, and as many as the next
four countries combined. The United States has more immigrants than
Canada has Canadians. Nearly 90 percent come from the developing
world, with eleven million Mexicans trailed, respectively, by Indians,
Chinese, Filipinos, Salvadorans, Vietnamese, Cubans, Dominicans, Koreans, and Guatemalans. Non-Hispanic whites, 83 percent of America
when Johnson signed the bill, account for 62 percent today. Much attention gets paid to the share of immigrants, about a quarter, who are here
illegally and less to the fact that most come through authorized channels.
With one in four children in the United States an immigrant or the child
of one, it's no exaggeration to say their future is America's.

In a thousand ways, large and small, Johnson wouldn't recognize the
society his pen stroke helped create. Immigrants brought a hundred languages to the Des Moines public schools, turned the South Side of Mil-
waukee from Polish to Latino, and raised mosques in the Washington
suburbs. In twenty-five years, the foreign-born population of Greater

Atlanta rose nearly 1,200 percent. Immigration changed the way Americans eat and the way they pray. It powered the rise of Silicon Valley and redrew the electoral map. It bred cosmopolitanism. It bred resentment. It widened class divides between the affluent, who are most likely to benefit from migration, and the less privileged, who are more likely to bear its costs. It made America more vibrant but less united, wealthier but less equal, more creative but more volatile. Shockingly, the demographic upheaval brought Barack Obama. More shockingly, it brought Donald Trump.

The United States is not alone. About 258 million migrants are scattered across the globe, and they support a population back home as big if not bigger. Were these half billion or so people to form their own country, it would rank as the world's third largest. Just since the turn of the century, their numbers have grown nearly 50 percent. While the movements of the nineteenth century were largely transatlantic, what stands out about migration today is its ubiquity. Ireland elected its first African-born mayor. Mongolians do scut work in Prague. The roster of recent Miss Israels includes one Ethiopian-born. "I went to bed in one country and woke up in a different one," wrote the Irish novelist Roddy Doyle, who peoples his stories of multiethnic Dublin with characters like Fat Gandhi, the Celtic Tandoori King. A few decades ago, migration seemed so irrelevant to international affairs that doctoral students in political science couldn't find professors to guide dissertations. Now it threatens to tear apart the European Union.

My own light bulb moment came in learning that remittances—the sums migrants send home—are three times the world's foreign aid budgets combined. Migration is the world's largest antipoverty program, a homegrown version of foreign aid. Mexico earns more from remittances than from oil. Sri Lanka earns more from remittances than from tea. About $477 billion a year now flows home to the developing world, an increase of more than sixfold in the twenty-first century.

Yet competing with the literature of gain is a parallel literature of loss. About half the world's migrants are women, many of whom care for children abroad while leaving their own children home. "Your loved ones across that ocean . . ." Nadine Sarreal, a Filipina poet warns,

> *Will sit at breakfast and try not to gaze*
> *Where you would sit at the table*
> *Meals now divided by five*
> *Instead of six, don't feed an emptiness*

Earlier waves of globalization, the movement of money and goods, were shaped by mediating protocols. The International Monetary Fund regulates finance. The World Trade Organization regularizes trade. The movement of people, the most intimate form of globalization, has the fewest rules. There is no World Migration Organization to say who has the right to migrate or what rights a migrant should have.

Migration disquiets the West, but demographic logic suggests it will grow. Aging societies need workers. Workers in poor countries need jobs. Rising incomes in the developing world give more people the means to move and instant communication spreads word of opportunity. Refugee populations have soared. Economically, incentives to move are profound. An unskilled migrant in the nineteenth century might triple his wage by moving to the States; his counterpart today can multiply his earnings six or seven times (even after accounting for the cost of living), a pay raise twice as high.

No country does more to promote migration than the Philippines, where the government trains and markets overseas workers, whom presidents celebrate as "heroes." More than two million Filipinos depart each year, enough to fill a dozen or more 747s a day. About one Filipino worker in seven works abroad, and the $32 billion that Filipinos send home accounts for 10 percent of the gross domestic product. Migration is to the Philippines what cars once were to Detroit: the civil religion. The *Philippine Daily Inquirer* runs hundreds of stories a year on Overseas Filipino Workers. Half have the fevered feel of gold rush ads. Half sound like human rights complaints.

"Remittances Seen to Set New Record."

"Happy Days Here Again for Real Estate Sector."

"5 Dead OFWs in Saudi."

"We Slept with Dog, Ate Leftovers for $200/month."

I WASN'T THINKING ABOUT migration when I arrived in Leveriza. I was thinking about rats and eggs, about how people like Tita endure such dire poverty. Migration was part of the answer. Emet came home during my visit and did all he could to stay. But he couldn't earn a living in Manila. Forced to choose between living with his children and supporting them, he returned to Saudi Arabia, a cycle he sustained for nearly twenty years.

What started as an act of desperation became a way of life. All five of Tita and Emet's children grew up to become overseas workers, and they are part of a close, extended family that stretches across the globe. Of the eleven siblings in Tita's generation, nine went abroad or had spouses who did. So far, twenty-four of their forty-one children have done the same. Most of what could happen to a migrant, good or bad, has happened to someone in the clan. Some lost marriages; one lost a limb. Others replaced thatched huts with cement block homes and hung their children's college degrees on the freshly painted walls. Tita has a grade-school education, but her sister Peachy earned a doctorate, with money that her daughter made cleaning cabins on a cruise ship. Peachy's husband's years abroad nearly destroyed their marriage; she understands migration's social costs. But when I asked if the sacrifices had been worth it, she articulated the unofficial family creed: "A good provider is one who leaves."

Soon after I left Leveriza, Rosalie started nursing school, which was possible (if barely) because Emet was away cleaning Saudi Arabian pools. She was twenty-four when she landed her first overseas job, at a hospital outside Mecca. By the standards of foreign workers in the Persian Gulf, Rosalie was in luck: nurses earn much more money, and suffer less abuse, than the migrants who go in much greater numbers as nannies, cooks, drivers, or maids. But Rosalie left nursing school with an overriding goal, to reach the United States. Two decades later, she was still trying, working in Abu Dhabi, along with her husband, and worried that she had become a stranger to her three young kids, who were living with Tita and Emet back in the Philippines. Then a hurricane slammed the Texas Gulf Coast and left behind a nursing shortage. Rosalie got her chance.

In 2012, I met her in Manila and flew with her to Galveston. Her husband, Chris, followed five months later with Kristine, Precious Lara, and Dominique (ages nine, seven, and six), who spoke little English and hadn't lived with their parents in years. They had to learn a new country and form a new family at the same time. I tracked their experiences on a near-daily basis for three years, following Rosalie in her hospital and the kids in the Galveston schools. Migration has become the defining story of the twenty-first century; by the accident of an old friendship, I had an intimate view. This was a journalistic endeavor but not an entirely arm's-length one; occasionally my presence shaped events I was trying to record. But our long relationship affords a perspective that conventional deadlines don't afford. Rosalie was a fifteen-year-old schoolgirl when I met her and a forty-eight-year-old nurse, wife, and mother as her story goes to print.

The politics of migration, at home and abroad, have radically changed since the project began. Britain voted to leave the EU, the Far Right gained a hold on the German Bundestag, and the United States elected a president who denounces immigrants in terms no president has ever used. The Trump administration muscled through a travel ban aimed at Muslims, separated mothers and children at the border, cut refugee admissions to the lowest level in four decades, assailed protections for immigrants brought to the United States illegally as kids, and erased the words "Nation of Immigrants" from the work of the immigration agency. No one can fault President Trump for hiding his views. He cut a 2018 campaign ad too racially inflammatory for Fox News. Among the labels he's attached to immigrants are "drug dealer," "terrorist," "animal," "gang member," "criminal," "rapist," and "snake."

Little about Rosalie, a four-foot, eleven-inch nurse, evokes the main American controversies. She never crossed a border illegally. She doesn't sport gang tattoos. To the challenges of assimilation, she brings advantages the poor and unauthorized lack. She's the kind of immigrant who is largely invisible in political debate but increasingly common. Since 2008, the United States has attracted more Asians than Latin Americans, and nearly half of the newcomers, like Rosalie, have college degrees. Every corner of America has an immigrant like her.

In a world where migration is a growing norm, it is tempting to call Rosalie's experience an ordinary one, propelled by a common mix of hope and doubt. But nothing about an immigrant's life is truly ordinary. The journey from a Manila slum to a Texas hospital spanned eighty-five hundred miles and a quarter century, and little that happened along the way went according to plan. For Rosalie, as for the world, immigration is a story filled with surprise.

PART I

THERE

Masses, Huddled

T he seventy-six hundred islands of the Philippine archipelago spill across a thousand miles of stormy seas, halfway around the world from the United States. Lush beauty suggests abundance, but bare survival was the twentieth-century norm, and extreme concentrations of wealth left most Filipinos struggling for that. In the early 1950s, a young boy on the island of Leyte slipped onto a crowded ferry to trade the certain desperation of farm tenancy for an uncertain life in the distant capital. It was the first of many journeys that would carry him and his children across the globe. He was newly orphaned. He didn't have a ticket. And his stomach hurt.

Emet Comodas, Rosalie's father, was the youngest of nine children born to landless farmers near the end of World War II. There was nothing yet on the horizon to suggest that a poor boy in an obscure corner of the developing world would grow up to exemplify a new age of mass migration.

Migration is as old as Exodus, but the mass migration of free labor is different and new. It took shape in the mid-nineteenth century when a special constellation of forces converged on the transatlantic world.

Population growth filled Europe with surplus workers; wage gaps gave the workers reason to move; cheap transportation made moving affordable; and migrant networks—friends and relatives—eased the way. Seemingly distinct, these forces came together to form a system, a program, a regime. From 1800 to the 1920s, nearly fifty million Europeans crossed the oceans, mostly for the United States.

But by the middle of the twentieth century, that era was dead. After decades of nativist furor, the United States in the 1920s all but closed its doors. Two world wars and a global depression additionally restricted the ability to move, and wage growth in the postwar years left those Europeans who could still get visas less likely to want them; they could do nearly as well at home. In the decade after World War II, annual admissions in the United States were down about 80 percent from their Ellis Island peak. Yet the same forces that had once triggered the great European outflows—population growth, inequality, cheap travel, and migrant networks—would soon arrive in the developing world and launch an age of global migration more pervasive than the first.

When Emet was four months old, in October 1944, the biggest battle in naval history exploded off Leyte's coast. The United States destroyed the Japanese fleet and lent the island a moment of newsreel renown as the place where General Douglas MacArthur, chased from the country two years before, waded ashore to keep his pledge: "I shall return." Otherwise Leyte was known, if it was known at all, for poverty severe even by Philippine standards. Poor soil limited crops, and typhoons wreaked havoc, but the biggest problem was man-made: large landlords controlled the most fertile ground and imposed terms that consigned a tenant to a life of feudal need and debt. "He is economically little more than a serf," wrote an American geographer who studied postwar Leyte.

Emet lost his mother when he was two and his father when he was eight, both to undiagnosed diseases. He was living with his brother when a relative of sorts—his sister-in-law's sister, Primitiva—visited from Manila and offered to smuggle him aboard the ferry and take him home. A shot of palm wine settled his stomach, and Emet prayed to the Virgin of Guadalupe for help in dodging the ticket takers. After a night of rough seas, the boat found the calm of Manila Bay, and Primitiva led him toward a sprawl of shanties called Leveriza.

Manila had once been "the Pearl of the Orient," a city with genteel colonial airs. The United States acquired it in 1898, after three centuries of Spanish rule. It had a stately cathedral, an old walled quarter, shady boulevards, polo grounds, cabarets, and breathtaking sunsets. Three years of brutal Japanese occupation brought wanton executions and outbreaks of famine, and a month of American liberation in 1945 left the landscape outright lunar. Hopelessly outnumbered, the Japanese dug in with suicidal resolve, while the Americans advanced block by block behind a cyclone of bombs and shells. A hundred thousand Filipinos died.

Some of the fiercest fighting occurred in Malate, an elegant precinct on the south side of town, beside tony De La Salle College and the giant Rizal Memorial Stadium. As the Americans advanced, Japanese soldiers massacred scores of civilians sheltered in the college chapel—survivors told tales of toddlers bayoneted—and dug foxholes in the stadium. American tanks blasted them out, but the shelling and retaliatory Japanese arson left the area in ruins. When the war ended, homeless families poured into Manila from the ravaged countryside and threw up shacks wherever the razed landscape allowed. The hovels on swampy grounds behind Leveriza Street, beside the college and the battle-pocked stadium, were unusual only for their prime location. It was a shantytown near the yacht club.

By the time Emet arrived, nearly a decade later, Leveriza occupied sixteen acres with a look of squalid permanence. The squatters had hammered together their shelters from whatever the city would yield—rotted planks, rusted signs, rice sacks, scrap wood, tarps. From a distance, the quilted textures and colors had the appeal of folk art. Up close, Leveriza was a trash-choked swamp overrun by warring gangs. "The living conditions are extremely bad," a team of researchers later wrote. "There are no water, drainage or sewer systems. . . . [T]he community is a maze of alleys and passageways. . . . Congestion is extreme. . . . Most houses have no toilets and the stench in some areas is terrible." Primitiva led Emet into the jumbled interior and told him he was home.

Despite the wartime damage, the Philippines's future seemed bright. Newly independent, it boasted high literacy rates, extensive public schools, rich natural resources, and higher incomes than Korea or Taiwan. It had a free press and an elected government. Many Filipinos spoke English, the language of global business, and the United States offered economic aid and preferential market access. Boosters saw "the next Japan."

Emet liked the tumult of urban life—the garish jeepneys, the Babel of dialects, and the men in the alleys throwing dice. Leveriza was ruled by gangsters and drunks, but Emet wore his geniality as a shield and was quick to make friends. Drawn to commerce more than to school, he spent much of his youth dodging traffic to hawk newspapers and cigarettes and dropped out at the start of high school. Primitiva was kind, but Emet's older sister eventually moved to Leveriza and insisted he stay with her. Nanay Dak was married to a drunk. She took the money Emet earned on the streets and hit him with a switch. Once, she bit him. When Emet wearied of the abuse, he would run away and sleep on a bridge.

Among the places Emet liked to sell cigarettes was Rizal stadium, the complex once shelled by American tanks. Lacking a vendor's license, he had to slip in before events and hide beneath the stands. The canteen manager admired his pluck and offered him a job as a waiter. With a bounce in his step from his first real job, Emet, now nineteen, was walking home through Leveriza when he saw a young woman in the alley ironing clothes. He had never seen anyone at once so beautiful and so frail. He was too scared to say hello.

Teresita Portagana came from a higher echelon of the Filipino poor. Her enterprising father, Venancio, had acquired a few fields in the neighboring province of Cavite, mostly through his own effort but also with the small pension his mother-in-law received from the American government because her husband, Tita's grandfather, died fighting the Japanese. Tita was born a year after the war's end and raised on the farm in a thatched hut. Ten younger siblings followed with the regularity of the seasons. Lean times made for lean meals—meat was a rarity—but a close family gave Tita comfort and protections that Emet, an orphan, lacked.

The Portaganas were a gregarious clan, quick to laugh at each other's expense and make friends. As the family introverts, Tita and her father stood apart. Much of her childhood passed happily beside him in the fields, where she absorbed his example of family devotion and bore the duties of the eldest without complaint. After six barefoot years in school—cash was too scarce to waste on shoes—she quit to help care for the younger kids. Her parents saw little point in continuing the education of a girl. When Tita turned sixteen, her father sent her to work in a Manila factory. She would live with an aunt and send home her pay.

Manila was only thirty miles away, but she had never seen the city. Her excitement vanished when she discovered where her aunt lived. Leveriza wasn't just ramshackle and chaotic; it stank. Bare-chested men leered from the alleys, and gangs fought with poison-tipped darts. The factory belonged to an American glove company that expected her to sew her four-finger sections at an unforgiving pace. About a quarter were rejected by supervisors so exacting that Tita came to see the United States as a nation of fastidious glove inspectors. Still, the cash felt empowering. She got paid on Saturdays and rode the bus home proud to be a provider.

One day the family got alarming news: Tita had a neighborhood suitor, a gang member named George. Her father raced to Leveriza and moved her. "One relative in Leveriza is enough," he said. George lost interest, but he had a friend who'd been admiring Tita from afar and awaiting his chance. His chances were slim: until Emet tracked her down, Tita didn't know his name. She considered him plain and "even poorer than a rat," and her father had barred her from seeing Lever-iza men.

But Emet proved gifted at ingratiation. He plied her with leftovers from the stadium canteen and sweets from the market. He finagled in-vitations to the farm and brought fish for everyone. Tita saw in his de-votion a hint of her father, and Emet saw in her happy family life comforts he lacked. Venancio liked Emet's ambition: he worked two jobs, as a waiter and street vendor, and talked of building a house. Though nothing warranted it, Emet had the optimism of a man whose break was just around the corner.

Tita was twenty-one when they married in November 1967, after a courtship of nearly two years. Emet bought a pig for a party on the farm, and they rode the bus back to a rented shack in Leveriza. Soon Tita was pregnant.

WHAT CARRIED TITA AND EMET to Manila, beyond the belching bus, was the greatest epoch of population growth in world history. It started about the time they were born and hasn't stopped. It tripled and quadrupled the populations of poor countries, urbanized the develop-ing world, and packed the slums of teeming cities with surplus workers. It was demography that propelled the Age of Migration: there's no mass movement without masses.

Since births were abundant but lives short, the key to population growth was reducing death rates. That's what suddenly happened in Europe in the nineteenth century. Science and industry led the way, with breakthroughs as simple as the wider use of soap. Cleaner water and the construction of sewers slowed the spread of disease. Better tools brought bigger harvests, and better roads and trains brought the harvests to market. Better-fed people lived longer lives. After death rates start to fall, families eventually have fewer children, but the demographic transition takes several generations. Meanwhile, populations soar. In the nineteenth century, the number of Europeans doubled, even as tens of millions of migrants left for the New World.

A similar package of lifesaving advances reached poor countries after World War II, but with the science now well understood, progress came much faster. Modernizers sank wells, cut roads, sprayed mosquitoes, and vaccinated children, and mortality rates plunged. At mid-century, life expectancy in low-income countries was forty-two years. By the century's end, it was sixty-three years. It took the world until 1800 to hold a billion people and 125 years to add a billion more—but just thirty-three years for its third billion, and roughly a dozen years each for its fourth (1974), fifth (1987), sixth (1999), and seventh (2012) billions. In the six decades after Tita and Emet were born, the population of the (mostly Catholic) Philippines grew especially fast, rising fivefold to nearly 100 million.

More people meant more cities. Venancio Portagana had eleven children and ten acres. The children couldn't all stay home to farm, and they didn't all want to. City life, for all its hardships, promised freedom, excitement, and dreams, however slim, of making it big. In the twentieth century, the urban population of the developing world rose twentyfold, to two billion. Over six decades, Manila grew from a city of 1.5 million to a megacity of nearly twelve million. Urbanization isn't essential for overseas migration—some people migrate straight from the village—but it does encourage it. Having already moved once, internal migrants have practice, and cities provide information and connections.

Teeming, the cities couldn't house the newcomers, so the newcomers housed themselves, wherever daring and imagination allowed—under bridges, atop medians, and beside railroad tracks. Just as Eskimos have multiple words for snow, Tagalog developed multiple words for the shantytown: *iskwater, estero, eskinita, looban,* and *dagat-dagatan.* Like Tita and Emet, about a third of Manila's residents lived in squatter and slum settlements, typically lacking rights to the land. With 250,000 people, Tondo Foreshore was Manila's biggest slum, but its most infamous was Smokey Mountain—a smoldering trash dump where 10,000 people lived and foraged in a hellish landscape. It was the most degrading place I've seen. I spent an Easter sunrise there, watching two candlelit processions of scavengers descend the stinking mountain of trash, one holding a statue of the veiled Virgin, the other the crucified Christ. They met in a chapel where a statue depicted Jesus as a trash picker. Fireworks exploded and the crowd cheered: Christ has risen! Christ has risen! My companion, a Filipino publisher, exulted, "Faulkner was right: 'Man will not merely endure; he will prevail!'" Amid the filth and stench, the priest reminded the praying scavengers that Jesus was with them: Cavalry had been a garbage dump, too.

Like the Dickensian tenements before it, the shanty was a brutish emblem of a brutish age. In the early 1960s, Manila's sanitation was so bad that cholera reappeared. Overcrowding and rats spread tuberculosis. Malnutrition was prevalent: 80 to 90 percent of slum families lacked an adequate diet. Infant mortality was dismayingly high. (Both of Nanay Dak's children died before age five.) Tondo was the epitome of overcrowding, but with 680 people per acre Leveriza was nearly 40 percent more dense. As much as crowds or malnutrition, what defined the slum was the absence of toilets. As late as 1980, about 40 percent of Metro Manila residents lacked them. People went where they would and pitched it where they could. Every ditch in Leveriza doubled as an open sewer.

Across the globe, development experts held conflicting views of the slums. Some saw them as degrading and morally ruinous, incubators of vice. Others praised them for finding innovative ways to integrate the rural poor in the absence of government services. Likewise, politicians split. Some courted the squatters' votes, even encouraged them to move in, but most saw blight and a danger to property rights. The bulldozer was a constant threat.

About the time that Tita first moved to Manila, the mayor launched a fierce campaign against the squatters who had occupied part of the old walled city, Intramuros, for nearly two decades. Wrecking crews descended in 1963, piled families and their dismantled shacks in the backs of trucks, and dumped them on a barren hillside twenty miles away, called Sapang Palay. There was nothing there—no homes, no water taps, no toilets, no jobs. The removal continued until nearly twenty thousand people occupied a site that the World Health Organization deemed "unfit for human habitation."

Some people in Leveriza thought their long tenure and political clout would spare them a similar fate. But given the land's valuable location, Tita wasn't so sure. She hoped to leave Leveriza, but not in the back of a garbage truck.

TITA WAS TWENTY-ONE when she had her first child, on the floor of a Leveriza shack. Her father wept when he saw his first grandchild lying in shantytown squalor. He named the boy Rolando and moved mother and child back to the farm, where cleaner air and helping hands awaited. Emet stayed behind to work at the stadium canteen, where he slept on the floor to save money, and visited on weekends. Tita missed him. After six months, she and the baby moved back to the city, and Emet rented another place in Leveriza.

This one was worse, with rats so aggressive they ate the bar soap. Pregnant again, Tita grew dizzy and weak, and a midwife declared her anemic. After a bleeding episode at three months, Tita took shots to prevent a miscarriage. But she went into premature labor and rushed to the public hospital where her daughter, Rowena, was born seven weeks early, weighing less than four pounds. Visiting the high-risk nursery every day, Emet panicked at all the dying infants. Against doctors' orders, he brought Rowena home. "If my baby is going to die," he said, "I want her to be with me." Tagalog folklore holds that children resemble what their pregnant mothers crave; Tita joked that she must have craved a tiger. Rowena proved fierce; she survived.

As a young mother with an ailing child and an introvert in a sea of strangers, Tita felt overwhelmed. Slum life was socially savage. When Tita had Rowena, an anthropologist trained at the University of Chicago, F. Landa Jocano, was doing fieldwork in a squatter camp nearby. His resulting study, *Slum as a Way of Life*, remains a minor classic. The Leveriza-like setting was predictably noxious—"wet and muddy" with a "nauseating smell" and crowded with "cardboard hovels." But what stood out was the conflict. Despite the Filipinos' reputation for prizing accord, husbands beat wives, gangs murdered gangs, and *tsismis*—gossip—ruled the alleyway. "Envy, jealousy, hatred, and other forms of ridicule" prevailed. It took a special social deftness to thrive. Lacking it, Tita withdrew. "I was talkless," she said. When she was twenty-four, her third child arrived, and the pattern of her difficult life seemed set, down to the baby's alliterative name. After Rolando and Rowena came Rosalie.

By 1971, when Rosalie was born, no one still saw the Philippines as "the next Japan." Hong Kong, Singapore, Taiwan, and Korea had lapped it in the development race. Before long, Thailand, which was much poorer in the 1950s, would have per capita income nearly three times as high. Gains in agricultural productivity had powered development in other Asian nations but eluded the Philippines, where landowners still ruled vast estates. With land and labor in equal abundance, the barons saw no need to innovate. They bought banks, factories, utilities, newspapers, and mansions in the capital and fashioned an oligarchic system of "booty capitalism" that rewarded connections over competition. The country's stupendous inequality *grew*. With a communist insurgency on the rise, the stagnation posed security risks. A prominent mission led by a Yale economist warned that absent "major structural change" the situation would prove "explosive."

The problem with the Philippine economy was Philippine politics, an armed competition for plunder rights. The parties were ideologically indistinguishable coalitions of power brokers who delivered votes in exchange for economic favors: tax breaks, tariffs, import licenses, low-interest loans, regulatory loopholes, monopolies, and government contracts. Vote buying made campaigns expensive, and private armies made them violent. The Election Day death count could reach hundreds. In the 1960s, *Time* correspondent Stanley Karnow met a young politician named Benigno Aquino, Jr., or Ninoy, who "cruised around town in a bulletproof limousine, its upholstery fitted with slots for machine guns." Every country has rich schemers, but the Philippines (unlike Japan or Korea) lacked an administrative state strong enough to resist. The Filipino oligarchs didn't just control the politicians. They *were* the politicians: President Sergio Osmeña Sr., Vice President Fernando Lopez, Governor Danding Cojuangco. When Congress convened hearings on land reform, seventeen of the twenty-one committee members were landlords.

The 1965 presidential race went to a young senator known for his guile and his beauty queen wife. Ferdinand and Imelda Marcos cast themselves as stylish modernizers after the Kennedys, but the Philippines wasn't Camelot. Marcos gained renown as a law student by persuading the Supreme Court to overturn his conviction for murdering his father's political rival. He moved into the presidential palace assailing corruption and began shoveling money into Swiss bank accounts; by the CIA's estimate, he stole as much as $10 billion. With the national debt already swelled by his pork-barrel projects, Marcos spent so much public money buying votes in his 1969 reelection campaign that he plunged the country into fiscal crisis. Inflation spiked, and compensatory cuts in government jobs further punished the poor. Proclaiming herself a civic beautifier, Imelda Marcos set out to sweep the shanties from sight with bulldozers and whitewashed walls.

Soon after Rosalie was born, Emet won a long-shot bet on a horse.

He used the windfall to buy his own Leveriza shanty, which was so rotted he burned it down and started over, though he didn't own the land. Tita had two more boys—Roldan and Rosalier—leaving seven people in a single room under a leaking roof.

Paradoxically, Rosalie has happy memories of an impoverished childhood in a place she loathed. Tita and Emet were loving parents. Relatives visited often, and the farm, two hours away, offered an escape to swimming holes and cousins. The boisterous Portagana clan gave Rosalie a sense of belonging. Tita did duty as the sober budget chief, while Emet played the indulgent father, sneaking the kids into the stadium pool or treating them to after-school bowls of rice porridge. "Sheer joy" does not exaggerate the happiness Rosalie felt when he brought home a pink toy watch. It was the best day of her childhood.

But even Emet couldn't make Leveriza feel safe. The house next door was so close Rosalie felt as if the mentally ill neighbor across the alley could reach through the window and grab her. For the rest of her life, she would fear sleeping alone. A gang fight left a corpse in the alley. Bare-chested drunks smirked and stared. Among the goblins of Rosalie's childhood was Nanay Dak's husband, an uncle nicknamed Tatay Sing—Daddy Drunk. He handed out candy when sober but left Nanay Dak cowering behind Emet's locked door when the bottle kicked in. When Rosalie learned to pray, she prayed to get out of Leveriza.

With Rolando away for long stays on the farm and Rowena chronically sick, Rosalie was a third child with the duties of the firstborn. It was Rosalie whom Tita sent to the market, Rosalie who scrubbed clothes, Rosalie who waited at the spigot for hours while the neighbors quarreled. She responded with a seriousness beyond her years. "You're always frowning," Emet would tease. Real disobedience never crossed her mind, but Rosalie did allow herself one small rebellion. She never called Rowena *Ate* (*Ah-tay*)—"big sister"—as custom required. As Rosalie saw it, *she* did the big sister work. Only in retrospect would the absence of the honorific hint at her larger ambition—her refusal to accept that her place in the world depended on the accident of her birth.

Although Rosalie's childhood was poor, city life subtly encouraged ambition in a way that farm life did not. Every block in Manila housed a college or technical school. When Rosalie was young, Tita's brother Fortz started an engineering course; the school let him work off his tuition, and he slept on Tita's floor. He didn't graduate, but Rosalie saw the family pride when he landed a job fixing copy machines and got sent to Japan for training. City life also promoted an awareness, if vague, of life beyond the Philippines. Long before she could see past the horizon, Rosalie sensed something out there. When a neighbor got a private water tap, Tita explained that the woman could afford it because her husband worked in a place called "abroad." Rosalie had a friend who was doubly blessed: her father worked as an international seafarer, and she had relatives in the United States. The friend went to Catholic school and got lavish Christmas presents from America. Rosalie knew the United States was special but assumed you had to be born there to benefit. The idea that you could move to a new country had not occurred to her.

WITH HIS SECOND TERM waning and the constitution barring a third, Marcos declared martial law. In September 1972, he abolished Congress, seized businesses, closed newspapers, and jailed opponents by the thousands, including his likely successor, Senator Ninoy Aquino. Marcos cast the move as an effort to sweep aside the communists and oligarchs and launch a "New Society." But his new powers, which indefinitely extended his rule, mostly gave him new ways to enrich himself. The United States, more concerned about its military bases than the dictatorship, went along. "We love your adherence to democratic principles," Vice President George H. W. Bush later said.

Emet liked Marcos and supported martial law. Filipinos were "hard-headed," he said, and needed a strong hand. The extra police quieted the Leveriza gangs. But job growth faltered, poverty deepened, and the 1973 Arab oil embargo worsened the economic crisis: oil prices nearly quadrupled in three months, boosting inflation and draining the country's foreign exchange.

With a surging population and a shortage of jobs, the Philippines had two of the conditions that can trigger mass migration. Marcos gave the process a shove. In a 1974 May Day speech, he warned that the country simply had too many workers and not enough work. His solution was to ship the workers abroad—to "undertake the systematic employment of Filipinos overseas" and "optimize the national benefits therefrom in the form of dollar remittances." A new government agency (the Overseas Employment Development Board) would place Filipinos in temporary contracts with overseas employers. While the program would only last a few years, until local conditions brightened, its aims were not modest. Overseas work, Marcos promised, "shall mean ultimate liberation" from "graft, abuse, and exploitation."

A government that told its workers to leave defied orthodoxy. By the early 1970s, global migration had started to rise: guest workers were well established in parts of Europe, and permanent settlement was increasing in the United States, Canada, and Australia. But migrants generally went on their own, not with their government's aid. (Korea, a modest exception, encouraged workers to go to the Persian Gulf with Korean construction firms.) Some regimes even viewed migrants as disloyal; the Soviets prevented people from leaving. To the extent that development experts thought about migration, they called it a problem—a source of brain drain. No one called it a solution.

But Marcos saw opportunity. Saudi Arabia and its neighbors already had ambitious building plans. Now there was no limit to what they could spend. They needed airports, power plants, hotels, hospitals, offices, shopping centers, and people to run them. Their workforces were tiny and untrained. Two-thirds of the Saudis were illiterate, while many jobless Filipinos had college degrees. The Filipinos would get paid in dollars and send the dollars home. For Marcos, labor export had the makings of a triple play: it would raise incomes, slow the insurgents, and shore up foreign exchange. In 1975, the program's first year, 36,000 Filipinos went abroad. By 1983, departures had risen to 434,000.

Emet envied the men who went. Their kids ate better, and their houses had new roofs. They came home sporting The Look—leather jackets, Ray-Bans, and cases of Saudi "hepa," skin yellowed by the reflection of gold chains. But migration is usually beyond the very poor. It takes connections to find a job and cash for a passport and medical exam. An industry of middleman recruiters sprang up, riddled with rackets and demanding high fees. Though the government capped the amount they could charge workers—they were supposed to collect mostly from employers—most ignored the limits and imposed significant charges, sometimes for jobs that didn't exist. Absent another winning horse, Emet saw little chance to work overseas.

For the workers left behind, the misery deepened as growth dipped to the lowest level in Southeast Asia. In eight years, the incomes of unskilled urban workers fell by a third. Emet switched to cleaning the stadium pool and made about $2.40 a day, more than most Manila slum dwellers. But even with a second job, peddling cooked food on the street, he struggled just to feed the kids. When Tita lacked fish, she served plain rice. When she lacked rice for three meals, she served two. When the rice ran out, she borrowed from the neighborhood lender, a giant Sikh they called the "Boom-Bai," at 20 percent a week. Rain poured through the roof so freely there was no dry place to sleep. Emet had lived a hard life without growing hardened—a mixed blessing given the indignities of his poverty. He worried most about Rowena, whose weak heart left her frail and needing medicine that he couldn't afford.

Tita's brother Fortz got the family's first break. Cold-calling on recruiters, he found one supplying technicians to a Riyadh firm that was putting the Saudis' vital records on microfiche. After years of fixing copy machines, he was an ideal candidate. The salary, $700 a month, was astonishing—about twenty times what he earned in Manila—with no placement fee. His father lent him the money for the medical exam, and half the extended family crowded into a rented jeepney for a tearful airport farewell.

Emet tried to disguise his jealousy. He borrowed to open a tiny store by the house, which Tita would help him run. The thief who emptied the shelves during Holy Week seemed to know they were busy reading the *Pasyon*, a twenty-four-hour life of Christ. Easter or not, it was the only time Emet felt capable of killing someone. When Rowena fell ill again, he asked God to heal her or take her to heaven. Soon after, Emet's boss stunned him: he asked if Emet was interested in going abroad. An American firm was starting a fitness program for the Saudi Air Force and needed a pool keeper in Dhahran. The boss knew the recruiter, who would waive the placement fee, and his monthly salary would rise tenfold, from $50 in Manila to $500 in Dhahran. "Yes," he said. "Yes! Yes!" He was so afraid of how Tita might react he didn't tell her for a week. Their baby was still in diapers.

Rosalie had just turned ten in 1981 when the family took another ride to the airport—not quite old enough to keep a brave face. She was a daddy's girl losing her daddy. Tita found hope in Emet's salary but fear in the prospect of facing Leveriza alone for two years. An enterprising photographer at the airport was peddling good-bye shots, but the few coins Tita and Emet could muster weren't enough. Tita spent them to enter a lounge where she could watch and wave as his plane took flight. Then she returned to Leveriza, drew the kids close, and cried.

TWO

Migration Fever

Emet landed in Dhahran after a ten-hour flight, worried about the worry on Tita's face and worried about Saudi Arabia. The orientation in Manila had warned that the heat and police were equally severe: no Bibles, no booze, and no *babaeros*—playboys. Workers who committed adultery could be jailed or lashed. He half expected airport camels but found only bored police who checked his bag for Bibles and smut and left his clothes in a heap. Emet got the message: Filipinos were too plentiful and cheap to bother welcoming.

Four decades earlier, the city hadn't existed. Dhahran was a sand dune outside the village of Dammam when American engineers began to sink exploratory wells. The first six didn't find much. In 1938, Dammam No. 7 struck gold, confirming that the tiny tribal kingdom sat atop unfathomable wealth. By the early 1980s when Emet arrived, the tri-city area (Dhahran, Dammam, and Al-Khobar) held 350,000 people, anchored by one of the world's richest corporations, Aramco, and guarded by King Abdulaziz Air Base, whose pools Emet came to tend.

He settled into a dorm beside the base, reserved for Filipinos. It had hot and cold running water, flush toilets, televisions, tennis courts, a cleaning service, and a cook. It was the nicest place he had ever lived—by Leveriza standards, palatial. Emet was miserable. First timers have it rough, and Emet's closeness to the kids made it rougher. Ever since his orphaned childhood, all he had wanted was a family, but to support one, he had to leave it. Veterans told him the loneliness would pass, but Emet, who was thirty-seven, doubted he could last a month.

Physically, the work was easy. He got paid on time and at the promised rate—neither a sure thing among guest workers in the Gulf, who were frequently defrauded and powerless to complain. Although moonlighting was technically illegal, Emet took a side job cleaning the house of a Saudi general. He arrived one day to a scene that inspired terror: a glimpse of the general's wife in flimsy nightclothes. He panicked and ran. "In orientation they said if the woman complains they chop the head, even if you didn't do anything." The general arrived hours later, puzzled to find Emet squatting in the courtyard, awaiting arrest.

THE TWO MAIN THEMES of Overseas Filipino Worker life are homesickness and money. Workers suffer the first to get the second. Some hung posters of dollar bills to remind themselves why they had come. One played a recording of his pig. Emet paced the mall and asked the Virgin of Guadalupe to help him pass the time. Eventually, he grew bold enough to make bathtub wine. Infidelity was on everyone's mind. A Tagalog pop hit, "It's So Painful, Brother Eddie," took the form of an overseas worker crying about his wife's affair: "I'm wondering why our two children are now three." Despite the watch of Saudi authorities, workers cheated, too. Unmarried couples bought fake marriage certificates, and rooms let by the hour on Friday mornings to treat "homesexness" while the Saudis were at the mosque.

After fourteen years of marriage and five kids, Emet and Tita had bonds that younger couples lacked. If Tita needed reassurance, she could find it in his constant letters and tapes. "I'm counting every minute, every hour," he wrote. "Every time there's an airplane in the sky, I say when I ride it again?" He yearned for news of the kids. Emet is a gentle man, slow to anger, but decades later, he would flare when he heard critics say that overseas workers deprive their children of love. "You cannot look at each other and say it's love if your stomach is empty—I *sacrificed*."

At first, single motherhood seemed more than Tita could bear. Frail and friendless, alone in the slums, she was a fretter with reason to fret. Rowena, now twelve, was constantly sick, and the baby, nicknamed Bhoyet, was just a year old. Since Manila's overcrowded schools started their split shifts at 6:00 a.m., Tita rose at 4:30 to boil the breakfast rice. She washed each child's uniform every day, with water Rosalie toted from the public tap. Emet's absence meant the difficult decisions were hers alone. Hitching a piggyback ride from school, Roldan, who was five, slipped from his brother's back, cracked his head, and vomited all the way home. Tita decided not to spend the meal money on a doctor. "By God's grace, nothing happened," she said.

The first time Emet sent money, Tita cried. In Manila, he made about $50 a month—in Saudi, $500, plus his moonlighting job. Tita stopped running out of fish and rice. She bought extra school uniforms so she didn't have to wash every day. She bought a closet to hang them in. After years of toothaches, she had seven teeth pulled and treated herself to dentures. She bought a fan to stir the stagnant air and a television after the neighbors complained about the kids watching theirs through the window. Rosalie loved television, but the ultimate luxury was the family's first bed. "I was ecstatic we could lay on something soft."

New comforts were part of migrant lore—"symbols of hope to neighbors and friends." After households sent workers to the Gulf, the share with televisions doubled. The share with stereos quadrupled. Two-thirds said they ate more meat. They built concrete walls and laid new roofs. Economists, who value investment, sometimes dismissed the purchases as "mere consumption." To the families there was nothing "mere" about it; consumption meant more to eat.

In Emet's absence, Tita's authority grew. When she hired a work crew to install a toilet, she revealed not only her prosperity but also her empowerment. Most labor migrants at this point were men; the rising autonomy of their wives was an unforeseen side effect. More than three-quarters of Filipino wives said their husbands' time abroad made them stronger. Women as far away as Egypt and India said much the same, although some fell into subjugation by male relatives. With a few pesos to share, Tita noticed that her neighbors afforded her a hint of the deference offered to people of means.

After nearly two years, Emet flew home in a crowd of workers who cheered when the plane set down. He brought chocolate for the kids, earrings for Tita, and a bag of duty-free cigarettes, his homesickness having made him a heavy smoker. Bhoyet, now two, considered him a stranger and cried at his touch, but Emet pretended not to notice. "I was too happy to be sad," he said. He threw himself a party, patched the walls, and replaced the roof. A few months later, when it was time to return, Emet learned he was jobless again. The recruiting firm had lost the contract.

It took a year of pavement pounding in Manila to find another overseas job, even with a reference from a Saudi Air Force captain who had praised his "fine performance" and "dedication and attentiveness." Emet pawned the earrings he had bought Tita, sold the kids' Nintendo game, and went back to peddling cooked food. But with no regular job, he was poorer than before he had left. When he finally got sent to clean pools in Najran, near the Yemen border, the whole family breathed a sigh of relief. Everyone was surprised at how much now depended on Emet being gone.

As Emet became a migrant, migration became a force. From 1960 to 1990, the world's migrant population doubled. More countries sent migrants, more countries received them, and the migrants brought rapid ethnic change. Plot the movements on a map, and witness a festival of arrows: West Indians to Britain, Turks to Germany, Chinese to formerly "White Australia." Public opinion leaned skeptical, but migration had a life of its own.

If the postwar migration were put to film, the opening shot might pan the wary faces of men docked on the river Thames. The five hundred Jamaican recruits who filed off *Empire Windrush* in 1948 were just looking for a paycheck in a war-racked country short on labor; unwittingly, they launched multicultural Britain. Nearly half a million West Indians followed over the next two decades—bus drivers, porters, factory workers, orderlies—and even more came from the Indian subcontinent. As citizens of the Commonwealth, migrants from the former colonies could move to Britain as they pleased. That freedom ended in 1962, but the movement did not, since British reunification laws let migrants send for their families. By the early 1970s, the country held 1.5 million colonial migrants and their children.

Other European countries needing postwar labor turned to guest worker schemes. Switzerland, France, and Belgium were among them, but the classic example is Germany, which in 1961 began recruiting Turks for "temporary" jobs. Since the contracts generally lasted just a year, no one imagined that Germany was seeding an ethnic and religious minority, an idea with zero appeal in a country so defined by its homogeneity. But once they started cashing German paychecks, the Turks had no more interest in leaving than the Germans had in training replacements. Accommodations were made. By 1973, Germany hosted 600,000 "temporary" Turkish workers, about half of whom had been there for at least seven years.

The oil shock ended the guest worker programs, but the workers didn't leave—not the Turks in Germany, nor the Moroccans in the Netherlands, nor the Algerians in France. Laws and sympathetic court rulings let workers bring wives and kids; more than half a million Turkish dependents moved to Germany in just three years. By 1975, the foreign population climbed to 7 percent in Germany, 8 percent in France, and 16 percent in Switzerland. "We wanted workers, but we got people instead"—so went the famous lament. The quotation belonged to the Swiss writer Max Frisch. The sentiment belonged to the continent.

The welcome could not be called warm. Racial violence exploded in Britain as early as 1958, when hundreds of whites rampaged for days in a West Indian section of London called Notting Hill. (Some called the mayhem "nigger hunting.") A decade later, a Tory MP named Enoch Powell likened immigration to national suicide and predicted racial violence. "It is like watching a nation busily engaged in heaping up its own funeral pyre. . . . Like the Roman, I seem to see 'the River Tiber foaming with much blood.'" The speech cost Powell his party post, but three-quarters of Britons approved, and Powell gained lasting renown among immigration opponents worldwide.

In France, North Africans languished in the worst jobs and crowded into shantytowns called *bidonvilles*. They launched work strikes, rent strikes, hunger strikes, and mass demonstrations and died in mob attacks. "The bodies of murdered foreign laborers regularly were fished out of the Seine," wrote the political scientist Mark J. Miller. "North African cafés were bombed and machine gunned." When a mentally ill Algerian killed a Marseilles bus driver in 1973, revenge squads bombed the Algerian consulate. Unlike in Britain, where both Tories and Labour worked to suppress racial backlash, anti-immigrant attitudes in France coalesced around far-right parties.

Unwelcomed is not the same as unwanted. Europe might not have liked migrants, but it liked having them do grubby jobs—pick crops, wash dishes, and mop floors. The idea that advanced economies used foreigners to do the dirty work was explored by the economist Michael J. Piore in his book *Birds of Passage*. He argued that natives disdain the low status of certain jobs even more than the low pay. Hiring foreigners to do the stigmatized chores eases the class conflict among natives but makes it politically harder to reduce the flows. By 1975, foreigners constituted 10 percent of Western Europe's labor force. "The last thing I worry about is losing my job to a Frenchman," scoffed a Malian worker during a Paris subway strike. "No Frenchman would do what I do for what I get paid."

The resumption of mass migration to the States differed in significant ways. It began later, focused on settlers not guest workers, and benefited from its initial framing as a civil rights issue. But one element of the experience was the same: unintended consequences. In signing the 1965 law, Johnson said mass migration was dead but launched a new migration age. More immigrants came in the 1970s than in the 1930s, 1940s, and 1950s combined—three-quarters of them from the developing world.

As in the past, population growth and rising inequality increased the incentive to move. In the second half of the twentieth century, rich countries added 380 million people, but poor countries added 3.2 billion. In 1960, America's per capita GDP was twelve times that of the Philippines; by 2000, it was thirty-six times as great. Steamships once made travel cheaper and safer; now airplanes did. Television was another migration-quickening force, since it globalized images of First World comforts. Even in the alleys of Leveriza, Rosalie could see what she was missing. By the end of the century, cell phones and the internet strengthened ethnic networks. Soaring numbers of refugees—fleeing postcolonial conflict and the proxy battles of the Cold War—increased the migrants' head count.

While public opinion generally opposed large-scale migration, Western governments didn't stop it. Migrant-friendly courts were one constraint. Foreign policy imperatives were another, like the United States' admission of Cubans and Vietnamese. And the dynamics of interest-group politics were very much in play. For decades, opposition was broad but not deep, while organized support was intense among a strange-bedfellows mix of business, ethnic, and humanitarian groups. In politics, intensity wins: legal and illegal, the movement continued.

As the monarchs of the Persian Gulf pondered migrant labor, nothing about the West's experience seemed reassuring—not the speed of change, the potential for strife, or the resistance to state control. "Roiled" is the usefully elastic verb that journalists often use to describe the conflict migration generates. The royals did not want to be roiled. As autocrats, they didn't have to worry about courts or legislatures, but they did have to worry about math. By 1980 or so, migrants made up 7 percent of the workforce in the United States and 11 percent in France—but 70 percent in the Persian Gulf. To keep the migrants from settling, Gulf countries barred them from buying businesses or homes and prevented them from changing jobs without permission. Only a privileged few could bring their families. Paths to citizenship didn't exist.

Still, hiring other Arabs, as the Gulf States initially did, posed political risks. Egypt was a source of socialist ferment. Palestinians were radicalized. Yemenis sometimes posed as Saudis and tried to stay. Relying on an Arab workforce could create pan-Arab obligations the oil states hoped to avoid. Asians offered an answer. They worked for less than Arabs, and the supply was virtually endless—if Filipinos got expensive or demanding, the rulers could hire Bangladeshis. Best of all, Asians could never fit in. In Europe, hard-to-assimilate migrants were a problem. In the Gulf, they were the solution. By 1985, nearly two-thirds of the Gulf's foreign workers were Asian, up from 20 percent a decade earlier.

Like the Europeans before them, Gulf leaders called the arrangement temporary. But cosseted by a rich welfare state, no Saudi wanted Emet's job cleaning the pool. Just as the 1970s recession did little to reduce migrant labor in Europe, the 1980s oil slump did little to reduce it in the Gulf. The migrant worker might have been temporary; the migrant workforce was not.

No country worked harder than the Philippines to export its people, and no people proved more eager to go. Remittances rose sevenfold in the first decade—a mere hint of the windfall to come. In its force and novelty, the program bore the imprint of its founder, Blas Ople, Marcos's labor secretary. With a gush of New Society hooey, he extolled overseas work for freeing "our feeling and thinking process from the long earthbound and isolated destiny of our people." But Ople was also a keen operator who lured talent to the "Department of Social Conscience" with idealistic talk of serving the poor. At its best, the effort had the poverty-fighting thrill of the Peace Corps: they were employing the masses! At its worst, it resembled a flesh-peddling scheme. Hosting a Middle East official, an Ople lieutenant relayed the client's request for evening entertainment—not one Filipina, but three.

Ople's creation, the Overseas Employment Development Board, was essentially a government job-placement firm. Government officials circled the globe seeking jobs and praised as "Dollar Earners" those who took them. "Armed with slide shows [and] photographic exhibitions . . . teams fan out month after month . . . securing proper contracts, and guaranteeing the quality and dependability of the skills," boasted *Wingtips*, a government airline magazine. Quick delivery was part of the pitch, and requests could be staggering in size. Fluor Daniel, the giant construction firm, needed ten thousand workers. Most Filipinos went to the Middle East, but by 1981 the board counted placements in 108 countries and vowed, with martial overtones, to increase its "market thrust."

The government wasn't just drumming up jobs but fashioning a brand—casting the Filipino as a genial hard worker, the best in low-cost labor. The Labor Department touted his "mettle, versatility, and temperament" and record as a "friendly and cooperative guest." *Wingtips* insisted that "Filipinos don't pose the problems that guest workers from, say, the Mediterranean belt have in Western Europe." They wouldn't riot or strike. Critics later called the sale of the happy, hardworking Filipino dehumanizing, an effort to turn people into remittance machines. But most Filipinos liked their country being known as the HR department of the world. Emet was boasting, not complaining, when he said, "Anywhere you go, you will find a Filipino!"

The government found so much demand for Filipino labor it couldn't fill all the orders. The role of private recruiters expanded. When Marcos created the program in 1974, officials planned to phase out private brokers by the end of the decade and have the government do the placement work. But the phaseout went the other way. The government continued its marketing blitz and let private recruiters fill most of the orders, under (light) regulation.

One result was the addition of the profit motive to the forces propelling migration—thousands of Manila labor agents with reason to see it grow. Another was the proliferation of scams. Shady labor agents were nothing new—they had plagued the recruiting for Hawaiian plantations seven decades earlier—but the ranks of the grifters grew. Restrictions on charging workers for jobs were widely ignored; the charges could reach thousands of dollars. Everyone had heard of a desperate family that sold its livestock or mortgaged its farm for a job that never materialized. So many hustlers peddled phony maids' jobs in Italy the government temporarily stopped sending them there. Countless workers fell victim to "contract substitution" schemes: after signing one contract in Manila, they were forced to sign another (often in Arabic) when they landed that offered less money. The abuses were so widespread that one Manila observer warned that "thousands upon thousands of unsuspecting and gullible workers" were "stranded and jobless on foreign soil." That observer was Ferdinand Marcos.

The industry was impossible to police, and no one imagined a man as corrupt as Marcos was trying. His cronies often owned the firms. Victims were often afraid to complain, fearing reprisals. Layers of subagents allowed swindlers to deny responsibility. Regulators could be bribed. A 1981 raid at the Labor Department found tens of thousands of dollars stuffed in desks and false books to hide the skimming from a workers' welfare fund. But the lack of prosecution suggested that the scheme had presidential protection. Ople's staff considered him honest, though in a government so compromised one never knew. Following the raid, he reorganized the program under a new agency, the Philippine Overseas Employment Administration, and appointed an aide with an honest reputation to run it. Patricia Sto. Tomas launched a three-year crusade to rein in the recruiters, which brought death threats but little lasting change. As she was leaving for a fellowship at Harvard in 1985, Marcos himself summoned her to the palace. A businessman had demanded exclusive rights to sell insurance to the workers and warned Sto. Tomas that he had pull. Manila was awash in such bluster, and Sto. Thomas ignored him. Marcos fixed her with a glare. "Are you hardheaded?" he said.

If the government couldn't police a thousand recruiters in Manila, it couldn't protect hundreds of thousands of workers across the globe. "Pitifully inadequate" is how Ople described migrant welfare efforts in the late 1970s. Reports of misfortune poured in from overseas attachés. Two hundred and eight road pavers in Iraq walked off the job for "nonpayment of salaries." Fifteen hundred Filipinos in Bahrain paid "exorbitant amounts" for jobs. A seafarer in Ontario lost both his legs. Six ballet dancers in Greece were told to "perform functions beyond the limits of morality." The Labor Department's Tokyo rep couldn't sleep. "Even at night, they call me up—at unholy hours," he complained to his bosses. "I have to take tranquilizers."

The Labor Department improvised. As a young troubleshooter, Marianito Roque spent months in Libya seeking redress for unpaid workers from Ople's hometown. When a worker died in Kuwait, Roque organized a weekend of covert gambling to raise money to send the body home. When the labor attaché arrived in Jeddah in 1981, he found hundreds of runaway maids sleeping on the embassy floor. With no budget to feed them, he had staff scour markets for discarded fish heads; they made *sinigang*—fish head soup. The attaché in Abu Dhabi housed runaway maids in his home.

Eventually, the government elevated the migrant protection work by giving it an agency of its own. The Overseas Workers Welfare Administration grew to boast a staff of nearly six hundred in sixteen countries. They ran orientations for departing workers, intervened in employer disputes, visited the sick and the jailed, and developed an expertise in wartime evacuations, starting in 1991, when it brought home thirty thousand Filipino workers from the first Gulf War. Still, with millions of workers overseas rare was the staffer who thought the agency equal to its outsized tasks. So thoroughly were pain and gain intertwined in the migrant experience that the agency's logo depicts the sun doing battle with the rain.

A departing worker does not say he is off to make his fortune. He says, "I'm going to try my luck."

TITA'S FAMILY WAS READY to try theirs. Fortz and Emet were the first to go, followed by Tita's brothers Fering, Bandoy, and Pablito; her brother-in-law Weny; her sister Vinya; and her sister-in-law Aurora, all in the 1980s. Others followed. They missed their children's birthdays. Some missed their children's births. Three of Tita's brothers missed their father's funeral while working in Riyadh and Jeddah. But even the least fortunate doubled his wage. There was no end to the tales they told.

Fortz was a big backslapping man who got hooked on the freedom of the rogue. His affairs became the stuff of family lore. He left for Riyadh with a daughter named Sheryl and returned with another named Sheralyn. Hoping to hide his extramarital affair, he asked Tita to raise the child, which she did for eight years. Reports of Fortz's girlfriends were so common his wife gave him a religious medallion to keep temptation at bay. "I admit, I have more than one, more than two, more than three," he said. But where others saw infidelity, Fortz saw fidelity: "It does not enter my mind to divorce my wife, to separate from my kids—no!" In all, he stayed gone more than thirty years. "Money is the secondary consideration—I like the life in the Middle East."

There was no rogue in the next brother, Fering, the family's family man. He had two children and a third on the way when he left for a Riyadh toilet factory. His earnings rose tenfold, and he saved enough to build his family a house with a toilet of their own. But he saw his children just once in five years. When the factory cut his pay and started hiring Pakistanis, who worked for less, Fering left. "I wanted to be there when my children went to school. I considered it a mission accomplished."

Bandoy's mission was never accomplished: his visits home only showed him what a stranger he had become. He left when his wife was pregnant and didn't see his son until the boy was five. "They weren't very comfortable with me," he said of his four kids. Bandoy worked as a Riyadh driver. The stories he could tell in good humor involved a substitute contract that cut a third of his pay, a trip to jail for a missing car registration (his boss's fault), and the injury he suffered fighting a burglar at his boss's house. The story he couldn't laugh off was the unkept promise of a raise. His boss brushed him off year after year until he quit in a rage. By the time he came home, his kids had kids. "I'm not mad at my employer; I'm mad at myself: Why did I stick it out?"

Bandoy's brother-in-law Danny felt as nostalgic as Bandoy felt betrayed. No chapter of his life could match the thrill of his years as a Saudi bookie. "I was one of the gambling lords of Jeddah!" He went as a worker but overstayed his visa and organized illegal card games for Filipinos, paying the brother of a cop for protection. The big money came from taking bets on the Thai lottery. With the numbers chosen in Bangkok, he couldn't be accused of cheating, and the odds ran heavily in his favor. Filipino nurses, working on commission, sold tickets in the hospitals. Danny cruised Jeddah with a driver and more money than he could spend. He survived for four years and came home in an amnesty for illegal immigrants. When I met him, he was penniless and aging, dreaming of past glories. "Sometimes when I'm alone, I think about how much money I had in Saudi. It felt like I was sleeping on piles of cash."

Danny took risks for vice; Rodel took risks for virtue. An evangelical convert, he had prayed for the chance to work abroad and promised God he would use the opportunity to spread the Good News. Underground Christianity in Saudi is even more dangerous than underground gambling. Members of the Jesus First Christian Ministry called meetings in code ("we have basketball") and took circuitous, James Bond–style routes to avoid the police. Even so, a leader was arrested before Rodel's arrival, and it took an Amnesty International campaign to save him from execution. Rodel was in Riyadh when I met his wife, Myra, who is Tita's niece. She smiled and showed off the kids' new Bugs Bunny sheets—just another happy homemaker buoyed by remittances. Then she started sobbing. "Both of us know it's very dangerous, but I can't stop him. That's where he's found his happiness."

Separations strained marriages. Tita's youngest sister, Chang Idhay, is a cheerful innocent whose husband was working in Saudi when they wed, making theirs a long-distance marriage from the start. Thirteen years and two children later, Chang got a call from a stranger who said their spouses were having an affair and sent pictures of the couple cozied on a Jeddah couch. Chang's husband denied everything, then stopped calling or sending money for the kids. "What he did to us was worse than if he had died," said their smiling nine-year-old, Jonvic. "Because he violated the Ten Commandments of God." After losing one parent, the kids lost the other: Chang left them with relatives and took a job in Abu Dhabi. (Years later, the couple reconciled.)

Tita's sister Peachy also had marital trouble. After two years in Riyadh, her husband, Weny, came home and confessed that he'd had an affair and conceived a son. Half-crazy with grief, Peachy wept for months. Weny groveled. Peachy forgave. They went on to have a son of their own, and Weny's sixteen years abroad built a house and educated three kids. Not knowing the story, I asked Peachy if being apart had been hard. "No—we're loving each other for ever and ever!" The next day she sought me out to tell the fuller tale. "I was not able to tell you the truth last night, because I was ashamed. I almost *died* at that time. You really go out of your mind when you have an OFW husband."

Having "almost died," she understood the risks of overseas work as well as anyone. But it was Peachy who insisted there was no other way: "A good provider is one who leaves."

FOREIGN JOBS PROLONGED the Marcos presidency but couldn't save it. The beginning of the end dawned on August 21, 1983, when Marcos's old rival, Ninoy Aquino, returned from exile in the States. Marcos warned him through Imelda to stay away, but Aquino donned a bullet-proof vest and brought a press entourage for protection. Soldiers led him off the plane and shot him in the head. The brazenness of the assassination unleashed forces that even Marcos couldn't control.

With the economy in ruins and foreign criticism mounting, Marcos called a snap election, and Corazon Aquino, a self-proclaimed "housewife," ran in her martyred husband's place. Sister Christine, her friend, led a campaign caravan through the countryside, and Tita joined the Leveriza women riding along—surprised at her own daring. A vote count so rigged it defied parody couldn't conceal Marcos's defeat in February 1986. The defense minister and a top general defected, and "a human sea" flooded the streets to keep the pro-Marcos forces from reaching the military base where dissidents took shelter. After a four-day standoff, the United States finally withdrew its support, and the Marcoses fled to Hawaii. Crowds ransacked the palace and uncovered Imelda's signature treasure: 1,060 pairs of shoes.

It was a remarkable moment, the "People Power Revolution," a spectacle of nuns staring down tanks and joyful crowds evicting a dictator. By coincidence, much of it unfolded outside the Philippine Overseas Employment Administration, down the street from the defectors' base. For a moment, people wondered if the end of Marcos meant the end of his overseas work program. Nationalist emotions ran high, and Aquino, a devout Catholic, worried about the strain on family life. But even devout heads of state can count. Aquino saluted the migrants as *Bagong Bayani*—"New Heroes." Annual departures rose more than 80 percent during her six-year term, and remittances more than tripled.

Emet was in Najran when Marcos fell. He still admired the old man but agreed it was time for a change. On his next contract, he moved to Jeddah, where he tended a pool for the pilots of Saudi Arabian Airlines. One day he answered a knock and found a familiar face at the door, grinning nervously. It was his eldest son, Rolando, who was supposed to be enrolled in a Manila technical school. At twenty-one, he had lost interest and persuaded his uncle Fortz to help him find a job. His arrival announced a new chapter in family life: the reliance on overseas work would continue in the next generation. "I want to try my luck," he said.

THREE

Girl Gets Grit

W hen I reached Manila in 1986, seven months into Aquino's term, the headiness of People Power had faded, and each day brought fresh reminders of the challenges that remained. Leftist guerrillas prowled the hills, right-wing colonels plotted coups, and nearly three million people swelled the Manila slums. After Sister Christine's clipped introduction ("if you don't want him, pass him on"), I had found my place among them. Tita let me move in, with an unwarranted apology for her hesitation, and gave me floor space between her nephew and the rats.

My study of the global poor shrank to a sample size of one: I was absorbed by Tita and her world. Language gaps and excessive politeness kept us strangers for the first few days. Then she enlisted my help in a glue-pot project, turning newspapers into paper bags. I botched the job so badly she laughed and threatened to mark them "Made in U.S.A." My ineptness put the household at ease.

My Tagalog was another punch line. Wondering if she was going to a protest, I asked if she was going to the *prutas*—the fruit. I pointed to the last scrap of fish on the table, meaning to say "all yours," and announced "that's mine!" With her English better than my Tagalog, we muddled along.

"See you later, alligator," I said one day.

"I don't know what means 'alligator,'" Tita said.

"It's like a big lizard."

She looked hurt. "I don't know why you call me big lizard."

The labors of a Leveriza homemaker were formidable. From my mat, I could hear her make breakfast before dawn and wrestle the laundry at midnight. Poverty had claimed most of Tita's teeth, but at forty she had the biceps of an athlete. She asked why I was always writing in a notebook. On a whim, I bought her one, and to my surprise she used it. One entry read in full: "I washed, I cooked, I went to bed." Another: "My tiredness is too tired."

Half of Tita's life revolved around household drudgery; the other, slum solidarity. Sister Christine's juggernaut group, Alay Kapwa (Serve Others), was a spirited effort to answer the question "What Would Jesus Do?" if Jesus were a squatter? The women (most members were women) prayed, marched, sang, staged political theater, sold handicrafts to the nuns' rich friends, and drew suspicion from the parish priest, who considered them subversives. Tita had an imposing title, member of "Exe-Comm," and was responsible for a dozen co-op stores, which sold sugar, rice, and eggs, subsidized by donors and craft sales. Her kitchen doubled as the Alay Kapwa egg depot, with an all-night fluorescent light as rat repellent. If she wasn't cooking or washing, she was staring scrunch-faced at the index cards on which she kept the books. When I took some Alay Kapwa women to a movie, Tita startled, cartoon-style, and slapped her head. I thought I had missed a Tagalog plot twist, but she had forgotten to record an egg sale.

Alay Kapwa had changed Tita's life. The nuns' main message—that the last were first in Jesus's heart—was revolutionary amid conditions that suggested otherwise. "We thought it was natural not to have a restroom, to live with 'flying saucers,' your roof leaking," Tita said. Remittances had boosted her self-esteem, but so did Leveriza's brand of liberation theology: if God had hope for the poor, the poor could have hope for themselves. I'm not sure what I expected to find in the slums. But it wasn't a woman in a worn housedress trying to live out the Gospel beneath a tower of eggs.

Alay Kapwa had awakened Tita's curiosity. Are all Americans rich? (No.) What do they think of Filipinos? (Generally, they don't.) Did I like the fish head she cooked for breakfast? (I lied.) When Sister Christine testified before the Philippine Congress, Tita went along. "Wow, the inside of the Congress is nice!" she wrote. She said that she had been putting a question to God: "Why if you love your Son are so many people fighting? Why are so many Filipinos poor?" It's the central dilemma of faith—why does an omnipotent God allow suffering?—and one with special urgency in Leveriza, where 80 percent of the children were malnourished. What had God answered? "Not yet," she laughed.

My time as Leveriza's journalist in residence, if that's what I was, proved formative, but I can't quite say what it formed. Certainly, no five-point plan. It was more like an encounter with grace. Tita faced crushing poverty without being crushed. As a reporter in the States, I had tried to understand what kept people from seizing opportunity in a society of plenty. As a reporter in Leveriza, I tried to understand how people seized opportunity where it scarcely existed. Our relationship was so unlikely I didn't know what to call us. Reporter and source? Tenant and landlady? Friends? One night a group of Alay Kapwa women and I walked past a Sheraton hotel where the chandeliers lit a gleaming dining room. The women laughed and teased me—I could enter while they could not. I laughed, too, but the real joke was class itself—however fleetingly, the divisions seemed absurd. To subvert them was rare good fortune. I might not have found Jesus in the slums, but I did have one epiphany: with her dentures in, Tita looked resplendent.

FOCUSED ON SLUM LIFE rather than migration, I was slow to appreciate its grip on the Philippine imagination. My Tagalog teacher left to be a nanny in Greece. Tita's sister Peachy was trying for a Texas teaching job. A Leveriza neighbor slipped me a note to say she was seeking an American husband for a "friend" (and implored me not to tell Sister Christine). I joined Tita on a mission to enroll a neighbor's son in kindergarten after the deadline; she got nowhere until the teacher, discovering an American in tow, demanded my phone number and asked me to get her an American job. "I'm sure you know rich people in the States!" I tried to laugh it off by telling the boy that she was taking my number in case he misbehaved—but she snapped, "I'm taking it because I want to work in the U.S."

A few months into my stay, Tita got word that Emet was returning. He'd been gone two years. She curled her hair and had a fitful sleep the night before he was due, only to awake to a call on a neighbor's phone: indefinite delay. Tita went back to her chores. "I was busy all day because 25 cavans of Sugar arrived," she wrote. "My head hurts. I've been thinking all day because Emet hasn't come." Three weeks of uncertainty followed until he walked off the plane. "At exactly 3:20," Tita wrote. "I'm happy this day."

I was out of town the day he arrived. When I returned, a cake awaited and he greeted me as an old friend. The house became a hub of cheerful activity as Emet gave the kitchen a concrete floor and put up cement block walls. Tita and Emet marked Holy Week by hosting a marathon reading of the *Pasyon* in thanks for Rowena's survival. Neighbors filed through to sing, sweat, and gossip, and Tita bustled about in a T-shirt that said, in Arabic and English, HEMPEL: THE KINGDOM'S LEADER IN PAINTS. A bloody Christ, not yet risen, slumped on a makeshift altar. On Good Friday, Tita joined Sister Christine on a daylong tour of the

Stations of the Cross that set each of Christ's trials in a different slum. With Emet's return, and Christ's redemption, Tita's world was right.

Having been gone four of the last six years, Emet was eager to stay. His youngest sons—Roldan, twelve, and Bhoyet, seven—hardly knew him. But his savings went faster than planned and his job hunt slower. His good cheer slowly faded. A World Bank project was coming to Leveriza, which gave him the chance to purchase the land beneath his home. He spent about $900 for the lot—and $125 to bribe a clerk to process the papers. Powerless, Emet seethed. He talked to an Alay Kapwa donor about starting a pool-cleaning business, but the plan fell through. "I don't like the rich," he griped. One night Emet came home in tears and punched the walls. "Before I was always bringing home something for the children. Now I'm just around the house—all day, all day." He complained that the egg light ran up the electricity bill. To save on books and uniforms, Tita asked Rowena to take a year off school. But Rowena secretly appealed to Sister Christine, who bought the supplies. Eventually, an American friend of mine hired Emet as a watchman. But she would soon be moving back to the States, and Rosalie, a high school senior, had her sights set on college. Emet's return to Saudi felt as inevitable as gravity.

When my year in Manila ended in 1987, we all said a difficult goodbye. There was no way to know if we'd ever see each other again. A postcard reached me a few months later with a 3-D picture of a camel. It was postmarked Jeddah. "I miss our companionship," Emet said.

IF YOU WERE PICKING a teenager with the drive to leave Leveriza, you wouldn't have picked Rosalie. Among the Alay Kapwa youth, Nilda was tougher, Irma a better student, and Reinaliza more outgoing. Rosalie was the quiet girl, the nun in Alay Kapwa plays. The C average she carried into high school showed no special academic promise. Hard work raised it to a B, but the most revealing part of her transcript wasn't her grades. Through four years of poverty and political upheaval, Rosalie never missed a day. "About high school is where I got grit."

Rosalie was so different from Rowena they hardly seemed sisters. Rowena was a pop culture maven, shrieking at the celebrity news. Is Lot-Lot going steady? Will Sharon leave Gabby? Rosalie joined the Legion of Mary and went door to door singing tributes to the Virgin. Her work in Alay Kapwa caught the attention of Sister Christine, whose interest made Rosalie proud. "She saw something in me," she said.

In fact, she saw a nun. As Rosalie started her last year of high school, Sister Christine encouraged her to join the Good Shepherds. Rosalie gave it serious thought: the marriage to Christ was appealing but not the vow of poverty. Sister Christine took the Alay Kapwa youth to Malacañang Palace, where Imelda's shoes were on display. Citing the sin of extravagance, Sister Christine lectured the teens on the spiritual freedom she had found in owning a single pair. Having come by her poverty more naturally, Rosalie was slower to see its blessings. She didn't need a thousand pairs of shoes, but a dozen or so might do, along with a new handbag.

The surest way for a Filipino woman to advance was to become a nurse, especially in the States. It was Americans who had forged the path. Going to war with Spain over the sinking of the battleship *Maine* in Cuba, the United States had acquired an Asian colony; rushing in to civilize the tropics, Americans established the first Philippine nursing school as early as 1906. Being trained in English on an American curriculum left Filipinos suited to work in the United States, and a few did so within a decade.

Their numbers soared in midcentury via a Cold War effort in cultural diplomacy called the Exchange Visitor Program. Meant to showcase American democracy, it offered foreigners two years of work or study but morphed into a backdoor way for hospitals to solve nursing shortages: in the late 1950s and the 1960s, more than eleven thousand

Filipino nurses came. Many married, got employer-backed waivers, or found other ways to stay, despite limits on Asian migration. By the time the discriminatory quotas were lifted in 1965, Filipinos had an established occupational path, and many had relatives in the States who could petition them on family visas. Migration is history's ripple effect: because American expansionists cried "Remember the *Maine!*" a Manila schoolgirl a century later set off to be an American nurse.

"Nursing, that's my choice to help and curing sickness," Rosalie wrote to me. "And to earn money and go abroad."

But nursing school was a stretch—in cost and in academic rigor. Rosalie started the entrance exam with a prayer and finished with a flurry of guessing. She needed an 80 to qualify and mustered an 82. "God helped me to finish," she wrote to me. In enrolling in a prominent school, Manila Doctors College, Rosalie aimed high and struggled. She felt "snobbed" by her classmates' brand-name clothes and private school confidence. In high school, even her English teacher lapsed into a "Taglish" mix, but "Ma Doc" was English only. Unable to do math while listening in English, she failed algebra. Tita took over the chores and told her not to frown, which made her frown more. Pressure mounted when Emet went three months in Saudi without getting paid. "Because not good company," Tita wrote to me.

Ma Doc students were warned their ranks would be culled after two years. To protect the school's pass rate on the national board exam, it dismissed students with averages below 80. Rosalie emerged from final exams with a 79.5. When two lists appeared outside the dean's office, her name was among those departing. She joined a group of crying classmates who rushed to a lesser, distant school and grabbed applications. Tita said maybe nursing wasn't meant to be, but Rosalie turned defiant. "I cannot give up," she said. The dean offered a surprise reprieve—salvation by upward rounding. "I knew then I would finish," Rosalie said. "God gave me another chance."

The second half of nursing school turns to practical care. Rosalie was happy to forget algebra but nervous on the ward, where mistakes could prove more costly. Doctors gave curt orders, nurses hazed the young, and Rosalie found it hard to witness her patients' pain. Only later would she consider her empathy a strength; as a student, it was another challenge.

Tita watched Rosalie's progress with the fear it was too good to be true. Missing the cut by half a percentage point seemed a likelier fate for a Leveriza girl than a place on the graduation stage. "I knew she would pass—but there was a tiny part of me that didn't know." Emet, in Jeddah, missed the ceremony, and Tita was so worried about her debts she tallied them on the back of Rosalie's graduation photo, where she apologized to God for fretting. "Don't ever think that I am losing my faith," she wrote. The pretty young woman in the picture wears a starched uniform and a three-quarters smile that a passing glance might mistake for simple happiness. It takes a second look to see the worry in her eyes, as though she knew the hurdles ahead.

THE FIRST WAS the board exam. Unless she passed, a degree meant nothing, and in some years half the test takers fail. Rosalie spent two months in a review course and nine Wednesdays at the National Shrine of Our Mother of Perpetual Help, petitioning the Virgin's aid. The results were announced months later in the *Manila Bulletin*. The first edition appeared at midnight, and it took six pages of agate type to reach the Cs. There, on November 19, 1992, the smudged ink announced a minor miracle: "Comodas, Rosalie." She needed a 75 and scored a 76.8. Rosalie was a nurse.

If anyone in her class was *not* hoping to move to the States, Rosalie hadn't met her. Her vision of it came from *Home Alone II*—Rockefeller Center and the Plaza Hotel. "I'm very much willing and dream to work and live there," she wrote to me. But she needed two years of experience first. Sister Christine pressed her into duty at the Alay Kapwa clinic, and Rosalie enjoyed the rise in her neighborhood stature. She also acquired her first boyfriend, a cousin's cousin named Ariel who had just finished seafarers' school. Rosalie found him frustrating—indecisive and intimidated by her status as a nurse. Still, she took a job at a hospital near his home outside Manila and lived with an aunt, hoping the relationship might grow.

A year after graduation, Rosalie took the American nursing test and failed. "I find it too difficult, especially the listening and writing English exam," she wrote to me. She took a review course and failed again, which was more worrisome. Rosalie could keep trying, but the course was expensive and family finances turned dire. Emet was home and unable to find another overseas contract. Her brother Rolando, back from Saudi, had a premature baby. Tita went deep into debt to pay for her grandchild's care. Next Tita's brother Fortz asked her to raise Sheralyn, his secret daughter from Saudi—another significant expense. Finally, a typhoon hit the farm. At fifty, Tita returned to the fields to help save the harvest. "I had no money, even centavo," she wrote to me. Rosalie's romance had stalled and so had her earnings: there were so many young nurses needing experience to go abroad that Philippine hospitals hardly had to pay. She earned about 64 cents an hour—$110 a month. Three years after graduation, Rosalie felt stuck.

In 1996, an uncle came home from Saudi and said a new hospital outside Mecca was hiring. A Manila recruiter was filling the jobs, and Rosalie passed the Saudi test, which was easier than the American exam. The placement fees were enormous (and beyond the legal limit), about nine months of Rosalie's Philippine pay. But Tita pleaded with a relative for a loan. By moving to Saudi, Rosalie would more than triple her earnings, to $375 a month. She wasn't giving up on the States, just delaying her plans. Ariel went to sea, and Rosalie, now twenty-four, figured the relationship was over.

By this time, so many relatives were shuttling back and forth to Saudi Arabia that leaving was less a daring gambit than a rite of passage. The only thing special about Rosalie's departure was her gender. Besides two aunts who had briefly worked as maids, all the migrants in the family had been men. Typically, women went to the Middle East as domestic workers, and everyone in the Philippines had heard stories of abuse. Arriving for her medical exam, Rosalie shared the waiting room with a returning maid, who offered some advice: "When the boss says jump, you jump. And when he says take your clothes off, you have to take your clothes off."

Rosalie's soft face hardened. "I'm a *nurse!*" she said.

NOT LONG AGO, a migrant worker was understood to be male. The title of a lauded book made the point: *A Seventh Man.* Arguing that Europe depended on foreign sweat (one in seven German manual workers were foreign), the illustrated essay, published in 1975, showed migrants swinging hammers, digging tunnels, and decorating drab dorms with topless photos—all men. But by the mid-1990s, when Rosalie went abroad, nearly half the world's migrants were women—more than half in the United States—and they increasingly went as breadwinners, not spouses. Perhaps nowhere was the feminization of migration more pronounced than in the Philippines, where the women's share among departing workers rose from 12 percent in 1975 to 72 percent three decades later. Today's seventh man would be a woman, changing a diaper or wielding a blood pressure cuff.

Migration feminized because work feminized: rich countries demanded more caregiving labor, which women disproportionately supply. Aging societies needed nurses. Working mothers needed childcare. By 2000, nearly two-thirds of American women with young children had wage-paying jobs, more than four times the share in the 1950s. Whether they worked by choice or to compensate for men's lagging wages, many needed domestic help. In Singapore, the number of Filipina maids rose tenfold in less than a decade. (In the Persian Gulf, the story was different: women generally did not work, but Filipina maids became luxury goods, a form of conspicuous consumption.) A demand for women in light-assembly jobs also quickened the trend. It's a bit strong to say, as the theorist Saskia Sassen-Koob did, that the feminization of migration marked "a new phase in the history of women." But it marked a new phase in many women's lives.

Migration is usually a mixed blessing, but for women the trade-offs were especially stark. Migration elevated their incomes, raised their status, and increased their power within their marriages. But it also took many away from their children, often to care for the children of others, and elevated the risks of abuse. Domestic workers were especially vulnerable, since they lived with their employers and worked outside public view. As a researcher with the International Labour Organization, Nana Oishi was hardly naive when she set out in the 1990s to study migrant women in Asia. But her resulting study warned, "I found myself stunned by the extent and severity of the abuse and exploitation."

The mistreatment of migrants, especially migrant women, was a dilemma for Filipino politicians. They couldn't appear to accept it. But they couldn't do much about it. In 1988, President Aquino banned domestic workers from leaving, but quickly retreated after protests from the workers themselves. Unable to protect them, she praised them instead, traveling to Hong Kong to celebrate nannies and maids as "heroes of our country's economy." Her successor, Fidel Ramos, took office criticizing the system that made Filipinos "the housemaids and janitors of more fortunate peoples." But soon after, he conceded, "overseas employment must remain . . . a pillar of national life." Stories of women abused overseas were staples of the Philippine press. Some virtually became household names: Maricris Sison (murdered while working in a Japanese nightclub), Sarah Jane Dematera (imprisoned in Saudi Arabia), Sarah Balabagan (sentenced to die in the United Arab Emirates for killing a boss whom she accused of raping her).

Whatever his qualms about overseas work, even Ramos couldn't have foreseen how a single murky case involving a domestic worker could imperil his presidency. The 1995 execution of a maid in Singapore ignited the worst crisis in the history of the labor program and the largest protests since the fall of Marcos a decade earlier. Flor Contemplacion was accused of strangling another Filipina, Delia Maga, and drowning the boy Maga looked after. Prosecutors said Contemplacion was angry because Maga refused to carry a package to the Philippines on an upcoming trip. Contemplacion mounted an insanity defense but was convicted of the double murder through her own confession and sentenced to hang.

At the time, the case drew only modest attention in the Philippines, which was used to stories of migrants in peril. More outrage focused on three Filipinos beheaded in Saudi Arabia for killing their employer, an accusation they denied. But shortly before the scheduled hanging, another Filipina maid came forward to say that Contemplacion had been framed. (In her telling, the boy had died in the bathtub, and his distraught father had killed Maga in revenge, then fingered Contemplacion.)

Despite the abundance of woeful migrant tales—or because of it—the story suddenly riveted attention: Contemplacion was cast as a martyr for her country's poverty and the government's zeal for remittances. Her status as a mother of four children swelled the anger. Ramos pleaded for mercy, but Singapore officials hanged her without delay as television stations in Manila played funeral dirges. Tens of thousands of Filipinos lined her funeral route. "She is a symbol of millions of Filipinos driven by poverty to take their chances abroad," said the bishop who buried her. "Their lot is pathetic. Their own Government neglects them."

It speaks to the growing importance of migration that the case nearly severed the countries' ties. The Philippine diplomats who handled the case considered Contemplacion guilty, but Ramos, yielding to public outrage, downgraded diplomatic relations. Hailing her as a "heroine," he donated a month's salary to her children and appointed a commission, which questioned her guilt and accused the government of systemic neglect. With congressional elections pending, it took the resignation of the secretaries of labor and foreign affairs for Ramos to preserve his majority. The message was clear: woe to the politician judged insufficiently devoted to migrant welfare.

After the elections, Congress rushed into special session to pass a migrant protection law, Republic Act 8042: the "migrants' Magna Carta." As a tool of damage control, it worked. The 1995 law said migrants could work only in countries where "the rights of Filipino migrant workers are protected." But it defined "protected" so weakly that every Persian Gulf country qualified. Its central assertion was plainly untrue: "The State does not promote overseas employment as a means to sustain economic growth." At best, the law might have given Philippine officials a bargaining tool but not one they used with much effect. Over the next decade, deployment of female domestic workers rose by nearly a third, to more than eighty thousand a year, and by 2005 women accounted for nearly three-quarters of new Filipino migrants (excluding seafarers). Remittances topped $10 billion a year. The government chose jobs over protection, but so, then, did the workers.

Perhaps no story does more to show the limits of migrant protection than the Philippines's shipment of bar girls to Japan. In the late 1990s, recruiters started giving young Filipinas short courses in song and dance and sending them to Japanese clubs, after the Philippine government certified them as "overseas performing artists." Their duties ranged from table-side flirting to outright prostitution. Some women went clear-eyed, but the recruiters targeted provincial teens, many of whom really thought they were being hired to sing. For all its paeans to worker dignity, the Philippine government turned seventy thousand scantily clad women a year into an export commodity. It wasn't the Philippines that ended the flesh trade but Japan, which did so only after the United States labeled it weak on trafficking. Remarkably, Japan acted over the objections of the Philippine government, which sent a protest delegation to Tokyo.

I once asked Marianito Roque, a future labor secretary, how to square the government's complicity in the sex trade with its pledges of worker protection. At the time, he ran the Overseas Workers Welfare Administration, which made him the head of the most celebrated migrant protection bureaucracy in the developing world. He shrugged. "The contract does not say anything about prostitution—that is a private matter between the employer and the employee. Nobody forces anyone to go abroad. Do they know what they're getting into? I think so."

ROSALIE LEFT FOR her first foreign job in 1996, a year after Flor Contemplacion's death. She was nearly twenty-five. She thought she should cry but was too excited at her first plane ride and the chance to live alone. Tita worried about sending a daughter abroad, but nurses worked in public and slept in dorms; they were safer than dancers or maids. Soaring above the cottony clouds made Rosalie feel weightless, but she landed with a jolt. Faceless in burkas, Saudi women looked spectral, a herd of dark ghosts. "There is such a people as this, all covered in black?" she thought. A hospital agent met the nurses and took them to a dorm outside Mecca.

Rosalie never fully settled in. The Makkah Medical Center wasn't ready, so she transferred to a sister hospital in Jeddah, then back to Makkah and later to Riyadh. The mental patients in Jeddah scared her, and Saudi men seemed uneasy with women touching their bodies. Not yet fully confident as a nurse, Rosalie was uneasy, too. Dorm life was tense. As the newcomer in Jeddah, she drew a creaky top bunk that left her scared to move. Riyadh was ruled by an aging tyrant with big feet the younger nurses secretly named *paa*—Tagalog for "hoof." Calls home were expensive, placed from booths with metered lines whose every click reminded her of the cost. Only one neighbor in Leveriza had a phone. After waiting for someone to find Tita, Rosalie would race through the call, too worried about the expense to concentrate.

What bothered her most was infidelity—"how widespread and openly people were committing adultery." The Filipinos' brazenness stunned her. "The people who betray their family forget the reasons they came in the first place," she said. She made friends, but not close ones; prayed a lot; and got known as an innocent more than a prude.

Rosalie's vice was shopping. Her first paycheck prompted a trip to the mall, where she saw a $100 watch with a shimmering blue face. It brought back her happiest childhood memory, of the plastic watch Emet brought home. A hundred dollars was more than a week's pay, too much for a watch. Rosalie left, but returned. "I had to have it."

Among the three cities, Rosalie was happiest in Riyadh because her father was there. Migrant labor being a young person's game, Emet, now fifty-two, had blackened his hair with shoe polish to persuade the Manila recruiters to give him another contract. A few times a week he appeared at Rosalie's dorm with a home-cooked meal. On weekends, they strolled the mall, carrying IDs in case they encountered the religious police; unless they were family, men and women couldn't mix. Although Rosalie wasn't sad when she left Manila, she cried when she left Riyadh. After so many years apart, time with Emet was precious.

Back in Makkah for her last six months, Rosalie was surprised at how many of her colleagues had paired off with boyfriends. She was nearly twenty-seven. Friends were marrying. Perhaps that helps explain her interest when Ariel, her old boyfriend, started to write. Rosalie wrote back. By the time Rosalie flew home in 1998, they were moving toward an engagement.

Rosalie had a happy homecoming. She liked the fuss that Tita made and the stature her earnings had lent her. But with her mind turning to marriage and motherhood, her nursing career seemed over. It would be hard to raise children on a nurse's schedule, especially with a husband at sea, and local wages weren't worth the effort. She enrolled in a teaching course and proceeded toward the *pamamanhikan*, Ariel's formal request to Rosalie's family for permission to marry her.

At the last minute, Ariel balked—or rather his mother did. His sister

was marrying, too, and *sukobs*—siblings getting wed in the same year—
were notorious for bad luck. His mother asked him to wait. Rosalie
thought the real reason went unstated: as long as Ariel remained single,
his mother got most of his paycheck. Rosalie was furious. "You're a
man—you should fight," she told him. With her extended family in on
her plans, her humiliation was complete. Ariel returned to his ship, and
Rosalie never saw him again.

Rosalie spent the next two years discovering how little was left for
her in the Philippines. After thirty-six years in Leveriza, Tita made a
bittersweet change and moved back to the farm. She missed Alay
Kapwa, but the family no longer needed to live in Manila for work or
school. She rented out the Leveriza house and built a new one beside her
siblings in the family compound. While Rosalie approved, the move to
the farm took her from friends. Teaching held no interest, and nursing
didn't pay. Dating was difficult. Most men she met had less education;
they struck her as weak. She and a cousin joined a group called Singles
for Christ. Her cousin got married—so did her sister, Rowena—while
Rosalie was left with a recurrent dream of standing at the altar beside a
tall man whose face she could never see.

Life as an overseas worker had prepared her for one thing: life as an
overseas worker. At twenty-nine, Rosalie failed the American nursing
test for the third time and returned to Jeddah. With Emet home for
good, the baton passed: it was her turn to support the family.

ROSALIE'S SECOND STAY IN SAUDI was lonelier than the first. Jeddah
was a pleasant city on the sea, and Rosalie was now bold enough to
bring a Bible. She slipped it in a pile of underwear, where she figured no
one would look. But with the novelty of overseas life gone, all that remained was the work and the fear that her youth was fading. There is
an honorable place in Philippine life for the dutiful daughter who for-

goes marriage to support her family. "Maybe this is God's plan," Rosalie thought. She also thought about the tall man at the altar and asked God for a sign.

On her thirty-first birthday, Rosalie joined some friends at a Chinese restaurant. Unlike Riyadh, Jeddah was liberal enough to allow a mixed-gender meal in a back room. A couple of Filipino men had invited the nurses in the hopes of finding girlfriends. After dinner, the group went for a walk, with the men trailing behind, in case the religious police appeared. "I was trembling," Rosalie said. By now, everyone had a cell phone; soon after, one of the men called. He hadn't talked much at dinner, but he was tall. Christopher Villanueva was four years younger and worked in a cement pipe factory. After another Chinese dinner, Rosalie decided he had a kind heart. And unlike wishy-washy Ariel, he was persistent. Ariel couldn't choose. Chris chose Rosalie.

Succumbing to a fast-paced romance was wholly out of character for Rosalie. But Ariel's dithering had eroded her faith in patience, and guest worker life rewrote the dating rules. She had few chances to meet other people, and her contract was coming to an end. They took to covert meetings and flew home five months later, engaged. The ceremony, in December 2002, was held in a four-hundred-year-old cathedral near the farm, lending it an air of tradition the courtship had lacked. Rosalie trailed a hectare of lace. Chris stood tall in a sheer *barong Tagalog*. Only later would they realize they didn't know each other very well.

MARRIED LIFE BEGAN with happy news; Rosalie was pregnant. She and Chris renewed their contracts and moved to a Jeddah apartment. Chris proved the better cook. He washed and ironed and walked her to work. "Sweet and caring" is how she described him. She had planned to have the baby in Jeddah but flew back to the Philippines at the last minute so she'd have more support. Chris followed the labor with calls from the factory floor. He was five thousand miles away when he learned he had a baby girl: Kristine Joyce Villanueva. Everyone agreed that the mole above her upper lip was an omen of good luck.

For all her training as a nurse, Rosalie found infant care overwhelming. Craving sleep, she relied on Tita and Rowena to a degree that surprised them all. As her maternity leave ended, Chris suggested she stay in the Philippines to retain their help. Breaking her contract was expensive—the penalty alone was two months' pay—and it sacrificed her salary. But Chris wanted to do the right thing for the daughter he hadn't yet met.

Just as she headed for a domestic interlude, Rosalie's life was overtaken by a series of shifting overseas plans. When Kristine was two months old, Rosalie spied an ad for jobs in the States. She could take a different test from the one she had failed. This test, called the NCLEX, was offered only in the United States, but a nursing agency was sending Filipinos to take it in Saipan, an American commonwealth. (The firm would pay for the flight and recoup the expense from American hospitals that hired the nurses.) A screening test showed that with a bit more study Rosalie could pass. In eighteen months, the agency said, she, Chris, and Kristine could be in the States as permanent residents. Her goal was suddenly at hand. "This will only be the start of everything," Rosalie wrote to me.

With Rosalie studying, Rowena did much of the baby care. After suffering her third miscarriage, she was yearning for a child. Suddenly the sisters swapped roles: Rosalie, the caregiver, was distracted and fatigued, while Rowena, the tough survivor, exulted in surrogate motherhood. Nothing had prepared Rowena for how much she loved Kristine. Rosalie "only gave birth to the child," she said. "After that I stepped in as the mother." Tita was surprised at Rowena's possessiveness but passed no judgment on whether it represented usurpation or abdication. Perhaps Kristine would be the lucky child with a surplus of motherly love.

Rosalie's progress in the nursing course stalled: it was going to take longer than she expected to prepare for the test in Saipan. Chris sent money, but finances were strained when Rosalie saw another ad, this one for jobs in Abu Dhabi. The jobs paid twice what she'd made in Saudi—so much that Chris feared a scam—and she had no trouble passing the Abu Dhabi test. Rather than stay home broke, she could work in Abu Dhabi and study for the American exam there. Chris could join her when he finished his contract, and Kristine could follow; for now she was safe on the farm. As Rosalie saw it, they were all still headed to the United States—only the route had changed.

One force Rosalie hadn't factored in was the guilt of the migrant mother, even one leaving to secure her family's future. Kristine was sleeping when she left. Tita told her not to worry, but Rosalie couldn't stop crying. At seven months, Kristine had never seen her father, and her mother was moving five thousand miles away. They would be three people in three countries—a family and a diaspora at once, the national dilemma writ large. "I'm sorry, I'm sorry," Rosalie said as she sobbed. "Mommy has to leave."

FOUR

The Guest Worker State

As Rosalie arrived in Abu Dhabi in 2004, a crew of foreign workers rushed to finish a new hotel. With twelve thousand workers from fifty countries, the polyglot army was no ordinary crew, but the Emirates Palace was no ordinary hotel. It was $3 billion of national swagger, with a dome larger than that of St. Paul's Cathedral and ambitions to rival the Taj Mahal. Even the chocolate had gilded flakes. It took ten full-time housekeepers to clean the thousand Swarovski chandeliers, and it went without saying they all came from abroad. From the German general manager to the Kenyan doormen, the emblem of Emirati pride was run by non-Emiratis.

No country relies on migrants more than the United Arab Emirates, where 88 percent of the population and nearly the entire private workforce is foreign-born. The tiny Emirates has more than eight million migrants—more than Canada, France, Australia, or Spain. A rags-to-riches story on a nation-state scale, it was a sleepy patch of desert until the 1960s, when it discovered it held 9 percent of the world's oil. Independence from the British followed, and seven semiautonomous sheikhdoms united around a common flag. The flashiest, Dubai, blended miniskirts with burkas and built the world's tallest building. But conservative Abu Dhabi had more oil and therefore more power. Just over a million Emiratis are supported by a generous welfare state, working (if they work at all) in cushy government jobs while legions of foreigners hammer and scrub. The Emirates is the ultimate guest worker state.

Guest worker programs make liberals uneasy, for good reason. They are undemocratic in theory and often abusive in practice. While the Emirates is much freer than Saudi Arabia, someone looking for a narrative of mistreatment needn't look far—no further than the army of construction workers toiling in the heat and sleeping in often-seedy desert camps. In 2006, thousands walked off the job at the Burj Khalifa, the country's signature tower, and rioted in the streets. Human Rights Watch reported that the workers, mostly South Asian, were deep in debt to illicit recruiters, unable to collect their dollar-a-day pay, and laboring in conditions "that are hazardous to the point of being deadly." A trade magazine counted 880 construction deaths in a single year.

Modest reforms followed, like midday breaks from the summer sun, but labor scandals remain rife. Investigating Saadiyat Island, the showcase development that lured branches of the Guggenheim and the Louvre, *The New York Times* found that "labor can resemble indentured servitude," with workers paying up to a year's salary in recruitment fees and living with as many as fifteen to a room. The problems start with the *kafala* system, which gives the employer control of the worker's visa. Migrants can't change jobs without permission, and anyone who quits or gets fired is subject to deportation. When bosses control immigration status, workers are at their mercy.

The flip side to the Emirates' story is that few countries offer foreigners more jobs. Its eight million migrants send home more than $19 billion. The remittances India receives from the Gulf rival the private investment it gets from the whole world. If the United States contained as many migrants relative to its native population, the number would exceed two *billion*. There's an iconoclastic argument to be made that the focus on abuses, however disturbing, obscures how much good a humane guest worker program could do. One of the iconoclasts who makes it is Lant Pritchett, a former World Bank economist whose slim manifesto, *Let Their People Come*, champions guest work not as a source of cheap labor but as a solution to global poverty. About 7 percent of the rich world's jobs are held by people from developing countries. Every increase of a percentage point would leave them more than $100 billion richer. I took a trip with Pritchett across Nepal, a poor, landlocked country where decades of localized uplift efforts—wells, toilets, goat husbandry—had yielded thin results. Then we met a Gulf worker home on vacation, and I noticed something different about him: he was the first villager I saw with a paunch. His father stood beside him and beamed. "He's full," he said. "Full all the time."

Depending on how you looked at it, Rosalie had either landed in another repressive, exploitative state or an oasis of opportunity.

ROSALIE LIKED ABU DHABI. It was much freer than she had imagined. She liked not having to cover her head or surrender her passport, as she had done in Saudi. She was astonished to find a Catholic church with Masses in Tagalog. She felt secure in the crowds of Filipinos and excited in the glittering malls. She arrived thinking that she was just passing through but stayed eight years, and as news of her growing prosperity spread, two dozen relatives followed—most of them straight to her door. A negative term for the force she unleashed is "chain migration." A neutral way to say it is that Rosalie's life in Abu Dhabi shows the power of "network effects."

Networks drive migration as surely as do planes or ships. People go where they know someone. Networks plant the thought of leaving. They offer the migrant a couch to sleep on and word of the job opening. In economic terms, they reduce the costs and risks of moving and increase the rewards. As a means of speeding people across the globe, networks are formidable, but as a set of relationships to manage, they're a challenge: the relative on the couch can be a burden. In moving to Abu Dhabi, Rosalie blazed a trail. What followed, in a rush of siblings and cousins, was a complicated story of solidarity and conflict.

For the first few months, Rosalie found Abu Dhabi easier than she had expected. Al Rahba Hospital had a new dorm and a light patient load, which left her time to study for the American test in Saipan. Chris had feared her salary was too good to be true, but the paycheck came as promised. The bank even waived the service fees when she agreed to take out a credit card and accept a $5,000 loan. Five thousand dollars! She had never seen such a sum. When a new batch of nurses arrived, Rosalie met another Filipina of humble origins upset about leaving her first child. Rosalie and Mylene became instant best friends.

The ease didn't last. After four months in a dorm, the nurses had to find apartments. At thirty-two, Rosalie had never searched for housing. The stipend was generous, but the market was tight; either the stress of looking or the Abu Dhabi heat gave her palpitations. She spent a night as a patient in her own hospital. When she finally found an apartment, one floor above Mylene, another nurse said she had claimed it first. Rosalie prevailed, but the conflict was unnerving. She spent most of the bank loan on furnishings and hoped to put the difficulties behind her.

But rather than abate, the anxiety grew, setting off a storm that she came to call a "spiritual crisis." Maybe it was guilt about leaving Kristine. Maybe it was fear about the looming test. Maybe it was living alone for the first time. But Rosalie was immobilized. She blamed "negative thoughts," "all the stress," low potassium, "lack of prayer," "evil spirits," and "the thought that someone evil is hunting me." After five months in Abu Dhabi, she had planned to go home for Kristine's first birthday and then fly to Saipan to take the test. She called the nursing agency to warn she might cancel the exam and boarded a plane to Manila still unsure what to do. "I'm really scared," she wrote to me.

The trip home only added to her worries. Kristine now called

Rowena "Mama" and treated Rosalie like a stranger. Chris, home from Saudi to meet his daughter for the first time, got the same wary treatment. When he hoisted Kristine to grab a goody bag, she howled until he put her down. He and Rosalie hadn't seen each other in more than a year. It was their first time together with their child.

Knowing Rosalie had money, everyone had a request; the financial pressures added to the strain. She bought a car for her brothers, a cow for her uncle, rice seeds for one of Chris's relatives, and furniture for Tita and Emet. (They alone didn't ask.) One friend of the family wanted money for tuition and another for reasons she didn't explain. "It's up to you, if you want to help," the woman said. But it wasn't up to Rosalie at all; there was a code of obligation. "You cannot say no," Rosalie said. When she returned to Abu Dhabi, she took another loan.

Upset about Kristine and uncertain about the test, Rosalie flew to Saipan. She lay awake the night before, with her mind randomly looping back to the same review question: *Should Tagamet be taken with meals?* (Yes.) The exam was enough of a local business that the taxi driver boasted that his clients always passed. That was one good omen. The first question supplied another: *Should Tagamet be taken with meals?* (Yes!) Rosalie asked Jesus to sweep the demons from the room and plowed through a hundred more. Tricuspid valve . . . metabolic alkalosis . . . Hail Mary . . . for Kristine's future. When time expired, the computer shut down, and Rosalie flew back to Abu Dhabi.

Finished with his Saudi contract, Chris joined her. They were at the breakfast table a few weeks later when the agency called. She passed. Suddenly it was all within reach: Hollywood, Disney World, the Manhattan skyline. "I was'nt [*sic*] feel good before taking the exam," she wrote to me. "But God really good and He has a purpose on why He gave it to me." A few minor hurdles remained, including an English test. But with visas and jobs in abundance, the agency said the whole family—Rosalie, Chris, and Kristine—could get to the States in as little as a year. No one imagined that seven years later Rosalie would be sitting at the same kitchen table, pondering the opaque ways of American immigration law.

FOR A WHILE they were newlyweds again. Chris had hesitated to quit his job and play the trailing spouse, but Rosalie had seen too many migrant marriages collapse to risk more separation. With Chris nearby, her anxiety vanished. Mylene's husband moved to Abu Dhabi, too, and the foursome joined a marriage-strengthening ministry called Couples for Christ. With her husband present and green cards close, Rosalie enjoyed a rare season of happy days.

One thing surprised her: Chris's slowness in getting a job. When they had met in Jeddah, he had worn dusty boots and driven forklifts; at six feet, he towered over most Filipinos. Rosalie had taken his work ethic for granted. But if hardship had given Rosalie the will to make things happen, Chris had learned to let things happen as they will. Adopted by an aunt and uncle—childless teachers who wanted a child—he was reared in small-town comfort two hours outside Manila. Content by nature and circumstance, he had none of the Filipino itch to leave. Chris was more interested in cockfights than classes and talked vaguely of starting a breeding business with his father. But Papa had a stroke when Chris was nineteen and though he lived for another two decades he never walked or talked again. Mama slowly sold off land to pay for his care; Chris drifted.

Perhaps because he was big, Chris was drawn to older friends, which proved problematic. He hung out with a neighbor named Joel, who was six years older and liked to gamble and drink. Mama steered Chris to a nearby college, where he spent seven years getting an engineering degree but skipped the board exam. Through political connections, Mama then found him a maintenance job at the power company. By then, Chris was almost twenty-five and saw that his partying was risky. Joel's brother, Rod, visited from Saudi and offered to get Chris a job; in addition to doubling his salary, Chris saw a chance to get away. Joel, staying behind, did time for selling drugs. That the job found Chris, not the other way around, is a telling detail. Latter-stage migration often works that way: once the go-getters go, it takes less drive to follow. Before he got to Abu Dhabi, Chris had never found work on his own. "He will easily discourage," Rosalie said.

Though she didn't fully notice at the time, Rosalie was sinking into serious debt. She got a big raise and took a second credit card. Then she got a third. With the Emirates' economy booming, banks were shoveling them out the door; the number of credit cards in the Emirates quintupled in five years. With high salaries and stable jobs, nurses were alluring sales targets; bank reps prowled the hospital parking lots. The easy credit posed dangers to migrants like Rosalie, who had little experience managing money and endless demands back home. Lured by gifts and teaser rates, few understood the cost. Counting fees, some borrowers paid 50 percent a year. Rosalie got a fourth card because Mylene sold them. A friend had seventeen. When the balances got high, the nurses would "top up," roll the debt into bank loans, and start afresh. After a year in Abu Dhabi, Rosalie owed $20,000—about a year's pay—and the automatic payments consumed a quarter of her check. But she earned so much she scarcely noticed.

As word spread of Rosalie's success, the family was eager to follow. Saudi Arabia required workers to find jobs before they came, but the Emirates made things easier; visitors could buy tourist visas and launch their job search there. Rosalie's younger brother Roldan, a go-getter from central casting, pleaded for a chance. Rosalie put his plane ticket and visa on her credit cards, and he handed out résumés billing himself a "hard-worker person." Though he had a degree as a computer technician, Roldan had never worked as one; a computer shop in Manila made him a driver. When an Abu Dhabi shop gave him a chance, an easy computer repair took him all day. But he learned quickly and soon had a shop of his own. Migration rewarded Rosalie for skills she already had, but for Roldan it worked differently; it let him develop hidden potential. He worked constantly, slept at Rosalie's apartment, and complained that Chris was still jobless.

Next came Rosalie's cousin Tess, one of her closest childhood friends. Tess had married a violent drunk and escaped by finding work in Singapore while her parents raised her two daughters. Noting Rosalie's success, she thought she might earn more in Abu Dhabi. Rosalie lent her money for the flight, and Tess found work as a nursing aide. A striver like Roldan, she moonlighted by babysitting and doing nails.

Rowena followed in the throes of a crisis: her husband had sent her a text ending their marriage. Whether the problem was her miscarriages or the return of an old girlfriend, Rowena never knew. She locked herself in the house and swallowed a bottle of pills, which brought nothing worse than a headache and a hospital bill that Rosalie paid. Feeling responsible for her sister's woes, Rosalie sent a ticket, and Tita looked after Kristine. When Rosalie's brother Bhoyet arrived, the fourth relative in a year, the household bulged with her kin.

Rosalie liked having family close and didn't notice the household dynamics were changing. Chris felt outnumbered, and his in-laws' speed in finding work underscored his own lack of progress. He considered himself a generous host. They considered him a loafer. Mostly they said so privately, but Rowena made sure he could hear. Chris's joblessness bothered Rosalie, too, less because of the lost income than the passivity it revealed. In one of the hottest job markets in the world, Chris went without work for a year. Finally, their Couples for Christ leader got Chris a job at the electrical firm where he worked; they shared an apartment in Dubai and drove home every other night. But the divide between Chris and his in-laws remained. "It did not start off in a proper way," he said. "They did not look up to me."

Though Rosalie had cleared the nursing test, to qualify for a job in the States she still had to pass an English exam. She took it as her siblings started to arrive and failed badly. She had "a partial command of the language" and was "likely to make many mistakes," the test indicated. "I failed too much in speaking and reading," she wrote to me. "I got so tense." She shrugged it off as a learning experience and figured she would do better next time. "Maybe God has a purpose," she said. "I'm pregnant."

For reasons she didn't much ponder, Rosalie felt in less of a hurry to move to the United States. A promotion had earned her another raise, and she was distracted by her pregnancy. She waited a year to retake the English test and shrugged when she failed again. Testy emails arrived from the nursing agency, which had sent her to Saipan and wouldn't recoup its investment until she got an American job; it chided her for delinquent paperwork and unpaid fees. "You are seriously putting into jeopardy your position," the agency warned. Rosalie ignored the messages. She still saw herself as a nurse in the States but didn't care when.

In the fall of 2005, Rosalie had her second child. She prayed for a boy and had another girl, Precious Lara. Rosalie gave birth in Abu Dhabi and planned to keep the baby there, but with Chris working, she lacked child care, and Lara came home from the nursery sick—coughing and crying all night. Feeling overwhelmed, Rosalie took her to the Philippines, where Tita could watch her with family help. Lara arrived so dehydrated they went straight to the hospital, and Rosalie soon returned to Abu Dhabi. She'd had seven months before leaving Kristine but only a month with Lara. Rosalie's life was scattered: she had a job in the Emirates, children in the Philippines, and plans for a future in the States.

Rosalie's trip home brought a visit from a former Leveriza neighbor who was selling real estate. Remittances had fueled a housing boom; developers chased overseas workers from overseas marketing posts, plying them with nostalgic reminders of home. New subdivisions lined the highway home with chic European names—La Melia, Athena, Athena Classic. Rosalie's neighbor took her to West Beverly Hills—"inspired by the classy and popular place in California, USA," the pamphlet explained. The model, splashed in pastels, had a white picket fence and reminded Rosalie of the Barbie sets she had coveted as a child—a Barbie set for $36,000.

Buying it was a bad idea on multiple grounds. With a job in Abu Dhabi and plans in the States, Rosalie was unlikely to return to the Philippines, and the house was too far from the compound to use on vacations. She was already in debt, and Chris was opposed. But Rosalie was sad about leaving another child, and what better symbol of domesticity than a white picket fence? She could borrow the down payment in Abu Dhabi and get a mortgage in Manila. Tita couldn't imagine a woman buying a house without her husband's approval, but Rosalie snapped, "He's not the one paying for it." In one impulsive decision, she plunged deeper into debt and further damaged her husband's pride. Looking back, she would call the purchase in West Beverly Hills "the worst decision I made in my life."

MIGRANTS HAVE ALWAYS sent money home or, like Rosalie, come home to spend it. But for a long time experts didn't think it amounted to much. They considered remittances small potatoes and possibly rotten ones—minor sums "wasted" on consumption or reminders of brain drain. About the time Rosalie moved to Abu Dhabi, a World Bank economist named Dilip Ratha set out to count the cash. As a migrant who regularly sent money to India, Ratha suspected the sums were substantial. But he was floored to discover just how large they were: in 2003, when Ratha first published his data, the $72 billion that poor countries received in remittances was more than three and a half times what they received in foreign aid; in a dozen countries remittances exceeded a tenth of the GDP. By 2018, remittances were projected to top *half a trillion* dollars, and thirty countries had remittances worth more than a tenth of GDP. As a share of the Tajikistan GDP, remittances were 32 percent.

No large country relies on remittances more than the Philippines. I once joined President Gloria Macapagal Arroyo at her annual airport ceremony to welcome home workers for Christmas. As the cameras rolled, a planeload of bleary men from the Gulf strolled down a red carpet, swapping puzzled looks for free rice cakes and a presidential handshake. Squeezing in an elevator beside Arroyo, I asked why she called the migrants "heroes." A president and the daughter of a president, Arroyo was a seasoned pol with a doctorate in economics. Her look suggested she considered me a dunce. "They send home more than a billion dollars a month," she said. (It's now nearly three times as much.)

As Ratha's annual surveys tallied the sums, a cottage industry arose to encourage remittances and maximize their impact. Egypt offered tax breaks to migrants who sent money; India and Bangladesh offered higher interest. Banks in Turkey and Brazil used remittance flows as collateral for corporate bonds. High on the agenda was cutting the cost of sending money and getting families "banked," to encourage savings, create capital pools, and establish credit histories. Optimists saw a potent new way to promote development, though not everyone was convinced.

The case for migration as a development tool starts with the migrants' loyalty. Between her mortgage and her support for her parents and kids, Rosalie sent home about a third of her earnings and more in emergencies. That's not unusual: researchers found Mexicans in the States sent 31 percent and Senegalese in Spain, 50 percent. The sums decline with time, but nearly a quarter of Latin Americans in the States still send money after twenty years. Since the money bypasses the government, it is less susceptible to corruption than foreign aid. It's also countercyclical: private investors pull back in bad times, but migrants send more.

Remittances cut poverty. That may seem obvious, but it's not: the poorest families usually don't migrate, and some migrants, being ambitious, would escape poverty anyway. But with the evidence in, the World Bank flatly states, "Remittances, in fact, do reduce poverty." The bank found poverty reductions of five percentage points in Ghana, six points in Bangladesh, and eleven points in Uganda—large declines. A study of seventy-one poor countries found that a 10 percent rise in remittances cut by 3.5 percent the number of people living in poverty. That's about twice as much poverty reduction as a similar rise in domestic growth achieves, since the latter is more easily captured by elites. Rosalie provided about two-thirds of Tita and Emet's monthly income of $430. Without her support, Emet's income (social security and the rent from Leveriza) would have left them at the poverty line. With it, they had an income three times higher.

Skeptics fear the money gets wasted on consumerist splurges (and sometimes it does). But migrant families also invest in housing, health care, and education. To analyze spending priorities, Dean Yang of the University of Michigan capitalized on a natural experiment—the sudden change in Philippine exchange rates in 1997, which boosted the value of remittances by about 50 percent. The windfall had little impact on consumption but "large effects on various types of household investments." School attendance rose; child labor fell; and families with remittances started more capital-intensive businesses. In Pakistan, where household spending favors boys, remittances left girls 5 percent taller; with more money, families fed them better. Despite fears, there's little evidence that remittances cause inflation or tempt recipients to quit jobs.

Concerns about migration once focused on brain drain. (A related fear is "brain waste"—Third World engineers driving First World cabs.) With twelve million skilled migrants from the developing world living in rich countries, the potential harm can't be ignored. But the debate has broadened to include "brain gain." As many as half of skilled migrants eventually come home, sometimes with new skills or connections. Brain gain boosted the tech industries in India, China, and Taiwan, which drew on the ideas, networks, and capital that return migrants brought. Counterintuitively, countries that send skilled workers overseas may even increase the number at home, by stimulating supply. As Filipino nurses prospered abroad, the number of schools and graduates soared;

most hoped to work overseas, but not all made it, creating a domestic glut. Migration didn't reduce the number of nurses in the Philippines; it raised it.

Though migration relieves poverty, it hasn't shown much ability to do what economists value most—raise GDP. Macroeconomic growth involves too many other things: taxes, trade, the monetary supply, education, taxes, war, and peace. By propping up rulers like Marcos, migration may even impede reforms (not that keeping people home to storm the barricades is a good alternative). Migration hasn't weakened the Philippine oligarchs or reduced corruption. The third president of the post-Marcos era, an action-movie hero named Joseph Estrada, was convicted of "plunder" for skimming tens of millions of dollars in taxes and bribes. Pushed from office, he was pardoned by his successor, Arroyo, who was charged with plunder herself. (She was elected to Congress and acquitted.) While brain gain reinforced growth in India and Taiwan, the growth was already under way; it's hard to find a case where migration alone triggered development.

Or it is if you define success in terms of place rather than people. Migration hasn't enlarged the Philippine economy, but it's enlarged the incomes of millions of Filipinos. That's development, too. A Filipino who goes abroad often raises his salary at least three or four times. An antipoverty program with a record like that would be the stuff of legend. "There are two possible ways to reduce global poverty: migration; and increasing people's wages while in their home country," writes Pritchett, the former World Bank economist. "Why should only one of these ways count as 'development'?" If you put the migrants back into the picture, "migration *is* development."

If migration is development, or a form of it, there are few better places to see its effects than Tita's family compound, a few lush hectares that once held nothing but coffee trees and the straw hut where she was raised. I hadn't seen Tita and Emet for nearly twenty years when I returned to write about them for *The New York Times*. I took a car from Manila and waited nervously in a small-town restaurant until an elderly couple with white hair and familiar grins walked in. In an instant, I felt home again.

But what a different home the compound was compared with Leveriza. A dozen cement block houses sat in a rough semicircle, each belonging to a different relative. Like an ocular version of carbon dating, a quick look yielded a fair guess of how long the owner worked abroad. The home without paint or windowpanes belonged to the brother who did two years. A tile roof and second kitchen suggested an absence of a decade or more. Thanks to Rosalie's exalted standing (seven years as a Middle East *nurse*), Tita and Emet boasted the compound's jewel, a three-bedroom pink bungalow with faux-marble floors, two kitchens, and a private water tank.

The house was nicer than any Tita and Emet had known, but quieter, too, with four of their five children abroad. "I am sad because they're in a far place," Tita said. Emet was especially susceptible to nostalgia for the bad old days in the slums. "I was happier then, because I was with my children." One reason Rosalie had left Lara behind was that she felt her parents needed children to love. Armed with her first cell phone, Tita had sent so many texts to the Emirates that she had worn off the keys. The guest room contained a wedding portrait of Rosalie, facing the camera with a confident look. Migration had given her more education, money, power, and prestige than Tita could have dreamed of on her wedding day. But Lara, then a year old, didn't play in the room and hardly knew the face.

Across the compound, the mix of comfort and discomfort was the same. There were bunk beds, stereos, big TVs, and the newest status symbol, braces. Half the teenagers attended private school, and most were headed to college. But schooling had a circular logic: parents worked abroad to educate kids, who got educated to work abroad.

Migration had brought development, to a degree that no one had imagined. And development brought more migration.

ROSALIE DISCOVERED she was pregnant again, with the boy she had coveted. Having left two children in the Philippines, she vowed to keep the third. Caring for the girls grew hard on Tita, who at sixty slipped on their shampoo spill and scalded herself. Rowena flew home to help and brought back Kristine, and Rosalie had her boy, Dominique. After years of long-distance motherhood, Rosalie had two children to raise.

Or maybe a child and a half. Kristine, who was three, considered Rowena her mother. She wouldn't sleep with Rosalie and Chris, and when Rowena left for work, she stood at the door crying, "Mama!" Rowena told Kristine to go to her parents but seemed pleased when the toddler refused. When Rosalie and Chris tried to coax Kristine into their bed, Rowena decorated her ceiling with glow-in-the-dark stars. She called Kristine *Ah-tay ko*, "my big girl," and composed a bedtime script they recited like a prayer.

> *Good night Ah-tay ko*
> *Good night Mama ko*
> *I love you Ah-tay ko*
> *I love you Mama ko*
> *Kiss Ah-tay ko, Super sexy in the whole world*
> *Kiss Mama ko, Super sexy in the whole world.*

It was a liturgy for two, without Rosalie. Until then, Rosalie had told herself she could make up for lost time, but doubts grew. "It is very difficult, because she is not close to me," she told me. When Kristine went to a parent, she preferred Chris, who courted her with a silly side that Rosalie lacked. With Kristine aloof and Lara away, Rosalie doted on her boy, Dominique.

Rowena's return left Chris surrounded by in-laws, feeling like a house-guest. A few months later he quit his job, complaining he hadn't received a promised bonus. *"Tamad,"* Rowena griped. *Lazy.* With Chris out of work, Rosalie made the monthly payments to his mother. Once she included extra for a life insurance bill, sending her mother-in-law more that month than she sent her parents. Rowena saw the receipt and howled. "We need to take care of *our* parents—not someone else's." Roldan and Bhoyet chimed in. Rosalie told them not to meddle without knowing that Chris had left the receipt on the counter to see what they would say. His in-laws' talk of helping *our* family only confirmed they didn't consider him part of it. He said nothing, even to Rosalie. "Chris will not talk," she said. "He will keep everything in his heart, and later it will burst."

It burst one morning before church. Kristine fussed while getting dressed and ran across the room. Rowena spanked her, and Chris snapped, insulting Rowena with a Tagalog obscenity so potent it nearly knocked her down.

"I'm her father!" Chris yelled.

"I'm not trying to take her," Rowena said, though she told herself she already had.

Chris apologized by text, but no one forgave or forgot. Roldan overheard him tell Rosalie her siblings should go. Rosalie refused: family was family.

The complexity of family life grew. Though Kristine and Dominique were in Abu Dhabi, Lara, almost two, was still back on the farm. When Rosalie visited for the first time in a year, she was shocked. "Lara is so thin, so black," she said. "I feel so guilty she's far away." She resolved to bring her to Abu Dhabi. But while Rosalie was home, Emet pulled a tooth with pliers and gave himself tetanus. Rosalie rushed him to a hospital in Manila, and he came home with a chronic nosebleed. The first two specialists detected nothing, but Rosalie insisted he see a third, who found cancer in his nasal passage. Chris's cousin, a doctor, offered to arrange cheap care, but Rosalie took Emet to the elite Makati Medical

City for seven rounds of chemotherapy and thirty-eight sessions of radiation, all of which had to be paid for on the spot. "Thank God I have children working overseas—otherwise I'd be dead," Emet said.

Emet's illness marked a turning point in Rosalie's finances. The treatment cost about $25,000—another year's pay—which she put on credit cards and covered with more loans. Brushed aside, Chris questioned the need for such expensive care. "Maybe she just wanted to show off," he said. Rosalie was nearly $50,000 in debt, not counting the mortgage for an empty house. The automatic payment consumed more than half her paycheck, and in the Emirates people who didn't pay their debts could be jailed. She scrapped the plan to bring Lara to Abu Dhabi, which required plane fare and babysitting. Rosalie didn't tell anyone, but for the first time since she got a credit card, she was scared.

By now, Rosalie had expected to be in the States, not in limbo and debt in the Persian Gulf. But after failing the English test three times, she had given up. She stopped filing paperwork, paying fees, or answering her agency's calls. O'Grady Peyton pleaded, cajoled, and threatened, and then sent a curt notice: "You have been dropped from the OGP-USA sponsorship program."

Rosalie was so close—why quit? She has given multiple answers. She liked Abu Dhabi and felt prosperous there. She got promotions and helped her siblings. She was distracted by her pregnancies. She grew tired of failing the English test—*really* tired of failing the English test. "I just said, 'Oh, I'm so fed up.'" Perhaps the truest explanation was the simplest: "I didn't feel ready yet."

The agency's dismissal grabbed her attention. "I apologize," she wrote, promising to retake the English test. "It's been my greatest dream to work in the U.S." I got her a tutor. Chris's mother wrote a prayer. Rosalie studied for months and failed for the fourth time. "I have a hard time telling this not good news," she wrote to me. "I feel so much disappointed." Her cumulative score passed, but her speaking score failed. Next she failed the opposite way: her speaking passed, but her cumulative score failed. Rosalie was mulling a sixth attempt when she learned she could superscore—combine the best marks from different tests. Sixteen years after graduation, four years after passing the nursing exam, Rosalie was eligible for an American visa.

But there weren't any visas, and there weren't any jobs. Rosalie's timing was exquisitely bad. A quirk of American immigration law pitted nurses against engineers for a fixed number of green cards. The tech boom had flooded the queue with engineers, adding years to the nurses' waits. (Congress had added some nursing visas in 2005, but they had run out.) Then, as soon as Rosalie passed the test in 2008, the U.S. economy went into a free fall. With American nurses clinging to their jobs, openings vanished. There was nothing to do but wait.

More relatives piled in. Rosalie bought a ticket for Chris's aunt, Tita Nanette, and hired her to care for Kristine and Dominique. Tita Nanette brought her nephew and son-in-law. Tita Nanette was tough. She accused Rosalie of working her too hard and warned Chris that his in-laws gossiped about him.

Next came Tita's youngest sister, Chang, whose husband had left her for a woman he met in Saudi. Chang brought Lara, who was now nearly four and the only child with whom Rosalie had never lived. Their arrival left a dozen people sharing a two-bedroom apartment with two toilets and one shower; they jokingly called it the Philippine embassy. But for the first time in married life, Rosalie had her husband and children beside her.

Long gone were the days when Chris had cooked and walked Rosalie to the bus and they felt like newlyweds. He went back to work, but surrounded by Rosalie's relatives and upset about her debts, he often seemed sour and withdrawn. Once they quarreled so badly Rosalie took off her wedding ring. Her siblings complained he acted secretive. But Rosalie put their gossip out of mind. She and Chris finally had their kids and a place in the visa line. Sooner or later—sooner, she hoped—they would be in the United States.

FIVE

The Facebook Mom

While Rosalie finally had her kids, most overseas Filipino mothers did not: the surge in mother-child separations was a source of national angst. To gauge the Filipino fear of migration and motherhood, consider the hit film *Anak* (Child), which follows the return of a Filipino nanny after six years in Hong Kong. Josie's family has fallen apart. Her husband has died, her children are adrift, and she no longer understands them. She brings basketball shoes to a son who plays chess and serves eggs to a daughter with egg allergies. Her oldest child, Carla, is a promiscuous, drug-abusing geyser of rage who denounces her mother as a "heartless bitch" and blames her for the family's problems. "Look at what all your precious sacrifice came to!" she screams. "Our lives are shit!"

Josie's two best Hong Kong friends have equally painful returns, one to a dissolving marriage and another to four drunk and lazy sons. No one respects them. Even the emcee in a karaoke bar mocks their cheap hairdos and subservient jobs. "What are you, *domestic help?*" While Josie tries to reconnect with her children, Carla pines for the weak father who couldn't support her and spurns the strong mother who did.

As her finances dwindle and a return to Hong Kong looms, Josie notes the double standard: "Have you ever wondered why, when a man is able to give his family food, clothing, shelter . . . people are quick to say what a good father he is. But if you're a woman . . . it's still not enough for you to be called a good mother."

Carla eventually straightens up and tells Josie that migrant mothers are the country's new heroes. But it's her ferocious resentment that makes the 2000 film memorable; even the reconciliation scene suggests the wounds remain. "I grew up without anyone to guide me—without a mother to tell me that I'm good, that I'm pretty, that I'm special," she says. "Nothing can take your place, not money or anything it can buy. You're our mother—*my* mother."

Rosalie's cousin Marites Aliscad—Tess—went abroad the year after *Anak*'s release, leaving two young daughters. Like Josie, she was taking up for a feckless man who couldn't feed the kids. Like Josie, she felt stigmatized as a nanny. Tess was stronger than Josie, who groveled to her bosses, and Tess's parents took better care of her kids. But the biggest difference between Tess and her fictional counterpart was technology. Josie wrote letters and waited weeks for a response. Tess enjoyed instant communication through calls, texts, and social media. Josie didn't know what her daughter could eat; Tess knew what her daughters ate for breakfast. Not all migrants have the same digital access or use it with such energy. But as migration feminized and digitized at the same time, millions of migrant mothers seized on technology to try to be two places at once. Tess embodied a migrant vanguard—the Facebook Mom.

ON THE SURFACE, Rosalie and Tess were alike—two four-foot-something, up-from-nothing Filipina breadwinners, making their way as migrants and mothers. But their ascents differed in an important respect. While Rosalie relied on a nursing credential, Tess had nothing to rely on but her wits. Savvy where Rosalie was shy, armed with a high social IQ, Tess conjured opportunity from thin air. She went abroad penniless and returned to renown within the family as "The Best Paid Nanny in Abu Dhabi."

They were born nine months apart to mothers who were sisters and best friends. Tess, if anything, grew up even poorer but more outgoing and self-assured. Her father was a butcher in Binakayan, an hour away, but the girls got together for vacations on the farm, where they splashed in muddy swimming holes and squirmed as their grandmother smoked cheroots with the lit end in her mouth and picked lice from their hair.

Tess liked to visit Manila, where Emet, her godfather, sneaked her into the stadium pool and scrounged coins for rides at the mall. Just nine when Emet went abroad but already a keen observer of class, Tess noticed the rise in her cousins' status. She envied the necklace with the gold R he brought back for Rosalie. Bold where Rosalie was shy, Tess asked Emet to remember her on his next trip. He did, with maroon earrings.

Like Rosalie—even more than Rosalie—Tess wanted to be a nurse. While Rosalie passed the entrance exam by two percentage points, Tess failed a year later by the same margin. With a few jots of a No. 2 pencil, the cousins' lives diverged. Tess settled for a course in midwifery, which she practiced with an energy born of stifled ambition.

Rosalie didn't date in high school; Tess fell for a traffic cop. Noel Reyes was six years older and drank heavily but looked dashing in uniform. Her parents pleaded with her to dump him; Tess thought "true love" could save him and pushed through to a wedding. She got pregnant immediately and had her first child, Marielle, on her twenty-first birthday.

Noel kept drinking and lost his job. When he drank, he got violent. He put a wire around Tess's neck and threatened to strangle her. He threw a knife at her head. Her prayers for his sobriety had no effect. "There was a time that I hated God—it was like, 'Lord, you are not listening to my prayers.'" After six years of marriage, she thought a son might prompt him to change but had another daughter. Shortly after

Noreene's birth, Noel threatened to blow up the house. Tess saw one way out: "Leaving the country was the only way I could escape him." Her parents moved to the farm to raise the girls, and Tess answered an ad for nursing aides from a Singapore hospital.

For all migrants, but especially mothers, moving brings losses and gains. Tess was twenty-nine years old and had never left the island of Luzon. Alone in a new country, she learned to talk to foreigners, sleep in a dorm, try new food, and navigate a city. She raised her pay tenfold, to more than $800 a month. As a person and provider, she felt herself grow. But as a mother, she felt herself shrink. The girls were eight and two when she left; she feared they would forget her. She bought her mother a cell phone and called constantly. "Are you showing my picture to the kids?" she demanded.

After two years, Tess came home for her first vacation, braced for disappointment. She had missed as much of Noreene's life as she had shared. But the four-year-old hugged her immediately and announced a plan: she would sleep with Tess one night and her grandmother the next, so both would feel loved. Tess returned to Singapore for another two years, modestly reassured.

As she did, her younger brother got the break of a lifetime: a job at an electronics factory in Taiwan. The jobs paid enormous sums but demanded enormous fees. The $3,000 the recruiters demanded (far beyond the legal limit) was more than Michael's annual pay in the Philippines. Families able to raise such sums considered them long-term investments, with the rewards in the out-years. Michael had always been the prodigal son, long on roguish charm but short on responsibility. Now married with a child, he could reinvent himself as a family man. His parents sold their house in Binakayan to raise the fee, and Tess paid for his medical exam.

Six months later Michael was back, with a fishy story about a sore knee. The family was in shock. He had quit the job, and his parents had lost their life savings. But the depth of the problem wasn't clear until the

gangsters appeared. Michael had drunk and gambled with such aban-
don he owed a Filipino loan shark in Taiwan as much as he had paid to
get the job. Michael panicked and went into hiding, and his father, worried that Michael would kill himself, guaranteed the debt. But only one
member of the family could muster that kind of cash. Tess wiped out
four years of overseas savings to keep her parents from growing sicker
with worry. "All the money I had in the bank, all the years I deprived
myself—all gone because of Michael. So from Singapore, zero."

As Tess's second contract ended, Rosalie was talking up Abu Dhabi;
she lent Tess the airfare.

THE COUSIN'S DIFFERENCES quickly showed. Despite her years abroad,
Rosalie found comfort in the familiar. No one would call her cosmopolitan. Tess had less education but more confidence and curiosity, better English, and an ability to read a room. She connected with people
and inspired their trust. She asked questions, empathized with her
bosses, probed without being intrusive. Rosalie got ahead by being a
nurse. Tess got ahead being Tess.

After a short stay with Rosalie, Tess found work in a maternity hospital as a nursing aide. The pay was low, and her bills were high with
Marielle in private high school. Tess picked up extra cash doing nails,
babysitting, and tutoring Arab children in English. Among the maternity patients she eventually impressed was the daughter of one of Abu
Dhabi's richest men, Obaid Al Jaber. When the sheikh and his family
flew to Paris on his private jet with an entourage of fifty, they asked
Tess along as an extra nanny. To go, she had to cancel her first vacation
home in two years, but she needed the pay. The Al Jabers offered her
full-time work, but the idea of being a nanny made her cringe. Tess was
a health-care worker.

She was working in a clinic the following year when an American
woman arrived in distress. With a year-old child and a colicky baby, the

mother was so sleep deprived she was nauseated. Tess began staying overnight so the woman and her husband could sleep. Christina Aboyoun felt burned by Filipino nannies—one had stolen from her, and another had quit—but Tess was smart and steady, reassuring like an old girlfriend. "From the beginning, Tess was different," she said. Christina's husband, Vince Gordon, was Australian. When they took a vacation in Brisbane, they asked Tess to come at premium pay. The trip meant skipping vacation again—she hadn't seen the girls in three years—but Marielle's college fees loomed. Reluctantly, Tess went.

The trip went so well that the Gordons asked Tess to move in and work full time. Tess declined. She worked part time for the Gordons for another six months, until Vince, a corporate lawyer who understood deals, finally asked what was the most she could ever hope the hospital would pay. Then he offered her considerably more—$2,200 a month, with four weeks' paid vacation. It was five times what she was making. Vince offered Tess nanny work at the starting pay of a nurse.

Still she hesitated. *Nanny.*

Tess drew a line down the center of a pad. Under "pros," she listed the girls' education, her parents' health care, and a chance to rebuild the leaking house. "Cons" amounted to a single item: pride. Tess extracted two concessions—no housework and time off in a few months for Marielle's high school graduation.

Flush with the raise, she bought the girls a new computer. Like lots of 2008 models, it had a gizmo called a webcam. "Once the realm of science fiction and boardroom meetings, videoconferencing at home is now highly sophisticated and, in many cases, free," *The New York Times* had recently announced. Rosalie got one, too, for Tita and Emet.

Older people in the compound, unsure where to look, filled the screen with noses and ears, but kids were naturals with Skype. When Tess made regular overseas calls, Marielle fretted about the cost. With the webcam, they could see each other and talk for as long as they wished. "It feels like Mommy's not far anymore," she said.

Tess liked it, too. It gave her the chance to ask more questions and wring more nuance from the answers. "Being a mom, you want to know exactly what's going on."

FILIPINOS FEARED THE WORST about mother-child separations; pop culture, like *Anak*, was alarmist. While politicians hailed migrant mothers as "heroes," the tabloids and telenovelas trafficked in stories of resentful, rebellious kids. In a coda to the case of Flor Contemplacion, the nanny hanged in Singapore, three of her sons received life sentences for selling drugs. "It highlighted all that could go wrong when the mother leaves," said Maruja M. B. Asis, a leading Filipino migration researcher. Concerns about the "left behind" kids went beyond the Philippines. The United Nations warned, "The loss of their mothers' nurturing and affection can take a huge emotional toll."

Fears are inevitable, but it's not clear that maternal migration hurts the kids left behind. While most miss their mothers, many eat better and attend better schools because of their mothers' earnings. Whether the loss outweighs the gain depends on the context—the strength of the preexisting relationship, the quality of the substitute care, and how much the family finances improve. Unauthorized migration is especially hard on kids, since mothers can't go home to visit. Children in Mexico and Central America often go a decade or more without seeing mothers illegally in the States, and the mothers sometimes form new families. But most Filipinos, like Tess, migrate through legal channels and have large extended families to step in. It takes a village, but the Philippines is a village society.

In 2004, Asis, of the Scalabrini Migration Center, published a nationwide study of kids with a parent abroad. Most did well—better on average than similar children with both parents home. The migrants' kids outperformed peers in school, enjoyed better health, and reported less anxiety or loneliness. They even bathed and went to church at higher rates. "The direction of the changes is for the better: improved economic status, the family being happier, more complete and closer," the study found.

But there was one important qualification: the benefits were more obvious when fathers went abroad and mothers stayed home. When the absent parent was a mother, the effect was unclear: on some measures their children did better than kids with parents home, while on others they modestly trailed.

A few years later, Asis did another study. Again the children of migrants on average outperformed nonmigrant peers: they were healthier and more successful in school, less likely to have psychological problems, and just as likely to be happy as children with both parents home. The main difference was that in the latter study, published in 2011, the children with absent mothers no longer lagged. "Contrary to earlier findings, the children of migrant mothers did as well" as those of migrant fathers and better than those with both parents home. Far from being ruined, they had the highest levels of on-pace schooling and positive socialization.

It was only one study, too little to support broad claims, and it wasn't clear why children of absent mothers showed no disadvantage. But a passing line in the report offered a clue. "Extraordinary developments" in communications—from cell phones to social media sites—helped both mothers and fathers "continue parenting from afar." Mothers, whose absence had been especially missed, had new ways to stay in touch.

Tess's life as a migrant mother unfolded in perfect sync with the digital revolution, which took hold with special zeal in the Philippines. In the four years after Tess went abroad, the number of Filipinos with cell phones tripled to forty-three million, and extraordinary rates of text messaging made the Philippines the "texting capital of the world."

Since landlines had long been prohibitively expensive—Marcos gave a monopoly to one of his cronies—the surge reflected decades of pent-up demand. Compared with the 1970s, the cost of overseas calls fell by as much as 99 percent. Tech culture and migrant culture were instantly intertwined. Smart, a cell phone carrier, courted the migrant population with an ad that showed a father coming home to a son who no longer recognizes him—every migrant's nightmare. But technology saves the day. The father steps aside and calls, and his familiar voice sends the boy leaping into Daddy's arms. Calling isn't as good as being there; in Smart ads, it's better.

The marriage of migration and technology is too new to be certain just how much the latter keeps families close. But in a revealing study of Filipino mothers in Britain, Mirca Madianou and Daniel Miller emphasize the sheer variety of ways mothers have to keep in touch in an age of "polymedia." Phone calls offer intimacy. Email works well for detailed instructions. Texts are ideal for saying something without having much to say; the chime says, "Thinking of u." Webcams appeal to young children. One migrant in the U.K. used a webcam to watch her father's funeral. Some mothers played virtual hide-and-seek with their kids. Mothers and daughters got together for online shopping trips. Many mothers left their webcams on for hours at a time, chatting (or not) with whoever wandered past.

It's tempting to think of the written letter and mourn the loss of deeper communication. Letters could be talismanic. Migrants clutched them to their chests and slept with them under their pillows. But every technology has strengths and weaknesses. Pen and paper wasn't just slow but often ritualistic. Migrants affirmed their devotion; children expressed their appreciation and vouched that all was well. "Tell me good things, OK—nothing bad," Josie tells her children in *Anak*. Even faithful correspondents came home to discover how much they had missed. It's easier for parents to pick up clues when they see their children's faces.

Webcams don't replace mothers. There's no mistaking the rawness of the loss, for mothers and children alike—mothers often suffer more than kids. Leaving for London, one Filipino mother was so worried about being forgotten she made her children look at her cesarean scar. "I said 'Look, this place is where you come out of, I nearly died before. So there's no other mother.'" While most mothers like new media, about half the children in the U.K. study were "ambivalent or negative." Even for mothers, the immediacy of the contact can increase the longing. Planning her daughter's first birthday party, one mother in Britain sent home the dress, chose the pink Barbie cake, and Skyped in. But the sight of her daughter blowing out candles upset her so much she hung up before everyone heard her sob. Being (virtually) there made it worse.

Still, migrant mothers, more than migrant fathers, grapple with guilt, and technology offers new tools for coping. The double standard that Josie bemoaned in *Anak*—that a migrant father is doing his duty while a migrant mother is shirking hers—is harder to sustain when the mother can call to complain about her aching feet. Tess's life abroad played out on twin tracks: she was a poor woman on the rise and a mother missing her kids. Instant messaging didn't make her whole. But it did make her feel less divided. As one of her counterparts in Britain said, it made her feel like a mother again.

TESS'S TRIP HOME for Marielle's graduation was her first in four years. She had left as Marielle started high school and returned to see her in cap and gown. Unlike the daughter in *Anak*, Marielle was everything a mother could want—dutiful, affectionate, and grateful for her mother's sacrifice. She had agreed to go to nursing school solely to fulfill "Mommy's dream," and she had gotten into De La Salle, one of the most elite. Tess swelled with pride.

But graduations mark passed time. Marielle was sixteen, focused on friends. For the first time, Tess found herself competing for her daughter's attention. Noreene, who was two when Tess went abroad, had no memory of living together. The ten-year-old was surprised that Tess didn't know her favorite color as her grandmother did. "You don't know me very well, but *Nanay* knows me," she said. It was an observation, not an accusation, but the truth of it stung.

Tess had kept in touch with the cell phone and webcam, but a new technology was gaining popularity. When she got back to Abu Dhabi, she and the girls got Facebook pages.

For a product first meant to ogle college girls, Facebook proved surprisingly useful as a vehicle of long-distance parenting. It supplied social context that phone calls lacked. Tess could see pictures of Marielle's friends and follow their banter. Unlike texts, instant messaging was free. Chatting wasn't as intimate as talking, but it took less energy and didn't require people four time zones apart to synchronize their schedules. Sometimes it was easier to broach sensitive subjects online than it was face-to-face.

With Facebook, Tess did feel more like a mother again. She used it to dispense beauty tips, enforce bedtimes, check the weather, pry into love lives, complain about headaches, broker disputes, and gush over grades. She urged Marielle to be nice to her sister: "Support her. Don't just tell her 'No.'" She advised her on the dangers of spiked punch bowls: "Don't take alcoholic drinks. Someone might slip a sleeping pill in." She fished for compliments: "Did you see my latest picture? What can you say about your mommy?"

"You're beautiful mommy," Marielle wrote back. "HAHAHA. Gold looks great on you . . ."

"Hahaha really?"

"You look young."

"But your mommy is getting old!"

"Age is just a number, 'mi."

One minute Tess was a girlfriend, swapping fashion tips, and next a sheriff, grilling her daughter on her Saturday night plans. As Marielle headed to a friend's house, Tess asked, "Are you going to sleep there?"

"Yes, I will go home tomorrow morning."

"Who are you going out with?"

"My high school friends. We're just going to eat out."

"But it's already late there right?"

"Yes, we will spend the night there."

"What time are you going to leave? Where are you going to sleep?"

Close your eyes, and you see the poor girl squirming to escape. "We have a place to sleep. I will text you. Mwah."

Mwah was the family noun and verb—long-distance love and the act of expressing it, heaped onto chat space in supersized portions.

"Muahhhh," Tess wrote. Also "Mwuahhhhh" and "MAMI LUVS YOU SO MUCH.... MWUAHHH."

Marielle responded with "Mwah, I love you so much," "mwaaaaah!" and "Big hugs! Mwah, mwah, mwah."

Noreene added, "Mwaps!" "Mwuh:))))))*," and "Thanks GOD for giving me a MOMMY like you.... i will never get tired hugging and kissing you, and im still lovin it like t'was the first time:)) . . . mwah:))*" (The extra exuberance seemed designed, in part, to soften news of a bad math grade.)

After a sojourn among the tribesmen of New Guinea a century ago, the anthropologist Bronislaw Malinowski coined the term "phatic" communication to describe how seemingly meaningless words can affirm a social bond. Tess's chats were gold mines of phatic communication. To follow them is to see how meaningful the meaningless can be. Sometimes Marielle just wrote "Mami!" to which Tess replied "*Anak!*" (In Malinowski terms, this forged a "communion . . . in which ties of union are created by a mere exchange of words.") A report that "our topping was boiled pork" was another way to say "mwah." When Marielle wrote, "I washed my underwear," Tess heard, "I love you." One night, Marielle pivoted from the topping report ("milkfish and beans") to nursing school, where she was caring for a dying patient.

"Mami, I have a code blue," she wrote. "The relatives said we should no longer resuscitate him."

"What a pity," Tess wrote.

"No one is even with him at the hospital," Marielle wrote. "His wife is in Japan, they have already separated. Even his children are not close to him."

"Were you thinking of anyone?" Tess asked. Marielle hadn't seen her father since her high school graduation, when he had shown up drunk.

"Yes, 'mi. I remembered Daddy. I felt sad for my patient and his conditions."

"Ah. Ok. So you remembered your daddy?"

"Yes, I remembered him. Daddy has high risk with kidney failure because he is alcoholic."

"I wonder what would happen to your daddy if he gets sick."

"Maybe I would still take care of him. He's still my Daddy after all."

Though Tess had every right to be bitter, somehow she wasn't. "I'm proud of you!"

In another exchange, Marielle confided that she had a suitor. "Our neighbor likes me," she wrote.

"Is he courting you?"

"No. I didn't let him. He just said he liked me, but I didn't let him go further."

"Is he not good looking? . . . Who do you like?"

"I don't know. HAHAH! He's just not my type. . . . I'm not really opening up to suitors anyway. I just don't want to."

"You don't want anybody to court you? You're a beautiful and smart woman."

"But I don't want to Mi . . . he seems like a loser/wimp. . . . And he doesn't seem aggressive about getting a job. Always drinking."

"What kind of suitor would you like anyway?"

"I'm OK with anything as long as he has handed his mother a diploma."

"Hahaha that's good idea *anak* . . . go ahead and sleep."

"Alright mommy, I'll just keep my Facebook on. . . . MWAH."

"Left behind" kids often live with grandparents, and generation gaps can widen when they span an extra generation. While Marielle was studying modern science, *Nanay* had a grade-school education and faith in old-school ways. Bathing at night was forbidden because sleeping with wet hair made it fall out. Sweeping at night chased away good luck. When Marielle got her first menstrual cycle, *Nanay* told her to jump down three stairs (she did) and dab her cheek with the discharge (she didn't) to limit the cramps to three days. When tensions over curfews arose, Tess took to Facebook to broker a peace. "Talk to her still and kiss her," she urged Marielle. "Elders are sensitive."

But Tess squabbled with *Nanay*, too. As her mother's blood pressure rose, Tess insisted on hiring a maid, while *Nanay* fretted over the cost. "I won't take no for an answer," Tess wrote. When the maid started, Tess reminded her mother to treat her worker well; they were mutual links in the global care chain. "Be nice to your household helper. Your daughter is overseas and wearing the same shoes."

Though Tess had been loath to become a nanny, her employers were generous beyond compare. The Gordons not only paid her five times the going rate but hired Tess's aunt and sister-in-law as maids and her brother as a driver. They let Tess work part-time as a preschool teacher to boost her earnings and growth. They brought her on summer stays in New York and flew her to San Francisco to see long-lost relatives. They even threw in spending money. In a region where some domestic workers are treated worse than pets, Tess's life was regal. In return, the Gordons got a smart, devoted caregiver whom the children adored. "She's worth it," Christina said.

But generous is not the same as easy, and Christina was not an easy boss. She was a research scientist by training and a competitive triathlete. She was particular about how she wanted things done. Despite his work as a corporate lawyer, Vince had the kindly air of a small-town vicar, while Tess fretted over Christina's moods. The work could be a strain.

Tess didn't want to burden the girls with talk of her sacrifices. Then again, she did, and Facebook chats gave her a way. "I want my daughters to know that I'm not always OK," she said. "They should be aware that I'm working so hard for them—they have to work hard, too." Marielle was the keeper of Tess's nursing dream. When her grades flagged, Tess urged her on.

"You can endure it, just as I am persevering here," Tess wrote.

"Yes, Mi."

"I'm crying now."

"Don't cry Mami. I'm persevering."

When the grades improved, so did Tess's mood: "(sigh) I'll have a nurse."

"Do great for Mami," she later implored. "So that all my suffering will end."

Marielle's response was always the same: "Yes, Mami."

FOR MOST OF HER LIFE ABROAD, Tess had made extraordinary sacrifices for modest gains. But after two years as The Best Paid Nanny in Abu Dhabi, Tess came home on Marielle's eighteenth birthday and delivered a statement: this migrant mother had made it. She bought her parents an SUV, emblazoned it with the girls' names, purchased the family fancy burial plots, and threw Marielle the biggest party the compound had seen.

For Filipinos, three birthdays matter most—the first, seventh, and eighteenth. Tess had been too beleaguered to properly celebrate the first two. For the third, she rented a tent and hosted 150 guests for Marielle's debut. Marielle wore a blue satin dress with eighteen decorative roses. Eighteen relatives offered toasts, followed by a court of eighteen friends. Rosalie, Marielle's godmother, filmed the event. Tita said the opening prayer. If guests felt jealous, they hid it; the family had helped raise Marielle and praised her success as their own. Tess's cousin Ariane, a cruise ship maid, joined in the toasts: "I feel like I'm celebrating a debut myself—like the entire family is."

When Tess took the mic, she made no effort to hide her pride or her pain. "I left Marielle when she was only grade three—now where is my daughter? She is studying in an exclusive school, at La Salle! It makes me happy and I am proud of myself because I am able to send my child to a prestigious school. And her major is no joke either!" Tess thanked her parents and the extended family. Then she acknowledged a feeling she hadn't expected—a wrenching sense of loss.

"You're all grown up now!" she told Marielle. "And you didn't grow up with me."

In a society anxious about migrant mothers, the film adaptation might have shown a resentful, drunken girl who raved about being abandoned. Instead, Marielle thanked "Papa Jesus" and promised to finish her nursing degree so she could give Tess the life that Tess had given her. "I will provide for you," she said.

A few days later, Tess flew the girls to Hong Kong for their first family vacation. Expectations for the trip ran high and were quickly exceeded. The girls had never ridden on a plane. They had never slept in a hotel. They took in Disneyland and strolled the harbor, but the real attraction was each other. For three days they were inseparable. Noreene was twelve. "It felt like all the New Years, Christmases, and birthdays she was gone were finally here," she said.

And then it was over. Tess was thousands of miles away, raising someone else's kids.

Two months later, the girls posted a Mother's Day slide show to Tess's

Facebook page. Set to Tess's favorite ballad, it mixed vacation photos with adages about the power of a mother. Here was the trio lingering over an elegant breakfast table. Here they squeezed cheek to cheek for a selfie in a cable car. "No words can express how much I love my mommy," Marielle wrote. "No one can measure her sacrifices for us. No one can replace her in our hearts." She signed off, "Muah, muah, muah."

Four time zones away, Tess awoke early, opened her computer, and cried.

SIX

The Visa

R osalie and Chris had a big fight—over her spending, his with-drawal, her siblings' gossip. Unable to contain her anger, Rosalie cried, screamed, took a leave, and rushed the kids back to the Philippines. Raised in an age when women expected less, Tita told Rosalie she was overreacting. "That's part of being married—working through your problems as a couple." Leaving the kids in the Philippines would only divide the family that Rosalie had spent years trying to unite. But Rosalie was too distraught to listen. "I was not thinking," she said.

Deciding that her marriage needed space, Rosalie returned to Abu Dhabi and asked her siblings to leave. "I want Chris to feel like he's the head," she said. She wasn't used to putting her needs before those of her family, and Rowena's howls compounded her guilt. Her brothers moved to a boardinghouse where eight men shared a room, and Rowena found a similar "bed spacing" arrangement. But for Rosalie and Chris, the new privacy offered little balm; each felt too betrayed. While their mothers urged them to reconcile quickly and quietly, the opposite occurred: a long-running drama that played out before family and friends.

"Talk about your situation has reached the four corners of the globe," Chris's mother complained.

If there was a fate Rosalie couldn't face, it was being alone. Solitude unnerved her, and she was proud to be a wife. But being together was nearly as lonely as being apart. "He says I'm not listening; to me, he isn't talking." She vowed to go; she resolved to stay. She talked in circles and exhausted her friends. With no jobs in the States and no decisions in her marriage, three shapeless years unspooled. All she could do was wait.

While adults can find themselves frozen, kids keep growing whether or not their parents are there to watch. Kristine was five; Lara, three; and Dominique, two. In leaving them with Tita, Rosalie had set herself up for years of distance and insecurity. When they missed her, she felt guilty. When they didn't, she felt alarmed.

Bed spacing was lonely and expensive; Rowena moved home and had Kristine to herself again.

> Good night Ah-tay ko
> Good night Mama ko
> Love you Ah-tay ko. . . . Super sexy in the whole world!

When Kristine entered the school beauty contest, Rowena picked her outfit and celebrated her triumph as "Miss Balubad." Rosalie hired a videographer and was left to watch the tape.

The kids missed Rosalie. Lara went to sleep one night hugging her mother's picture, and Kristine wrote a prayer: "Please Papa Jesus, bring my mother home." Kristine's homework included English vocabulary. "Moment": "The *moment* I am with my mother I feel so happy." As Rosalie left after one visit, Dominique cried and tried to go with her— back to "the abroad." But they missed her intermittently, with the fleeting attention of kids. The bad part of the good family life in the compound was that it gave Rosalie competition. While Chris could lure the kids to the computer with funny faces, Rosalie lacked the gift. "I'm the serious type, so maybe they think I'm boring."

Her frustration boiled over one day when the kids were too busy playing to come to the webcam. *"You better pay attention!"* she screamed. *"If you do not talk to me, I will not call you again!"* Alarmed, Tita herded the kids to the screen, where wide-eyed and frightened they watched their mother weep. *"You are my happiness! I'm just asking for your time! Talk to me!"* Rosalie apologized, but the incident only left her more depressed. "Sometimes my emotions I cannot control. I feel so guilty."

For two years, the kids stayed with Tita and Emet. By the third year, Chris's mother announced she was taking Lara—"with permission or without." She was alone with a bedridden husband and insisted, "I want a companion here." The last thing Rosalie wanted was more family division, but with Chris supporting his mother, she felt powerless to resist. Lara started first grade two hours away.

WITH FAMILY LIFE FROZEN, Rosalie's only sense of progress came on the job. Al Rahba Hospital was outgrowing its start as a sleepy outpost. Eager for Western skills and prestige, the government hired a Johns Hopkins management team to shake off the desert dust. Rosalie's new boss was a hard-charging Australian nurse who judged her too valuable for the underused VIP ward but too timid for her own good. She gave Rosalie a promotion and made a project of toughening her up. "You're a nurse—stand up for yourself!"

To everyone's surprise, Rosalie did. When a doctor made an offensive joke (something about her mother), Rosalie confronted him and filed a complaint. Her boss celebrated when Rosalie forced another doctor to re-sterilize his hands after touching his phone. "She stands up for her patients, and I'm really proud of that." A Western feminist and single mother, the older nurse urged Rosalie to stand up in her marriage, too. Rosalie was proud of her growth but noted a dilemma: the assertiveness prized on the job was the quality Chris resented.

One of Rosalie's patients was an Emirati who tried to kill herself when her husband took a second wife. Rosalie urged her to be strong. "Don't let the other woman win. Your children need you!" She added that she understood marital strain: "We are the same." Rosalie left the hospital aglow, as if God had used her to save a life.

In a stroke of marketing genius that year, Coca-Cola flew home three Overseas Filipino Workers and filmed their surprise reunions. Red Coke vans met them at the airport and whisked them to their astonished families. A caregiver saw his twelve-year-old son for the first time in eleven years. A nursing aide surprised her daughters after nine years away. They laughed, cried, and hoisted glasses of Coke. "Where will happiness strike next?" the commercial asked. Gorgeously shot, it's the most moving soft drink ad you'll ever see, but even Coke's careful editing couldn't erase all signs of strain. The boy hesitated to return his father's hug. The daughters looked more shocked than elated. A close look suggested what Rosalie feared—separations take a toll.

After three years apart, Rosalie resolved to bring the kids back. Bit by bit, her marriage was mending. When Chris decided to take the engineering board exam, Rosalie made a tape recording of the study guide so he could listen in the car. She exulted when he passed. "That's the best decision I ever did for Chris—I was part of his success." Chris agreed; they would get the kids when the school year ended. With hopes fading of getting to the States, maybe happiness would yet strike in Abu Dhabi.

BEFORE ROSALIE MOVED THE KIDS, Rowena got sick. She rushed to the hospital with an ovarian cyst the size of a cue ball—a poisonous mass that could kill if it burst. Rowena had known she was ill but lacked the money for care. Given her weak heart, doctors had to speed through the operation, but all was well, except for the bill that Rosalie got. "In a case like this, you have to help," Rosalie said. "Thanks God she's OK."

Rosalie was at Mass two days later when her cell phone rang. Rowena had a blood clot in her lung. With the family gathered around, she had thanked everyone and slipped into a coma-like state. The doctors put her odds of surviving at 50 percent. Racing to the airport, Rosalie posted a Facebook prayer that awarded Rowena the title she had always withheld. She called her *Ah-tay*—"big sister."

By the time Rosalie got to the Philippines, two things were clear: Rowena would survive, and she would need a degree of support that only Rosalie could provide. I met Rosalie in the compound as she transformed the kitchen into a cross between an ICU and a shrine. Rowena came home to a new hospital bed surrounded by five-foot oxygen tanks, a Sto. Nino, and a Black Nazarene. Between the hospital, the equipment, and the statues of Jesus, Rowena's illness added $10,000 to Rosalie's debts, which had grown so high that she and Chris began illegally subletting their bedroom and sleeping in another room.

The episode ended Rosalie's bid to reclaim the kids. "Rowena is saying she cannot survive without the kids by her side." Tita agreed they should stay. "What about us?" Chris protested. "What about *our* condition?" But Rosalie would not fight her ailing sister. Her children were not her own.

As it happened, Tess had flown home, too; her husband had died. Another woman might have gloated over her abuser's death. Noel died in ruin, while Tess had the girls in braces and drove an SUV. But the girls cried, and though Tess had seen him just twice in eleven years, she felt more grief than she could explain; some part of her still loved him. "I can't say I'm OK," she said. The girls wanted to give their father a dignity in death that he hadn't found in life, so Tess arranged the burial. "It's their last time to show their dad they still love him." Rosalie and Tess weren't just honored daughters and mothers; they were insurance policies.

They flew back to Abu Dhabi together. With ten of us squeezed into the eight-seat SUV to take them to the airport, we crawled up the highway, past the shantytowns of the old Philippines and the remittance-built malls and subdivisions of the new. Drop-off parking is limited to two minutes, but the car was filled with pros. We didn't overstay. "Love you! Mwah!!" Heading back to the compound, I asked Tess's daughter Noreene what part of the visit she had most enjoyed. Noreene is the born-to-shop child who had talked Tess out of her new Lacoste watch. I figured she would say the trips to the mall.

"Sleeping together," she said. The three of them—Tess, Marielle, and Noreene—had shared a twin bed.

"And when we are sleeping, we are embracing," Marielle said.

As Rosalie waited (and waited) in Abu Dhabi, the number of global migrants surged past 200 million, more than twice as many as when Emet first went abroad. But their impact couldn't be gauged by numbers alone. Though still just 3.2 percent of the world's population in 2010, migrants were more consequential than ever before—more economically potent, more culturally pervasive, more politically salient. They came from more places and went to more places; they arrived in diverse, proliferating streams: high skilled, low skilled, legal, illegal, students, refugees, brides. Even countries in which international migrants were a small share of the population, like China and India, often grappled with large external migrations that could pose similar issues, like language barriers, discrimination, or the need for various permits, which many migrants lacked. No one imagined that migration would soon catapult the host of *The Apprentice* into the White House or pull Britain from the European Union. But its force grew more evident every day.

I started keeping a chronology of the ways large and small migration was sculpting events. It spilled across hundreds of pages:

1995—Europe starts abolishing border controls, moving toward free internal movement.

1996—José becomes the most popular name for baby boys in Texas.

2000—Fifty-eight immigrants being smuggled into Britain die in the back of a truck.

2005—One in seven Korean births occurs to a foreign-born mother.

2006—Argentina legalizes 750,000 Bolivians after six die in a factory fire.

2011—Anders Behring Breivik, an anti-immigrant extremist in Norway, kills seventy-seven people, mostly teens.

Captivated by migration's reach, I spent a few years at *The New York Times* exploring its impact beyond the United States. One of my first stops was Cape Verde, a tiny island nation off the West African coast where the number of people abroad rivaled the number at home and almost everyone had a close relative in Europe or the States. Migrant money sustained the economy, migrants' votes changed elections, and the most famous song by the most famous Cape Verdean venerated the national emotion—"Sodade," or "longing." Lofty talk of opportunity abroad mixed at café tables with jaded accounts of false documents and sham marriages. Cape Verde was a Galápagos of migration, a microcosm of the force remaking the world.

On a hillside in the city of Mindelo, an old woman beamed at the furniture that a son in Rotterdam had sent. By the airport, a teenager studied Dutch; to join his mother in the Netherlands, he would have to pass a test. By the beach, a struggling entrepreneur was staring at empty tables; injured in New Jersey, he had used the insurance money to start a restaurant. From a hovel with no water or lights, Manuel Gomes hustled change for his HIV meds. He had moved to Rhode Island as a child, sold drugs, and been deported to a world no less foreign for having been the place of his birth. "You have a Cape Verdean here who would cut his right arm off to go back," he said.

The theme of the island was mobility—but immobility, too. As migration grows, the desire to migrate can grow even faster, and barriers were rising. Cape Verdeans strolled the Avenida da Holanda, but the song on the radio warned, "Holland belongs to the Dutch."

> *Watch out*
> *Because they can make you go back swimming*
> *And you'll get home with seaweed in your teeth.*

A defining feature of modern migration is its geographic reach: migrants go to places unaccustomed to receiving them. Southern Europe, a classic migrant source, was suddenly a migrant destination. In two decades, migration doubled in Greece, quadrupled in Italy, and rose by a factor of eight in Spain. In famously insular Korea, it grew more than 2,000 percent.

Ireland is so defined by *emigration* that statues of the starving stalk the Dublin quay, to honor ancestors who fled for America in the famine of the 1840s. But the boom years a century and a half later brought a homogeneous island of red-haired Marys and blue-eyed Seans: the demographic version of an extreme makeover. With Polish housekeepers, Latvian farmhands, Filipino nurses, Chinese traders, and sub-Saharan asylum seekers, the immigrant share of the Irish population was nearly as high as that in the United States. As in America, the immigrants spread out: sixty Irish towns had foreign-born populations of at least 20 percent.

I was writing about an Irish-born teen whose undocumented parents faced deportation, a circumstance with abundant parallels in the States. Cork-born and proud of it, George-Jordan Dimbo studied Gaelic, ate rashers, played hurling, prayed to the saints, and papered his walls with awards from parochial school. And if the government won its case, he would be moving to Africa. His parents had come illegally from Nigeria.

"Dear Justice Minister," he wrote when he was nine. "I heard my

Mommy and Daddy whispering about deportation. Please do not deport us."

"Remember," he added. "I am also an Irish child."

Ireland's dash to diversity brought little of the conflict found elsewhere in Europe; his mother's Yoruba headdress was an accepted sight at the Synge Street school. Not long after George arrived, a classmate confided that he disliked black people.

"But I'm black," George said.

"No," the boy said. "You're Irish."

We usually think of migrants as people who move from poor countries to rich ones. But nearly as often migrants move from one poor country to another. Nepalis dig Indian mines. Nicaraguans build Costa Rican homes. Farmhands from Burkina Faso work the fields in Ivory Coast. "South to South" migrants typically start poorer than migrants to rich countries, earn less money, and suffer more abuse. Yet their earnings help sustain some of the poorest people on the globe.

Their struggles could be seen on a muddy hillside in the Dominican Republic where hundreds of Haitians lived in shanties and tended the banana fields. (One reason there were so many jobs for Haitians is that a tenth of Dominicans live in the United States.) Among the Haitians was Anes Moises, who had worked in the D.R. for a decade, always illegally. Farm bosses paid him $5 a day and told him that Haitians stink. Soldiers had called him a dark-skinned "devil" and deported him four times. A recent attack had left three Haitians burned to death in reprisal for a murder.

But with per capita income in the D.R. six times greater than in Haiti, Moises had answered each expulsion by hiring a smuggler to bribe the border guards. "We are forced to come back here—not because we like it, but because we are poor," he said. "When we cross the border, we are a little better off. We are able to buy shoes and maybe a chicken."

Shoes and maybe a chicken—imagine an existence so meager you would risk your life crossing a border for that. It's common for social theorists to celebrate "agency," the ability of poor people to shape their fate. Does anyone exercise more agency than a migrant who refuses to accept as fate the random geography of birth?

Migrants die by the thousands crossing deserts and seas, but they also pay more subtle costs. I accompanied Dilip Ratha, the World Bank remittance expert, to his childhood village in India, where monkeys prowled the rutted roads and rain poured through the school roof. By any standard, Ratha was wildly successful: he commanded a salary in Washington a hundred times greater than what he could have earned in Sindhekela. But home was no longer just home; it brought obligations and judgments. Old friends wanted money. A younger brother had squandered his help. His aging father feared being left to die alone. His sister fretted that he ate with a fork. Relatives in the village spoke Sambalpuri, meaning they couldn't communicate with his Venezuelan-born wife and American sons. Globe-trotting technocrat, a village boy made good, Ratha belonged fully to neither of his worlds. "On bad days, I do feel lonely in a way that I can't explain," he said.

A distinctive aspect of modern migration is the degree to which it defies government efforts to restrain it. Even legal flows often grow larger than intended, and illegal movement persists everywhere. A government's failure to control its borders erodes faith in government itself. It stirs populist suspicions of shadowy "elites" said to be profiting from the flow. It invites demagoguery. The message to disgruntled citizens becomes this: your government has sold you out for cheap fruit pickers.

By the time I launched my travels, anti-immigrant parties were well established in Europe. In 2002, Jean-Marie Le Pen, a Holocaust denier, stunned France—and the world—with a second-place finish in the presidential election while complaining the French were expected to "crossbreed" with "the population of the Third World." Le Pen later said of immigrants, "Monsieur Ebola could fix this in three months." In Austria in 2000, another politician who spoke sympathetically about the Nazi past, Jörg Haider, led his party into the governing coalition. Of illegal immigrants, he said, "This has to be our priority, to eliminate them uncompromisingly." In Holland, Geert Wilders, who by 2011 headed the third-largest party in Parliament, said Islam was "not a religion" and the Quran was "worse than Mein Kampf."

The far-right, anti-immigrant parties attracted lots of notice, but most scholars cautioned against overstating their influence. "Radical-right parties are successful only in a minority of European countries," wrote the political scientist Cas Mudde in 2012. Even where they had attained office, their impact on policy had been modest; they hadn't reversed their countries' transformation into multiethnic societies.

America had nativists and demagogues, too, but none that had made a big mark on the national stage. Some people thought America's immigrant heritage helped stifle nativist appeals. Others cited the two-party system, which smothers insurgencies. Either way, it was comforting to know the hate-flecked rhetoric of the European Right—Wilders later campaigned by calling immigrants "Moroccan scum"—wouldn't get far in the States.

ROSALIE HAD WAITED SO long to reach the States she had all but forgotten what she was waiting for. Waiting was just what she did. She passed the nursing test in 2004 and got in line for a visa. She passed the English test four years later. She reached the front of the visa line in 2010, but there weren't any American jobs. Now it was 2012, eight years after she came to Abu Dhabi, and she talked about the United States as if it weren't quite real. She asked me if California was a safe neighborhood. She wanted to move to San Francisco because there were Filipinos in L.A. She learned on Google the economy was good in a place called "Dah-ko-tah." Did I know it? Was it warm?

In April 2012, the nursing agency sent her a note about a job in Texas. The University of Texas Medical Branch, an academic health center in

Galveston, was opening a new medical-surgical ward and staffing it with foreign nurses. Rosalie was working nights and sleeping all day. She didn't respond. A few days later the agency called: this is real—get on it.

Rosalie completed an online assessment and felt it didn't go well. But the hiring committee in Texas was pleased. On the downside, the ensuing report warned that Rosalie could be slow to adapt and tense under pressure. But it judged her "conscientious, dependable, reliable, and organized," aggressive about patient safety, and said her clinical knowledge was good. She got the highest marks for integrity that the scale allowed. Having worked with Filipino nurses, one of the Texans, Ruth Ann Marr, felt as if she knew her—"a good Catholic girl," shy in social settings, but diligent on the job. The committee screened sixty applicants to hire about twenty. It ranked Rosalie in the top ten.

The hospital scheduled a Skype interview and sent practice questions. Rosalie and I spent hours on the phone honing her answers. We made bullet points, timed her responses, compressed them, and timed them again. Asked to describe a difficult patient, she talked about a businessman with a broken leg who had cussed the staff. "I would just try to understand his pain and give him medicine so he could sleep," she said. "Before he left, he apologized to us—he was happy about our care." Asked about patient advocacy, she described her efforts to keep an injured construction worker from being rushed back to India. His company balked at the cost of his care, but she got the hospital to insist he wasn't well enough to travel. Asked about an experience that challenged her beliefs, Rosalie mentioned the Emirati wife who tried to kill herself. "The case challenged my values because I believe God is the only one who can take a life. There was darkness all around her. I tried to open up the light, just a little bit."

Rosalie invested in a new blazer and a trip to the salon. She borrowed a lamp to warm her face on camera and posted sticky notes to remind herself to smile. With Chris away, she asked her aunt Chang to sit off camera for support. I wasn't sure how the interview would go.

Her English could be confusing, especially on the phone. She mixes up "he" and "she," says "one staff" when she means "a nurse," and resorts to the phrase "that one" as inscrutable filler. "I reminded the doctor to wash his hands" could come out as "I told to him that one." But she is luminous when she smiles, earnest, conscientious, and caring. I didn't know which Rosalie the interviewers would see from such a distance.

They saw the right one. Every question came from the practice list, and when Rosalie said of the Emirati wife, "I tried to open up the light," she could see three heads in Texas nodding. The committee asked if she had any questions. We had practiced the answer.

"When can I start?" she asked.

She was filling me in right after the interview when the agency called and offered her the job. Night shift, med-surg, $30 an hour. She would qualify for a green card—permanent residency—and so would Chris and the kids. (The agency would buy her ticket, and she would pay for the others.) It was midnight in Abu Dhabi. The agency urged her to give notice immediately. She had eleven weeks to get to Texas.

After years of moving too slowly, events now moved too fast. She had to travel to Manila to get the visas at the American embassy and then hurry to the States. She wasn't sure where Texas was. She discovered Galveston was on the sea and fretted about hurricanes. She saw pictures of houses there with holes in the walls. "What do you call that one—fireplaces? Why do they have it? Is it very cold there?"

The biggest unknown was Chris. Having felt disrespected as a trailing spouse in Abu Dhabi, he wouldn't commit to reprising the role. Without him, Rosalie didn't think she could manage the kids. Eventually, he said he would finish his contract and bring the kids five months after Rosalie. But she wasn't certain he would.

Shortly before she planned to go, Rosalie stopped by the Abu Dhabi Commercial Bank. Before she could leave the Emirates, she had to designate a financial guarantor for her debt. Between Emet's chemotherapy, Rowena's operation, her parents' house, and trips to the mall, it had swollen to nearly $60,000. The Emirates treated bad debt as a crime, and thousands of foreign workers had gone to jail when they couldn't pay the bills. Two nurses Rosalie worked with were among them. A severance payment, a month's pay for each year of service, would cover about half her debt. But until she paid the rest, the bank could block her exit visa. She'd be stuck in Abu Dhabi and possibly arrested.

With Chris still angry about her spending and unwilling to help, Rosalie planned to use her brothers as financial guarantors. They would legally commit to making the payments, and she would take over from the States. But the Pakistani bank clerk warned they didn't earn enough to qualify. "Just leave," he whispered. She didn't need an exit visa to take a vacation. If she flew home and then resigned, she'd be free before anyone could stop her. Just some advice, he said, from a man who had seen too many migrants behind bars.

Rosalie didn't see herself as someone who made furtive escapes. But she lacked a better idea. She decided to leave in five days and repay the debt from Texas. A few nights later, her friends threw a going-away party, unaware of how soon she was going. Moved by their friendship, Rosalie made a surprise apology: she'd been avoiding them, because seeing mothers with their children made her sad. From their looks, she discovered they knew. Mylene gave her a Mother Mary medallion and told her to send Coach bags from the States.

Prudence and embarrassment dictated discretion. Chris moved her luggage to the car before dawn so the watchman wouldn't see, and Rosalie deleted her Facebook page. She called me on the way to the airport, sounding wistful. She had given birth to two children in Abu Dhabi, brought relatives, made friends, tripled her income, and grown as a nurse. But she was fleeing like a fugitive. "It was never my intention to leave this way," she said.

The hospital expected her at work in a few hours. When she emailed her supervisor after boarding the plane, the lies gave her English the tremors:

I want to apologized for my emergency leave without noticed. I couldn't afford to give an advance noticed for the very urgent reasons. I have crises to resolve immediately in my country. It is a very personal matter and was revealed to me by my family only this Saturday. . . . My presence needed so badly. It was too difficult to decide. . . . It was beyond my will.

Tita was startled when Rosalie walked in, three weeks ahead of schedule.

FOR ALL THE TALK of "open borders," they don't seem so open to people trying to cross them—not even to someone as privileged as a Filipino nurse. With her credentials in order, Rosalie was *visa eligible*. What she lacked was the physical visa itself, a three-and-a-half-by-five-inch passport sticker that would get her past the armed guards at both ends of her journey. For that, all five Villanuevas—Rosalie, Chris, and the kids—had to appear at the U.S. embassy in Manila. I flew to the Philippines to watch.

It's hard to overstate how forbidding the American embassy is or how prominently it figures in the Filipino mind. It's the gateway to opportunity, but marines guard the gate. The complex hugs a central stretch of Manila Bay, with a chancery that resembles the White House. But its most revealing feature is the line of visa seekers outside, which stretches down the boulevard in rain or sun like a fixture of the cityscape. In popular culture, the embassy is the place where Filipinos go to get rejected.

"What is the purpose of your visit to the United States?" the officer asks in the comic film *La Visa Loca*.

"I want to attend the funeral of my grandmother!"

"I want to join the *American Idol*!"

The rejection mounts. *Denied! Denied!*

"I want to see snow," the next applicant pleads.

"But it says here you're going to Hawaii."

With Rosalie's application already vetted by the agency, the Villanuevas' visit was supposed to be routine. But with visas nothing can be taken for granted. "Pray for us!" Rosalie shouted as the car left the compound. Everyone was in high spirits, like a team with a big game to play. Kristine, who was almost nine and practicing her English, had a laptop open to her Facebook page. "Mommy, how do you spell 'successful'?" She posted a message: "I hope the interview is successful."

Rosalie wasn't sure if the embassy would interview the kids, but drilled them anyway. "When the consul asks you, what will you say? You want to go to the U.S.?"

"Yes," Kristine said. "Because I want to have a U.S. visa."

"What else?"

"And I want to go to a school in the U.S. Because I want to see your country."

"I want to get a life!" Lara giggled.

"Lara, no joking, no laughing! Don't be naughty tomorrow! Practice again: Why do you want to go to the U.S.?"

We stayed at a hotel nearby and reached the embassy at 6:00 a.m., half an hour before the appointment. It was raining, and the line for tourist visas already stretched past the covered walkway, to the benefit of the umbrella hawkers. As applicants for immigrant visas, the Villanuevas were sent to an entrance with no wait, x-rayed, patted down, and admitted to a vast windowless vault, a Gringotts of consular treasures. The room was the length of a stadium, with seventy-four counters in a saw-toothed pattern, each sealed by security glass. There was no door between the waiting room and the work space. The petitioners and the petitioned were set apart like different species.

"I'm nervous already," Rosalie said.

She was heavily rouged and wearing her lucky blazer. Dominique was slicked in hair mousse, and the girls wore bobby socks and patent leather flats.

"I'm excited to go to your country," Kristine told me. "I don't see school in U.S. and I want to see."

"What do you think it looks like?" I asked.

"There's a beautiful" was her answer.

An electronic billboard directed traffic. Window 48 asked for medical records. Window 38 asked Rosalie to recopy twenty pages of forms. At seven thirty, she learned she owed an additional $1,620. Rosalie thought she had paid half, but there was no record of the money. At eight, Rosalie bowed her head: "Lord, I hope that the interview will be fine and hopefully no more problems." Window 53 sought her nursing test results, original and copy. She had them, with her police clearance, birth certificates, and a pile of other existence-affirming documents in a binder she clutched as if it might run away.

I had asked the press office for a briefing on the visa operation. As Rosalie waited, a courteous man appeared and offered me a tour on the condition I identify him only as an "embassy official." He seemed custom-made for the job—crisp, articulate, proud of the rigorous process, yet empathetic toward the people going through it. The embassy screened more than a thousand people a day. Although Rosalie's documents had already been sent to New Hampshire for inspection, he warned of possible delays. "There's a fifty-fifty chance she'll be told that she's missing something," he said. "It's an extremely detailed process, and it's very bureaucratic." I wasn't sure if that was a boast or an apology.

So far, Rosalie had talked to Filipino staff, but the final interview had to be conducted by an American foreign-service officer. It typically lasts about two minutes, and it was the only part of the process I wasn't allowed to see. It occurred during my tour and involved nothing deeper than "When did you pass the NCLEX?"

"You got your visa!" the officer then told Rosalie. "Congratulations!"

The embassy official took me to meet the officer a few minutes later. She couldn't have been more different from the martinet in *La Visa Loca*. A former Peace Corps volunteer and social worker, she talked up the satisfaction she felt at welcoming people to the States. "People have been waiting a long time for their interview, and they've gone about it, by and large, the right way. Once they talk to me, their journey is complete. I'm the light at the end of the tunnel. . . . I do like being able to facilitate—the dream is a little strong—but I find the work very fulfilling." In the Fortress of No lurked an Angel of Yes.

Rosalie got the visa! Twenty-five years after we met . . . twenty years after nursing school . . . eight years after she joined the visa queue . . . against all odds. It seemed as if someone should bang a drum or pop a cork. Instead, we filed out in the rain with hungry children demanding lunch. "What is the name of that woman?" Rosalie said. "She is so *nice*." Rosalie's brother Rolando pulled up with the car. "From now on you speak dollars!" he said. Rosalie seemed sobered, as if the significance were sinking in. "It's been a long time—this is the accomplishment of our dreams," she said. Then, as if the question had just occurred to her, she asked, "How is life in the United States?"

IT WAS OVER. Except that it wasn't. Rosalie had been promoted from *visa eligible* to *visa approved*. But she didn't have the precious sticker itself, the high-tech, tamperproof treasure. The U.S. government would affix it to her passport after further, unspecified security measures even the Angel of Yes was not at liberty to disclose. She said it could take two weeks. With her Texas employer in a rush, Rosalie was scheduled to leave in twelve days. The problem was more complicated than that. To board the plane, Rosalie needed proof that she had taken a Philippine government class meant to brief her on American life (and encourage remittances). It was offered daily, but she couldn't take it until she got the visa. She faced a double bottleneck.

"*Bahala na*," Rosalie said. *What will be, will be.* She went about packing, praying, saying good-byes, and fretting over fireplaces and hurricanes. A week passed, then ten days. And then she was out of time. On the morning before she was scheduled to leave, I returned to the embassy to interview the nice consular officer about the challenges of visa work. It was 9:15 a.m. The Commission on Filipinos Overseas started its last class for emigrants at ten. Even if Rosalie got her visa that afternoon, she'd still be blocked from her flight for want of a sticker that showed she had taken the seminar.

Over the years, my relationship with Rosalie had blended the roles of participant and observer with no set script; I helped and I took notes. The journalist in me wanted to let events run their course. She wouldn't get the visa in time. She wouldn't make the plane. She would miss the orientation in Texas. She might even lose the job. The costly delay would make a point about the difficulty of crossing borders. Long waits, security glass, triple vetting, caprice—such are the norms. There was no line Rosalie could stand in, no number she could call.

But the Angel of Yes might be able to help. I hesitated. I was there as a journalist, not an advocate. But Rosalie had been waiting for twenty years, and the red tape could be costly. When I explained the dilemma, the officer left the room, then returned to say the visa would be ready by the end of the day. In the meantime, she had arranged for Rosalie to join the seminar. Rosalie dashed to the class, and the officer and I finished the interview by talking about the service work she had done in a nearby slum. "It was really eye-opening. There are a lot of people living in really desperate circumstances."

I waited outside the embassy that afternoon when Rosalie picked up the visas. She came out shaking. "Oh my God, I need water!" A Filipino clerk had handed her the passports, and the Angel of Yes had stopped by to wish her well. "I was *trembling*. I was checking the names so carefully. Oh my God, I said to myself, 'This is really it—it is true, I leave tomorrow!' I said, 'Thank you, thank you, thank you.' Oh my *God*."

The plane was leaving in twelve hours. Chris and the kids had six months to follow or the visas would expire. The most valuable three-by-five sticker in the world fixed Rosalie's picture beside the Capitol with snippets of constitutional text floating in the background.

We the People . . .
Blessings of liberty . . .
Form a more perfect union.

Rosalie caressed it and whispered, "The United States of America."

PART II

HERE

SEVEN

Immigrants, Again

The visa that Rosalie clutched was the product of a 1965 law that once again made America a nation of immigrants, but only after its authors promised it wouldn't. The law's appeal was mostly symbolic. It sought to fix legislation from the 1920s that was designed to keep out Italians and Jews, not trigger mass migration from the developing world.

But after opening the gates wider than expected, Congress opened them wider still. For decades, both parties helped expand legal immigration and lightly policed those present illegally. About 320,000 people a year arrived legally in the 1960s—but 625,000 in the 1980s, nearly 1 million in the 1990s, and more than 1 million so far in the new century. In 1970, the foreign-born share of the population had dropped to 4.7 percent, the lowest level on record. It's now 13.7 percent, the highest in more than a hundred years.

Rosalie wasn't a typical immigrant but only in the sense that nobody was. The average immigrant a century ago was a penniless European in a big city. Now the foreign born are economically diverse, ethnically varied, and geographically scattered, with a majority in suburbs; there are slightly more women than men. Immigrants cut lawns, pick crops, diaper babies, transplant organs, and build rocket ships. Hispanics illegally in the country dominate the discourse, but among new immigrants Asians have quietly outnumbered Latinos for a decade. While Rosalie didn't represent every immigrant, as a college-educated Asian woman she typified a share that was growing.

For decades after the 1965 law, immigration played little role in national politics. Most Americans, if asked, favored low levels but had more pressing concerns. With both parties internally split, neither pushed the issue as a source of partisan advantage. A conservative as definitional as Ronald Reagan welcomed "millions of immigrants from every corner of the Earth" as a sign that God had raised up America as a City on a Hill. A generation later, conservatives who otherwise claimed Reagan's mantle ushered in an age of backlash politics.

As Rosalie arrived in 2012, the backlash was accelerating. The 9/11 attacks had joined fear of terrorism to fear of foreigners, and a full-throated nativism found its racially charged voice on talk radio and cable TV. By 2016 it conquered the White House, where Donald Trump placed the full weight of the presidency in the service of his shopworn bigotry. If all you knew about immigration came from politics, you'd think the country was in an especially bad place—angry, bitter, and mean.

At the level of daily life, however, the story was different. Economically, immigration brought winners and losers, but most researchers judged it modestly beneficial to the country as a whole. Socially, the power of American assimilation remained the envy of much of the world, aided by a post-civil-rights-movement ethos that promoted minority advancement. Culturally, new food and entertainment made the homogenized past seem blanched. Racial divisions remained, of course, and growing inequality hardened class lines for immigrants and natives alike. But ethnic life was fluid: by the second generation, virtually everyone spoke English, and intermarriage was high.

Perhaps in no place was immigration on more surprising display than the twelve-county swath of red-state America that Rosalie was about to make home. Nearly a quarter of the Houston area's seven million people—and a third of the workforce—was foreign-born. It was the Houston metro region, not Los Angeles or New York, that ranked as America's most diverse. Foreign doctors brought renown to the storied medical centers; foreign engineers helped drill the wells. Nearly as dependent on immigrants as it was on oil, Houston embraced its majority-minority status with business-class boosterism, while Hindu temples rose in the suburbs. The "open-arms approach has worked for Houston," the *Houston Chronicle* enthused.

To miss either element—the talk-radio nativists or the *quinceañera* dress shops in Houston's Gandhi district—is to miss half the contradictory story. The contradictions *are* the story. The politics of immigration was broken. But immigration itself—tens of millions of people gathered from every corner of the earth—remained an underappreciated American success.

THE STORY OF A DOOR OPENED begins with the story of a door closed, in response to the greatest wave of immigration in U.S. history. About a million people a year arrived in the decade ending in 1914, more than double the pace of the 1890s. (Relative to the population, the arrivals were more than twice as high as they are today.) Pushed by poverty and persecution and pulled by smokestack jobs, immigrants and their children filled three-quarters of the great cities like New York and Chicago. Eager for cheap, pliable labor, industry wanted them.

Patricians saw crises—tenements, corruption, and drink. What alarmed them more than numbers was the newcomers' ethnicity. Seventy percent of the "New Immigrants" were southern or eastern European. Proponents of Anglo-Saxon superiority considered them nonwhite. Italians, Poles, Slavs, and Jews, they were "beaten men from beaten races," warned the president of the Massachusetts Institute of Technology.

Anti-immigrant bias in a nation of immigrants wasn't new. It predates the country itself. Every colonial historian knows that Benjamin Franklin called the Germans of the 1750s the "most ignorant Stupid Sort" and warned they would "Germanize us instead of our Anglifying them." Railing against the Irish "Papists in our midst," the Know-Nothings in 1854 sent a hundred members or allies to Congress. The Chinese Exclusion Act of 1882 not only halted new arrivals but banned Chinese from citizenship. Whether anti-Irish or anti-Asian, the critics accused immigrants of stealing jobs and imposing foreign cultures.

What distinguished the Progressive Era critics was their claim to scientific expertise. Informed by the growing study of eugenics, scholars like Edward A. Ross thought they could spot the foreigners' inferiority by visual inspection: "In every face, there was something wrong—lips thick, mouth coarse, upper lip too long." By 1911, Senator William Dillingham's congressional panel produced forty-two volumes of research, including a *Dictionary of Races or Peoples*, which warned that the "impulsive" Italians had "little adaptability to highly organized society" and mulled the problem of "the Jewish nose."

Efforts to restrict immigration had been building since the 1890s, but the industrializing economy produced an "insatiable drive" for workers, whose arrivals generally tracked the business cycle. It took a special run of events to close the door. World War I and the Russian Revolution deepened the suspicion of foreigners, and the industrialists' hunger for cheap labor gave way to their fear of Bolsheviks. In 1917, Congress flatly banned most Asian immigrants and imposed a literacy test to keep out unwanted Europeans. When too many proved able to pass it, Congress imposed quotas. The Reed-Johnson Act of 1924 gave each nationality an annual cap based on its share of the 1890 census, a date chosen to keep out the southern and eastern Europeans, who had mostly come later. Immigration fell by more than half, and the arrival of Italians and Poles by more than 90 percent.

Along the southern border, a different migration system evolved, much of it seasonal and unsanctioned. The quotas didn't apply to the Western Hemisphere. Mexicans faced other restrictions (the literacy test, laws against public charges), but enforcement was typically light, especially when farmers needed labor. "When we want you, we'll call you; when we don't—git," is how one foreman described the rules. With farm labor short during World War II, Congress formalized the circular flows with the bracero guest worker program. Weak wage and safety protections allowed widespread abuse. But unwilling to be bound even by weak contraints, many planters hired illegally, encouraging the illicit flows.

A constant in immigration policy is that it's slow to change. The quotas endured, despite their unconscionable role in thwarting Jews trying to flee the Holocaust. Liberals argued the blatant racism of the quotas undermined American leadership of the Cold War: the United States pledged to defend Italy and Greece while discriminating against Italians and Greeks. But Congress reaffirmed the quotas in 1952 over Harry Truman's veto. When the Soviets invaded Hungary in 1956, Dwight Eisenhower used obscure parole powers to admit refugees. So unworkable was the law that Congress passed thousands of "private bills" to reunite constituents' families. But the public favored low immigration, labor resisted competition, and southern conservatives dominated Congress. The quotas remained.

Immigration crept onto the reform agenda as labor's opposition eased and concerns for civil rights rose. Eager for the ethnic vote, John F. Kennedy published a 1958 book called *A Nation of Immigrants*, which denounced the quotas as "an indefensible racial preference." But as president, Kennedy was wary of antagonizing southern Democrats with whom he had other battles. He didn't propose a new law until shortly before his assassination.

Succeeding him in 1963, Lyndon Johnson was wary, too. Unlike the struggle for black civil rights, the issue produced no mass protests pushing him to act. Aides prevailed by framing immigration as part of his broader agenda on civil rights and democracy—a bid for the moral high ground at home and credibility abroad. Six weeks after taking office, Johnson called for abolishing the quotas, saying Americans should ask immigrants, "What can you do for our country?" not "In what country were you born?"

Just as it took extraordinary events to impose quotas, it took extraordinary forces to remove them: a powerful president at peak influence, Cold War competition for moral authority, the logic of civil rights, and the desire to burnish the legacy of the martyred JFK. Even then, Johnson faced formidable obstacles. Senator James Eastland of Mississippi, the Senate point person, was a segregationist with no interest in ethnic diversity, and his House counterpart Michael Feighan was a Cleveland crackpot who had considered JFK soft on communism. Remarkably, Johnson got Eastland to cede control to a young Ted Kennedy, and Feighan's resistance ebbed after the Democrats' landslide in 1964 gave them the option of going around him.

Still, reformers made a cautious case—not that diversity was good, but that it wouldn't occur. "The ethnic mix of this country will not be upset," Ted Kennedy said. Robert F. Kennedy, the attorney general, predicted that after five thousand Asians arrived, "immigration from that source would virtually disappear." The administration said that at least 90 percent of the newcomers would be white.

Feighan agreed to eliminate the quotas but secured a last-minute change. Johnson wanted a system that favored people with job skills. Feighan gave three-quarters of the visas to people who already had relatives in the States. If most immigrants were family, he figured, the ethnic order would persist; the quotas would continue under another name. Conservatives praised him for slyly preserving the status quo and liberals cried betrayal, but Johnson was eager to claim victory. He signed the 1965 law beside the Statue of Liberty, hailing the paradox of a breakthrough law whose impact would be tame.

It's hard to recall another law that so fully did the opposite of what its sponsors promised. Ted Kennedy said yearly arrivals would remain "substantially the same." Over three decades, they more than tripled. Rather than nine-tenths coming from Europe, nearly nine-tenths came from elsewhere. Since 1970, the Filipino population has risen by more than a factor of ten, Mexicans by a factor of fifteen, and Indians by forty-seven. More than sixty immigrant groups number 100,000 or more—the size of small cities—from Bosnians and Burmese to Thais and Turks.

Critics later charged that lawmakers hid their radical designs, but the truth is less flattering. As the journalist Tom Gjelten wrote, "None of the people involved . . . understood what they were doing." Lawmakers failed to grasp three dynamics of the system they created: prospering Europeans saw little need to leave; a growing middle class in the developing world had means and motive to move; and family preferences did little to stop them. Feighan thought he had created a mirror: new Americans would look like the old. But a quarter of the visas went to people with skills, regardless of family ties, and most came from the developing world. Once they arrived, they could bring relatives, who could bring relatives, in a process that critics called chain migration. There were annual caps, but some immigrants, like spouses of citizens, didn't count against them. The family visas that Feighan considered brakes became accelerators.

Congress also created unintended consequences along the southern border when it ended the bracero program in 1964. Unions rightly despised it as a source of cheap and exploited labor. But growers wanted workers and Mexicans wanted work: the seasonal movement from Mexico continued, now without legal sanction. Soon after, Congress put the first caps on the Western Hemisphere, further restricting the ability of Mexicans to migrate legally. Together the end of the bracero program and the imposition of caps did less to stop Mexican movement than make it illicit. In effect, the United States created two immigration systems: a widened front door and an unlatched rear entrance. Unauthorized entries soared.

Even as immigration grew faster than expected, Congress passed three remarkably expansionist laws in a single decade. In 1980, it revamped the refugee program, normalizing admissions at high levels. In 1986, it legalized three million illegal immigrants. In 1990, Congress expanded legal immigration by a full 40 percent and even added a "diversity lottery," with fifty thousand visas a year for underrepresented nationalities.

Unlike in 1965, when lawmakers didn't know what they were doing, they now knew perfectly well they were expanding a system that mostly admitted people from the developing world. Whatever explained the politics wasn't public opinion: in national polls spanning more than a decade, support for increased immigration averaged about 6 percent. The curious result was a system at once open and closed (and little understood). It was open to people with the right relatives or skills but closed to almost everyone else, including millions of poor Mexicans along a two-thousand-mile border. As illegal immigration soared again, critics said migrants needed to get in line. But for most there was no line.

In retrospect, part of what stands out about the expansive politics was the lack of grassroots influence. Deals were shaped by interest groups (ethnic advocates, faith alliances, business associations) and brokered by congressional leaders. Divisions within the parties muted the discord between them. (Democrats were split between ethnic groups wanting more immigration and unions wanting less; Republicans juggled business interests that wanted cheap labor and traditionalists wary of change.) Critics were right when they later complained that elites pushed sweeping change on an unsuspecting society. But the change was generally positive. "The research findings are clear," insisted a bipartisan commission that helped forge the 1980s consensus. "Immigrants, refugees and their children work hard and contribute to the economic well-being of our society . . . strengthen our ties with other nations . . . and powerfully demonstrate to the world that the United States is an open and free society."

"Open and free": the words point toward two other expansionist influences—the Cold War and the civil rights movement. On the right, a welcoming refugee policy (for Cubans, Vietnamese, and Eastern Europeans) became part of the fight against communist regimes. On the left, a welcoming immigration policy was seen as part of the quest for racial justice. By framing immigration as an issue of ethnic equality, not economic competition, the 1965 law muted opposition from African Americans and others who might have viewed immigrants as rivals for jobs and clout. Illegal immigration remained contentious, but the much larger rise in legal entry generally was not. With only modest debate, a foreign-born population of fewer than ten million in 1970 grew to thirty-one million by the century's end.

FOR ALL THEIR DIFFERENCES, the new immigrants had much in common with the old—including the label "New Immigrants." Late twentieth-century America didn't expect Mexicans and Filipinos, but the early twentieth century hadn't expected Russians and Poles. The newcomers in both ages were labeled nonwhite. Both groups faced doubts about their willingness to learn English, even as they did, and both faced accusations of criminality, despite arrest rates lower than natives. Both were judged inferior to their predecessors—less hard-working, less loyal, and less willing to assimilate.

The differences between the eras are instructive, too. Some differences work in the current group's favor. The Ellis Island–era migrants arrived in an age of open bigotry, while their successors inherit civil rights laws and a pluralistic culture that offers more ways to fit in. The earlier immigrants were virtually all poor, whereas nearly a third of today's are college graduates like Rosalie. More than one in eight has a graduate degree—slightly more than natives.

On the other hand, about a quarter of today's immigrants lack legal status, a problem virtually unknown in the Ellis Island age. Today's migrants also face an economy hostile to the unskilled. The Ellis Island migrants came to an industrializing country that needed their brawn, and their descendants inherited a postwar age of broad prosperity. Now the distinctive feature of economic life is inequality. Education matters more than ever, and more than a quarter of the foreign born lack a high school degree. To succeed, their children will have to make rapid progress in an age of weak public schools.

ETHNIC CHANGE BROUGHT ethnic strain and fractious local fights. The Los Angeles suburb of Monterey Park became the first American city with an Asian majority after promoters advertised it abroad as the "Chinese Beverly Hills." Affluent buyers arrived from Hong Kong and Taiwan, development quickened, and home prices rose. There was still enough comity in 1985 to earn the city a national award for tolerance. A few months later, civil war broke out over proposals to limit Chinese signs and make English the official language. "Will the Last American to Leave Monterey Park Please Bring the Flag?" a bumper sticker asked. A leader of the English-only drive was a local official named Barry Hatch, who called Chinese signage "one bold slap in the face" and fought the library's acquisition of Chinese books. "We created this nation," he said. "We are going to hold this nation. And people who come, welcome. But don't overpower us with your traditions, customs, loyalties. Don't *dare* overpower us." But Hatch eventually decamped to Utah, and a successor as mayor, Judy Chu, became the first Chinese American woman in Congress.

Unlike the California culture clash, tensions along the Texas Gulf Coast were primarily economic and quick to turn violent. After the fall of Saigon in 1975, thousands of Vietnamese refugees moved to the Gulf of Mexico to work as fishermen. Their willingness to endure long hours at low pay made them tough competitors, and their heedlessness of local custom added friction. Often illiterate even in Vietnamese, they bumped the Texans' boats and poached hot spots informally reserved for those who found them. Tempers flared.

In 1979, a Texas crabber in the town of Seadrift physically attacked a Vietnamese counterpart, who shot and killed him. Vigilantes burned Vietnamese boats and firebombed a Vietnamese house. After a jury agreed the defendant had acted in self-defense, Klansmen burned crosses and piloted a shrimp boat around Galveston Bay, cloaked in robes and hoods and carrying guns. As in Monterey Park, the immigrants were legal, but that only added to the rub: natives complained the government had betrayed them by importing competition. Within a few years, the Vietnamese ruled the market, and the outworked Texans were shell-shocked by defeat.

Conflict was common—accommodation, too—but localized. For most of the 1970s and 1980s, immigration played little role in national politics, unlike in Europe, where far-right parties fed on the issue and governments responded with restrictions. The 1988 Republican Party platform said, "We welcome those from other lands who bring to America their ideals and industry."

The populist backlash, curiously missing from American politics, began in California in 1994 with the state in deep recession. The Reagan-backed amnesty of the previous decade had promised to curb illegal immigration by penalizing employers who hired unauthorized workers. But business clout kept enforcement lax, and illegal immigration soared. Those who had reluctantly accepted legalization in exchange for tougher enforcement felt betrayed. The Los Angeles riots in 1992 showcased deadly ethnic tensions, and a drumbeat of national news highlighted other immigration-related problems: Haitians headed to Florida in rickety crafts; jihadists attacked outside the headquarters of the Central

Intelligence Agency in Virginia and the World Trade Center in New York; and two would-be attorneys general were disqualified for hiring undocumented nannies.

Still, few Californians ranked immigration a major concern. For a backlash to occur, something has to elevate the issue and focus the discontent. Saddled with dismal poll numbers, the once-moderate Republican governor, Pete Wilson, did the trick by making illegal immigration the centerpiece of his reelection campaign. The grainy footage in a highly publicized ad showed furtive figures racing across the border. "They keep coming," the voice-over warned. Then Wilson embraced a ballot initiative that would deny government services to unauthorized migrants and bar their children from public schools. Proposition 187 was blatantly unconstitutional—the Supreme Court had ruled in 1982 that schools can't turn away undocumented kids—but potent in a state with a million unauthorized immigrants (and climbing). It passed in a landslide, and Wilson salvaged a second term.

The backlash seemed poised to spread. Though Prop 187 was strangled in court, the 1994 elections gave Republicans control of Congress just as some Republicans were questioning legal immigration, too. The GOP platform morphed from one sunny paragraph to nine stormy ones, demanding English as the official language and the end of birthright citizenship. In 1996, Patrick J. Buchanan, who had questioned America's ability to assimilate "Zulus," won the New Hampshire primary. But by the end of the year, restrictionists were in retreat. They won some significant victories (including huge cuts in public aid for legal immigrants and a ten-year ban on people illegally in the States for more than a year) but not the biggest ones: there were no new penalties for hiring illegal workers and no reductions in legal immigration. The leading immigration-control group complained its hopes had been "dashed."

One reason the restrictionists faltered was the influence of business: in the tightest labor market in a generation, employers wanted everyone from dishwashers to engineers. Another was the ethnic vote. Motivated in part by Prop 187, an additional 1.3 million Latinos registered nationwide by 1996, and in California more than 80 percent voted Democratic. Pete Wilson never won another election, and the Golden State turned deep blue. "For the first time in 20 years, there was little whining about the paltry turnout of Latino voters," the *Los Angeles Times* observed. "Thank God and Gov. Pete Wilson, not necessarily in that order."

FAR FROM WANING in the 1990s, immigration soared—legal and illegal alike. The foreign-born population grew nearly 60 percent, the largest single-decade rise since the mid-nineteenth century. The number of illegal immigrants more than tripled as the job market boomed, the Mexican economy crashed, and the devalued peso tripled the purchasing power of the dollar. Rather than slow illegal immigration, the 1986 amnesty probably sped it; newly stabilized, the beneficiaries could send home for relatives. A subsequent hardening of the border intended to keep the unauthorized out also kept them in, by making it too risky to go back and forth. Estimates of the undocumented peaked in 2007 at 12.2 million, about 4 percent of the U.S. population. (It has since modestly declined.)

The most striking change wasn't scale but geography: the immigrants went everywhere. Previously, about two-thirds had settled in five traditional states, led by California and New York. The 1990s brought "new faces in new places"—millions of newcomers to corners of the South and the West with no tradition of immigration in their civic DNA. In two decades, the foreign-born population rose fourfold in Alabama, Kentucky, Nebraska, and South Carolina; fivefold in Arkansas, Georgia, Nevada, and Tennessee; and sixfold in North Carolina.

Immigration shifted because opportunity did; the immigrants followed the jobs. Facing global competition, manufacturers moved to low-wage states. Exurban construction boomed. Migrants chopped chickens in the Piedmont and wove carpet in the Georgia hills. Refugee resettlement sent Afghans to Nebraska and Somalis to Maine. As usual, migration attracted migration: once some people settled, others followed. It wasn't quite true that every state was a border state, but it increasingly felt that way.

Few explosions of diversity were as startling as a stretch of U.S. 23 north of Atlanta known as the Buford Highway—"La Buford" to the Mexican shoppers in the Asian strip malls. Its modest apartments had once catered to blue-collar whites, but dying factories (GM, Kodak, Frito-Lay) brought falling rents that attracted refugees and other immigrants. Whether this felt like revitalization or invasion depended on your point of view. When *The Atlanta Journal and Constitution* visited the "improbable melting pot" in 1992, it found thirteen languages in an elementary school, a restaurant selling tacos with cow brains, and police chiding a Vietnamese man for skinning a goat in his carport. The mayor of Chamblee rued the change—the city of his childhood was gone—but his counterpart in Doraville called immigrants a boon. "They've really helped our economy, especially with taxes."

America was hundreds of Chamblees and Doravilles—a crazy quilt of rapid change. Conflict was inevitable, but into the twenty-first century studies of "new destinations" emphasized the positive. "The overall picture still shows a significant degree of acceptance and even of a positive reception," wrote two leading scholars in 2008. They saw little likelihood that "new barriers to immigration will be enacted."

AFTER THE POPULIST BACKLASH in the 1990s, George W. Bush ran for president in 2000 as a different kind of Republican, with Spanish in his stump speech and talk of immigrants as neighbors. "Immigration is not a problem to be solved," he said. "It is the sign of a successful nation." Bush liked Latinos and was reelected governor of Texas with nearly half their votes. He thought their faith, family closeness, and enterprise made them proto-Republicans. As president, Bush befriended his Mexican counterpart, Vicente Fox, and began working on a plan for a new legalization and a guest worker program, in exchange for Mexico's help with border security. Fox pitched the idea to the U.S. Congress on September 6, 2001.

Five days later, foreign terrorists killed three thousand people, and the politics of immigration was never the same. Bush's focus shifted to the war on terror, and Republican hard-liners grew. In fearful times, restrictionism grows.

A restrictionist movement, long in coming, finally hit full stride. The improbable story of its organizational growth begins in the 1970s with a Michigan doctor and amateur naturalist worried that population growth hurt the environment. From his obscure perch in the hamlet of Petoskey, John Tanton went on to help found all three major immigration-control groups, starting in 1979 with the Federation for American Immigration Reform, or FAIR. (The other two are the Center for Immigration Studies and NumbersUSA.) Mindful that bigotry had plagued early twentieth-century efforts to restrict immigration, Tanton pledged to avoid race and focus on color-blind issues like job competition. That went nowhere. But a new Tanton group devoted to English-only campaigns drew mass support; the culture wars paid off. Soon Tanton was making the racial arguments he had pledged to avoid, warning of the "Latin onslaught," expressing an interest in eugenics, and telling a white donor he feared "the decline of folks who look like you and me." When news surfaced that FAIR had taken money from the Pioneer Fund, which promoted theories of whites' genetic superiority, centrist support vanished. FAIR found its home on the populist right, with its signature event an annual gathering of conservative talk show hosts.

FAIR's evolution was emblematic; it both symbolized and advanced the rightward lurch inside the GOP. While Bush hailed immigrants as "energetic, ambitious, optimistic people," Representative Tom Tan-credo of Colorado called for banning them—legal and illegal—"until we no longer have to press 1 for English." His House caucus attracted more than a hundred Republicans. Another political entrepreneur, Sheriff Joe Arpaio of Maricopa County, Arizona, earned his renown by arresting Latinos based on what a federal court later found to be egre-gious racial profiling. He housed prisoners in tents in the Phoenix heat, dressed them in pink underwear, and marketed his folksy cruelty on Fox News, selling himself as "America's Toughest Sheriff." Virginia senator George Allen referred to an Indian American working for his opponent as a genus of Asian monkey. "Let's give a welcome to *macaca* here," he said, in a frat-boy jibe that helped cost him the election. Jihad-ist attacks in Madrid (2004) and London (2005), and immigrant riots in the Paris suburbs (2005, 2007), bolstered concerns that immigration posed a security threat.

Bush's battle with his party peaked in 2007 when he resumed the push for a "comprehensive" bill that would have offered a path to legal-ization for nearly twelve million people. Gone were the days when elite opinion shaped cloakroom deals. Mass rallies on the left drew hun-dreds of thousands, while talk radio and Fox News denounced "open borders" and "shamnesty." While the backlash of the 1990s faded, this uprising marked a structural shift within the GOP.

What had changed? For starters, the situation on the ground: the immigrant population had continued to rise, illegal immigration had soared, and new destinations had made immigration a national issue. Compared with the 1990s, business's need for labor had waned and so therefore had its moderating influence among conservatives. More im-portant, the 9/11 attacks had raised new security concerns. The internal dynamics of the GOP had also changed; it was more uniformly a party of southern and rural conservatives, and (unlike Bush) most saw immi-grants as Democrats, an electoral threat. They faced a network of interest groups and conservative media that demanded a tougher line. "We will deport you from office," the talk-radio host Michael Savage warned wavering Republicans.

One force *not* driving the backlash was public opinion, which was increasingly immigrant friendly. In more than a dozen polls from 2001 to 2014, the share of Americans who said immigration was good for the United States ranged from a low of 52 percent to 72 percent. In both the expansions of the 1970s and 1980s and the backlash of the new century, congressional action ran counter to public attitudes.

Bush viewed his party's shift with dismay, lashing out at people who "don't want to do what's right for America." He all but called his party's base racist:

> Look, when you grow up in Texas . . . you recognize the decency and hard work and humanity of Hispanics. And the truth of the matter is a lot of this immigration debate is driven as a result of Latinos being in our country. . . . I'm deeply concerned about America losing its soul.

But three-quarters of Senate Republicans voted no, and the bill died. The GOP wasn't the party of stump-speech Spanish anymore.

Soon it was out of power. The unlikely rise of Barack Obama, the son of a Kenyan sojourner and a white woman from Kansas, suggested that America had moved beyond pique over pressing 1 for English. But Obama encountered the same resistance as Bush. His unexpected toughness on deportation in his first term angered the left but mollified no one on the right. Republicans even blocked a bill to legalize the "Dreamers," hundreds of thousands of immigrants illegally brought to the United States as children—a cause that many had once supported. Still looking for an achievement as he sought reelection in 2012, Obama resorted to executive powers he had suggested he lacked to give some of them temporary protection. In 2013, another attempt at "comprehensive" reform died, this time in the GOP House. The fate of 11 million undocumented migrants was left to another day.

What no one imagined was that day would be ruled by Donald Trump, who spent the Obama years pushing the lie that the first black president was born in Kenya and therefore ineligible for office. Trump may not be the most anti-immigrant president in history, but he's certainly the only one to kick off a campaign calling Mexicans "rapists." Bush feared that America was "losing its soul" when crude nativism conquered cable TV. He didn't know it would conquer the Oval Office, too.

THE AMERICAN "SOUL" is hard to define, but the left likes to think it's progressing—that the "arc of the moral universe is long but bends towards justice." Maybe not. The political theorist Rogers M. Smith describes America's racial politics as the constant clash of opposite traditions—one democratic and inclusive, the other illiberal and discriminatory. The result is the triumph of neither but the persistence of both, in a "none-too-coherent mix."

"None too coherent" captures the country that awaited Rosalie as she arrived in the summer of 2012, with Obama gliding to reelection and Trump stoking birtherism. As Washington deadlocked, the battle moved to statehouses and city councils, where more incongruity reigned. Some created sanctuary cities; some passed show-me-your-papers laws. The story was none too coherent in another way, too: the politics of immigration was bitter, but community life generally was not. Most places, most of the time, made immigration work.

In metro Houston, Rosalie would find a place where change had been rapid, profound, and mostly welcomed as a source of economic growth and cultural vitality. In three decades, the immigrant population had grown 500 percent. Nearly a quarter of the population was foreign-born, with whites (40 percent), Latinos (35 percent), blacks (17 percent), and Asians (6 percent) all in the minority. (Latinos soon outnumbered non-Hispanic whites.) Nearly half the metro area's kids were children of immigrants. Touting its minority-majority status, boosters called Houston the future—a "bellwether," a "microcosm," "America on demographic fast-forward."

Immigrants had helped save the city, and Houston seemed to know it. The oil bust of the mid-1980s caused one of the worst local crashes in American history. Houston lost about one in eight jobs. Owners of the overbuilt apartments were so eager for renters they offered immigrants English lessons. To diversify beyond energy, the city invested heavily in projects that drew on foreign labor, including the world's largest medical center (foreign doctors and nurses) and a giant port (engineers and traders). With dozens of hospitals and institutes joined in the Texas Medical Center, Houston employs nearly as many people in health care as it does in energy. A third of the metro area's workforce, and more than half its construction workers, are foreign-born. "Whether we are talking about unskilled or highly skilled workers, the fact is that Houston depends on immigrants," the head of its leading business group told Congress.

Once synonymous with honky-tonks and rodeos, Houston now sells itself as a hub of cultural diversity. Only about half the area's foreign born come from Mexico or Central America, with Indians, Vietnamese, Chinese, Nigerians, Filipinos, and Pakistanis prominent in the mix. Schoolkids board the bus from homes where a hundred languages sound. Along with evangelical megachurches, Houston boasts a five-hundred-acre Buddhist center, seven Sikh *gurdwaras*, a Zoroastrian cultural center, and dozens of suburban Hindu temples. It has a quarter million Muslims, who are mostly educated and affluent.

As a microcosm of immigration, Houston is a microcosm of its problems, too. Thirty percent of the region's immigrants, and nearly half its Mexicans, lack legal status. More than one in seven kids has a parent in the country illegally. One of the deadliest smuggling incidents in American history occurred a hundred miles away in Victoria, where nineteen people died of heat stroke and suffocation in the back of a tractor trailer, the youngest seven years old. More routine abuses are woven into the low-wage economy. Shipley Do-Nuts, a local chain with three hundred stores, admitted in 2008 that more than 40 percent of its employees were unauthorized; in multiple lawsuits, immigrants have accused managers of calling them "wetbacks" and making physical threats.

Still, on the whole, Houston has been welcoming. In 2017, Rice University, which has tracked local opinion for nearly four decades, found that "no matter how the questions are worded," Houstonians hold "increasingly positive attitudes towards immigration." Nearly two-thirds agreed that immigrants "contribute more to the economy than they take" and that immigration "mostly strengthens, rather than threatens, American culture." Local officials have been supportive, and so has the *Houston Chronicle*, which ran a yearlong series in 2015 on the region's immigrants with scarcely a word about political conflict. It pointed to Houston as "a place where the immigrant experience is a point of commonality—not a source of contention."

IF POST-1965 IMMIGRATION has worked better than politics suggests, Filipinos offer an overlooked study of its success. Compared with natives, the two million Filipinos in the United States have more education, higher employment, lower poverty rates, and less divorce. Their average household income, $90,000, is nearly 50 percent higher than that of native-born Americans. More than 70 percent speak English "very well," and 85 percent are present legally. They intermarry and integrate. For most of the post-1965 period, their numbers trailed only Mexicans. But measured against groups of similar size, like Indians or Chinese, they are virtually invisible. Few people remember they were once called savages and subject to mob attacks. One era's scape-goats can become another's model minority.

Filipinos are here because we were there, as the scholar Yen Le Espiritu notes. The United States planted the seeds of migration almost as soon as it seized the islands, sending elite students, called *pensionados*, to study in the States and enlisting Filipinos as naval stewards. (By 1970, there were more Filipinos in the U.S. Navy than in its Philippine counterpart.) Hawaiian planters started recruiting Filipinos in 1909 after anti-Asian fervor halted the flow of Japanese; more than 100,000 Filipinos went over two decades. Congress banned most immigration from Asia in 1917, but as American nationals Filipinos were exempt. Tens of thousands went on to California farms or Alaskan canneries. They were mostly poor and virtually all were men.

By the 1920s, eugenic thought held sway. Filipinos were alternately portrayed as childlike and savage—sexual predators who stalked white women at halls where they paid the women to dance. "Positively No Filipinos Allowed," announced West Coast hotels. In 1930, the Chamber of Commerce in Watsonville, California, warned that Filipinos—"ten years removed from a bolo and a breechclout"—were undercutting wages and chasing white girls. "If the present state of affairs continues there will be 40,000 half-breeds in California," it said. Four hundred white men rioted for days, beating Filipino workers and shooting one dead. As anti-Filipino violence spread, politicians blamed Filipinos: California passed new anti-miscegenation laws, and Congress capped Filipino immigration at fifty people a year.

After Filipinos and Americans fought together in World War II, the most virulent racism waned. Independence followed in 1946, and low immigration quotas remained, but many Filipinos came outside the restrictions, as war brides, navy men, or exchange nurses. By the time Congress opened the door in 1965, there were more than 100,000 Filipinos already in the States, perfectly positioned to petition relatives under a system that Congress thought would keep Asians out. Since the Philippines had lots of English-speaking professionals, others got work visas. If the old Filipino American community was sweat stained and stooped, the new group lived in suburbs and wore stethoscopes; it was 60 percent female. The NO FILIPINOS signs didn't just disappear. It was hard to imagine they had ever existed.

As a Filipino nurse, Rosalie embodied this often overlooked, mostly uncontroversial stream of immigration, which benefited her, her patients, and her family and fulfilled her lifelong dream.

And she had no idea it would be so hard.

EIGHT

Hard Landing

The flight from Manila was bumpy and cold. Rosalie wore a parka and knit hat, looking bound for the Arctic, not Texas in summer, and snacked on cookies she called *biskwits*. Landing in Detroit, we proceeded to separate immigration lines. I found her at her second checkpoint, where a gangly agent was trying to capture her fingerprint. He loomed over her by a foot. "Relax," he said, laughing, as she extended a digit stiff as rigor mortis. "Welcome to the United States."

"For a long time I've been waited!" she said.

"You can work, you can travel, you can study." The agent, who was African American, bristled at his final task: recording Rosalie's race. "What is this, 'Asian . . . Caucasian'? Everybody's the same—*maganda*!" Everybody's beautiful.

"You speak Tagalog!" Rosalie said. Only a few words, but she appreciated the effort.

Her next encounter played out like a vaudeville routine. The Customs agent asked why she had come.

"For an employment," she said.

"For *unemployment*?"

Rosalie beamed. "Yes! For my job!"

A flash of suspicion gave way to a laugh. He smiled and waved her along.

Though Rosalie had spent twenty years thinking about the United States, everything about it seemed strange: the visa came without operating instructions. Stopping in Washington, we visited "the White Palace," where the president works, and the Lincoln Memorial. She had never heard of Abraham Lincoln. A plaque marks the spot where Martin Luther King Jr. said, "I have a dream." She had never heard of Martin Luther King Jr. She was surprised the planes did not serve mango juice. She was surprised to see no Filipinos.

The Washington suburbs, where I live, struck her as "quiet." This was not a compliment. "Everybody's busy with their own work. I think before you visit another person, you have to set an appointment." She had been warned that Americans took independence to extremes—they sent away their children at eighteen!—and the do-not-disturb neighborhood vibe stoked her fears. "People are very liberated." "Liberated" meant "alone." "I think if I find a Filipino community, it will be good."

A few days later we flew to Texas, on another flight without mango juice. Rosalie pulled out a prayer kerchief with a Tagalog version of Psalm 91. ("He is my refuge.") The interstate from Houston crosses Galveston Bay and opens onto an eyesore of fast-food joints and body shops; the GPS led us past a burned-out shack the size of a slave cabin. "Termites?" Rosalie asked.

She had rented an apartment in advance from the agency's list. The manager was a cheerful beach hippie who suggested we eat at a "hole in the wall." Rosalie looked alarmed. "Hole of the wall?" The manager advised her to get a roll of quarters for the washing machine. Rosalie did not know what quarters were, never mind a roll of them. The hole in the wall served poor boys. "Why not 'poor girls'?" She called Walmart "Hallmark" and was paralyzed by the choices of crackers—dill, rye, sea salt, or olive oil? It was July, but Rosalie wore a sweater everywhere.

World travelers aren't always worldly. Rosalie wanted rice with breakfast, lunch, and dinner. She was disappointed that the Golden Corral didn't serve *pancit*, Filipino noodles. "A Filipino bakery!" she exulted, at the Mexican *panadería* sign. Rosalie had lived abroad for most of her adult life but always in Filipino cocoons. She had never seen a place where Filipinos were so scarce. After three days in Texas, she felt something going wrong. "I feel homesick."

IF THE LACK of *pancit* was one disappointment, the cityscape was another. "It is not a place you'll be excited to see," Rosalie said of Galveston. She had pictured the cityscape of *Home Alone 2*—Rockefeller Center and the Plaza Hotel—and landed in a luckless blue-collar town with 47,000 people and a vista of vacant lots.

Galveston was not designed "with habitation in mind," wrote a native son. It's a barrier island just three miles wide, in the center of a hurricane zone, and slowly sinking into the sea. The Indians had sense enough to stay on the mainland and make the dune a hunting and burial ground. The freewheeling Texans who followed had grander plans, lured by the harbor on the island's coastal side.

The port made Galveston stupendously rich. By the 1870s, 95 percent of the state's trade goods crossed its docks. Immigrants poured in—Germans, Russians, Scots, Czechs, and Poles—and merchant barons lived in European splendor. The city boasted eight newspapers, three concert halls, and an opera house, along with the state's first medical school. Galvestonians like to boast that their forebears strolled gaslit streets when Houston was still a mud hole.

And then, devastation. The hurricane of 1900 remains the deadliest natural disaster in American history. It killed almost a fifth of the population—six thousand people—and destroyed half of the city's buildings. While less determined (or deluded) city fathers would have fled, Galvestonians dredged the ocean to raise the town's elevation and put up a seawall. But the glory was gone. Houston expanded its own port, and Galveston's economic rationale disappeared.

Decade by decade, it withered. An empire of Depression-era speak-easies slowed the decline, and a downscale tourist trade endured. But the city's population stopped growing in 1960 and fell 15 percent by the century's end. Poverty rose. Once the grandest city between New Orleans and San Francisco, Galveston today isn't even the largest in the county—just a humid curiosity with a silty beach. Some glorious old architecture remained, and the city kept the University of Texas Medical Branch, the research complex that grew up around the medical school. But while immigrants generally look to the future, Galveston "knows its future can never equal its past."

In 2008, another hurricane hit, with Katrina-like consequences. Galveston's seawall faced the Gulf, but Ike's storm surge attacked from the opposite side and swamped the island. Eighty percent of the homes were damaged. Sixteen percent of the residents never returned. With marooned boats littering its lawn and dead cows on the helipad, UTMB, the county's largest employer, suffered more than $700 million of damage. The emergency room closed for nine months. By the time it reopened, hundreds of nurses had left for other jobs.

They weren't easy to replace, given the island's forlorn state and competition from Houston's renowned hospitals. UTMB recruited from as far away as Nebraska and Florida, with signing bonuses of $5,000. But the best nurses wouldn't come, and others wouldn't stay. "We just can't keep them here," complained Chelita Thomas, a nurse manager. "And the ones we get here, they're not good. They're absent all the time. They're tardy, they're lazy, they fight."

Four years after Ike, patients were still backing up in the emergency room due to the shortage of beds. The hospital was building a new ward and needed nurses to staff it. UTMB had a nursing school, and faculty wanted jobs for their grads. But David Marshall, the hospital's head nurse, said that he couldn't safely staff a ward solely with new nurses. He had worked with Filipinos and admired their skills. "I thought maybe the international pipeline was a way to get some experienced nurses here," he said.

Rosalie arrived in the second of three groups, each about a month apart; they totaled twelve Filipinos, six West Indians, and a child of Cambodian refugees from Montreal. Except for the Canadian, they came from poor countries, but most had already been working abroad, in cosmopolitan hubs like London and Dubai. They agreed with Rosalie that Galveston was "not a place you'll be excited to see." One cried at first sight. Another vowed to finish her two-year contract in Galveston and then "move to the United States."

But Rosalie was happy to be part of a group, even if the group was unhappy. At her first Mass, the scripture conveyed Jesus's command to go forward with nothing but sandals and a staff and cure the ill. She felt she had obeyed. "I left and let God handle everything. I know God has a good plan."

THE NURSES WERE IMPRESSIVE, especially those from the Philippines, where nursing is more prestigious than it is in the States. All had four-year degrees, which are optional in the United States, and many had graduated with distinction. Their disappointment with Galveston was the flip side of their idealism about the States. "Growing up in the Philippines, you are trained to think America is the best," Rosalie said.

Orientation fell in unlikely fashion to two tough-talking Texas blondes, neither of whom had ever pictured herself a Gulf Coast Jane Addams. Ruth Ann Marr had worked with Filipinos and found their Tagalog chatter clubby and rude. But this group was so earnest they had won her over with their Skype interviews. "These nurses are going to be such a breath of fresh air," she told everyone. In training, they called her "Ma'am," which sounded like "Mom," and when they walked behind her like ducklings the name morphed into "Mommy Duck."

When a few American nurses complained that the foreigners were taking local jobs, Mommy Duck let them have it. "They said, 'Well, isn't one of them *Muslim?*' Yeah, what of it? If you can pick out which one of these nurses is Catholic and which one is Muslim by the way they treat their patients, then I'll see the relevance of this conversation. Didn't you take your EEO class?"

If anyone would resent the foreigners' success, circumstances might have nominated Michelle Times, a down-on-her-luck Texan hired to help them settle in. After a divorce, brain tumor, and layoffs at Dell, she was forty-six years old, living with her parents, and transporting patients across the hospital for close to the minimum wage. But she was startled to see how many people each of the nurses helped support. "They care for each other in a way that Americans don't even think about." When a store sold a nurse a cracked TV, she marched in and solved the problem Texas-style. "I had to go see the HMFIC!" she reported back to baffled looks. *"The Head Mother Fucker in Charge."*

"I hear a lot of flak about these people taking jobs," she said. "Well, if we had qualified nurses, they wouldn't be coming here."

Rosalie's start at the hospital brought more confusion about American life. She was disturbed by how many old people worked—doctors in their sixties. "To me, they should take rest." She was alarmed to learn poor patients cadged food to take home. And she was surprised to find a transsexual on the staff, which she had never seen in the Middle East. "Everything is accepted here—you are free, even gender-wise!"

At the same time, she loved the emphasis on patient satisfaction. With Medicare tying payments to patient surveys, the hospital had a protocol for boosting scores. Nurses should "AIDET." (*Acknowledge* patients by name, *Introduce* themselves, discuss the *Duration* of the stay . . .) "I love this AIDET!" Rosalie said. Boilerplate tools of customer service seemed an odd source of uplift for a homesick immigrant. I knew Rosalie was conscientious—she would want to keep her patients safe—but did she really care if they were *satisfied*? She answered with pure earnestness. "I'm working for my family to make a living, but when I'm working with a patient, I don't think of money anymore. I won't think of anything but care for my patient. I will always thank God for giving me the opportunity to be part of this noble profession."

Rosalie moved into patient care under the guidance of a preceptor. She prayed for a Filipino but got a hard-charging American who had served as a navy nurse. They worked a twelve-hour overnight shift and shared four patients. There was a little confusion when Rosalie called the patient "she," not "he"—a common mistake since Tagalog pronouns are gender neutral—but mostly the first night with Judy passed smoothly. "She's very good and accommodating. She teach me a lot," Rosalie said. To make things easier for patients, she Americanized her name to "Sally."

The second night was busier. A patient with a tracheotomy couldn't talk. A patient with dementia wouldn't stop talking. One needed to be turned every two hours; the other quoted scripture all night. American nurses have more authority than Rosalie was used to, and Judy urged her to use it. "Maybe you can do a stool test," Rosalie told a doctor. "Don't say 'maybe'; say 'he needs a test,'" Judy told her. A patient with a spider bite needed a painkiller, but the resident wouldn't prescribe one. Judy said, "Don't suggest, *insist*—you know more than him." Judy kept asking, "Are you mad at me?" but Rosalie insisted she wasn't. "Judy is a really good motivator," she said. She went home and googled "overcoming shyness."

Ten days later Rosalie said, "My preceptor's driving me crazy!" She had worked three nights in a row, each a strain. On the first, Rosalie got upset when Judy criticized her in front of other nurses. ("I've been a preceptor, too. It is not professional.") On the second, Judy questioned Rosalie's dosage of a medicine. Rosalie had it right, but Judy's tone stung. On the third night, Judy chided her as Rosalie struggled to get a catheter into a woman's urethra. In Abu Dhabi, doctors had done it. Rosalie succeeded but fumed at having her competence questioned in front of a patient.

News of the conflict reached Chelita, their supervisor. Having come from the Philippines three decades earlier, she understood how challenging the transition could be. She thought Judy was being too rough. When Judy took a leave, Chelita let Rosalie finish training with a Filipino preceptor. They brought *pancit* for dinner, closed the break-room door, and talked Tagalog. "It's so relaxing," Rosalie said. "You're so happy."

WHILE ROSALIE SPENT her first summer in Texas, her cousin Tess, still a Facebook Mom, spent her third as a nanny in New York, where her employers had an apartment. The Gordons, generous as always, bought her a ticket to Texas. A relative's visit did Rosalie good. Tess spoke better English and navigated the United States with greater ease; her presence felt reassuring. They swapped family gossip, decorated Rosalie's apartment, and traded impressions of the States.

Both were surprised at the poverty. Rosalie had seen a panhandler with a sign that said he was jobless and hungry. "I don't know how to react. This is a place of opportunity for me. Why they cannot find just a simple job?"

"When I saw them in New York, I thought the same thing," Tess said. "Because you think people in the U.S., they're all having a good life." She couldn't understand why family didn't step in.

"I wanted to give him some money, but you know I'm so shy—I don't know if it's allowed," Rosalie said. She lowered her voice and repeated the story about patients stashing food. I asked why she whispered. "I don't want to offend the people here."

After four years as a nanny, Tess was restless. With the death of her estranged husband, she was free to remarry (the Philippines bans divorce) and wanted an American husband. She asked if I knew anyone she might date. "If I can bring my kids here, we are all [in] a green pasture."

The three-day weekend floated by amid talk of Coach bags, Tagalog soap operas, and the sacrifice of being apart from their kids. As we lingered in a sunny café, I marveled at the determination that had brought them so far; in an old picture of the three of us on the farm, they look like waifs.

Tess grew bold enough to order a beer and asked me again about dates. Rosalie said she drank beer once and it made her feel silly and light. "I wish I could tolerate the feeling. Any little thing I will laugh."

When it was time for Tess to return to New York, I drove her to the airport, thinking again how strong she was and how skillfully she moved between worlds—rich and poor, adults and children, Americans and Filipinos. I'd never seen her flummoxed.

She told me to be sure to call my kids. Then suddenly she was sobbing.

"*I wasn't there!*"

She wasn't there for the girls' first crushes. She wasn't there for their first menstrual periods. She wasn't there for their games, meals, homework, illnesses, tests. "I look at my kids, and I really don't know who they are!" It still bothered her that Noreene had pointed out that Tess didn't know her favorite color. "I really don't know what's their interests! I don't know their favorite food. Only my mom knows that, because I wasn't there!"

Texas flew past at seventy miles per hour while Tess mourned the childhoods she had missed. "They're all grown up; they're busy hanging out with their friends. I'm very close to them, and my girls are very sweet. But I missed out!"

It ended as suddenly as it began. Tess was calm again. In a few hours, she would be back in New York, caring for a richer woman's kids. "That's life. If I didn't work abroad, yeah, we're all together, but what if we're starving?"

The next day, Marielle looked at her phone with mild alarm. "Do you love your Mommy even if I'm far away?" the Facebook message asked.

"What kind of question is that, mommy?" she replied. "OF COURSE I DO!"

ROSALIE'S UNHAPPINESS GREW. The bills in America were bigger than she expected; the malls were farther away. It was hard to get around without a car, and she didn't drive. She lived near the beach but scarcely went. "Maybe I will get lost." The drone of English made her head ache. When the priest criticized *The Fountainhead* in church, she thought he was criticizing fountains. What health plan to buy? What retirement plan to pick? Freedom to choose felt like freedom to fail. With other nurses struggling, too, gatherings turned into gripe sessions. One quit and returned to England.

Rosalie's biggest fear was that Chris wouldn't come, and without him she didn't see how she could bring the kids. He had said he would, but she wasn't convinced. "Chris isn't calling me anymore," she said one day, crying.

She retreated into the familiar—Filipino food, Filipino television, Filipino Facebook friends. There are 7,641 islands in the Philippines. Her apartment felt like the 7,642nd. She kept purple yams in the refrigerator and Tagalog soaps on TV. She kept Skype open to the family as background noise. You could sit in Galveston and hear the roosters crow thirteen time zones away.

During previous moves, her loneliness had been at least partially offset by having more money to spend. In Texas, she barely broke even. Nominally, her salary doubled, but unlike in Abu Dhabi her earnings were taxed, and she had to pay her own housing and health insurance. ("What is this 'deductible'?" she wondered.) If she finished her contract and joined the staff, her earnings would jump, but that was two years away.

Yet requests from home poured in. Everyone knew American nurses were rich! A storm destroyed her parents' roof. Emet was hospitalized. Tita's brother Bandoy died; there was a collection for his funeral. Even as she sent home more than half her pay, she disappointed family and friends. "When you tell people you don't have any money, they will not believe you." Tita's best friend in Leveriza was dying of kidney disease. When Rosalie failed to help with the medicine, Tita took out a loan to save face. "I said this is from Rosalie—otherwise she would think we didn't want to help."

I arrived one night to find Rosalie eating dinner on the floor. She had returned her rental furniture to save money and was streaming a show called *Extreme Couponing* for bargain-hunting tips. The couponing would have to be extreme, indeed, for her to retire her Abu Dhabi debts. Rosalie had left owing nearly $60,000 and told herself she could pay. Now she saw no way. The bank recouped half its loss by taking her severance pay, and she ignored the follow-up demands. Neither defiant nor contrite, she just put it out of mind. She couldn't return to Abu Dhabi without risking arrest.

If you've ever gotten what you really wanted only to regret it, you may understand Rosalie's special strain of misery. Her homesickness was tinged with shame. "People tell me, 'Oh, you're so lucky you made it to the U.S.!' I can't complain and tell them I'm lonely here. They expect me to tell them happy stories." Only Tita had the empathy to imagine hardships in the promised land, and even her sense was faint. The inability to share her loneliness made Rosalie lonelier. "Maybe if I could turn back the time I would not come."

"Maybe" soon disappeared. "Take me back to Abu Dhabi! I wish I did not leave!"

———

ROSALIE'S DOUBTS HAD AMPLE PRECEDENT: regrets are as central to immigration history as steamship trunks. "O God, where is my homeland?" sang a Hungarian in Cleveland a century earlier. Hard work, disappointing pay, the fear of never seeing family again—the European migrants now lauded as models of assimilation had the same complaints. "I am always sad and lonely," a Polish man wrote. An Irishman gasped, "You mean to tell me this is America?" A Russian said, "Had [I] known it would be so bitter for me here, I wouldn't have come." A Lithuanian newspaper advised, "Let us return."

Many did. As early as the 1750s, Benjamin Franklin fretted that return migration would thwart the colonies' growth. Charles Dickens, returning to England from his U.S. tour in 1842, was startled to discover the return migrants below deck:

> Some of them had been in America but three days, some but three months, and some had gone out in the last voyage of that very ship in which they were now returning home. Others had sold their clothes to raise the passage-money, and had hardly rags to cover them. . . . The history of every family we had on board was pretty much the same. After hoarding up, and borrowing, and begging, and selling everything to pay the passage, they had gone out to New York, expecting to find its streets paved with gold; and had found them paved with very hard and very real stones. . . . They were coming back, even poorer than they went.

It's a measure of immigration's success that most people assume the newcomers were quick to adapt. But as the historian Mark Wyman has shown, between 1880 and 1930 a quarter to a third of Europeans went back—roughly four million people. Among Italians, the share might have been as many as half. Migration has always been laced with ambivalence and pain.

Some migrants returned with full purses and some with broken hearts, but both groups risked finding more disappointment at home—there were reasons they had left. "I was surprised and indignant on seeing that people do not bathe in villages," a returning Pole complained. If the New World had mocked them as backward, old-world authorities feared they carried subversive ideas about egalitarian styles of worship or democratic politics. Some came back to America. What a historian said of the Europeans could be said of Rosalie: "At home, their dream was of America; in America, their dream was of home."

THE FIRST PLACE in Texas Rosalie felt at ease was the hospital—not because the work was easy, but because she felt equal to its difficulties. The job increased her confidence, even if she didn't know it. One reason America generally integrates migrants better than Europe is that the migrants are more likely to have jobs. Work can help immigrants broaden their contacts, learn the language, and grasp a new culture.

A few local nurses resented the foreigners for taking jobs that they thought Americans should have and accused them of being inept. One Filipino nurse didn't know how to start an IV, a task her hospital had left for doctors. Another was unfamiliar with a device that retracts used needles. When she searched for the missing needle in the patient's bed, her preceptor dressed her down. A third started an MRI before typing the patient's name in the computer, though she added it later. A drumbeat of complaints reached Chelita: "They're not safe!"

Having once been the target of similar complaints, Chelita was skeptical. She had arrived in a small-town Texas hospital so green she tried to do her banking on foot in drive-through lanes. Even the clerks had hazed her. "I had to kneel down to send my blood to the lab—and I'm the nurse." In staffing the new ward, Chelita had added the Americans for experience but considered them malcontents. "They aren't nice people." She warned the foreign nurses, "If you don't stand your ground, they'll bully you."

The Filipinos considered their detractors lazy and thought the Americans gave them the hardest cases in hopes they would fail. One of Rosalie's tribulations involved a morbidly obese man who needed an enema. "His buttocks—it's like how many kilos already? You have to push to see where is the rectum. You cannot do this alone!" When Rosalie asked for help, the Americans went on break, violating her solidarity code: unless it put her own patient at risk, Rosalie never refused a nurse's call. "They will make you suffer. It's because we are new and because we are foreign. They hope we give up."

If so, it would take more than a fat man's enema. Unlike other parts of American life, bullying summoned Rosalie's determination, not her doubt. She was the charge nurse one night when the ward was short staffed. Ideally, one nurse should handle no more than four patients; each already had five when the admissions desk tried to send another. Rosalie refused, citing safety. "We already have one who fell." The clerk threatened to call Chelita, but Rosalie stood firm. "They keep dumping all the patients to us."

One night Rosalie saw a name on the roster and winced. Harold Samuels was an aging alcoholic who abused everyone. He had mocked Rosalie's English, accused her of "wasting" his blood, and threatened to have her fired. "Go back to where you belong!" he screamed at another Filipino. But at 4:00 a.m., he smiled and asked about her family. He didn't quite apologize but confided he was always in pain. She told him more smiling would help and went home feeling that she had broken through, in accordance with God's plans.

Four months after Rosalie arrived, the hospital opened the new ward and reminded the nurses that revenue rose with patient satisfaction scores. The Americans helped with a brief transition. When the two groups mixed, unit 7B had mediocre ratings, but on the first month the foreign nurses worked alone, their patient scores soared.

Chelita exulted. "That's a big deal! They've heard the comments: 'It's not going to work.' They have a chip on their shoulders." She bought pizzas to celebrate, but everyone was too busy working to eat.

TESS HAD A DIFFICULT SUMMER. The Gordons' two-bedroom apartment was roomy by Manhattan standards but lacked the privacy of the house in Abu Dhabi. The kids were messy, Christina seemed tense, and Tess was bored. "I'm getting burned out," she wrote to Marielle.

The death of Tess's uncle had the family upset. Bandoy, Tita's younger brother, was just fifty-four and the first of the eleven siblings to go. He was a man of inexhaustible friendliness with the compound's biggest smile. His passing marked a dubious generational milestone: just as Bandoy had missed his father's funeral while working in Saudi, now his son, in Saudi, would miss his.

Tess was in the park, on the phone with Rosalie about the funeral, when James, the Gordons' four-year-old, scraped his toe. Tess got a Band-Aid and paid the situation no mind. But as she and Christina entered the building a few days later, a woman pulled Christina aside for a word in private. Tess took the kids upstairs, and when Christina caught up, she said the woman had accused Tess of being neglectful—talking on the phone instead of watching James. Christina told Tess the woman had said, "If I were you, I'd get a ticket and send her back to the Philippines."

Christina was angry. She'd been telling Tess to stay off the phone when she watched the kids. They deserved her full attention. Tess was angry, too. She had raised James since he was a baby. Why would Christina listen to a stranger—because they were both wealthy and white? Where Christina saw a distracted nanny, Tess felt the sting of caste.

More hurt feelings followed over Tess's dating prospects. Responding to her requests, I arranged for her to meet a friend for coffee. Christina googled him and warned that he was too educated. Tess took it as another insult: you're a *nanny*.

On the day of the scheduled get-together, Christina and Tess took the kids to the dentist. James got scared and flailed. Christina emerged from the treatment room and tried to tell Tess not to let him drink, but before Tess understood, it was too late. He would have to repeat the treatment. Christina yelled at Tess in front of the waiting room.

When she called me an hour later, Tess was so upset she was threatening to run away. She would find an under-the-table job. She would find someone to marry. The humiliation was just what she had feared when she left her midwife career: nannies were *nothing*. She couldn't stop crying. Her reaction seemed extreme—she had suffered worse—but the blow to her pride made her question years of painful choices. She arrived to her coffee a wreck.

Cooler heads prevailed. Bosses were bosses, her father said. Sometimes they got upset. He hadn't heard of any as generous as the Gordons. He reminded Tess she had tuition to pay. Christina apologized and insisted that Tess was part of the family. This wasn't true, but it was more than a lie; they were bound together in a knot of need, affection, and gratitude.

Still Tess felt the strain. "Do great for mami," she wrote to Marielle. "So that all my suffering will end."

CHRIS FINALLY DECIDED: he was coming to Texas. He still had misgivings about following his wife, but his relatives warned it would be folly to pass up a green card. Their insistence proved persuasive where Rosalie's had not. He flew from Abu Dhabi to the Philippines to get the kids, with a month to reach the States before their visas expired.

"It's so hard to wait longer, even a day!" Rosalie said. She transferred to an apartment with a second bedroom and bought a car from another nurse so Chris could drive. She bought Disney outfits for all the kids and was especially excited to see Dominique. "I always say thanks to Jesus he gave me a boy," she told another Filipino nurse. "But I love them all."

"It's 1 percent better with a boy," her friend agreed.

As the kids' departure approached, a pall fell over the compound. Tita and Emet, who had raised the kids, knew they wouldn't be coming back. Rowena knew it, too, and Kristine was all she had. While Tita and Emet kept a brave face, stoicism was not in Rowena's toolkit. "God Almighty, help make me strong!" she wrote in a Facebook post.

At nine, Kristine was ambivalent. She thought a move to America might bring her fame as a fashion designer—"I'll get a chance to achieve my dream," she wrote—but she was filled with Rowena's pain.

On her last night at home, Kristine papered the house in sticky notes, each a paean to the aunt who had raised her. "Mama, I love you." "Mama, I miss you." "Mama, don't cry." She typed a message for Rowena to read after she left. Then they read it together, crying in bed.

> I will cry because you won't be next to me when I go to sleep, *Mama ko*, but even when I'm already in America I won't forget you. . . . I will always love you . . . because you took care of me for the last 9 years. *Mama ko*, take care of yourself. Ma, take your medicine at the right time, OK. And don't stay up late. Give yourself enough rest. . . . I love you so much.

If Kristine sounded like the parent, Rowena wept like a child. Lara was puzzled by the fuss. She didn't want to say so amid the mourning, but she was excited to go. She was seven and had always wanted to live with her parents.

Twenty-four hours after leaving the compound, Chris and the kids landed in Detroit, to spend the night. It took hours to find the shuttle to the Rodeway Inn; they were looking for "Road Wai." It was forty-three degrees, warm for December. The kids had coats, but Chris shivered in shirtsleeves. A black woman at the bus stop told him it was good to see a man taking care of his kids. The comment struck him as odd.

Rosalie couldn't think straight. She confused the date, then the hour. Michelle Times, the nurses' problem solver, drove her to the airport ninety minutes late. Chris and the kids were sitting on the curb. After five months in Texas alone, it was the moment Rosalie had imagined— shouts, hugs, a fresh start. Michelle said she "glowed like a bride." The first stop was KFC, where jet-lagged kids nodded off eating French fries. But they were together. In America. At last. "Thanks God," Rosalie said.

NINE

Just Like a Family

appiness so pure was rare, and Rosalie was smart enough to savor it. She was happy when the kids played, happy when they quarreled, and happy when their shallow breaths rocked their chests at night. When there were errands to run, they ran them together, as if it took the whole platoon to buy a loaf of bread. Texas law required families of five to rent two bedrooms, but the Villanuevas used neither. They shared a mattress on the living room floor, Filipino-style.

The Christmas season was packed with Filipino parties, each a spread of familiar food and Tagalog chatter. Chris and the kids had landed in a transit zone; they were no longer in the Philippines but not quite in the States. It's a Filipino tradition to cook something sticky and sweet to bind the family in the New Year. When Rosalie tried a flan that flopped, the kids joked that it looked like *puto*, the rice cakes served with pig's blood stew. Rosalie laughed along: rice cakes are sweet and sticky, too.

The celebrations obscured the challenges that remained. Rosalie had brought children she didn't fully know to a country she didn't know at all. The kids had to learn English. The parents had to learn to parent. Migrants often have competing desires. Rosalie wanted the kids in

America but feared they would Americanize. She wanted to be a hands-on mother but quickly felt overwhelmed by motherhood. As the Villanuevas left the transit zone for Texas, the challenges would grow.

It was obvious which child was the former beauty queen. Kristine reigned as if she still wore the tiara. She was saucy, bossy, long and leggy, purposeful and proud, with a toughness that belied her nine years, and she ruled her siblings with regal disdain. The beauty mark above her pouty lips offered a hint of Marilyn Monroe. Tin-Tin arrived with an ardor for Hello Kitty, Barbies, exclamation points, and anything pink, and she was eager to use the English she had learned in Philippine schools. She spoke it with a syntax that conveyed exuberance. She was "so very, very excited" to see America and so "very, very happy" when her father cooked. She was "so very, very proud" of her visa that she taped it to the wall.

But her situation was very complex. She had gained her "mommy" (Rosalie) but lost her "mama" (Rowena), to whom she was especially devoted. Bereft at her loss, Rowena didn't make the separation easy. The kids had hardly landed before she called in tears and complained of feeling forgotten. If Kristine was slow to answer her texts, Mama Wena froze her out. "My Mama wena angry to me," Kristine told her diary. "I feel sad mama is crying. I said to mama I'm soo very sorry. Please don't be angry to me."

Her younger brother, Dominique, or Boy-Boy, was what his nickname implied: all boy. A rough-and-tumble five-year-old, he arrived in Texas jumping on beds, hiding in hampers, and worshipping the superhero Optimus Prime. He spoke no English and wouldn't try, and his picky eating earned him a second nickname—*ayoko*, or "I don't like it." Rosalie made no effort to hide her special feeling for him, but Dominique idolized his dad, down to the matching tank tops. When the girls fretted about hurricanes, Boy-Boy told them not to worry: Daddy would chase the storms away.

It's telling that among the kids only Precious Lara lacked a nick-

name. She was a classic middle child, stuck between boisterous book-
ends and used to being overlooked. Though named for a real beauty
queen, Lara had no interest in pageants—she wore her hair straight and
her clothes un-frilled—and among the kids she had spent the least time
with her parents. While Rosalie had raised the other kids in Abu Dhabi
for several years, she had taken Lara home as a baby. In the Philippines,
Lara was sent away again, to spend a year with Chris's mother. Kristine
had Rowena to dote on her, and Dominique had Rosalie, but Lara ami-
ably generated her own sources of contentment. In the length of her
dinner-table prayers, she resembled another earnest middle child—her
mother—though Rosalie was slow to see it.

Rosalie and Chris vowed to preserve the kids' "Filipino values."
What this meant wasn't wholly clear, even to themselves. Retaining the
ability to speak Tagalog was on the list, and they made a rule, soon ignored, that the kids speak nothing else at home. Other Filipino values
included respect for elders, obedience to parents, religious faith, placing
family needs above individual desires, and socializing with other Filipinos. Independence and free thinking, American traits, were *not* Filipino
values. "Even you are in America you keep your Filipino values," Rosalie told the kids.

Galveston students aren't confined to their neighborhood school;
they can enroll wherever there's an opening. Rosalie had no idea how to
choose, but a Filipino woman at Mass told her of a school with several
Filipino teachers. It was half an hour away, but the prospect of Tagalog-
speaking adults addressed a major fear—that Dominique, unable to ask
to use the bathroom, would "spill the *ureene*." Although Oppe Elementary was in high demand, Rosalie walked in just as it got three rare
midyear openings. With luck and the help of the ethnic network, the
kids landed in the island's best elementary school.

Rosalie signed them up but didn't send them the following day. The
next day she kept them again; she had worked all night, and it was raining. When the kids didn't appear on day three, the school called. Even

Rosalie didn't seem to know whether she was tired, confused, or afraid to let go. Tita fretted: the shooting of twenty children in Connecticut had made the Manila news. She wondered if that was near Texas.

At 7:20 a.m. on day four, Rosalie and Chris walked three nervous children to their classrooms. Kristine hid behind a nervous smile, and Lara squeezed Rosalie's finger like a life rope. When Rosalie got home, she panicked: she had forgotten to arrange Dominique's bathroom pass. She texted the Filipino gym teacher, who hurried to his class. At the end of the day, the kids emerged happy, and two grandmothers exhaled half a world away: Boy-Boy had not spilled the *ureene*.

THE FOREIGN-BORN CHILD with little English passing through the schoolhouse door—in their arrival at Oppe Elementary School, Rosalie's kids were reenacting a classic American rite. As far back as the early republic, supporters of public education called it essential to nation building in a country with a broad ethnic mix. Immigration helps explain why the United States led the world in democratizing education. With no common history, language, or religion, Americans created common schools to forge unity. It's standard to say "diversity makes us stronger," but the rise of public education is a concrete example. Everyone benefited.

At first, public schools emphasized civics, to prepare a diverse population for the duties of democracy. As the cities swelled with tenement poverty in the Ellis Island years, the focus turned to cultural assimilation—not just English acquisition, but hygiene, order, and decorum. The effort could get heavy-handed. In disparaging immigrant culture, the Americanization movement often came between parents and kids, a problem that Jane Addams denounced and Rosalie instinctively feared. But despite episodes of bigotry, most educators embraced immigrants, whose numbers brought them funding, prestige, and power. Progressive Era education was alive with daring: buildings rose; the school day lengthened; talent rushed in. Addams called schools "the great savior of the immigrant district."

Now the goal of education is different: to enable economic success. It's a tougher task with greater individual stakes, and no one would call public education a force in ascendance. The main feature of today's educational landscape is inequality. While low-income students have always trailed privileged peers, the difference in outcomes is growing. That's because inequality has grown: the rich are richer and more segregated in neighborhoods with high-performing schools. It's also because academic work is more demanding, which favors students with educated parents. The issue in education isn't nativity—children of affluent immigrants excel. The issue is class. Education, a force meant to erode class barriers, now fortifies them.

The biggest controversy in immigrant education involves students with limited English, who account for about 10 percent of the K–12 population. About three-quarters are Latino, and most are low income. Like Kristine, many speak conversational English but lack academic proficiency. There have been fierce fights over how much instruction these students should get in their native language—whether bilingual or English-only approaches work best. Some recent evidence gives bilingual programs a nod (although fewer than a third of English-language learners receive any bilingual instruction). But the bigger point is that most non-English speakers are in weak schools no matter the language of instruction. Nationally, English-language learners drop out at about twice the average rate.

If you doubted the schools' ability to serve poor immigrants, the history of the Galveston district would offer scant reassurance. Its troubles had been driving middle-class families from the island for decades. As Rosalie arrived, more than 70 percent of the students who remained qualified for free or reduced-price lunches, and nearly one of six spoke limited English. Dealt a difficult demographic hand, the district played it poorly. Two superintendents resigned under pressure in a four-year stretch, and the state ranked the high school "academically unacceptable" for three of four years. The publisher of the local paper likened the district to "a listing ship." The program for English-language learners was in special disarray, prompting a state investigation. Only 19 percent of Spanish-speaking eighth graders could pass all the state accountability tests.

Had Rosalie's kids spoken Spanish, they could have gotten bilingual instruction before moving to a regular class. But for Tagalog speakers, there was one option: sink or swim.

KRISTINE WAS SURE she could swim. Her English was a point of pride, and she spoke it well for a child just arriving in the States. But she was upset to discover it wasn't as strong as she thought. Retreating behind a demure smile, she tried to hide how lost she felt. A popular girl named Lauren came to the rescue by declaring Kristine her friend. The young teacher, exasperated with her class, also liked Kristine, perhaps projecting onto her traits associated with Asians as a "model minority." "I said, 'She's going to be sweet,' and she is," the teacher said. "She really does want to learn, unlike some of these other kids."

If at school she shrank, at home Kristine swaggered. "What we study here in fourth grade would be *high school* in the Philippines," she messaged a former classmate. Soon she posted a video on her Facebook page that announced in English she had forgotten how to speak Tagalog. Rosalie was incensed and ordered its immediate removal. Insulting the language of your elders was *maarte*—pretentious. It offended "Filipino values." Kristine crept from the scolding but returned to imitate a surfer she'd seen on TV: "*What's up, duuuude?*"

The brave front disguised big conflicts. Kristine had swapped not only countries but mothers. She felt responsible for Rowena's pain. Rowena was anguished over losing Kristine and perhaps afraid that without the kids she would lose Rosalie's financial support. (Unable to work regularly, she relied on it heavily.) When Kristine showed Rowena a new doll on Skype, Rowena said she should have sent the money to her instead of buying toys. When Kristine didn't feel like talking one day, Rowena got mad and hung up. Kristine called back, pleading, "Mama, Mama, I'm sorry! I'm sorry!" But Rowena gushed over Lara until Kristine ran crying from the room. "Mommy, I don't want to talk to Mama Wena anymore," Kristine told Rosalie.

Her first school project presented a set of autobiographical questions. Kristine wrote of happy things—pink dresses, puppies, and family celebrations—but hinted at hidden conflicts. Asked to describe an act of bravery, she recalled abandonment: "When I growing up, my mom and my dad is not there." Asked about a pet, she changed the subject to Rowena's near death: "They said she was died. I cried and sad." Yes, she wrote, she would like to be a princess because of the "pretty dresses." But, she added, "peoples all over the world are poor," and even if you're a princess, "you can't help them." If that seems like a lot in a fourth grader's head, it's just what she could explain in English.

As school went on, Kristine was caught between her waxing ability and her waning confidence. She could decode words well enough to seem fluent but often didn't know what they meant. Whenever her teacher said "keep your book out," Kristine put hers in her desk. It took a Filipino teacher to explain that *itago*, Tagalog for "to keep," means to stash or hide away. Asked to describe a "pet peeve," Kristine wrote about her dog. Halfway through fourth grade, she read at a first-grade level.

One day the teacher paired up students and asked them to describe fanciful inventions. Kristine's card said "can opener." Her partner's said "squirt gun." They were supposed to imagine a way to combine the objects—make a squirt gun can opener—but Kristine didn't know what either one was.

"Maybe you can squirt the gun and make the can opener move," her partner said.

Kristine smiled. "I think that all the people have powers," she said. Her partner did most of the talking before the class, but the teacher insisted that Kristine take a turn.

"You touch this one, and when it rolls," Kristine began.

"When it rolls . . ."

"When it rolls . . ."

The whole class exhaled when the rest of the sentence came. "When it rolls, it open the can."

Her partner was kind. "Your illustration is better than mine," she said.

Another classmate was harsher. Asked his favorite part of a story that Kristine wrote, he replied, "I didn't have one."

Within a few months, Kristine was less *maarte*, more self-doubting, and more volatile outside school. "It seems like Tin-Tin is more shy now about speaking English," Chris said. At an after-school stop for French fries one day, the ketchup bottle made a bathroom noise and sprayed Kristine's nose. The whole family laughed, including Kristine, until someone said, "Let's get a picture." Her eyes turned wild with hurt.

"It's just a joke," Rosalie said.

"When somebody hurts me, that's how you respond—you *laugh*?"

Rosalie looked as if she'd been slapped.

"It's true, though—you're laughing at me!"

"Just stop, *right now*," Rosalie said.

While mother and daughter sat in hurt silence, Dominique grabbed the fries.

DOMINIQUE MADE NO PRETENSE of speaking English, or any other language. He spent a month in kindergarten without saying a word, then turned to his teacher and asked in English, "Mom, can you tie my shoe?"

His classmates gasped. "He can talk!"

His youth was an advantage, but so was his teacher—a maestro with twenty-three years in the classroom and a catalog of tricks to help kids learn. Rather than meander back from lunch on the 106th day of school, the kindergartners counted off 106 steps, an exercise that kept order, practiced counting, and gave them an intuitive feel for the number.

Kristine's teacher disciplined with threats, Dominique's with diversion.

"Put your finger on your nose if you've ever heard the word 'platter'!"

"Gimme a three if you're ready to try this!"

"Tickle your chin and give me a grin!"

Crisscross-applesauced, Dominique spent his days touching his nose, tapping his head, and singing out the days of the week. The gap with other students narrowed.

"Academically I'm not concerned," his teacher said. "He's got the intelligence to pick it up. It's more important for him to feel comfortable."

It worked. By the end of kindergarten, his *ayoko* phase was over. He remained a picky eater but complained in English, "I don't *like* it."

LARA'S TEACHER EXULTED WHEN she learned she was getting a Filipino student. "Fresh-off-the-boat Filipino? Wow!" Karen Jobe had gone to high school in Singapore, where her best friend was Filipino, and she pictured what she was getting: a polite girl from a churchgoing family who respected teachers. That's what she got, down to the dainty white sweater. When Ms. Jobe called time-out, Lara's hands were the first to fly into the overhead T. "She's a sweet, sweet girl—I need a few more like her!"

Indeed she did. Even a single disruptive child can slow a class, and eight of Ms. Jobe's second graders were chronic disrupters. She arose every morning at 4:45 and looked spent by 9:00 a.m. "I have to stay on them all the time or they will run us over." I tried to be an inconspicuous note taker—to the extent that a reporter can be inconspicuous typing notes in a room of seven-year-olds. But when Ms. Jobe turned her back, one boy would half shout across the room, *"Yo, fast-typing dude! Wassup??"*

Lara made the best of things, grabbing onto whatever Ms. Jobe offered, from Mars to the Berenstain Bears. In the Philippines, her class had seventy students. In Galveston, there were twenty-four and a classroom full of books. The best thing about America, she said, is "I get to read."

The slowest eater in the family, Lara liked to linger at the table, pick at her rice, and talk about the day's lessons. Lingering with her offered a chance to hear what was on her mind. "Helen Keller was awesome!" she announced one night. For a second grader learning a language, the quest to be understood struck a note. "Helen Keller made them realize even if you're deaf and blind, it doesn't matter—you can do something."

The class had also studied Rosa Parks, whom Ms. Jobe had called a "hero." But civil disobedience drew a skeptical review from a girl raised to respect authority. "I don't think so she was a hero. She didn't listen to the policeman. Maybe she was tired." Besides, Lara said, heroes wear capes.

A growing vocabulary, like a pair of glasses, snaps a fuzzy world into view. Lara read a book about a villain, Echo, who victimized a good girl, Halo, by repeating her words: Echo echoed Halo. Lara got the drift from the pictures but didn't know the words "echo" and "halo." When I told her, she lit up and reread the book, shouting whenever the evildoer repeated the heroine's words.

"Echo!"

"Echo!"

"Echo!"

"*I* told her that," Kristine said with contempt.

But progress doesn't come in straight lines, not for an immigrant girl straddling languages and cultures. After a few months, the improvement in Lara's test scores mysteriously stalled. "She should be doing better," Ms. Jobe said. Perhaps the problem was one of abundance. Lara's mind was full of new stuff—synonyms, homonyms, two-digit subtraction problems, penny biographies—and it would just take time to sort it all out. The synapses were working around the clock.

But Lara also hinted at a different dilemma: the classroom disruptions were getting her down. Ms. Jobe had to scold them all day. "It makes me sad when Ms. Jobe gets mad at the class a lot." Jane Addams had famously pleaded for patience with the chaos in immigrants' lives, but Lara found the need for patience ran the other way. "Why are Americans so *bad*?"

As the end-of-the-year field trip approached, Ms. Jobe passed out permission slips. "Ask Mom or Dad or Grandma or whoever to send it in," she said. The "whoever" wasn't meant to be snarky but to acknowledge the complexities of American family life. One student had a father in prison. Another was being adopted and changing both his names. Yet another regaled the class with stories of her mother's latest boyfriend's kids. "Kids that have two loving parents?" Ms. Jobe said with a sigh. "I can't count to four." After years apart, the Villanuevas hardly embodied convention, but by local standards they looked awfully solid. "Every time I see them, I see them together," Ms. Jobe said. "They seem really close."

The point bears mulling. Lara was both the most foreign student in the class ("fresh-off-the-boat Filipino") and in an old-fashioned, Norman Rockwell way the most classically American—the earnest, obedient girl with a shiny apple on her desk. In coming to Galveston, Lara didn't find the idealized place her mother had imagined. But as some immigrants have always done, she brought it with her. She was what she came to find.

AS THE KIDS SETTLED into school, Rosalie found family life harder than she had guessed. They weren't just learning to live together in a new country; they were learning to live together, period. "We've got to learn how to be parents again."

The two-bedroom apartment was cramped. Unwashed dishes spilled from the sink, and toys covered the floor. The clutter sapped Rosalie's energy, and her fatigue increased the clutter. Rosalie worked nights but slept only half the day before the kids came home and woke her. The kids were kids—unruly. "They will run; they will scatter all the things," Rosalie said. "Plus there's nobody to help us." In the Philippines, scores of relatives kept watch. In Texas, they were alone.

Chris, who had always played the easygoing dad, wasn't used to setting discipline. One day the girls launched a grape-throwing war. When his call for a cease-fire went unheeded, he lost his temper and swatted their legs. Their crying woke Rosalie, whose shouts added to the din. Other Filipinos had warned they would go to jail if they spanked the kids. They didn't, but their fear of a police raid was real. When a neighbor knocked to complain the kids were noisy, Chris momentarily panicked, thinking the cops were at the door. Rosalie worried that if the school learned they slept together, she would be charged with child abuse.

One morning when Lara wouldn't wake up, Rosalie started to shout. "Why are you shouting?" Lara asked, which made Rosalie shout more. Chris found Lara in the bathroom, crying. Rosalie and Chris realized that shouting had become the norm. "Sometimes when I'm yelling at the kids, I'm not even aware," Rosalie said. That afternoon they did something not all parents can do: they apologized. "If you see Mommy and Daddy doing that, you can say, 'Not allowed,'" Chris said. Compliance wasn't perfect, but the atonement helped.

Although Rosalie was deft with willful patients, she was flummoxed by a willful child. Grocery shopping one night, Rosalie put off Kristine's request for a teddy bear, telling her to wait until payday. Kristine got so mad she wouldn't leave the store, then stood in the parking lot beside the car. "*Get in*," pleaded Rosalie, afraid the whole city was watching. Chris put the car in gear, pretending he would drive away. "Don't leave, *Ah-tay*!" Lara sobbed. By the time Kristine surrendered, everyone was shaken. Rosalie started in on a lecture—you *humiliated* us—then dropped her voice to a hushed plea. "We are just five, alone in a new place. We have to take care of each other."

As she learned to be a mother, Rosalie faced competition. She didn't discourage Kristine's attachment to Rowena—she wanted her sister to feel loved—but she couldn't help feeling cheated of affection. When Rosalie did buy Kristine a teddy bear, Kristine named it "Mama Wena." On Valentine's Day, Kristine made a card for Rowena that professed her "Amazing Love!" To Rosalie she wrote, "Thank you for your hard work." She didn't mean to slight her mother. She just tended to overlook her.

Sometimes Rosalie didn't know how to accept the affection she got. For homework, Lara had to write her a letter. When Rosalie awoke from a nap, Lara read it aloud:

> *Dear Mom,*
> *Thank you for working so hard mom for us.*
> *Thank you for kipping us safe.*

Suddenly Lara got the giggles. She couldn't get the words out. Rosalie frowned and said, "I cannot understand you."

> *When you got mad at us we just laugh.*
> *You just laugh too.*

Lara was now laughing so hard she fell off the couch. A funny face or a tickle attack might have fit the occasion. But Rosalie felt slighted. "You did not tell any of the things Mommy do for you! In Abu Dhabi, all the time, I'm crying! Mommy miss you. Mommy love you! I did not hear good words!" Lara sidled away wounded, but Rosalie couldn't let up. "And when Mommy's sleeping, you shouldn't wake Mommy up! And you should clean up! It's too messy!"

A few minutes later, Rosalie cuddled Dominique and smothered him in kisses. "If Boy-Boy gets lost, Mommy will cry so much." Lara mostly shrugged it off, but Kristine watched the doting on Dominique with an unforgiving eye. "It bothers me a lot—she's so overcare," she said. In her journal, she wrote, "Mommy always think Boy Boy is the most important. . . . Boy Boy is the star, important, you can't fight him."

Uneasy around Americans, Rosalie and Chris kept the kids from socializing outside school. The only houses where the kids could play were those of other Filipinos. But American culture isn't easily kept at bay. Kristine, the fashionista, found a phone app that allowed her to dress her avatar in hot pants, a bustier, and spiky heels. "That's me," she said. I arrived one day to find her watching an R-rated film about teenage girls who dare each other to shoplift, drink, and "go to third base." Rosalie was sitting beside her, absorbed in a Tagalog Mass on her phone, while Kristine followed the flesh show through half-covered eyes.

There were trashy movies in the Philippines, too, but more adults to supervise, and the kids mostly played outside, which Rosalie forbade in Galveston. When Dominique took up video games, Chris bought *Grand Theft Auto*, which came with a label that read, BLOOD AND GORE, INTENSE VIOLENCE, NUDITY, STRONG LANGUAGE, STRONG SEXUAL CONTENT, USE OF DRUGS AND ALCOHOL. (Was that a warning or an ad?) As Rosalie and Chris napped, Dominique took his virtual self to a strip joint where the hostess wore pasties and asked, "You want a little action, sugar?" It fell to Kristine to grab the remote and steer him to the exit.

AT THE END of fourth grade, Kristine found her social place. Academic progress came and went, but the frozen smile melted and out came a note-swapping, secret-sharing preadolescent who never wanted for recess friends.

On the trip to the water park at the end of the year, Kristine and Lauren agreed to swim together, then reluctantly let a third friend join them. In the aftermath, a crisis set in. The interloper told Kristine that Lauren was only *pretending* to like her. They weren't really best friends.

"Why is this happening to me?" Kristine asked her diary.

She mulled the problem for days, wondering whether to confront it, ignore it, or withdraw in defeat. Finally, she handed Lauren a note, with a picture of a crying girl. "You hate me—yes or no?" she wrote. "I want the truth."

Lauren didn't know what she was talking about; the third wheel had concocted the story out of jealousy. "My problem was really solve," Kristine wrote. Magnanimous in victory, she even forgave the instigator, because "I'm not a kind of people who doesn't care who is sad."

The episode marked a turning point. Kristine could hold her own in matters of social intrigue. Next year she would move to middle school, a world of cliques, crushes, hormones, shifting Metternichian pacts, and girls shouting, "OMG!" Kristine was ready.

IF FAMILY LIFE WASN'T always what Rosalie had pictured, sometimes it was. One day, the Villanuevas piled into the SUV and drove to a wildlife park. They saw antelopes, giraffes, and rhinoceroses, and Lara pointed out a humped "caramel," like those she had seen in picture books. The highlight was a picnic in the back of the car, repurposed as a family cave. It wasn't quite big enough to hold everyone, which was part of the appeal; they squished. "The family that stays together—stays together," Rosalie said.

About that time, a woman from the Chamber of Commerce came to a parents' meeting at school to talk up all that kids can learn from starting a lemonade stand. *Planning, budgeting, responsibility.* Once a year, Galveston kids don yellow T-shirts and line the streets for Lemonade Day, the chamber's effort to encourage young entrepreneurs. A community drive to groom children for success was just the sort of thing Rosalie had hoped for in the States—sunshine and upward mobility.

Another Filipino nurse agreed to join forces with Rosalie. With five kids between them, they launched the High-Five Lemonade Stand.

There was one problem: Rosalie had never heard of lemonade. She went home and watched YouTube.

"Location, location, location," the lemonade lady said. Picking a spot would be key. The city reserved hundreds of sites, and the High-Fivers got a good one, on the beach by the inflatable slide. "Think outside the box" was another chamber tip. The city didn't allow the stands to sell food, but Rosalie missed that stricture. Festivity in the Philippines is served on full plates. The High-Five menu included spring rolls, spaghetti with liver paste, and neon-red Manila hot dogs served bun-less on a stick.

Halo-halo was bound to follow. The drink is to Filipinos what lemonade is to Americans: a sweetened expression of national identity. Tagalog for "mix-mix," it blends crushed ice and condensed milk with a grab bag of trimmings that meets the most stringent definitions of "outside the box"—purple yam, green and red Jell-O, kidney beans, cheese, and coconut string. It looks like a Mardi Gras float but feels like a scavenger hunt. Imagine drinking a milk shake with a pile of spare parts on your tongue. What better way to embrace the American spirit than selling Filipino drinks on the beach?

It was unseasonably cold for May when the group set up. Foot traffic was sparse. Rosalie had worked all night and was woozy with fatigue. The wind played havoc with the shade canopy and threw sand on the neon hot dogs. Kristine strolled the beach with samples, but the cups leaked, and a hairy man yelled at her for waking him up. By mid-morning, the ledger looked like this:

Spring rolls: $0

Spaghetti with liver paste: $0

Bright red hot dogs on a stick: $0

Lemonade: $4

Halo-halo: $0

But as a foray into American life, Lemonade Day was too important to entrust to Americans. The High-Fivers had spread the word on the Filipino grapevine. Nurses on duty phoned in lunch orders; Chris made deliveries. An avuncular Filipino named Kuya Teddy sauntered by. He couldn't remember when he'd last had *halo-halo*. He declined Rosalie's offer of the drink, then downed it with a dreamy look. It tasted like boyhood beside Manila Bay.

"Oh my God—what is *that*?" A gawker strolled past. Lost in his reverie, Kuya Teddy ignored him and dropped $100 into the box.

The immigrant experience follows a crooked path. What started as an effort at Americanization became an exercise in ethnic solidarity. A celebration of individual enterprise became a lesson in the power of the clan. Cold weather and tired kids cut the day short, and Rosalie was asleep before the car got home. But High-Five cleared a profit, and a picture of the kids handing the school a poster-size check from a print shop went up on the family Facebook page, where a making-it-in-America narrative was carefully tended for consumption back home.

Lara was too shy to sell anything, but she applauded the adventure. "When Mommy and Daddy were in Abu Dhabi, I missed them a lot. Now Mommy, Daddy, Boy-Boy, *Ah-tay*, and me are all together."

"Just like a family," she said.

TEN

The Good Nurse

An elderly woman spied Rosalie across the produce aisle. "Sally! Remember me?"

Rosalie did not.

"GI bleed," the woman said. "*Bad* GI bleed."

Rosalie smiled. "Room 13! Central line!"

It had been six months.

"You remember now! Yeah, *bad* GI bleed."

"Yeah, because it's like *whoo-hoo-hoo*—it's a *big* blood!" Rosalie said.

"*Bad* GI bleed," the woman said.

"And your family is really so supportive," Rosalie said. "Yeah, I remember. Room 13."

"Oh, you were *excellent*," the patient, Jeanette Dotson, went on. She had even returned to the hospital to say thanks, "but they said you wasn't there."

Surrounded beside a mound of broccoli and unsure what to say, Rosalie offered some juicing tips. "Take more vegetables—the *coo-cumber* is good. And some apple or celery. I check it in the YouTube. I don't want to see you back!"

"I don't want to be back," Ms. Dotson said. "But I'd love for you to take care of me again."

As Rosalie resumed her shopping, I lingered to ask what had merited such praise. Kindness in a time of vulnerability makes an impression. "Some people might be like 'unh-uh'" with so much blood, "but she had no hesitation. You can tell that she really loves to take care of people. It wasn't like 'this is just my job.'" Among the moments that had touched her was their farewell: "She let me know she'd pray for me. There was just something about her that was very special."

If produce-aisle accolades are surprising, so is the reliance on foreign nurses. Rich countries usually tap immigrants for low-wage chores that natives scorn, while nursing is a respected profession with average salaries of $70,000 a year—just the kind of stable, family-supporting work you'd expect to find the besieged middle class ready to fill. "The notion that we would have to import nurses makes absolutely no sense," Barack Obama once complained.

But for half a century or more, the story of nursing has largely been the story of a HELP WANTED sign. Supply has frequently lagged; demand has consistently soared. Since 1960, health care has risen from 5 percent of GDP to nearly 18 percent, and the number of elderly Americans is growing by more than a million and a half each year. A generation ago, the United States employed a million registered nurses. Now it employs more than three times as many.

Women once turned to nursing because there were limits on what else they could do. (Even now, more than 90 percent of nurses are women.) By the 1970s, most first-wave feminists regarded the field as retrograde drudgery and turned to other careers. Bad working conditions in the 1990s, driven by cost cutting in managed care, discouraged more people from becoming nurses. When conditions improved, a shortage of spots in nursing schools slowed the supply; there weren't enough professors or clinical sites where student nurses could train. By the beginning of the twenty-first century, about a third of the workforce growth, fifteen thousand nurses a year, came from overseas. The Great Recession eased the nursing shortage—Americans held on to their jobs—and efforts to expand the pipeline have doubled the number of annual graduates. But localized shortages persist, and a wave of retirements looms. An expert panel has predicted that foreign nurses are likely to remain "a permanent feature of the nursing workforce."

The use of foreign nurses is an international norm: aging societies need the caregiving labor, and women from the developing world are eager to supply it. In the first six or seven years of the twenty-first century, nurse migration rose threefold in Canada, fourfold in the United States, and sixfold in Australia. Among a group of about twenty mostly rich countries, the average country gets 7 percent of its nurses from abroad. That's a lot of foreign nurses. A quarter of the nurses in London are foreign born and trained. "The Philippines must be half-empty—you're all here," Prince Philip joked at a London-area hospital. By 2008, Ireland, a classic nurse supplier, got nearly *half* its nurses from overseas. Migration begets migration: Jamaica sends nurses to the United States and Britain and hires them from India and Cuba. In the United States, about 8 percent of registered nurses were born and trained overseas, like Rosalie. They are virtually nonexistent in some states but a fifth of the workforce in New York and New Jersey and a fourth in Nevada and California. Among migrant nurses nationwide, more than a third are Filipino.

Critics raise three main concerns about relying on foreign nurses. One is brain drain: source countries could be depleted. That may be the case in some places, like sub-Saharan Africa, but the Philippines has a nursing *surplus*. It trains many more nurses than it can employ.

A second fear is that foreign nurses will displace natives or depress their wages and clout. In theory, there's no such thing as a nursing shortage—just a shortage at a given wage. Raise the nurses' pay or improve their working conditions and the market will supply more nurses. But health care isn't a free market. It's a heavily regulated social good whose costs and benefits are opaque. Hospitals that raise wages have limited ability to pass along costs (since their fees are largely set by government insurers), and patients don't shop for nursing in a market setting; they go where doctors or insurers send them.

Perhaps without foreign nurses, hospitals would have no choice but to raise pay and attract more Americans. But it's equally likely, if not more so, that they would just scrape by with worse staffing and riskier care. Overseas hiring is typically a last resort—the opposite of cheap labor—since recruiting costs are high and foreign nurses, who have more education than natives, often command higher salaries. In Galveston, the University of Texas Medical Branch paid Rosalie's agency $60 an hour for the foreign nurses, more than 50 percent above what it paid local nurses. The hospital had every incentive to hire Americans first.

A third question is the quality of the foreign nurses' care. Like Rosalie, each has to pass a demanding set of clinical and language tests. Still, some arrive with gaps in their experience or heavy accents. While managers often praise their attitudes and skills, there's been little study of how their care compares with that of native nurses. Two economists found that Filipinos (though not other foreign nurses) commanded higher wages than natives and that the premium "reflects actual quality differences"—the Filipinos were better nurses. But a team of health researchers found a heavy reliance on foreign staffing could be detrimental in certain circumstances. While the scant evidence is inconclusive, about 70 percent of migrant nurses have four-year degrees, compared with half of American nurses, and research has shown that more education generally improves patient outcomes. Research also shows that numbers matter: the higher the staffing ratios, the better patients do. If the alternative to foreign hiring is fewer nurses, the practice almost certainly saves lives.

Shortly after the new ward opened, the hospital gave me a set of scrubs and a chance to watch Rosalie.

SHE ARRIVED ONE NIGHT half an hour early for a briefing from the day nurse. Three patients awaited, with a fourth on his way from the emergency room. Handoff is serious business. A misunderstanding about tests or drugs can put someone's life at risk. The women huddled beside the nurses' station and talked above the ringing phones.

Room 10 held a ninety-two-year-old engineer with a broken arm who was too weak to walk and constipated from pain medication. "He's *really* unstable," the day nurse said. "I gave him an enema. His wife is sleeping beside him on a cot. She's really involved in his care."

"He's alert?" Rosalie asked.

"Oh yeah! He told me it's a second marriage," the nurse told Rosalie. "They travel all over. They go to clubs! But they just go to dance, not drink." Rosalie considered the day nurse flighty and steered the talk back to his chart. "What about his blood sugar?"

Room 12 held an eighty-year-old man with end-stage renal disease. "His kidneys barely work—actually, they don't," the day nurse said. He'd been skipping dialysis, and the toxins in his blood left him confused and defiant. "I took his blood around noon—it took a half hour to bargain with him. If he refuses, let him refuse. I'll take it in the morning."

The patient in room 13 was only fifty-two, but diabetes had wreaked havoc on his limbs. He'd lost his left foot a year earlier, and surgeons had just amputated a gangrenous right toe. "They dressed the wound this morning—it looks nice," the nurse said. But she warned he could be prickly. PLEASE KNOCK BEFORE YOU ENTER: he'd posted an all-caps sign after a nursing aide walked in while he was peeing. Ignoring doctors' orders, he insisted on prescribing his own dosage of insulin.

"Mmmmm," Rosalie said, disapproving.

"He wants to feel in control," the nurse said.

Rosalie absorbed the details with a seriousness that bordered on the somber. Then she went to meet her patients, full of cheer. "Hi, my name is Sally! I'll be taking care of you tonight!"

The engineer with the broken arm scowled. "I want to go home!"

"Yes, of course," Rosalie said.

"I have four bedrooms—the biggest is eighteen by twenty-four."

"You're a lucky man!" said Rosalie. "We'll work hard to get you back."

The kidney patient, sedated with morphine, dozed through her greeting.

Rosalie knocked on the door that said KNOCK, and the man with the amputated toe invited her in. "I'm a male," said Augustus Brown, explaining the privacy request.

"Of course!" Rosalie nodded. "This is your home!"

Mr. Brown said he'd been a diabetic since he was ten, and the disease now ruled his life. Before it left him disabled, he'd been a Baptist preacher and a social worker and run a business detailing cars. He was African American and spoke in the cadence of the black church. God had "manifested himself" in his life. The hospital was "effectuating" his tests. His body language, like his door sign, demanded respect.

The doctor had prescribed forty units of insulin. Mr. Brown took thirty, saying he knew his body best. Rosalie smiled and avoided an argument. "I'll let the doctor know," she said.

He softened. "I'll try to be a model patient," he said. "Your job is hard enough. You don't need somebody acting the fool."

Things got busy. Rosalie brought a stool softener to the constipated engineer and returned to change his diaper. She admonished the dozing kidney patient to wear safety socks. "No falling!" She fetched Mr. Brown's blood thinner and showed him the small needle. "Can I give this one to your tummy?" she asked.

The new patient arrived, a Mexican man with limited English. He'd passed out and hit his head after days of flu-like symptoms. His wife said he was in the United States illegally and lacked health insurance. A new admission is a lot of work. Rosalie asked about his language, his religion, his education (sixth grade), his occupation (construction), his food intake, and his stool output. His energy flagged, but she worked to connect.

"I'm whatchacallit—*Católico*," he said.

"I'm Catholic, too!" said Rosalie.

She was three hours into her shift before she ran to the bathroom. "No time to pass *ur-reene!*"

At 11:00 p.m., Rosalie checked on Mr. Brown, the amputee, who was distracting himself by watching a show about a repo man. After losing one foot, he feared his newly severed toe portended the loss of the other. The wounded foot hung off the bed. Rosalie raised it to avoid swelling, eavesdropped on his bowels, and checked the feeling in his remaining toes, of which there was little. "I won't feel it tomorrow, either," he said. "Diabetes is an unkind disease."

When Rosalie gave him his cough medicine, he changed the subject to Job.

"That is one of the scriptures I could identify with," he said. "Job went through a lot of stuff. His health, wealth—he lost it all one day. He still didn't curse God. He praised God. And because of his faith, God rewarded him double."

"God is just," Rosalie agreed.

"Whatever his will is, I accept it."

By midnight the lights had dimmed, and the nurses' station was quiet. Everyone squinted at screens and clicked on drop-down boxes, recording each pill popped and pillow fluffed. Charting takes hours out of every shift. "If it's not documented, it didn't happen," the managers say.

At 1:30 a.m. someone screamed, "*I want my chicken!*"

Rosalie ran to the kidney patient. "You want your children?" she said.

"I want my chicken!" The toxins were playing with his mind.

"Oh, your *chicken*," Rosalie said. "I'm sorry. I wish to give you the chicken, but I don't have the chicken."

"You don't have chicken?"

She offered vanilla pudding.

"I want my chicken and I want it now!"

Rosalie fetched a dose of morphine, but he was asleep by the time she returned. She went back to charting.

"I want my chicken!"

"He's wet," said Rosalie. She changed him and gave the morphine. "Thank you for allowing me," she said.

At 2:30 a.m., a Filipino nurse from another ward stopped by to talk about her recent trip home. Chatty colleagues cut into charting time; Rosalie fended her off. At 3:00, she turned the engineer in bed, which startled his sleeping wife. "It's OK, Mommy," Rosalie said. At 4:00, she helped another nurse clean a soiled patient. At 4:50, she knocked on Mr. Brown's door to examine his foot wound.

"First time I've looked at it," he said. "It's hard to see. It's like a re-premonition"—a reminder that the whole foot could go. "I'm just thanking the Lord—whatever he allows."

"It's always a blessing when you think of God," Rosalie agreed.

"I remember when I was dealing with my first amputation—I was very conscious of wearing sandals. People will stop and stare. It's pretty bad, you know."

Mr. Brown was OK. Then he wasn't. His blood pressure spiked, and he stammered. Rosalie looked alarmed. "You're shaking. Are you having pain?" He pulled the covers over his head. "I'm about to go into t-t-turtle mode."

Rosalie called a doctor and grabbed some morphine. She fed it into the catheter in his arm, but the line leaked. She looked for a suitable vein but couldn't find one large enough to get the needle in.

Mr. Brown pleaded. "We have to do something—it hurts."

"I'm sorry. Just relax, sir. Breathe."

Another nurse tried and failed. Rosalie called a nurse from the ICU trained to give difficult injections. Mr. Brown grimaced and shook. "Can you make sure she comes fast?" he said. "I think about my Jesus and all he went through—it helps me not to complain."

A nurse on the unit got the morphine in just as the specialist arrived. ("Can I go?" said the ICU nurse, snarky at the false alarm.) Mr. Brown stopped shaking. "It feels so much better," he said. "We give thanks for nurses and doctors. I often wonder what the cave people did."

"Thank you for your patience," Rosalie said.

It was almost six thirty; the day nurses filed in. Rosalie hugged the engineer's wife ("Take care, Mommy!") and gave the delusional kidney patient his meds with no talk of chicken. She told the day nurse that Mr. Brown needed morphine but didn't mention Job. He was asleep when she left, so a night of shared confidences ended with no farewell. "He's a good man," she said. She went out into the sun-scrubbed morning with a satisfied yawn.

In describing their search for the sublime, Celtic pilgrims talk of "thin places" where the distance between heaven and earth narrows and the presence of God is more readily felt. Rosalie, the almost nun, worked in a thin place.

CAPTIVATED BY THE INTIMATE TOIL, I visited as often as I could. It showed me a new side of Rosalie—assured, assertive, socially skilled. Perhaps the hospital had nurses more clinically advanced, but it couldn't have many who were more diligent. At home, dirty dishes sat for days; at work, she was a hand-scrubbing zealot. Outside the hospital she seemed overwhelmed; at work, in command. When a patient buzzed at midnight as she sat down to eat, another nurse offered to answer. "I'll be the one," Rosalie said, and hurried to the room. Some people seem born to do a certain job. Rosalie seemed born to be a nurse.

She left a patient at eight thirty one night and said she'd be back with his medicine by nine. "She'll do it too—you watch," he said. He had fasted all day for a test that got canceled and was feeling at the mercy of events. At 8:59, Rosalie reappeared. "Right on the money!" he said. "To me, that shows they care. I tell you, I love seeing her come around that doorway with that smile on her face."

Supervisors sometimes described Rosalie as serious to a fault. There are worse faults. An audit found that the emergency room had admitted a patient at risk of a stroke without checking his ability to swallow, a serious oversight. Rosalie caught it and did the exam, which led to a soft diet and therapy. "Rosalie, great save," the auditor wrote.

Chaos erupted after midnight when a hallucinating man tried to climb out of bed while tangled up in wires and protective boots. He was eighty but nearly overpowered the nurses. Rosalie, who got to him first, needed four others to restrain him.

"Please, please, let me go home!" he said.

Rosalie tried to hold his hand. "Mr. Marshall! Mr. Marshall! It's sleeping time."

"Please make them take me back! That's all I ask."

"You're in the hospital."

"Stop the car!" he shouted. "Stop yourself!"

He offered the nurses $20 for a ticket home and made a fist-over-fist motion, as if pulling himself to freedom. "Hello down there!" he yelled.

A couple of nurses giggled. One complained he had hurt her hand. No one knew what to do. He had reacted badly to an anti-hallucinogenic drug, and the resident had decided not to try another. "Leave him," one nurse said. "In two minutes, he'll be right back" trying to escape. One of the Filipino nurses asked if I now understood the difficulty of their work. "It's hard to earn money," she said.

"Money, money, money," laughed a Filipino nursing aide.

Rosalie broke the impasse. The delusional man wasn't her patient, but she called the doctor and insisted she come. "He's really agitated," Rosalie said. The doctor tried a new medication, which quieted Mr. Marshall for the night.

ROSALIE'S PATIENTS hailed from more corners of America than she had known to exist. One night she cared for a former marine who waxed in near-pornographic terms about his shore leave in the Philippines. "*Whoo doggie*, did we get drunk and laid and everything else!" Rosalie nodded. "It's a hard job to be a marine. You'd be outside all the time, fighting for freedom!"

A rowdy white family arrived one night talking about their "big black-ass dawg." When Rosalie asked the elderly patient her age, her daughter said, "*I'm* kicking sixty in the ass!" The black woman across the hall had a tattoo of an angel for a brother in prison ("he's still my angel") and a fiancé whose pants fell to his thighs. Rosalie bustled between the rooms and kept both groups happy. "You OK, Mommy?" she asked the white woman, then flattered the black woman's "awesome" gold tooth. "I've had it since I was thirteen!" the patient said.

The potential for conflict ran high when Rosalie got an eighty-three-year-old woman who was furious about being "disrespected" by a nurse on another floor. "If I could have gotten out of the bed, I would have tried to kill her with my bare hands," she said. Then she asked Rosalie to store her dinner in the nurses' refrigerator. "It's *Loosiana*-cooked, and it'll be sour in the morning," she said.

Storing the food would violate infection-control protocol. Not storing it could reignite the patient's fury. Rosalie returned with a bucket of ice and a pledge to change it all night to keep the food dry. "Thank you, ma'am," the patient said. After Rosalie left, she added, "She's got a nice personality. If they respect you, you respect them."

While the old woman with the Louisiana cooking wanted respect, an old man with a broken nose wanted company. Walter Yardley had taken a fall in his job as a janitor. His partner had been dead for five years. The last of their cats was dying. All he did was go to funerals.

"Everybody's dead—all my friends, family," he said.

"So we are your family here," said Rosalie.

He misunderstood. "No, there's no family."

"We are the ones," Rosalie said. "We are here for you."

"Oh, oh—*you're* my family! OK. I'll go for that!"

"So you can talk to us. You can call us, OK?"

He did—every fifteen minutes, all night. "I'm forever on the button," he admitted. "I call too much, but it's always a smile. I even got her to sneak me a bit of pudding. This is one of my better stays!"

Of the nineteen new foreign nurses, Rosalie's English was the weakest. In theory, that created risks. A landmark study published in 2000 found that nearly 100,000 Americans a year die from preventable medical errors and emphasized the importance of communications in clinical settings. "I'm still have doing," she told the lonely janitor, meaning she had things to do. When she gave another patient his "blood tinner," he snapped, "Can you speak English?" When a woman blamed her husband's cough on "the BP plant," Rosalie thought she was talking about a bush, not a refinery.

But for the most part, Rosalie and her patients communicated fine. They were much more likely to compliment her kindness than criticize her grammar. "It's like she feels your pain," said the woman who wanted to kill her previous nurse. When a patient awoke from a neck operation, the first thing she saw was Rosalie's face. "I remember just looking up and thinking, 'She's got the kindest eyes,'" she said.

"Her patients love her," said Chelita, her supervisor.

I asked patients, in private, whether they minded foreign nurses taking American jobs. It was a common complaint in politics but not on the ward. None said they did. If anything, the bias ran the other way—toward the assumption that foreign nurses worked harder and provided better care. Mr. Yardley said the hospital would have hired Americans if it could. "If there are people out there who are qualified, where the hell are they?" After multiple hospitalizations, he favored Filipinos. "You can look at a person and tell if they enjoy what they're doing. And if they're just here for a paycheck, you can tell that too."

Of course Rosalie *was* in it for the paycheck, but not for the paycheck alone. Nurses have long debated whether to cast the field as a profession or a calling; some find the latter condescending, an insult to their skill. Rosalie said that for her the calling matters more. "If you do something good for others, you're doing something good for God."

One night as Rosalie settled in, a cry hit the nurses' station. *"Arrg-ghh!"* It sounded like a cartoon pirate. "Your baby is crying," another nurse teased.

"It's Mr. Reese," Rosalie said, bustling to his room.

The fifty-seven-year-old man couldn't walk, talk, or understand what people said to him. His large head seemed too heavy for his neck and lolled to the side. He wore a diaper and ate from a feeding tube. "Oh, you're wet!" Rosalie said. "I'm going to change, OK?" She felt bad that no family visited.

Rosalie powdered his bottom, fixed his feeding tube, brushed his teeth, and moisturized his lips. He let out three rhythmic grunts: "unt-unt-unt."

"Unt-unt-unt," she repeated. He smiled as if in on the joke.

"You better be good to us!" she said. "And smile all the way!"

Hours later came another pirate cry. Rosalie changed him again and pushed a bottle of formula into the feeding tube. It was late, but the radio was on. Rosalie fed him ice chips and stroked his head. "Oh, I want to dance!" she said.

Someone passing the room in the next few minutes would have seen a curious sight: a short woman in a yellow infection gown, swaying beside an invalid's bed and offering compliments he couldn't understand. "I like your hair—curly on top. You're handsome!"

The feeding and changing went in the chart. The dance was just between them.

ONE NIGHT ROSALIE didn't eat dinner until 1:40 a.m.—pasta Alfredo with cheesy bread. Another nurse brought *pancit*, so Rosalie had noodles with noodles, which she ate in a rush. When I noted that Lara wanted to be a nurse, Rosalie frowned. "I want them to have a different job. Pay is good, but it's really hard on the family. I don't want them to experience what I experience, working all the time."

If Rosalie's calling was real, so was her fatigue. In Abu Dhabi, she mostly worked days and didn't have the kids; she could sleep. In Texas, she went to work with bloodshot eyes.

While the work was taxing under any circumstance, the foreign nurses remained convinced they were treated unfairly—forced to work more shorthanded shifts and care for sicker patients. Each unit was set up for sixteen beds and four nurses, so no nurse would have more than four patients. But 7B nurses were often "floated"—sent to fill vacancies on other wards—which left the unit understaffed when its beds filled. Some thought they got picked on because they were foreign and some because they were new, but everyone felt hazed.

Chelita agreed. One month, she found that 7B worked at less than full strength fifteen times, while a similar unit did so just once. "It's because they don't say anything. They get stepped on all the time." She added, "It's not just the numbers; it's the patients they have—they're really difficult." One night the short-staffed crew got seven admissions, when two or three is a lot. "Oh my God," said Rosalie. "We were really so much like overwhelmed." As I walked in one night, the Filipino charge nurse spat, "I'm refusing the patient!" and slammed the phone. Each nurse already had five patients; another would have given someone six. "It's unsafe!" the nurse said. If extra load caused mistakes, "we could lose our licenses!"

Job-related stress has existed forever, but in the 1970s it got a name: "burnout." A psychologist named Christina Maslach later developed a test to detect the condition, to which nurses are especially susceptible since it tends to accompany work that involves empathy. By some estimates, as many as 40 percent of nurses meet the Maslach Burnout Inventory's definition of the syndrome. Caring for very sick patients is one risk factor. Working short staffed is another. Working twelve-hour shifts is a third. Rosalie did all three.

Symptoms include headaches, stomachaches, chronic fatigue, sleeplessness, and shortness of breath, all of which Rosalie had. She came to work on a few hours' sleep, survived on a diet of Nexium and rice, gained weight, battled reflux, and waited out migraines in empty patient rooms. "When I come home, I'm already low-batt. Sometimes I feel depressed. I feel exhausted." A needle prick could give her HIV. A mental lapse could cost her a license. "I make one mistake, we're doomed— my kids' future, it's done," she said. Chelita noticed the strain. "It's like she's overwhelmed."

Rosalie popped two giant vitamin tablets one night and went to work on four hours' sleep. The evening started with just two patients— one with AIDS and a leaky stomach plug, the other an engineer with cirrhosis. His failing liver increased the ammonia in his blood and left him disoriented. He'd been trying to pee in a capped bottle. The day nurse, an American, warned he was less lucid than he appeared. "He's an inventor," she told Rosalie. "He's made a crapload of money!"

Rosalie pulled me aside and whispered. "What's that—a *crapload* of money? I can sense it means this man is rich, but why 'crap'?"

Rosalie gave the engineer a cheerful greeting, promised a laxative to purge the ammonia, and urged him to stay in bed to avoid a fall. "I want for your health," she said.

Fred Callahan had silver senatorial hair and a matinee idol's smile. He nodded as if he understood. "Gotcha!" he said.

Rosalie was charting at 11:00 p.m. when a bed alarm rang. Mr.

Callahan was up. Rosalie hurried to his room and guided him back to bed, with his two hundred pounds sagging on her frame. "I don't want any broken bones here!" she said. "That's why we say, 'Call, don't fall!'"

"Gotcha!"

"Thank you for understanding!" Rosalie sounded chirpy and lingered too long, almost as if she were flirting. It wasn't like her to seem insincere. Later, she explained: during his last stay she'd been busy with another patient, and he'd complained to a supervisor that she'd been inattentive.

Rosalie was working with her three favorite nurses, all Filipino. At midnight, they sat in a row, charting. One fussed that the equipment clerk had given her flak for filing back-to-back requests, instead of submitting them together. "The doctor just put in the second order. What am I supposed to do—*guess*?"

"She's just like that, *Ah-tay*," Rosalie said.

Another nurse had vacation photos from a Caribbean cruise. Everyone cooed and said in Tagalog that her husband looked handsome. A third slipped away to the break room to call the Philippines, where her father had just had a stroke.

The bed alarm rang. Mr. Callahan was up and in a fog. Rosalie steered him back to bed and covered him with a blanket.

"How's the blanket business?" he said.

"Can you tell me where you are?" Rosalie asked.

"No."

At one thirty, the nurse with the ailing father worked a calculator, worried about his bills. The alarm sounded again, and Rosalie found Mr. Callahan wobbling around his room, flushed and shaking. His temperature was nearly 103. "Oh, wow, you're hot," she said. She called a doctor, who told her to give him an enema.

At three thirty, she started working up a new patient. At four thirty, she checked Mr. Callahan's temperature. The enema had worked. At six, she got another patient, a drummer who had been drinking all night and had heart palpitations. He was hard of hearing, and the intake interview was slow. Rosalie looked exhausted. Her English started to slip.

"Do you afraid anything?" she asked.

"Wallet, how much your money?"

"Who will gonna take you home when you release?"

Her attempt to say she was giving him a blood thinner needed translation. "I'm going to give the five thousand initial bolus."

He shrugged. "Sounds good."

The ward hummed to life as the day shift walked in. As Rosalie was finishing her charts, a doctor asked her a question. She stared blankly. "Dizzy," she said. Then she grabbed a water bottle, splashed her face, and slumped facedown on the desk.

Her pulse was up, and her blood pressure was down. The nurses wheeled her to the break room, laid her across two chairs, and covered her with a blanket. "So sleepy," she said. Advice poured in. Go to the ER! No, the urgent care! Eat first, sleep first, drink water. "Too much *pancit*—that's the problem," one nurse teased. Someone remembered that she'd recently left early with a migraine. "Make sure you get a checkup, Sally, because it's too frequent."

"Maybe the stress," Rosalie said.

Half an hour later, a nurse helped her into a wheelchair and pushed her into the elevator beside the buzzed drummer, who was headed for a test. I pulled up the car, and Rosalie lay in the backseat with her legs elevated, to quicken the blood flow to her head. She took off two nights, as scheduled, and reported for her shift.

"ROOM 13: MS. OLA-EUNICE JOHNSTON, sixty-nine," the day nurse began. "She has a history of stroke—multiple strokes. She doesn't walk and she's not peeing. She hasn't peed since Thursday morning."

Rosalie frowned: almost thirty-six hours.

"The bladder scan said like 950"—milliliters of urine—"but I cathed her and only got 250 out."

"Only 250?" Rosalie asked.

"I know, it's not enough."

"She's oriented?"

"Oh yes—she's *very* nice."

Rosalie introduced herself but got pulled away. I stayed behind and heard a story out of Zora Neale Hurston. Raised in a family of Louisiana sharecroppers, Ms. Johnston had plowed behind mules, chopped cotton, and gotten married at fifteen. When I asked what her husband did, she said, "Nothing but hit me in the head." She left school in ninth grade but later got a GED and in midlife became a nursing aide. She was taking classes in hopes of becoming an RN when a back injury left her disabled. "After all that hard work I did, I never got a chance to make $5 an hour."

I asked how she felt about foreign nurses getting the job she had hoped to have. "I admire anybody and everybody that tries to get up a little higher!" Though she was black and they were Filipino, she considered them part of the same clan—the tribe of low-born strivers. "Don't stop! Keep going! You hear people say a lot of Mexicans have jobs. Yeah, 'cause they want to work! Anybody that wants to get higher, I'll go with them!"

Rosalie was busy. A new patient had a rare blood disorder, and a Vietnamese woman, depressed and crying, needed a translator. By the time Rosalie got the bladder scanner and returned to the room, Ms. Johnston had news. "I was finally able to urinate."

Rosalie inspected. "It's a success! You did a good job!"

For two days, Ms. Johnston had been searching for the word to describe the feeling in her leg. Without it, she feared the doctors wouldn't believe she was having seizures. "It's not 'swollen'; it's . . ."

"Tight?" said Rosalie.

"Tight!" Ms. Johnston said. "That's it!" She wrote the word and clutched it like a gift. *"Tight, tight, tight!"*

When Rosalie returned the next day, Ms. Johnston was in a chair. She had urinated twice and walked the hall. "You're up!" Rosalie said. Rosalie attributed the improvement to positive thinking. "When we are depressed, our body is not responding. But if we are telling, 'I can do this,' then every day you can progress a little bit."

"Mm-hmm," Ms. Johnston agreed. She had told the doctor her leg was "tight," and he believed that she'd been having seizures.

Rosalie didn't like Ms. Johnston's cough and inspected her nostrils. "It's red inside." She called the doctor and warned that the blood thinner he prescribed might cause a nosebleed. He changed the medication.

After fetching it, Rosalie yawned and said absentmindedly that she had gotten only two hours of sleep. She gave Ms. Johnston a bedpan, to measure the urine output. "The day nurse said we didn't need that anymore," Ms. Johnston said.

"I just want to check," Rosalie said. She later told me in private that the day nurse had just finished nursing school. "There are some things she needs to learn." Ms. Johnston had a private comment, too: the day nurse was fine, "but Sally, she be in here with me more."

Later, Rosalie fluffed Ms. Johnston's pillow and offered her juice. "Oh, you're good—*good*," Ms. Johnston said. "I like your glasses. Did I see you with glasses before?"

"When I have a headache, I have to use them." Rosalie rubbed Ms. Johnston's arm. "You sleep now," she said. Then she slipped off to the break room to call Emet and remind him to take his medicine.

Ms. Johnston had one more thing to say about Rosalie, but the word went missing again. "She's just . . ." After a few false starts, it came to her. "She's a *nurse*—that's what she is."

ELEVEN

Ruffled Feathers

As Rosalie left for work one night, Chris walked in with a laundry basket and ran to stir the soup. After four months in Texas, he was still unemployed and trying to pretend he didn't mind the domesticity. Rosalie made the money. Chris ran the house. He did all of the cooking, some of the dishes, and most of the wash. (Bathroom cleaning he left to Rosalie.) The other nurses' husbands were doing much the same. Chris was a patient and tender father who enjoyed the kids, but being cast as a househusband bothered him. He knew from the start, "People will say, 'Why is he like that—why is he only at home? Why does he allow his wife to work when he did not find a job?'"

Many aspects of modern migration echo the past, but the inversion of gender roles is new. Men have historically led the way, either alone or with families in tow. Their place in society changed, but their stature within the family endured. (Irish nannies in the early twentieth century formed a rare migrant stream composed of working women, but they arrived young and single, not leading husbands.) As more men followed their breadwinning wives, in the United States and beyond, couples like

Rosalie and Chris found themselves on a new frontier—pioneers in gender relations.

It was an uncomfortable place to be, with few role models and scant precedent. Raised in a culture where male authority reigned, the husbands couldn't match their wives' earnings, especially in a new country with no contacts or credentials. Some settled for menial jobs, and some stayed home to watch the kids, while the nurses worked exhausting hours and tried to keep the men from feeling marginalized. If the couples didn't always respond with grace, they were working without a script.

Unburdened by expectations, Chris liked Galveston. It was provincial, but so was he. He liked a town with weedy lots and plenty of parking space. Rosalie had no illusions that she understood American life, but Chris prided himself on his grasp of American ways. He assured Rosalie that if they kept their receipts, the government would repay them for their groceries. He delighted in the local stores' return policy— you could use things and take them back because "America is the home of the free." I wasn't surprised that he didn't know the story of Martin Luther King Jr. I was surprised to hear him tell the kids that King was literally king—"the King of America!"

He declared with cheerful certainty that he knew which universities were the very best: Harvard and "Uck-lah."

"Uck-lah!" he repeated, to my puzzled look. "U-dot, C-dot, L-dot, A-dot."

Like most of the newly arrived Filipinos, Chris was surprised to find the United States more racially diverse than it looked on TV. "There's not too many white people, right?" he said. The Filipinos were wary of the city's black neighborhoods, but Chris made a point of hailing the black traffic guard in the carpool line. The kids called the officer "Mr. Yomaman" because whenever Chris saw him he rolled down the window and yelled, "Yo—my man!" He had learned from movies that "this is the greeting of the black Americans when they are so happy to see each other."

As it had before, Chris's job search got off to a slow start. Rosalie tried not to push. She didn't want him to feel, as he had in Abu Dhabi, that she was faulting his efforts. New to the American job market, he didn't know how high to aim. His résumé expressed a desire "to actively participate in a company wherein I can apply my outmost knowledge and skills." He sent a copy to blue-chip Schlumberger, which thanked him for his inquiry. When the GE website froze, he stopped looking at it. Several of the husbands suggested he join them at Whataburger; Chris talked of applying but didn't. With Rosalie's earnings, he saw no urgency. "He's not lazy," Rosalie said. "When it comes to work, he really works. He's just so shy to talk to people. He always makes me be the one to talk."

One morning with Rosalie beside him, Chris stopped in at a beachfront resort and discovered it needed a "maintenance engineer." He handed Rosalie the application. "You write," he said. She must have written something good because the hotel asked him to come back in two hours for an interview. His excitement was obvious. "Do you think I need to go home and change?" he asked Rosalie. He was wearing a tank top and jeans.

"Much better," she said, surprised that he had to ask.

Chris returned in a collared shirt and fretted that if the interview lasted more than two hours, he'd be late to pick up the kids. Fifteen minutes later, he was back in the waiting room with a forced laugh as the manager silently walked past. Something had obviously gone wrong.

Chris said that when he told the manager about his work in Abu Dhabi, supervising a maintenance crew, the boss took offense: "You are trying to apply for my job." He needed someone to fix stuff, not supervise. "You should have specified 'technician'—not 'engineer,'" Chris shot back. The discussion ended there.

"Man, I was excited. I thought this was going to be it," Chris said. "I was really dressed up, too."

A few months later, with Chris still unemployed, Rosalie griped to me about his passivity at a volume he seemed likely to overhear. "That's what I hate about Chris right now: he's not keen about searching for a job." She'd heard about an opening in a bank, but by the time he applied, it was filled. "I want him to search and search the internet, but he doesn't. If you try for a hundred companies, maybe one will give you an answer." When Chris wondered if he should give up, Rosalie bristled. "I don't want to be the only one working."

I'd passed onto Chris a lead that hadn't worked out. A friend of a friend knew the owner of a new Galveston hotel who said he would give Chris a job. But after meeting with Chris, the personnel manager said he was overqualified for the only position he had, as a "houseman," or janitor. He pledged to call back if bartending opened up. Chris hadn't heard from him. After Rosalie's complaint, I dropped the owner a note to say that Chris was still looking. The next morning, the hotel called. The houseman's job was his.

Grocery shopping when his phone rang, Chris sounded flustered. "What is the time of the work will be started there, sir? I thought there's a bartending? No? OK, OK—houseman."

He hung up and said nothing.

"At last—a job!" Rosalie clapped.

"I wonder if I'll have free lunch at the hotel or pack my own?"

"First day, just pack," Rosalie said. Chris nodded and resumed shopping.

After school, he told the kids. "Daddy—I'm so proud of you!" Kristine said.

"Would you be ashamed of Daddy if I worked as a janitor?"

"No!" they shouted.

By the time he called his mother at night, his voice had a touch of swagger. He had landed an American job!

Rosalie was pleased, but one detail bothered her. When the hotel had asked Chris to come in right away and fill out some forms, Chris said he had an appointment at the bank. "Why didn't you prioritize the job?" she had asked. "You can always go to the bank later." She wondered what it was about men; they're supposed to be strong, but they often seemed lost.

FEMINISTS ONCE SAW THE RISE of the breadwinning female migrant as a hopeful trend. If men lost their economic dominance, patriarchal arrangements would erode: as women shared the bills, men would share the chores. Parity would gain. "When the two are working, the woman feels herself the equal of the man in ruling the home," explained a Dominican woman in New York in the 1980s.

The story has proved to be a lot more complex. Paychecks usually do give migrant women more clout than they had back home, but the changes have been modest and fragile, with gains on one front offset by losses on another. To sift the ethnographic record is to see how painful men find their lost status and how far their wives go to buck them up.

The battered male ego is the focus of Sheba George's study of nurses from Kerala, an Indian state where men are used to dominant status, as breadwinners and rulers of the home. While the women arrived in the States to high-status jobs, their downwardly mobile husbands became "completely dependent on their wives." They stopped working or languished in lowly positions. Some men responded by sharing chores, but others demanded more subservience from their wives, to compensate for their lost status. To bolster their husbands' self-regard, some nurses even pretended not to know how much money they made. "I really like it that I don't think she has any idea about financial matters," one husband explained. "When she makes more money, I feel a little inferior. I don't know why."

Among the Keralites, the biggest change in gender relations occurred in church, the center of community life. There the marginalized men fought back, by segregating the sexes during worship and excluding women from leadership roles. For men with no other place to shine, the church offered a coveted stage. Christmas caroling, a tool of fund-raising and evangelism, was a prestigious Keralite event. In India, both sexes sang, but caroling groups in the United States were bastions of male power—"by men for men," a "highly physical experience" some-times enhanced with alcohol. (When some teenage girls slipped in, one man griped, "I guess Indira Gandhi is still in power.") The men's desire for church titles was so great it drove schisms; congregations split to create more leadership slots. The women mostly went along, either be-cause they were too tired to care or to keep the peace.

My desk holds a stack of studies two feet tall examining gender roles across the ethnic rainbow. The details vary but support a common theme: migration increases the power of women and provokes a jealous reaction from men, who rebel in unpredictable ways. Cecilia Menjívar focused on poor Salvadorans in San Francisco, where women were quicker to find jobs and resentful husbands and boyfriends lashed out by reducing their household support. One husband demanded gas money to take his wife to work. "You know, women become too important here," he said. "So I said [to her] go to hell. I don't give her anything now."

Pyong Gap Min studied middle-class Koreans in New York, where families became newly reliant on women's earnings. The men were "frustrated over their inability to support their families" but unwilling to surrender "their patriarchal authority." Some sought status by running expensive campaigns for positions in church and ethnic groups. Others turned to "excessive drinking, golfing, and gambling" or blew large sums on fawning bar girls. Contrary to stereotypes of the harmonious Asian family, the Koreans suffered high rates of marital conflict and divorce.

Despite their fabled machismo, Dominican men in New York did surrender some household authority when their wives became provid-ers. But the men considered the power sharing temporary—to cease once they could support the family alone—while women sought to pre-serve their gains. Sherri Grasmuck and Patricia Pessar found that men scrimped and saved to move back to the Dominican Republic, but women tried to buy homes and appliances that would anchor them in New York. About a third of the couples divorced, with "the struggle over domestic authority" the leading source of strain.

As men rue their lost status, some migrant women forgo equality to maintain family unity. Among Vietnamese families in Philadelphia, Nazli Kibria found that men suffered a "deep and widespread sense of malaise" when their wives took jobs. ("Here, the woman is the king and the man holds a position below the pets," one Vietnamese man complained.) But rather than demand equal treatment, the women took pains to reinforce male authority. That's because they wanted to preserve the men's financial help and because they thought their children needed strong fathers to protect them from America's sexualized, materialistic culture. If it took a propped-up patriarchy to resist Madonna, so be it.

Gender relations weren't on my mind when I met Rosalie's colleagues in Galveston. But almost all the families were dealing with tensions from the men's downward mobility. One nurse was married to a stay-at-home dad known for his obsessive jealousy; she told other nurses he scrutinized her clothes after work for signs of infidelity. Another stay-at-home husband protected his ego by pretending not to have one. "She's the boss— I'm the man-wife," he said. Yet another, who'd surrendered a good position abroad in medical sales, drove to his job as a janitor in a new Lexus. (He didn't last long.) When I met with the husband of a Jamaican nurse, he brought a scrapbook of his college soccer career, as if to preempt any question of his masculinity. He had an MBA but worked as a Walgreens clerk. "I jog a lot to deal with the stress," he said. "I'm not as angry as I ought to be."

Chris didn't drink or golf; he did the laundry and was anything but violent. By the standards of old-world patriarchy, he was a model of equality. That's not to say that Rosalie's earnings hadn't hurt his pride. He asserted his masculinity in his own quirky ways. Among them was a devotion to smelly lunches and trips to the rooster farm.

CHRIS BOUGHT a new shirt and arrived early to start the janito-
rial job. "I feel sorry for Chris," Rosalie said. "In the UAE, he is the
supervisor of the cleaner—now he's the one who cleans." But his boss,
Ron, was welcoming, and the work wasn't hard. He cleaned the lobbies
and public bathrooms in two adjacent hotels and shuttled linens to the
housekeepers. It paid only $7.60 an hour, but the schedule let him take
the kids to school and pick them up. "I'm happy to be working there."

The problems began on the second day, with a bowl of fish head
soup. The housekeepers complained about the smell and teased Chris
for eating rice with his hands. Given his umbrage, they could have been
talking about his mother, not his lunch. "Of course I will take rice!" he
told them. "'Cause I am Filipino, not an American!" They dubbed him
the "Fish and Rice Man," and he took to eating quickly and alone.

The tension was partly racial. The housekeepers were poor and
black; they struggled to understand Chris's accent and slang, and he
struggled to understand theirs. When they asked him to take the trash
from their carts, he felt probed for weakness and refused: he said that
was their job. They continued to complain about his lunch. "I wanted
to say your comments are ugly like your face," he seethed. "I just ignore
the black women. The Latinos are more trustworthy."

In the second week, the hotel manager, Cathy, summoned him to
remove some hallway trash. He finished mopping and arrived five minutes later to a dressing-down. He hadn't known she was waiting. "If I'm
the one giving you orders, you do it right away," she said. Chris bristled
and complained privately that she should have gone through Ron, his
supervisor, instead of approaching him directly. "Maybe I hurt her ego
because she's a manager and I didn't take her order right away." He got
along fine with the men at work.

Outearned at home, surrounded by chiding women at work, Chris
found his joy where he could—in a field full of strutting roosters. He

leaped at an invitation to visit a farm. Cockfighting, wildly popular in the Philippines, was illegal in the States, but some Filipinos held clandestine bouts or made money breeding the birds and shipping them home, where Texas cocks were prized. Chris had grown up with cockfighting culture. Legend had it that his family had won its land in the betting pits, and his happiest days as a kid were spent at fights with his father. He still owned roosters in the Philippines. "It goes with our blood, our ancestors."

Visits to other farms followed, often with the family in tow. Rosalie and the kids sat around bored while Chris stroked the birds and talked shop with the breeders. In his free time, he watched recordings of professional tournaments. Each battle was a brief, deadly affair fought by birds with daggers on their legs—a cloud of feathers and blood to the amateur eye but a dance of beauty and courage to the fan. Rosalie shrugged. As men's diversions go, cockfighting was tame—cheaper than golf, healthier than strip clubs. "He's a crazy man, crazy for chickens," she said. "That's his passion. Let him be."

The most famous scholar to explore cockfighting was the anthropologist Clifford Geertz, who did his fieldwork in Bali in 1958 and described the fight, and the rituals around it, as a stage upon which men expressed the animality of their ids. "The deep psychological identification of Balinese men with their cocks is unmistakable," he wrote. "The double entendre here is deliberate. It works in exactly the same way in Balinese as it does in English, even to producing the same tired jokes, strained puns, and uninventive obscenities." When Balinese men gather, "half or more of them will have a rooster in his hands, holding it between his thighs, bouncing it gently up and down . . . ruffling its feathers with abstract sensuality." The fight itself was "a bloody drama of hatred, cruelty, violence, and death"—a display of "the narcissistic male ego writ out in Aesopian terms." Cockfighting in the Philippines played the same ego-affirming role and also had political overtones as a form of resistance to colonial regimes that tried to ban it. It made sense that a man who felt himself henpecked would find comfort in gladiatorial pursuits.

The maids continued to insult his lunches. One asked him not to eat until she left the break room. Chris kept quiet, but his boss, Ron, found out. He disliked the maid and insisted that Chris file a discrimination complaint—discrimination against his food. "Everytime I take my lunch in our pantry & we eat all together Ms. Reva the housekeeper she always give a comments against my food," Chris wrote. "I feel so embarrased [sic] for that." When Chris saw the housekeeper later that day, she was crying because her hours had been cut. She soon left the job.

Race, as well as gender, was part of the rub. The housekeepers were mostly BOI—"born on the island," meaning poor and black—a group widely disparaged by white bosses. "If you've talked to many BOIs, you know there aren't many of them who are pleasant and presentable," Ron told me. "Some of these girls, they're mean black women, and when they say something, it's scary."

More conflict followed when Cathy, the manager, told Chris to wash the break-room dishes. He refused, saying the dishes belonged to the housekeepers, who should clean up after themselves. "If you want to fire me, OK," he said. Ron backed him up and posted a sign that said CLEAN UP YOUR OWN MESS!! but Cathy then treated the housekeepers to lunch and omitted Chris. Though he didn't want to eat with them, he felt humiliated by the snub.

After two months, Chris quit. The work was dirty and the pay was low, but those were issues he could handle. Conflict with female authority was not. "I feel degraded. Much better to leave early than to punch people in the face." Rosalie agreed he should go before he got into a fight.

TESS, STILL THE GORDONS' NANNY, was back in New York for another summer and came back to Galveston to visit. She arrived just as Chris quit, bursting with news. It concerned an online beau.

Still looking for an American spouse, she had placed an ad on an online dating site in Abu Dhabi and drawn a response from an American businessman. "I am the mysterious man from your dreams, the man whose eyes spoke to you," Christopher Daniels wrote. "I'm generous, loving and lovable, sensitive, faithful, kind, fun, intelligent and erudite. . . . I can be very bitchy when pushed, but I cry easily, too."

She hadn't expected *that*. "I read your email Chris, and I was so impressed," she replied. "I could say I'm a good catch!"

He lived in Glasgow with a six-year-old son after losing his wife and daughter in a car accident. He and Tess had been writing almost every day.

Tess recounted their digital courtship to Rosalie with feigned indifference. "If he's serious, I'm serious; if he's just playing, I'm just playing." But her excitement was too great to conceal. After five weeks of emails and two phone calls, he was coming to New York to see her.

Over breakfast, Tess read Rosalie some of her suitor's messages, which had arrived in red italics:

> I knew I love you the moment we talked for the first time. I felt our hearts connect and our chemistry was amazing. I fall more and more in love with you every single day. . . . I love the way you touch and kiss me, murmuring sweet things on my neck. . . . Marry me.

Rosalie pretended to be shocked. "You answer him already?" she said. "He's your boyfriend now?"

"What's he going to do—jump on me over the internet?" Tess said. "We'll see where we end up." A friend had married a Texan whom she had met online. "Fiancé visa is the quickest way to come to America."

Rosalie's favorite Tagalog soap opera was about a nanny who married a rich man. They laughed at the parallels and sang the theme song—"Romance, I'm willing to take the chance"—but Rosalie was more skeptical than she let on. So was Christina, Tess's boss. Her online search found no American businessman named Christopher Daniels in Glasgow, and the mailing address he sent didn't appear to exist. Tess had never asked the name of his company or what it did or why an American in Glasgow would be searching a Middle East dating website.

She spent much of the weekend checking her phone. "Where are you, Christopher Daniels?" she groaned.

For the second year in a row, I drove Tess to the Houston airport. The previous year she had wept about the separation from her kids, but this trip was filled with anticipation. Noreene, who was fourteen, had joked about changing her name to Daniels. The mystery man might just be "playing," Tess said, but "my tummy is upside down."

Three days before his scheduled arrival, Tess got a 6:00 a.m. call. Christopher Daniels had a long tale, which he told between sobs. He had traveled to Nigeria and brought his young son, who had gone out at midnight for ice cream, fallen down the stairs, broken both arms, and injured his back. They couldn't come to New York. Half-asleep as she listened, Tess focused on one suspicious detail: Who lets a six-year-old go out for ice cream at midnight? When she told him to send a picture from the hospital, he seemed miffed.

"I don't know if it's true or not," Tess said a few hours later, though deep down she did.

Christopher Daniels never sent the picture. He didn't solicit money, though perhaps that was part of the plan. Tess asked no further about his son. At the end of the day, he complained about her silence and declared the romance dead. "It's so sad darling," he wrote. "I thought you loved me."

Tess had moved on. "I think it was *scam*," she said. With a Filipino accent, "scam" sounds like "scum."

WHILE ROSALIE HAD AGREED that Chris should quit, his joblessness increased the tension at home. He resented his dependence. She resented his lack of appreciation for her financial support. It was the same dynamic that had strained their marriage in Abu Dhabi. She had hoped things would be different in the States.

On a hot August day, the tensions boiled over. As Rosalie came home and slept after work, Chris lingered beside me at breakfast and vented about her profligacy. "She will spend and spend and spend." He even said he had quit in part out of frustration with her lack of restraint: there was no point bringing in money she was so quick to waste. Exhibit A was a $100 back massager. "Where is it now? In the corner!" He had known she wouldn't use it but complimented himself on holding his tongue.

Rosalie awoke a few hours later and aired the mirror-image grievance: Chris had the nerve to criticize her spending when she supported the whole family. He even griped about her back massager! "He's always commenting but not doing anything." She went into the bedroom to pray, but the sight of a broken dresser made her cry. She wanted a new one but knew Chris would resist.

The dam burst. "I don't know where to find my happiness!" The house was a mess. She couldn't sleep. Her body ached. Her family was ungrateful. "Every dollar I've earned, it's my blood, sweat, and tears!" She veered between English and Tagalog. She toggled between "I" and "you," as if a less personal pronoun could off-load the pain. "You feel unloved! The kids, you cannot control! . . . You don't get *appreciated*, like a simple back massager."

To the trained ear, the word was a clue: feeling unappreciated is a sign of nursing burnout. (A true-false question on the test for nursing burnout is "I don't feel I'm appreciated.") Rosalie continued through sobs. "Nobody *appreciates*. . . . That's why I keep telling my kids, 'Mommy's working hard for you.' . . . You feel *unappreciated*. Since the beginning, I feel that Chris did not *appreciate*. . . . Sometimes you don't know what will make you feel happy, feel loved, feel *appreciated*."

The sound of Rosalie's crying reached the girls, who crept into the bedroom. "Are you OK, Mommy?" Kristine asked.

"I'm OK as long as you give Mommy a hug and a kiss every day," Rosalie said.

"And don't scatter your toys!" she told Lara.

"And eat faster your rice!"

The girls swapped alarmed looks and melted from the room.

"Sometimes I feel like I'm not spiritually good!" Rosalie went on. "I don't want to say I'm depressed or anything like that. With my patients—that's the only time I feel I'm doing good with somebody. I can give hope to my patients! I can give care!"

It took her a long time to calm down. By midday, the kids were so bored that Lara was literally walking in circles. The apartment pool waited outside the door, and the sea was a few blocks away. I decided to take the kids to the beach and urged Rosalie to come. She had just passed two hours bemoaning the lack of family time but decided to stay home and clean. The house was so *cluttered*. If only she could get the toys off the floor, maybe she would find some peace.

After the kids went to sleep that night, Rosalie announced, to no one in particular, that things weren't so bad. "It feels like I'm not happy, but I am. All I ever prayed for before was to have my children back with me. Now they are here."

CHRIS GOT A LEAD on a job—not from the want ads, but from a more venerable source: a guy he met at the Filipino food store. When it comes to connecting immigrants and jobs, formal channels are fine, but the ethnic network is formidable.

Chris's new friend, Kuya Bebing, was a retired city worker whose wife had been dead for three years. He was lonely and eager to help. Soon, he was stopping by the apartment, dispensing advice. When he learned that Chris needed work, he introduced him to his friend Kuya Ben, who worked at the wastewater plant. Both men were a generation older than Chris, flattered by his attention, and impressed that he had an engineering degree. Kuya Ben set off with singular drive to get Chris a wastewater job.

It was only an entry-level maintenance post, but Galveston was building an expensive new plant, and Kuya Ben told everyone that an engineer would help ensure it got proper care. Chris had a good interview, but the city made a tentative decision to fill the job from within. Kuya Ben was livid. He reminded his boss that in two decades he'd never asked a favor; he hadn't sued even when a scalding had left him hospitalized for two months. He got so mad he flung a hammer and left. It seemed like an extraordinary push for a mere acquaintance. I wondered what was behind it.

The issue was still unresolved when the two older men stopped by to swap stories and plot strategy. Chris served *crispy pata*—fried pigs' knuckles—and a bottle of red wine. Kuya Ben wore an air of kindly sadness and talked about an earlier life as a seafarer: he'd learned to woo girls in port by reciting Shakespeare. Sonnet 18, his go-to, had won him a kiss from a white girl in Brazil. "Shall I compare thee to a summer's day? Thou art more lovely and more temperate." His fourteen-line recital across a pile of pigs' knuckles was word perfect.

Kuya Ben was equally poetic on the subject of wastewater technology, which he understood, with cause, as the cornerstone of modern civilization. He all but resorted to iambic pentameter in recounting the virtues of the chlorine contact chamber and anaerobic sludge. The plant was all that stood between man and darkness, Galveston and Manila Bay. "If nobody like us will do the job, society will be in trouble! Water is the most helpful thing God creates—water is life!"

Kuya Bebing cut in. At sixty-five, he was engaged to a woman in the Philippines half his age and debating whether to marry. "Fifty-fifty, I think she just wants to come to America."

"Of course—what do you think?" said Kuya Ben. Still, the marriage could work.

"I told her, no *bola-bola*," said Kuya Bebing—no teasing about her intentions. "I want someone who's going to stay with me for life. It's kind of hard to lose a wife—kind of depressed."

As the older men told tales, Chris grasped his role: fry the pork and listen respectfully. Kuya Bebing left at midnight to call his fiancée, and Kuya Ben told more sailor stories and seethed at the hiring impasse. "I told my supervisor that we *need* this man. We are getting old. He can help us."

"If the job will come to me, it will come," Chris said. "I don't want from all the pushing they will have a high expectation from me."

Kuya Ben recited another poem, about Filipino valor, then disappeared into the night. "We still have a chance," he said.

THE MIX OF SHAKESPEARE and *crispy pata* was sui generis, but the force behind it was not: ethnic networks are the engines of modern migration. They're the bottom-up version of globalization, moving people across the globe and into housing, jobs, and schools. They explain why many Mexicans in New York come from Puebla and those in Chicago come from Jalisco or Michoacán and why workers in Sussex County, Delaware, come from not just Veracruz but a particular Veracruz village. Migration is a story of connections.

· The persistence of ethnic connections in hiring defies expectation about how the modern world should work. Rationalists like Max Weber predicted the triumph of objectivity: the personnel office would sort applicants along quantifiable measures of merit. Economists in the Milton Friedman mold thought the magic of the market would connect workers and jobs. Network theory says not so fast: it's who you know that counts. Natives tap connections, too, of course, but their networks are broader and less intense and often compete with meritocratic ideals. The ethnic connection is often the only connection immigrants have.

Studies of immigrant employment often turn out to be studies of ethnic bonds. The sociologist Mary Waters found a Manhattan cafeteria that hadn't advertised a job in nine years. It relied solely on referrals from its West Indian workforce, while ignoring anti-nepotism rules. Philip Kasinitz and Jan Rosenberg surveyed the Brooklyn waterfront and found that by the time most jobs were posted, they had already been filled, typically by word of mouth from immigrant employees. "They bring in their friend, their cousin, their uncle, whatever," an employer explained. Networks thrive because they deliver: they give migrants opportunity and employers quality control. A worker vouches for his nephew only if he's sure he'll show up.

If there are losers, they tend to be native-born blacks, whom employers view less positively and who lack the same dense connections and loyalties. In a study of low-wage workers in Michigan, Sandra Susan Smith found that blacks absorbed their employers' prejudicial views; they, too, assumed that Latinos worked harder and often hesitated to recommend black friends. For natives and immigrants alike, the decision to help turned less on their closeness to the job seeker than on the candidate's attitude. They helped people who "were personable and easy to get along with . . . who listened well; who were honest, humble, and credible." Those are precisely the qualities that Kuya Ben saw in Chris, telling his boss he was "sincere and respectful," "very humble," and "I guarantee he will not be a disappointment."

The final score was Kuya Ben, 1, Max Weber, 0: Chris got the job.

ON THE SURFACE, it seemed a classic tale of ethnic loyalty. But the story nagged at me. Something seemed amiss, both in the academic emphasis on ethnic solidarity and in the specifics with Kuya Ben: Why would he go to such lengths for someone he hardly knew? Modern scholarship celebrates ethnic bonds, but there's a downside to solidarity, too. Earlier researchers, from Robert Park to Oscar Handlin, warned that insularity could isolate newcomers and inhibit mobility. History suggests that solidarity is easy to overstate. Poles in nineteenth-century

Chicago fought over church control to the point of "physical assault and riot." Whole libraries document the enmities among New York Jews— religious versus secular, Ashkenazi versus Sephardi, Socialist versus Communist.

Indeed, one of the most revealing modern studies exposed how fragile ethnic ties can be. Studying Salvadorans in California in the late 1980s, Cecilia Menjívar expected to find a private safety net for people fleeing war and poverty. Instead, she heard constant complaints of betrayal from migrants who said that other Salvadorans had turned them away or exploited them. The conflict was so at odds with the academic literature that Menjívar doubted her own findings. "I thought, 'Oh my, I must not be doing this right,'" she told me. Her resulting book, *Fragmented Ties*, argued that many of the migrants were too poor and beleaguered to help those who followed and warned against "overly romanticized notions of immigrant unity and solidarity." The book has the ring of truth, but few scholars followed in her vein.

Behind its polite facade, Galveston's Filipino community was riven by fissures and feuds. Filipinos who spoke Tagalog were wary of those who spoke a dialect called Visayan. Democrats called Filipino supporters of the GOP "brown-man Republicans." The Filipino association existed on paper but hadn't mustered enough unity to stage an event in more than a decade. Its scholarship fund remained unspent because the group couldn't agree how to use it. A past president told me he'd lost his Filipino friends because they resented his financial success. "You know the culture—envy, envy," he said. The Filipinos had turned out on Lemonade Day partly because the nurse families were new and being recruited by competing factions. "The Filipinos here hate each other," Chris said.

Those divisions only made Kuya Ben's devotion to Chris all the more curious. But whenever I asked why he had pushed so hard, I got the same unconvincing explanations: Chris is humble . . . the plant needs him . . . he's a fellow Filipino. Then, one night when we had dinner alone, he told me the fuller story: he had helped Chris in part because it enhanced his own stature within the ethnic group. Kuya Ben felt disrespected by more educated and affluent Filipinos, who mocked him for being five three and working at the sewage plant. "They think I know nothing, I am a piece of shit." His reputation had suffered from a falling-out with a Filipino friend, whom he accused of spreading lies about him to curry favor with a wealthier man. The conflict had hurt him so much that he blamed it for a bout with cancer. "It's the most painful thing that happened in my life. The gossip scattered everywhere."

But if he delivered for Chris—an educated man, an *engineer*—he could show his Filipino detractors his clout. There was nothing subconscious about his motivation. He had no trouble spelling it out. "The reason I help Chris—he is intelligent, he is respectful, he is kind, he is from the same province as my wife. And one of the reasons also, I want them to know I can help somebody get a job. I want them to know I can help an engineer." It was a story of ethnic solidarity and rivalry in one: Kuya Ben championed one Filipino to settle scores with others.

Chris knew nothing of the intrigue. He accepted the job without asking the pay, bought a pair of steel-toed boots, and reported to the plant, where the work took him down a hole known as the scum pit.

TWELVE

Inferring America

Immigrants are often lauded as extraordinary people, self-selected for ambition and daring. They board the *Mayflower*, flee the tyrants, enrich their new land with their striving. But a second kind of immigrant story merits celebration, too. It's the story of common people who achieve uncommon things simply because their new home is a bit freer or fairer or more open to their gifts. As she started third grade, Lara was a seemingly ordinary kid poised for extraordinary growth because her teacher nourished a quality that others had ignored or suppressed: her curiosity.

At the start of the school year, she simply looked scared, a pencil-thin girl with solemn eyes and black hair so straight it might have been ironed. As other kids slouched and chattered, Lara eyed the clock. "My hand is sensitive nervous," she wrote in class. "It gets sweaty." Despite her rapid progress in English, Lara still read below grade level and started in the lowest of the four reading groups. But she was the only student to greet her teacher walking in, hug her walking out, and thank her for sharpening her pencil. "Impeccable, impeccable manners," Ms. Morgan said.

They weren't an obvious match. Margaretanne Morgan was the school expert on hard-to-discipline kids. Lara was the least hard-to-discipline kid in East Texas. But Ms. Morgan's gift for control made Lara feel secure, especially after the unruly class the previous year. As organized as Rosalie was overwhelmed, Ms. Morgan made school an oasis of order. She wasn't bubbly—she talked to students like adults—but seriousness about learning can supply its own warmth. "I don't know how to describe it, but Ms. Morgan really made me feel special," Lara said. "She treated me with respect."

Ms. Morgan, who came from Ontario, noted another bond: they were both immigrants.

At the start of the year, Ms. Morgan read the class *The Juice Box Bully*, a story that focuses on a new kid in school who picks on others to keep them from picking on him. Asked what a book is "about," most third graders summarize the plot. Lara extracted a lesson. "The theme of this book is not to be rude. We should show good character."

Next, Lara read a story about a bear who builds a tree house alone, after friends refuse to help. Choosing from a list of adjectives, Lara called him "sensitive" and "friendly" but added a word not on the list. In letting his friends come to his house, the bear was "forgiving."

"She understood they were still friends—that's a higher-level skill," the reading teacher said.

"Don't steal," Lara wrote after one story.

"Don't be bad in school," she wrote after another.

One of Lara's favorite stories involved a turtle who tricks a spider into fishing and steals his catch. Lara emphasized the abstract unfairness of stealing but also the tangible hurt it caused. "The lesson I learn is don't trick somebody because they will fill bad when they now."

Her spelling would catch up. Her empathy was advanced. "After reading that, I said, 'I don't have to worry about you,'" Ms. Morgan said. "She's got so many skills that other kids don't have.

"She's behind but she's ahead."

Two months into the year, Lara made her first friend. "My very, very, very, very own best friend," she told Dominique, urging him to get one, too. "She's kind, she's friendly, and she never tells our secrets." Or so it seemed. When the friend quickly proved too bossy, Lara relegated her to "frenemy" status and proclaimed herself Best Friends Forever–Sisters Forever with a cheerful, undemanding girl named Audrey. They sealed their bond with a secret handshake under the lunch table. The decisiveness of the switch, and the endurance of the friendship, spoke to Lara's growing social skill.

Our talks fell into a routine. "How's school?" I'd ask.

"*Wel-lll . . . ,*" she'd begin, as if struggling to answer a question so immense.

"*Prr-retty great!*"

Third grade rewards curiosity. The work is less literal than in earlier years and packed with variety. Ms. Morgan liked to present herself as an unschooled peer who shared her students' wonder at the discoveries. "There's a word here, guys, that's really tough—the girls "adorned" their hair with flowers. I've never heard that word before, so I need to use the rest of the sentence to help me figure that out." She moved on to geometry. "Perimeter just gets me so excited! . . . There are going to be some brain explosions! Let me get out my brain poncho." Cursive: "Are you dying to learn the *R*? Will you beg me?"

Lara was captivated. "Hair" versus "hare," counting by twos, the planetary order—what other kids learned or didn't and left at school, she brought home to discuss. "I have so many thoughts! I'll tell you everything."

Ten weeks into the school year, Lara moved up to a harder reading group. The sweaty palms were gone. "I got a zero on my spelling test," she bragged. "Two zeros and a one!"

"How's school?" I asked.

"*Wel-lll . . .*"

"*Prr-retty great!*"

One day when we stopped for an after-school snack, Lara sprang a sneaky question. "Do you know how to *infer*?"

I frowned as if trying to remember. "I'm going to teach you how!"

She paused to dip a fry in her McFlurry and increase the suspense. "It's like when you say, 'Oh, it's cold—it's really snow outside.' I didn't *tell* you what season it is. But you can *infer* it's winter."

She stabbed the air with a milky fry, marking the triumph.

"You see? It works!"

KRISTINE WAS OFF to middle school, where orientation had an air of organized chaos as the fifth graders marched through the locker-lined halls in rumbling platoons. They came in every size and color—hulking girls, elfin boys, prepubescent, and fully formed—and hormonal change was on everyone's mind. "Bring some deodorant," the gym teacher warned. "*Not* cologne," the English teacher said. "It doesn't cover up the smell." The eighth graders were twice Kristine's size. "These kids can eat her alive," Rosalie fretted. But not for the first time, the fears of the immigrant parent were lost on the child. Kristine glimpsed the future and liked what she saw. When the librarian called her a "cutie," she beamed. "Yes, it's true!" she said.

Kristine had finished fourth grade with a surge of social confidence. At a swim trip at the end of the year, a classmate tried to break up her friendship with Lauren, but Kristine had deftly withstood the challenge. Then she spent the summer honing her identity as a Girlie Girl— a fashionable, feminine popularity seeker, clad in pink. She carried a Hello Kitty notebook, wrote stories about princesses, and decorated them with hearts. Her favorite cartoon character was a rich girl who shopped.

Scott Collegiate Academy, Galveston's main middle school, occupied an aging low-slung building in the center of the island. Three-quarters of its students qualified for subsidized meals, but Scott didn't feel like a

poor urban school. It strove for a homey feel, with 475 students and a
ferret named Ricky—part of an office menagerie. Academically, its defining feature was the unevenness of the faculty. A history teacher
thought the Loyalists were loyal to George Washington. A sub screamed
like an alcoholic parent. But the librarian drove students to reading fes-
tivals, and the math maestro could have taught geometry to the ferret.
To an unsettling degree, learning depended on the luck of the draw.

At the start of the year, I found Kristine huddled in the cafeteria before class with Lauren and a group of new friends.

"I'm a tomboy!" Lauren said.

"I'm a fighter!" another girl said.

"I'm an artist!"

"I'm a Girlie Girl!" Kristine said.

"Girlie Girl is like whenever you like flowers and bows and you're
always messing with your nails and drawing hearts," Lauren explained.
"I'm not usually friends with Girlie Girls, but me and Kristine just
clicked."

With so much emphasis on identity, it proved handy to have one.
Kristine marched off to class with a pink notebook, pink nails, a Hello
Kitty thumb drive, and a pink ruler stamped "BFF." She looked like a
conscript in a Girlie Girl army, fresh from the quartermaster's tent.

At the end of the first week of school, a message appeared on Rosalie's phone. Kristine had a new friend. "Hey," it said.

Then: "Hay, hay, hay."

Then: "Hey, text me. CALL ME. TEXT ME."

Kristine raced to answer. "Soooooo!!!!!!!!!!!!!!!!!!!!!!!!!!!!!!!!!" she wrote.

"OMG," her friend replied. "Soooooooooooooooooooooooooo!!!!!!!!!!!
!!!!!!!"

Rosalie frowned and demanded her phone.

"Can I text you later?" Kristine wrote.

"TEXT ME RIGHT NAW!"

"I think she spelled 'naw' wrong," Lara said.

"No, that's our thing," Kristine said.

Lara shrugged. "That's not my thing."

Rosalie was uncomfortable with the girl's aggression and vaguely subversive tone. But Americanization would be hard to stave off. Kristine soon had a phone of her own.

As she started fifth grade, Kristine's reading level lagged by a little more than a year. That was pretty good for a non-native speaker: at the 25th percentile of Texas students, she outperformed many of her native peers. But Texas fifth graders face their first high-stakes test. To reach sixth grade, Kristine would have to pass the State of Texas Assessments of Academic Readiness—the STAAR test.

The previous year had brought the school a scare. The principal had expected about 70 percent of Scott's fifth graders to pass on the first try. When less than half did, careers were on the line. The school tore up the daily schedule and marched kids through a month of cram sessions until a retest permitted a collective exhale. The new school year had hardly begun before teachers were strategizing about the spring exam. Kristine was among the kids they considered a coin toss.

No one doubted her smarts, but her English was like spring ice, weaker than it appeared. She bantered and joked (and texted) in slang, but her vocabulary rendered much of what she read opaque. The class tackled a Swedish folktale about a "distraught" wife with "gnarly" fingers and a "quivering" voice. Kristine shrugged. On a vocabulary exercise, she defined "pre-arrange" as a fruit and "emphasize" as a size—small, medium, large, and *emphasize*.

The risks she faced went beyond the STAAR test. Kids who enter school as non-native speakers typically find themselves in a race to stave off discouragement long enough for their language skills to catch up. Even with strong starts, many falter. Researchers who followed recent immigrants in San Francisco and Boston found that many started well, but two-thirds experienced a decline in academic performance within five years. The question wasn't whether Kristine would learn English. It was whether she would learn academic English quickly enough to stay invested in school.

Within a few months, the frustration showed. "Kristine is struggling in my class, and I know it is comprehension," her English teacher told me. The science teacher noted that Kristine could explain her answers but couldn't write them. Her math teacher caught tears in her eyes as she grappled with long division. She tried to reassure her that "you're not the only one struggling."

Her frustration went beyond long division. Her teachers all knew she was missing someone she called her "second mother." Asked to draft a thank-you note, Kristine addressed hers to "Mama Wena . . . for all this years that yoo take care of me." Asked to invent a state, she wrote, "My state's name is Rowena." (The capital was P.K., for Pinkish Fashion, and the economy revolved around shopping.) Asked to describe something sacred, Kristine wrote about a gift from Rowena, "because she's really important." For another writing exercise, she wrote, "Mama wena, i want to say that I love you soo much. It's a hard dission for me that I go to America."

Kristine would go days hardly thinking of Rowena, only to feel stricken—by Rowena's complaints of feeling forgotten, by her pleas for help ("I don't have medicine . . . hu, hu, hu"), or for no reason at all. Given her brave front, it was easy to forget that she was just a ten-year-old girl in a strange new place still mourning a loss. When Rosalie was late to meet the school bus one day, Kristine cried and refused to get off, holding up the route. "I was afraid somebody would take me," she said.

At a fragile moment, the math teacher stepped in with an offer of extra help. Melody Fabian ruled her class with a commanding mix of warmth, authority, and hard candy. She viewed unsolved math problems like unmade beds—they offended her sense of order—and admired Kristine's spunk. They met in after-school sessions that mixed math, girl talk, and Jolly Ranchers, and Ms. Fabian went the extra mile in a literal sense by driving Kristine home. She would have helped in any case, but the STAAR test added extra incentive and so did a crisis at home. Her husband was dying of cancer, and Kristine's spirit took her mind off her problems. "It's better to be focused on someone else," she said.

Kristine's math problem was English. When Ms. Fabian read the word problems aloud, Kristine's grades rose from Fs to As. The downward spiral stopped. It was impressive to see what a modest intervention could achieve and sobering to think how many kids don't get it. The STAAR test would still be a challenge. But it was months away, and her confidence was growing. Kristine drew a picture of herself as a grateful princess with a beaming heart and labeled herself a "Rock Staar."

CHRIS PACKED A BIG FISH LUNCH and went to work on some of the oldest sewer lines in Texas. Wastewater was a Galveston priority. The system's collapse during Hurricane Ike had blocked residents' return to the island for a week, and the city was spending a fortune to build a state-of-the-art plant while racing to fix broken pipes, some a century old. For the maintenance crew, long waits alternated with bursts of intense, nasty work. It was the life of an infantry grunt, split between boredom and muck.

Chris liked it. Fixing things made him feel as if he were using his engineering degree. Like the army, the culture was male, multiracial, and mordant toward authority at the top. The crew leader, Mike, was Mexican American, and the senior maintenance man, Frank, was black. Both had interviewed him, liked him, and given him points for his ties to Kuya Ben. At the hotel, Chris had worked alone, encircled by female antagonists. In wastewater, he joined a blue-collar fraternity, the brotherhood of broken pipes. If there was a strain, it involved English. The less he understood it, the more he smiled. His nickname at the plant was Smiley.

Chris had been on the job for just a couple of weeks when a pump gave out at the end of his shift. He was supposed to leave at four thirty, but it would take until midnight to fix it. With Rosalie scheduled to work, Chris was in the uncomfortable position of telling his boss he had to babysit. He worried he might have to quit. But Mike understood. "Family comes first—we can handle it," he said. Chris couldn't imagine a supervisor in Abu Dhabi or Manila saying such a thing. A family-friendly wastewater crew—it was something else to like about the States.

Chris earned his wastewater cred in a place called the Scum Pit. The narrow chamber, fifteen feet deep, collects putrid liquid and debris as the wastewater moves through the plant. When the pump at the bottom stopped working, someone had to climb down and remove it. As the new guy, Chris felt obliged to volunteer. He descended the ladder wearing thigh-high boots and elbow-length gloves, a meter to measure gases, and a harness in case he slipped or passed out. The water topped his protective gear and sloshed around his feet and hands. The smell made him queasy, and the broken pump shrugged his rope. Frank picked up where Chris left off and emerged triumphant with the lassoed apparatus; he was dripping from the wastewater bath.

The Battle of the Scum Pit left them bonded. They likened themselves to the stars of *Rush Hour*, a buddy movie about two cops, one black and one Asian. Frank said he spent more time with Chris than he did with his wife and pretended to be insulted when Chris tried to repay a loan of a dollar. Frank played a song called "My Nigga" on the truck radio. Chris heard it as "My Nigger!"—which was how he greeted Frank, loudly and warmly, when he walked in the plant. Frank laughed and yelled back, "My Filipino!" When Chris chose Thanksgiving for Dominique's birthday party, Frank went out of his way to attend. He was the only American there.

One evening Chris took the family on a sunset tour of the plant. He strode the grounds like a resort manager, pointing out vats and pumps and saluting the marvel of activated sludge. Half a dozen tanks squatted beside Galveston Bay, some placid and some boiling with ire. "It smells like farts' eggs!" Dominique said. Rosalie pulled her shirt over her nose. Kristine took selfies. Chris named the tanks, explained what they did, and pointed at a grate. "They call this one Scum Pit!"

As the kids ran to the car to escape the bugs and smell, Kuya Ben, the only worker on duty, returned to a favorite theme—sanitation as mankind's salvation. A few million dirty gallons a day flowed in; a few million clean gallons flowed out. "If nobody like us will do this job, you will be in trouble!"

The kids returned to prowl the catwalk and eye the sulfurous vats. They held their noses and took turns trying on Chris's hard hat. One of the trucks had a mechanical lift. Chris found the keys, and the kids climbed on for a sunset thrill. Up and down they went, laughing on the makeshift carnival ride beside the Scum Pit.

TO A DEGREE UNMATCHED in the family, Rosalie kept American society at bay. The kids settled into school, and Chris made a Texas friend. But the person who brought the family to America was most wary of Americanization.

Often she just felt lost. She dragged herself to a meeting one morning after work, to hear about the benefits the nurses would get if they finished their contracts and joined the staff. "We really don't have a 401(k); it's a 403(b)," an administrator explained. "You can do the traditional or the Roth."

"Mmmm," Rosalie said, unaware the topic was retirement plans.

Dentists were another dilemma. The kids had never seen one in the Philippines. Dominique needed seven teeth pulled, Lara needed ten, and Kristine's intermittent toothaches kept her from school.

I wish my teeth isn't hurting anymore
I wish my teeth isn't hurting anymore
I wish my teeth isn't hurting anymore

She wrote it twenty times on a page. Dentists wanted thousands to treat the kids. Rosalie bought dental insurance, but most clinics wouldn't take it. When one said the co-pay was 20 percent, Rosalie couldn't figure out if that was her share or the insurance company's. She got so frustrated she left.

Homework was equally intimidating. "I'm not so good with adverbs," she sighed to Kristine. One afternoon, the kids arrived home from school, pulled out books, and launched an impromptu reading contest, laughing and drowning each other out. Dominique had a phonics reader, Lara had a book about pharaohs, and Kristine a graphic novel about boy-crazy girls.

"Kip picks up sticks!"

"Egyptian farmers build the pyramids!"

"Let's list all our crushes!"

Their lines wove together like a fugue. But Rosalie was on her phone reading about a Philippine scandal called the Pork Barrel Scam: top politicians had stolen hundreds of millions of dollars in antipoverty funds. Her mind was half a world away.

Soon after, Rosalie and I had lunch with a retired Filipino nurse who had brought her family to Galveston in the 1960s. Like Rosalie, she was a devout Catholic who had vowed to preserve her children's "Filipino values." But she found America a difficult place to raise a child. I had spent months reassuring Rosalie that nothing she did as a parent would make the state take her kids, only to hear the retired nurse say that her husband's fights with their rebellious, pot-smoking son had attracted child welfare officials. The boy had grown up to suffer through multiple marriages and unsuccessful jobs, and his mother blamed Americanization. "He adapted to everything—including the wrong things." Despite the woman's devotion to the church, none of her children were still practicing their faith.

Sex, drugs, and apostasy—the story touched all of Rosalie's fears.

She was still fretting when she arrived home to find Dominique playing *Grand Theft Auto.*

"Promise when you grow up you'll be a good boy only. Not bad boy! No drugs, no drinks! You will not making Mommy cry!"

The answer came from his avatar. "Watch out, motherfucker!"

Rosalie didn't hear. "Promise? Promise?"

ROSALIE COULDN'T CONTAIN her excitement, and neither could several thousand other Filipinos. Houston was getting a Jollibee, the Philippines's most popular fast-food outlet. (Think McDonald's with *halo-halo*.) Opening night resembled an ethnic riot. The Villanuevas drove an hour and couldn't get in. They returned the next morning and found traffic snarled for blocks. When Rosalie finally got to the front of the line, she was breathing so heavily the cashier asked, "Ma'am, are you OK?" Jollibee wasn't a fast-food joint but a time machine. "It's just like being back in the Philippines!" Rosalie said. She brought $100 of chicken and burgers back to the Filipino nurses.

Rosalie returned the next week and the week after that. But with every visit Jollibee tasted less like deliverance and a bit more like fast food, once with the rice undercooked. It was possible to read the waning thrill as good news: perhaps she missed the Philippines less than she thought.

As signs of adjustment go, fading Jollibee fever was modest. But there were others, including a growing resistance to Rowena's pleas. Within a few months, Rowena asked for a washing machine, blood pressure medicine, seed capital to sell dietary supplements, help in reclaiming pawned jewelry, money to rent an apartment in Manila, money for a coffee business in Leveriza, money for Tita's birthday lunch, and money to help their brother run for neighborhood counselor—all on top of the $350 a month Rosalie always sent. "Please, I beg of you," Rowena wrote.

Rosalie admired her sister's courage: another woman so sick might have given up, rather than chase a succession of long-shot business schemes. Bereft after losing Kristine, Rowena had willed herself on. But Rosalie, was eager to focus on Texas. She didn't respond. "Whether you send small amount or big amount, there's something to complain."

One morning after work, Rosalie rushed to school, where Kristine was singing in the Veterans Day show. If any American holiday reflected "Filipino values," this was it—a tribute to the elders. As the band played and the veterans marched in, someone handed Rosalie an American flag. She thought of Sister Christine, who told the Leveriza youth group to consider it a symbol of *imperyalismo*. But Rosalie was now a Texas mom and starting to admit what she had quietly known: the kids were going to stay. "Land where my fathers died," Kristine sang. "Land of the Pilgrim's pride." Rosalie gave the mini-flag a wave. "I'm starting to feel a little more American," she said with a laugh. It was hardly the last word on the subject, but she was shocked to hear herself say it.

AFTER NEARLY A YEAR in the States, the Villanuevas made their first trip outside Texas. Chris had a cousin in New Jersey whom he hadn't seen in two decades. Rosalie had never met her, but *Ah-tay* Pinky was a legend—a nurse who became an American citizen, secured green cards for her parents, and settled into a prosperous life raising three American-born daughters. With a husband who was also a Filipino nurse, they had two good American salaries. Relatives saw them once a year in Christmas cards that bespoke affluence and style. Rumor had it they owned four cars!

Everyone knew that *Ah-tay* Pinky had made it, but her daughter's debut was like nothing Rosalie had seen, with a sit-down dinner at the Marriott, a video tribute, and a court of attendants in feathered head-bands for the *Great Gatsby* theme. Rosalie's discomfort was palpable. "It's too extravagant," she whispered. In a roomful of dark-suited men,

Chris alone was short sleeved and tieless. He left the table to stand in the hall, where he wouldn't have to make conversation.

Then came flurries—just enough to pass as the Villanuevas' first snow. The five of them rushed to the patio and danced about coatless, shouting from the cold and excitement. With a picture rushed onto Instagram, the evening was declared a success.

After the dinner, dancing, and toasts, the relatives gathered for photographs. Two weeks earlier, a monstrous storm had hit the Philippines and killed more than six thousand people; the grim pictures from Typhoon Haiyan were still flooding everyone's Facebook pages. I fell into a conversation with Pinky's father, Prospero, a Protestant scourge of Catholicism who said the Philippines was being punished for worshipping graven images—its obsession with the Virgin Mary was idolatry. "God is mad at our people." (Rosalie stiffened and muttered, "I love Mama Mary.")

Old enough to remember Americans liberating Manila in 1945 and handing out chocolates, Prospero lauded his adopted land. "You can see how well Pinky's doing. That's the dream of the parents!" Then he segued into a litany of complaints: the kids are fresh; they ignore their elders; if you spank them, people call the police. His son-in-law had spurned his parenting advice. "I will tell you the truth: I feel bitter—my heart is bleeding." The pivot, from celebrating American life to listing its disappointments, was so seamless he didn't seem to notice that he had changed the story line. The photographer arrived, and Prospero stood proud and smiled.

The following morning was set aside for a trip to the Statue of Liberty, in a party that included Chris's aunt Tita Amor. At seventy, she was battling cancer, and her first visit to the States had the feeling of a last wish. Her son, a physical therapist in Illinois, said his earnings were all that was keeping her alive.

"Every family should have one person outside the Philippines to send money," Pinky agreed. "That's why I went to nursing school. It was our ticket out."

It was ferociously cold at Liberty State Park, with gusts of forty miles per hour. The few hundred yards from the parking lot to the ferry felt like a mile of tundra, but Tita Amor bent her head and advanced against the gale. As we thawed on the ferry, I realized Rosalie didn't know that the statue was known for welcoming immigrants and offered a quick explanation. There was no time to linger: Chris was rushing to catch a plane back to work. A hurried photo wound up askew, with the family huddled beneath the torch-bearing arm, as if sheltered in Liberty's armpit. Rosalie spent as much time in the boat gift shop as she did at the statue; it was run by a Filipino! But Tita Amor declared her life complete. "If you've been to Liberty, you've been to America—I can die now," she said.

The next day, Pinky took her remaining guests into Manhattan. Rosalie walked up Fifth Avenue into the country she had imagined all along. Rockefeller Center! The Plaza Hotel! Just like *Home Alone 2*. She shopped in Times Square and had dinner in Chinatown. "This is America—not Galveston!"

There were ten of us heading back in the SUV when someone mentioned the Pork Barrel Scam, which was still all over the news. In the land of Ferdinand Marcos, it takes a lot for corruption to shock anyone. But the combination of the typhoon's mass death and the politicians' mass theft had united Filipinos worldwide in a convulsion of disgust. "They're *evil*, these people," Pinky said. "They are taking millions and millions, and there are beggars who don't even eat!!"

For three days Pinky had been an unflappable hostess. Now she angrily jumbled her thoughts, swerving between guilt and donor fatigue. "Why am I here when they're still suffering?" With Facebook, the pleas for help never ceased. "They cry to you: 'I need this, I need that,' and then they say, 'Oh, you don't care anymore.' I don't want to *read* it anymore." If fortunes reversed, "would they take care of me?"

The questions weren't meant for answers: the giving would never be sufficient, and the guilt would never disappear. The issue wasn't just corrupt politicians and ungrateful relatives. It was inequality. Those who pass the nursing test get four cars and a *Gatsby* debut. Those who don't face the typhoon. Immigrants can't erase the unfairness; they just live with it. And bit by bit they start to feel more like Americans.

Rosalie went home with a suitcase of souvenirs. Two Statues of Liberty appeared on her shelves, and a third went to Lara's teacher, Ms. Morgan, an immigrant who explained its significance. Lara excitedly told Rosalie, who had forgotten what I'd told her on the boat. "I learned from the kids it's a symbol that all are welcome here!" When I asked Rosalie if she felt welcomed, she sounded as though moving to the States were the most effortless thing she'd ever done. "Yeah, everybody enjoying the same rights and freedom here. . . . It was easier than I expected."

TEN DAYS AFTER SHE returned from New Jersey, Rosalie bought a new car. It was surprising not least because she still couldn't drive. She had failed to learn on the SUV but reasoned she could do better with a smaller Honda Civic. She may have had other motives: Chris had admired Pinky's fleet, and three of the Filipino nurses in Galveston had just bought new cars from the same dealership. If a new car provided a badge of success, she wanted one whether she could drive it or not.

Rosalie didn't tell anyone back home. She put a picture on Facebook and studied the silence. "Nobody posts, 'Wow, you got a new car.' Nobody 'likes' it. Nobody said anything." Rosalie was hurt but not surprised. "They're just worried if it'll be a reason to send them less money."

Four days before Christmas, Rosalie got a long, fiery text from Rowena. "Why didn't I get Christmas money? I was hoping this would be the time I can lower my debt . . . and of course I get nothing. . . . You were the one I was counting on. That's fine. It's just hurtful. It's a never-ending pain in my heart."

Rosalie shrugged and went out to practice driving. "She's just trying to make me feel guilty. It's like *Ah-tay* Pinky says—sometimes you feel tired, you feel pressured." She had already sent $500 and would send more the next day. For now, a new car awaited, with a rosary on the rearview mirror and a Statue of Liberty on her key chain. "Fasten your seat belts, passengers!" she laughed, and circled the town in slow, satisfying loops.

THIRTEEN

Moral Hazards

I t's a symbol that all are welcome," Rosalie said about her Statuette of Liberty. Or was it? Rosalie's period of adjustment ran roughly from mid Barack Obama to early Donald Trump—chronologically a blip but politically the equivalent of a geologic age. The foreign-born population topped forty million, and a movement to restrict immigration, once confined to the margins, captured the GOP.

While its political success was new, its arguments were long in the making. Someone unfamiliar with the movement's literature might be surprised at the sheer breadth of its concerns. Detractors variously argue that immigrants displace workers, undercut wages, stifle productivity, increase crime, quicken sprawl, spread disease, abet terrorism, and fray social ties. Among the obscure polemical disputes was one about the statue itself, which many restrictionists contend isn't a symbol of welcome at all but an exercise in "myth-manufacturing."

It's true that the statue's French promoters were looking not to honor immigrants but to celebrate bilateral friendship and the blessings of liberty after the tyranny of Napoleon III. The statue was dedicated in 1886, six years before the opening of Ellis Island. Emma Lazarus's 1883 poem—"Give me your tired, your poor, Your huddled masses"—was inspired by Russian pogroms and auctioned off to help pay for the pedestal: *she* certainly saw the statue as a welcome to immigrants, and so did the immigrants themselves as they streamed into New York Harbor. But for a while, the poem was forgotten. It wasn't mentioned at the statue's dedication or displayed at the site for nearly two decades, and it wasn't given a prominent place until 1945, long after the open door it celebrated had closed.

If you feel stirred by a lifted lamp greeting the tempest tossed, the historical ambiguity won't matter. Symbols gain meaning from lived experience, and generations of Americans have experienced the statue as a tribute to the country's immigrant roots—to opportunity and the ancestors who seized it. If you consider immigration a threat, you might think the statue tells foreigners to mind "the rule of law" or to "stay and fight for their own peoples." Restrictionist writing had long made that case, but it was startling to hear it in the White House briefing room. "The poem that you're referring to was added later," Trump's aide Stephen Miller lectured reporters. "It's not actually part of the original Statue of Liberty."

Given how much immigration has risen in recent decades, it's no surprise to hear demands for new limits, especially in an age of stagnant wages and terrorist threats. Over the years, I've intermittently engaged with restrictionist leaders, liked some of them, and sympathized with some of their concerns. The movement runs the gamut from toxic provocateurs like Ann Coulter, who rues that immigrants are "overwhelmingly poor brown people," to folksy Roy Beck, the founder of NumbersUSA, whose slogan is "no to immigrant bashing" but yes to "economic fairness" for American workers. A generation ago, some of their concerns, like the fear that immigration would hurt native workers, came from the left. (Barbara Jordan, a civil rights leader and former Democratic congresswoman, chaired a commission that in 1995 called for cutting legal immigration by about a quarter.) Amid so much rapid change, anyone who says he's never questioned some aspect of immigration probably isn't being honest. Diversity is a value but a preference, too; there's no objectively right amount.

At the same time, a large academic literature suggests immigration has helped the American economy and that most immigrants are assimilating well—as rapidly as their historical predecessors, if not more so. The evidence is strongest on the issues that draw the greatest concern, like whether immigrants are learning English (they are) or increasing crime rates (they're not). Are they undercutting wages? Not for American workers overall; it's possible that immigration reduces the wages of the least-skilled workers under some circumstances, but the evidence is mixed. Restrictionist lit has merits. It offers some poignant portrayals of changing small-town life. It rightly notes that immigration benefits elites more than the working class. It castigates the left, at times with cause, for anti-enforcement militancy. But there's not much room in its worldview for someone like Rosalie: legal, filling a vital unfilled job, and toting a Statue of Liberty key chain.

Although they approach it from different directions, left and right do share one fear: that some of the poorest immigrants—or especially their children—will assimilate downward into an ethnic underclass, characterized by poverty, alienation, and violence. Worst-case scenarios conjure the kind of ethnic rioting that has periodically exploded across northern Britain and the suburbs of Paris. Two overlapping problems confront the most disadvantaged immigrants. One is the very low level of education, which depresses their wages and hampers their children in school (and because they live in poor neighborhoods, those schools typically stink). Another is the lack of legal status, which ensures their exploitation and deepens their poverty. Many are doubly disadvantaged, lacking education and legal status alike.

There are about eleven million unauthorized immigrants in the United States. They are raising about five million children, most of whom are American citizens. (About 7 percent of all children in the

States have an undocumented parent.) If even a small share falls into something like an underclass condition, the consequences would be tragic, for them and society. Some Americans see them as lawless invaders, some as victims of poverty and violence, and some as victims of unjust conditions the United States helped create. But whatever one makes of their reasons for coming, nearly two-thirds of the people here illegally have been in the country for a decade or more. They are deeply embedded in American life and not about to "self-deport." A million or more—the so-called Dreamers—were brought to the States as children. They did not choose to break the law. The United States is the only country they know.

The restrictionist movement that crested with the election of Donald Trump offers the undocumented two responses. One is invective—the use of the presidential bullhorn to brand them as "rapists" and "terrorists." The other is fear—an expanded campaign of "attrition by enforcement" to ensure that no one feels safe. "Every illegal alien must understand that he or she may be deported at any time," wrote Mark Krikorian of the Center for Immigration Studies, the doctrine's architect. Trump revoked the protection offered to about 700,000 of the Dreamers (he was stopped in court), loosened the rules that kept most enforcement targeted on criminals, and urged agents to be less discriminating in arrest. Fear was the stated goal. "You should be uncomfortable," the country's top enforcement official warned the unauthorized. "You should look over your shoulder."

And why not—what part of illegal don't you understand? As a policing plan, more pressure makes sense. As a social policy for a large and vulnerable share of the population, it courts disaster. *The New Yorker* spent a year following the children of a woman deported to Honduras as they grew depressed and stopped going to school. UCLA researchers surveyed thousands of teachers nationwide and found reports of declining grades and rising behavioral problems among children of immigrants, with spillover effects on the whole school. One teacher wrote of a student "who had attempted to slit her wrists because her family had been separated." Another taught a fourth grader who said "her mom is teaching her how to make food and feed her baby sister in case the mom is taken away." An art teacher said students were drawing pictures of their families being hunted.

A narrative of spite and a campaign of fear—if you were trying to create an underclass, could there be a better way?

PERHAPS THE MOST COMMON restrictionist complaint is the one most easily disproved: "Immigrants don't bother learning English." It's true that English is vital to national cohesion and that the size and replenishment of the Latino population make Spanish more prominent than previous immigrant languages. But there's overwhelming evidence that immigrants rapidly learn English. "Today's immigrants are actually learning English faster than their predecessors," the National Academy of Sciences concluded.

The Academy is a group of scholars chartered by Congress in 1863 to give Abraham Lincoln scientific advice; its reports, written by committee, are the definition of academic consensus. It found that nearly half of immigrants, like Rosalie, arrive already knowing English. That's either because they're from countries, like India or the Philippines, where English is widely spoken or because it's the global language of commerce and culture—that is, because English is so *not* in peril.

Researchers found English acquisition "near universal" among children of immigrants in New York City and warned it "can happen *too quickly*," since the loss of their earlier language can weaken parental authority. The Academy did worry about "linguistically isolated" households, in which no adult spoke English very well, a problem that can slow children's progress in school. Still, its overall finding was unequivocal: "Immigrants and their descendants are learning English."

Another common charge is that immigrants disproportionately com-

238   A GOOD PROVIDER IS ONE WHO LEAVES

mit crime. As far back as the 1990s, Roy Beck warned that crime was one of immigration's "most insidious costs." But crime rates in the 1990s plunged. A decade later Mark Krikorian called the research on crime "inconclusive" but insisted that "whatever the facts" an influx of poor "young foreign men means many of them will have trouble with the law."

Actually, the research isn't inconclusive. As the National Academy puts it, a "large body of evidence" shows that "immigrants are in fact much *less likely* than natives to commit crimes." That evidence spans nearly a century and covers a variety of ethnic groups, historical circumstances, and differences in legal status. Cities where immigration grew fastest in the 1990s "experienced the largest decreases in homicide and robbery." Crime rates do rise among the immigrants' children (a sign of assimilation), but they are "generally lower than or very similar to the crime rate of the native-born."

Beyond the fear of crime is the fear of *reconquista*—the worry that Latinos will return the Southwest to Mexican control. It's not a prospect that weighs heavily on most Americans' minds, though it arises often in anti-immigration writing. "The *reconquista* of Alta California by Mexico is well advanced," warns Patrick J. Buchanan, the conservative populist and three-time presidential candidate. Samuel Huntington, the late Harvard political scientist who was perhaps the most academically distinguished immigration critic, thought that "demographic *reconquista*" was more likely than a formal secession but considered the latter a possibility.

Ethnic groups do influence politics. American Jews fortify American support for Israel. Anti-Castro Cubans help keep the United States in a hostile posture toward Havana. In 2000, they might even have delivered Florida, and hence the presidency, to George W. Bush; in a race won by 537 votes, the state's 850,000 Cubans were incensed by the decision of a Democratic president, Bill Clinton, to repatriate a Cuban boy named

Elián González, whose mother died bringing him to the States. By comparison, the Mexican American influence on politics has been tame.

The real issue about politics is that immigrants overwhelmingly vote Democratic and could therefore pose an existential threat to the GOP. Few facts better explain the ascent of the party's anti-immigrant wing, which has abandoned all hopes of courting them. Ann Coulter writes, "There is simply no reason for Republicans to legalize 30 million people"—the number is about a third as high—"who will vote 8–2 against them." The Center for Immigration Studies warns Republicans that, "Many demographers believe Texas will turn blue if we continue our high rate of immigration." Shortly before the 2016 election, a future Trump aide named Michael Anton published a pseudonymous essay warning, "The ceaseless importation of Third World foreigners . . . means that the electorate grows more left, more Democratic, less Republican, less republican, and less traditionally American with every cycle."

Are opponents of immigration racist? The accusation, common among their critics, makes some of them seethe. They say they are *defending* minorities, who compete with immigrants for housing and jobs. Many quote Frederick Douglass from 1853: "Every hour sees the black man elbowed out of employment by some newly arrived immigrant whose hunger and whose color are thought to give him a better title to the place." (Douglass later became a vocal supporter of immigration: "The apprehension that we shall be swamped . . . does not seem entitled to much respect. Though they come as the waves come, we shall be all the stronger if we receive them as friends and give them a reason for loving our country.")

But others say that keeping America white is the point, and properly so. "For European-American society and culture to persist requires a European-American majority, and a clear one at that," wrote John Tanton, the restrictionist movement's great organizer. Peter Brimelow's 1995 bestseller, *Alien Nation*, griped that "when you enter the INS waiting rooms you find yourself in an underworld that is not just teeming but is also almost entirely colored." Huntington feared that Latinos bring "lack of initiative, self-reliance and ambition." Coulter spends half her time complaining about charges of racism and half her time fueling them: "People notice when their little girls are raped and killed by Mexicans, their Arab shopkeepers commit honor killings, their Hmong neighbors are pimping out little girls and clubbing German shepherd puppies to death, their Indian landlord is importing concubines, and their Chinese acquaintances are murdering their wives out of 'humiliation.'"

It's a mistake to think that opposition to immigration is inherently racist. But if you're looking for racism in the movement, it isn't hard to find.

DO IMMIGRANTS THREATEN jobs and wages? They take jobs but create jobs, too, so analyzing their impact is complex. A foreign-born gardener might displace a native, but if an abundance of gardeners helps landscaping firms thrive, overall employment might grow, to the benefit of bookkeepers and botanists. Still, a growing economy might not grow evenly: among natives, low-skilled workers are most likely to pay a price.

In economic terms, the issue is whether the immigrants complement natives or substitute for them. It's not always clear which role the immigrant will play. Foreign construction crews may seem like direct substitutes for natives doing the same jobs, but they become complements if their work creates opportunities a half-rung up the ladder—as the drywall business expands, the Americans, with better English, may supervise the Mexicans. (Immigrants, being more mobile, also tend to settle in areas that have the most jobs, which reduces direct competition.) A concentrated influx increases the risks that American workers will be harmed—it can take businesses time to adjust.

The National Academy, sifting the evidence, reports the overall effect on American wages is "very small," but adds, "some studies have found sizable negative short-run wage impacts for high school drop-outs." Other studies did not. Most economists think the effect is modest even for low-skilled workers. Larger forces include weak unions, a declining minimum wage, outsourcing, stagnant rates of educational advancement, and technological change. One prominent economist (David Card) found immigration has had *no* impact on the wages of low-skilled workers. Another (George Borjas) calculates "a wage reduction of at least three percent" and possibly much higher in unusual circumstances. The Academy found the impact "highly dependent" on the local labor market.

Maybe the economists aren't measuring right. On the surface, Chris's experience as a janitor bolsters the case that immigration hurts minorities. When he and the black housekeeper clashed, she was the one penalized. His boss explained his preference for immigrants in racially explicit terms: "Some of these girls, they're mean black women." Likewise, in getting the city job through the ethnic network, he might have taken a spot that otherwise would have gone to a native applicant. (Even though Rosalie took a job the hospital couldn't fill, some local nurses thought she had displaced an American.) The counterargument is that if immigrant labor brings Galveston cleaner water and better hospitals, businesses will invest, the community will grow, and the whole city will benefit. If too much immigration risks displacement, too little risks stagnation.

Do immigrants impose fiscal costs? The National Academy mulled the issue for 240 pages and concluded . . . it depends how you count. Immigrants boost federal coffers (they pay more taxes than they collect in benefits) but impose costs on cities and states (largely for schools). In the second generation, however, state balance sheets turn positive as the investment in schooling pays off. The impact depends greatly on the newcomers' level of education. An immigrant lacking a high school education will cost federal, state, and local governments $225,000 over seventy-five years, counting his or her descendants. But a college-educated immigrant like Rosalie produces a net gain (taxes paid minus benefits received) of $504,000. Taken together, the five Villanuevas and their descendants will provide federal, state, and local governments a boost of $2.5 million.

Yet another economic concern is that immigrants stifle innovation. If cheap farmhands abound, why invent harvesting machines? Restrictionists used to hail Japan as a model—a high-income, low-immigration society with a technological edge. But after two "lost decades" of stagnation, it's hard to find anyone calling Japan a model now. ("Productivity growth has steadily eroded in almost every sector," warns McKinsey & Company.) Hampered by a shortage of construction and farm workers, Japan recently announced a plan to admit more immigrants.

ECONOMICS, HOWEVER IMPORTANT, isn't the main restrictionist concern. The hot-button issues are cultural: the fear that assimilation is failing (that *we're* conforming to *them*). People who see a broken melting pot make three main arguments: that immigrants don't fit in the way they used to, that society's leaders no longer make them adapt, and that technology encourages them to retain foreign identities. All three have a surface plausibility that fades when measured against real lives—certainly when measured against Rosalie's.

One version of "they won't assimilate" says the immigrants have changed. "The important thing" about earlier immigrants is "they were of European descent," argues Lawrence Auster in *The Path to National Suicide*; they shared certain "unifying myths" with each other and the United States. (They also shared ancient enmities, spoke different languages, and practiced different faiths.) Another version of "they won't assimilate" is that America has changed—advanced so far that immigrants from the developing world can't catch up. Krikorian credits the immigrants' pluck but worries about their "premodern habits and assumptions"; he warns "there is a larger gap between the lifestyles and assumptions of today's new arrivals and today's American norms than was the case in the past." But actually the opposite is more often true: given the reach of global media, cultural distances have shrunk. Many immigrants arrive pre-assimilated, as the Villanueva kids did—straight from a Philippine farm with Barbies and Disney CDs. Huntington fears that immigration has grown too easy; it lets in people who lack commitment to American ideals. "Those who chose to cross the Atlantic had to have the energy, ambition, initiative, and willingness to take risks." Huntington concedes that "ironically" people who come illegally "do need those qualities"—they often risk their very lives. But even for a skilled, legal immigrant like Rosalie, the flight from the slums hardly lacked for daring and ambition. She didn't retch her way across the Atlantic, but she labored her way across the Middle East for nearly two decades, sustained by a vision that placed America on a pedestal. "The U.S. is the dream," she said.

Some people worry that multiculturalism undermines assimilation, that liberal elites tell people not to adapt. The restrictionist ideal is Teddy Roosevelt, who said, "There is no room in this country for hyphenated Americanism." American culture is clearly more diverse than it was a century ago. But that's mostly a good thing. Coercive forms of assimilation can trigger ethnic resentment, as they do in Europe, or come between parents and their kids, as they did in the American past. ("We were becoming Americans by learning how to be ashamed of our parents," wrote Leonard Covello, an Italian-born educator who attended New York City schools in the first decade of the twentieth century.) Henry Ford made his workers cross a stage in ethnic garb, enter a mock melting pot, and emerge in suits waving American flags. Now they might show up in turbans or dreadlocks.

At the same time, civics isn't as endangered as its defenders fear—certainly not in Texas, where the Villanueva kids started their day with pledges of allegiance to both the Texas and the American flags. "Schools today are failing utterly to pass on the history and heroes and legends of our past," Krikorian warns. That's news in Galveston, where Kristine studied George Washington's rules of civility, Lara pondered Rosa Parks, and Dominique came home from first grade to announce that Abraham Lincoln "gave a speech called the Spaghetti Address." (Though he bollixed the title, he noted correctly that Lincoln was the sixteenth president.)

Can assimilation survive Skype? The fear is that cheap calls, cheap flights home, and the rise of dual citizenship promote a "transnational" identity. If you stream telenovelas and call home every day, you won't commit to the United States. While Roosevelt warned of hyphenated Americans, Huntington feared "ampersands"—immigrants with "two languages, two homes, and possibly two loyalties." He worried about middling naturalization rates and described remittances as a betrayal. "The billions of dollars that ampersands send abroad are also billions of dollars they do not invest in building homes, establishing businesses, creating jobs. . . . Money talks, and . . . the remittances flowing out of America do not speak English."

By those standards, Rosalie was an ampersand. She called home near daily, watched Manila TV, and sent her parents thousands of dollars for food and medicine. She literally lived in two worlds at once; I once watched her keep up a long conversation with Tita, mostly in Tagalog, as she accompanied Kristine through a medical exam and questioned the doctor in English. Did her contact with the Philippines slow her transition or ease it? The latter seems more likely. Her initial homesickness would have been worse without the ability to call the kids. Her support for her parents didn't weaken her attachment to Texas but lent it added purpose. Even with Skype, the kids forgot Tagalog so quickly the calls home grew strained.

Even Chris, the most reluctant immigrant in the family, encouraged the kids to quickly sink psychological roots. They were crossing the bay soon after they arrived when a bird hit the car; Dominique started talking about the birds back home, which made Kristine homesick. "This is not our country," she said. "I want the Philippines." Chris answered in Tagalog but not as an ampersand. "No, the time will come when this will be our country. You'll realize on trips to the Philippines that *it's* the other country now."

WHAT THREATENS ASSIMILATION isn't Skype but class—or more precisely class and legal status. Among Mexicans, the largest immigrant group, more than half lack high school educations, and about half are in the country illegally. Conservatives aren't the only ones who have warned of an ethnic underclass. As early as 1992, the left-leaning sociologist Herbert J. Gans warned that the children of poor immigrants faced the same barriers as native minorities—bad schools, dead-end jobs, street culture, discrimination—and might join them "in standing jobless on street corners." The sociologists Alejandro Portes and Rubén G. Rumbaut warned of "a rainbow underclass."

It is important to remember that most children of immigrants are succeeding. There have been two major multiethnic studies of the second generation, both mostly positive. Portes and Rumbaut followed fifty-two hundred kids in California and Florida and found "the new second generation seems to be achieving and adapting well." Two-thirds lived in intact families, virtually all spoke English, and their average grades were better than those of natives. Philip Kasinitz and three colleagues studied thirty-four hundred kids in New York City. "In every case, the second generation young people we have studied are doing at least somewhat better than natives of the same race."

Even among low-income Latinos, the large group most at risk, there is considerable progress. Average schooling among Mexican men rises from 9.4 years in the first generation to 12.6 in the second—a big gain. College completion rates nearly triple. One concern is that Mexican mobility seems to stall in the third generation, which could be either a sign of trouble or a data quirk; it's hard to track third-generation Mexicans because the most educated often intermarry and identify as white (which leaves a downward bias in the group that remains).

Still, the corner of poor and undocumented is a rough place to grow up, and lots of places have been busy passing laws to make it rougher. The good news is that after many years of rapid growth the number of people in the country illegally has been stable for a decade—actually down about 12 percent from its 2007 peak. The bad news is that nearly eleven million people are trapped in conditions that worsen poverty, destabilize communities, and threaten lifelong harm to their (mostly American) kids. "Parents' undocumented status," the National Academy warns, "can have negative effects on children's socioeconomic outcomes, cognitive development, and mental health." The impact is "sizeable and debilitating."

Accustomed to thinking of immigrants as achievers, I had doubts about the downward mobility thesis but took it for a test-drive of sorts in a Salvadoran suburb of Washington, DC, known as a stronghold of MS-13. Two-thirds foreign-born and Latino, Langley Park, Maryland, is a transient place with few community leaders and little community. Poverty and lack of legal status undermine parents' authority; weak authority abets gangs. I was following a student with a gang history trying to get a GED. At nineteen, Jesselyn Bercian had a smooth, friendly face, an eighth-grade education, and an ex-boyfriend in prison for murder.

Her parents had slipped across the border in the 1980s to escape the Salvadoran civil war. Her mother cleaned houses, her father painted them, and they believed in American opportunity. "You can achieve what you want here," her father said. But born in the United States and conscious of her identity as a low-income Latina, Jesselyn grew up thinking otherwise. Slow to read, she had struggled in school, cut class to drink, and found her niche in a clique called the Pure Crazy Gangsters. She scorned her parents' dirty jobs ("I'm not going to scrub someone's toilet") but lacked the skills to do better.

The problems of youths like Jesselyn are sometimes called a failure to assimilate. As she told it, the story might better be described as assimilating to the wrong things—to crime, school failure, and expectations of racial defeat. The most striking thing about the story was the way she had self-consciously adopted the adversarial pose of poor, streetwise blacks: she had celebrated friends as "my nigga" and labeled enemies "crackers," "bamma," and "whyte."

"I thought the American Dream was just meant for white people," she said.

"If you're Hispanic, people already expect you to steal, to fight, to be rude, to be ghetto. If everyone thinks wrong of you, eventually you're going to start thinking wrong about yourself."

In the three months I followed her, Jesselyn got a job, lost the job, quit the GED class and returned, attended the funeral of a friend murdered by a gang, broke up with her "fiancé," went back to her childhood church, reconnected with the Pure Crazy Gangsters—and got the equivalency degree. The gang girls complained, "You talk like a white girl." Her future was anyone's guess.

This is the assimilation story to be feared, that some children of the poor and unauthorized, unwilling to accept their parents' menial labor but seeing no better prospects, will succumb to poverty, alienation, and defeat—to the lure of the Pure Crazy Gangsters. American policy is now designed to make them and their communities poorer and more afraid.

It's true that legalization poses a moral hazard: it could encourage more people to come. The lack of a legalization is a hazard, too: it leaves millions of immigrants, and their American-born children, facing a modern Jim Crow. If they assimilate downward to an underclass, don't blame dreams of the *reconquista* or multicultural elites. Blame a campaign of cruelty that made a cracked melting pot a self-fulfilling prophecy.

FOURTEEN

Second-Generation Ampersands

Kristine's history teacher, Mr. Mallory, began most classes with a writing exercise he called a Do Now. "Where do you get your motivation?" he asked. "I don't know, because I don't know what motivation mean," she wrote. Mr. Mallory was cute; she decorated her response by drawing a girl batting her eyes and sticking out her tongue. Stumped again a few days later, Kristine just shrugged. "What, sorry, didn't get it," she wrote. One Do Now moved her to earnestness as she urged "all people to be kind, sharing loyal, Honest . . . belive in god." Another summoned her swagger: "I never treated unfairly in my whole life. Becous im the oldest." Asked to imagine a country she ruled, she reverted to the Girlie Girl: "I want [it] to be pretty and many mall and happy."

Every middle schooler is a collection of parts that don't quite fit, an identity in the making. For Kristine, moving to a new country made the assembly harder. There were more identities to choose from in the United States than in the Philippines—nice girls, smart girls, mean girls, Girlie Girls, artists, tomboys, teacher's pets. And there were fewer people keeping watch, no compound full of cousins and *lolas*. While Lara's

Filipino and American selves lived in harmony, Kristine's collided. Sometimes "my country" meant the States, sometimes the Philippines. Sometimes she wanted "Mama" (Rowena) and sometimes "Mommy" (Rosalie). "I didn't want to leave Mama Wena, but I also couldn't leave my parents," she said. "Either way it's sad." Ms. Fabian's math tutoring helped, but classwork could be hard to follow.

As Kristine's frustration mounted, she launched a series of minor rebellions—ignoring assignments, disrupting class, and affecting a scatterbrained personality in a bid for popularity. She modeled herself after a cartoon version of the tweener life. Long gone was the meek foreign girl who had arrived a year earlier with a stiff smile. She wanted to be one of the glamorous, wisecracking divas she saw on TV. Perhaps Kristine would have experimented with her identity just as energetically if she wasn't foreign-born. To varying degrees, all kids do. But it's harder to find your place in a place you don't know. Even by the standards of middle school, Kristine's teachers found her personality shifts abrupt.

"Ms. Fabian, there's a thingy here!" she yelled one day in math. She meant a new keyboard key. "There's a thingy here! There's a thingy here!"

"Ms. Fabian, do you know what day it is?"

"Ms. Fabian, do you know what time it is?"

"Ms. Fabian—am I the quietest one in the class?"

Moving on to science, Kristine left the room twice and launched a pen sword fight. In English, homework was chronically incomplete, and she failed four consecutive tests. "I have a question for everyone," she yelled at the end of one class. "Am I the quietest one?" The class groaned. She'd been repeating the line for a week, as if to announce the bold new self. It was a running joke, a sign of new comfort, and an impediment to getting anything done.

As rebellions go, Kristine's was mild and likely to pass: no one remains her middle school self forever. Ms. Fabian saw the unruliness as a show of new ease, but the English teacher, Ms. Sherrod, shook her head. "She's becoming *Americanized*."

ONCE, THAT WOULD HAVE BEEN a compliment. The classic version of Americanization is called straight-line assimilation. It's a three-generation tale as central to national mythology as the Boston Tea Party: the immigrants struggle amid poverty and bias; their children awkwardly straddle two cultures, embarrassed by their parents' old-world ways but unable to win full acceptance in the broader society; the third generation, Americanized, completes the rise—classically with a white-collar job and a house in the suburbs. The story imparts two lessons: the descendants of immigrants advance and do so by blending in. To assimilate—to *Americanize*—is to progress.

Straight-line assimilation was the reigning narrative of the mid-twentieth century. If you picture the age, you can see its appeal. Half a century had passed since the masses had streamed through the harbor. Learned men had warned that the exotic tribes would never adapt, but they had done so decisively. A unified country had beaten the Nazis, with Smiths and Joneses sharing foxholes with Kowalskis and Mancinis. (In the film *Unbroken*, the Italian American war hero Louis Zamperini comforts a dying crewmate by telling stories of his mama's gnocchi.) In a postwar world of ethnic enmity, America was a marvel. Groups that had warred for centuries abroad lived as neighbors in New York and Chicago. A Russian-born Jew (Irving Berlin) wrote "God Bless America" and "White Christmas." A Catholic became president. The American Century, in all its might and glory, rested on the force of straight-line assimilation.

Somewhere in the 1960s, the assimilation story fell from favor. In retrospect, its faults are clear. It overstated the acceptance that immigrants had won and understated the hardships they faced. It equated conformity with upward mobility, ignoring the satisfaction or success to be found in the ethnic enclave. It idealized WASP culture. It overlooked race. (Much of American history is the story of efforts to *prevent* black assimilation.)

Race riots, Watergate, and Vietnam discredited the establishment that the assimilationists lauded—who would want to assimilate to that? Scholars condemned "the blight of assimilationist ideology" and celebrated ethnic struggle. Ozzie and Harriet gave way to Kojak and Columbo, heritage travel, and klezmer bands. Assimilation seemed wrong as an explanation of what did happen and offensive as an explanation of what should happen. As the sociologist Richard Alba notes, even the Statue of Liberty did a metaphorical about-face: once meant to signify a break with the past, it became a symbol of enduring connections.

The resurgence of ethnic identity was heartfelt and meaningful but no sign that assimilation had failed. On the contrary (as scholars like Herbert Gans and Mary Waters have noted), Americans could celebrate their ethnic heritage precisely because it meant so little. It didn't affect where they could live, whom they could marry, or what jobs they could get. "Symbolic ethnicity" flourished, but divisions faded: intermarriage rose, discrimination fell, and residential enclaves dispersed. Americans of mixed lineage had "ethnic options"; they might emphasize their Irish heritage in one context and Italian roots in another. Given the difficulties the Ellis Island immigrants and their progeny faced, their assimilation is more accurately described as "bumpy line" than straight. But bumps and all, assimilation prevailed.

Kristine's generation faces a different world and may follow a different pattern. In some ways, assimilation is more challenging: economic mobility has waned; legal status is often an impediment; and most of today's immigrants are racial minorities. (Lots of Ellis Island immigrants were labeled nonwhite, too, but as Europeans they and their descendants were less visibly distinct.) In the past, mass media promoted common identity; in today's narrowcast world, *pluribus* triumphs over *unum*. But other differences between the ages make assimilation easier now: immigrants have civil rights protections their predecessors lacked (Sicilians didn't have affirmative action); many arrive like Rosalie, already middle-class; and mainstream culture is much more diverse, making it easier to fit in. From alt-Latino playlists to Ganesh mouse pads, there are lots of ways of being American.

Two schools of thought have shaped the academic debate about how children of immigrants are faring. Both believe the majority is succeeding—performing well in school, securing jobs, and integrating into the broader society. But one group, led by the sociologist Alejandro Portes, has emphasized that Americanization carries risks. "American schools and neighborhoods may promote a set of undesirable outcomes," he wrote (with coauthor Rubén Rumbaut). The longer immigrants are in the States, the more likely they are to smoke, grow obese, or commit crimes. In the most dire cases, the authors warned, the children of immigrants, facing the same problems as poor native minorities, might assimilate into a multiethnic underclass. Ms. Sherrod had nothing like that in mind when she fretted about Kristine. But even her mild concerns turned straight-line assimilation on its head: she saw Americanization as the problem, not the solution.

A rival camp is more optimistic. The children of immigrants they studied not only outperformed children of natives from similar racial backgrounds. They did so despite having parents with much less income and education. How could that be? Philip Kasinitz and three colleagues argue that children of immigrants often enjoy a "second-generation advantage" over native peers. Two parts of the argument are familiar. One is that immigrants, self-selected for ambition, pass along their drive. The other is that the intensity of ethnic networks provides support that natives lack. But the researchers also saw a third force in play: living at a cultural crossroads encourages creative new ways of thinking. Children of immigrants often "combine the best of both worlds"—their parents' and their peers'—or even "create something wholly new." They innovate in ways that "can be highly conducive to success."

In academic circles, the two camps have warred, criticizing each other's class biases, political judgments, and sampling techniques, but inside the Villanueva family each theory offers a helpful way to think about a different daughter. Kristine's experience provided a small reminder that Americanization isn't always beneficial: she assimilated energetically but to the flighty ways of American middle school girls. Lara, by contrast, blended her Filipino and American selves in ways that gave her an edge. She was second-generation advantage personified.

LARA LINGERED AT THE TABLE one night and picked at her rice. "I sort of agree with Rosa Parks," she told me. This was news. The previous year, she had resisted the thought that a lawbreaker could be a hero. But by her second Black History Month, Lara had revised her view. "It wasn't, like, fair for the black people to sit in the back, because they paid the same amount of money. Abraham Lincoln said the slavery was over, and the South didn't want the slavery to be over—I think the white peoples didn't want to work." With another bite, she praised Parks's courage, and also her manners: "When the American said, 'Get out of my seat,' she said no, but she didn't use a bad word!" Through a Filipino lens, Lara made Rosa Parks the Civil Rights Hero Who Didn't Curse.

Lara was Americanizing, too, but with little of the conflict that beset Kristine. Her Filipino and American selves were partners, not rivals. Kristine experienced migration as division, a set of painful choices—English versus Tagalog, Rosalie versus Rowena. For Lara, migration was addition—protests and politeness, McDonald's and Jollibee, grandparents on Skype and parents beside her. Her Filipino traits included her manners, her religiosity, and an immigrant's belief in opportunity, which can be empowering even when not wholly true. They also included the benefits of a two-parent family, which social science suggests can be considerable. ("American families are a mess!" Lara's teacher, Ms. Morgan, complained.) From her American side, Lara got a reduced sense of gender and class constraints and a classroom a third as large as that in the Philippines. Above all, American culture offered Lara a license to ask questions.

Nothing about her life in the Philippines had encouraged her to probe. On the contrary, a classroom with seventy kids had little time for raised hands, and children were taught to respect their elders, not interrogate them. "Look it up on the Google," Rosalie would huff, when Lara asked if fish slept or why Saturn has rings. "Mommy gets really annoyed when I ask her questions. She answers, '*Tssss*.' I think that means, 'Just don't ask me questions.'" Ms. Morgan loved questions. She invited more.

Curious how she had grown curious, Lara formed her own assimilation theory: America had scared her into asking questions. She felt lost when she arrived in Texas and frightened that she would have to repeat second grade. "I told myself I should be interested right now because I didn't want to do it all again." Being interested became a habit. Put differently, straddling two cultures gave rise to new ways of thinking. Lara was explaining in an eight-year-old's terms what the Kasinitz camp had argued about the creativity of New York City: "Innovation . . . occurs when different traditions come together, where no one way of doing things can be taken for granted."

Lara not only embodied second-generation advantage; she spelled it out. When the third graders made acrostics of their names, Lara's celebrated fusion.

The *L* stood for "Loves Books," an American attribute.

The *R* stood for "Respect," which she brought from the Philippines.

The *A*s were for "Awesome" and "Adventurous"—which is how the blending of her worlds made her feel.

MIDWAY THROUGH FIFTH GRADE, Girlie Girldom began to feel confining; Kristine sought a sharper edge. If Lara's identity grew organically, Kristine's was a product of conscious design—mulled in her journals and tested on Instagram, the standard laboratories of fifth-grade American girls. In her notebooks, she called herself "honest" and "joyful" but also "lazy" and "mean." Meanness was a boast: she was tired of being that nice immigrant girl. "My classmates say, 'Kristine, it's not like you!' I said, 'Back off—I changed!' Because before, I'm not talking too much and can't say words that everybody says. So now I'm a Kristine who will fight for herself! I'm a Kristine that if you step on me, I'm gonna step on you." Literally: when a classmate stepped on her foot and told her to shut up, she did the same. "I said, 'Why don't *you* shut up?' I was being really mean! But not *really* mean—I was *acting* mean."

To the work of trying on new faces, Kristine took a literal approach. She snapped selfies by the thousand and posted them on Instagram accounts like "kristinecute" and "swelfwe.queen." She practiced poses and named them like pets. For Fish Mouth, she gave an exaggerated pucker. Duck Face required flat protruding lips. For Hands on Chin, she cocked her head and turned pensive. Hamburger Face required a coquettish bite of the tongue: "Your teeth are like the bread *thingamajiggy* and then your tongue is like the hamburger." What united the poses was an air of insouciance—the carefree self-satisfaction that true beauty conveys to denizens of lesser realms. She tousled her hair, tilted the camera, and peeked from behind a peace sign. "No offense, but I take gooder selfies than my cousins," she said. My cousins: even as she honed an American identity, tension with the Philippines was never far from mind.

Kristine's Barbies, like Kristine, straddled two hard-to-reconcile worlds. Lots of girls construct doll fantasies. Not many use them to explore the guilt they feel for escaping the poverty of the developing world while leaving loved ones behind. Kristine's stories revolved around a poor family named the Fashion Fashionistas (Ernesto and Carol), who lived in a cardboard box and scavenged in a dump called Mountain High Trash Can. The setting bore a striking resemblance to Smokey Mountain, the infamous Manila squatter colony. Despite the surrounding squalor, the Fashionistas were quite stylish and went shopping abroad in their private plane. Their five children spoke perfect English and were all beautiful and kind.

"Not really *all* kind," Kristine said. "Two are like me—bossy, lazy."

"You just admitted it—you're lazy!" giggled Lara, the Barbie stage-hand.

The Fashionistas were happy and close, despite their poverty. Their oldest daughter, Stacy, had a rich boyfriend who sneaked away from home to visit in his tux; his parents didn't want him dating the poor.

Kristine, narrating the story, said she, too, lived at the dump. "I just feel more comfortable there." Then she changed her mind and flew off in the Fashionistas' plane to join them in the rich country. To Kristine, poor Filipinos transforming themselves into rich Americans required no explanation. It had the authority of feeling true.

Like Kristine, Stacy Fashionista, the Barbie, had a mother who was a nurse (also president of the world). Her father was a genial man caught in a world of changing gender roles.

"I'm the dad!" he said.

"I'm the boss!" said her mom.

"Oh, sweetie," the dad doll said, "I don't want to spend another night on the couch!"

But unlike Kristine, Stacy could visit the poor country instantly, whenever she wanted. Mostly her visits went smoothly, but occasionally Stacy felt burdened by the needs of those back home. When she caught a maid in the poor country wearing her shoes, Stacy beat her—Kristine dramatized the scene by grabbing the maid doll by the ankles and banging her head on the floor. *Thwack. Thwack.*

"You're only the prettiest girl in the poor country—but I'm the prettiest in the whole world!" Stacy-Kristine said.

"Ow, ow, ow, ow!" the maid screamed.

"I don't want to see your face anymore!" Stacy tossed the beaten maid on the dump. Then freed from the burdensome reminders of the poor, she flew back to the rich country and decorated her room in Hello Kitty.

"Stacy is a little mean," Kristine said with a shrug.

For a while, the Fashionistas magically lived in both worlds. But eventually they felt the need to choose: rich or poor, English or Tagalog? There were no bilingual Fashionistas. With little fanfare, they settled in the rich country, where Stacy's dramas revolved around trips to the mall and excuses for not doing homework. I asked Kristine how often they talked to people in the Old Country. "The Old Country doesn't exist anymore."

THE CURIOUS KID was on a roll as she finished third grade.

In early January, she discovered facts and opinions. "Fact is something you can prove, like 'If you go to Arabia, you see the camel.' And opinion is something you can't prove, like 'fun,' 'better,' 'pretty,' 'should.'"

"What's a fact about your life?" I asked.

"I got AB honor roll again!"

In late January, she encountered Clara Barton. "We're learning about heroes!" Heroines, actually—which added to the excitement. "Women weren't treated fairly, so Clara Barton entered the battle. Clara Barton didn't really fight, though—when the soldiers got hurt, she gave them a bandage. Clara Barton started the American Red Cross."

Lara debated, mostly with herself, which of her heroines was greatest. Rosa Parks didn't swear, Helen Keller didn't quit, and Jane Addams helped immigrants—but Harriet Tubman rescued others, *"even though they weren't her relatives."* Every Filipino understands sacrifice for family, but selflessness toward strangers offered her a glimpse of a new moral universe. "She did the really, *really* right thing."

February brought more questions. "Is the Leaning Tower of Pisa ever going to collapse?"

"Is Galveston an empire?"

"Do nurses have to be caring? Maybe I'll just be a doctor."

March raised the nature-nurture debate. "I learned something new— learned and inherited! You *learned* how to type fast. But I *inherited*

Mom and Dad's black hair." Kristine, playing *Shopaholic: Hollywood*, didn't look up from her phone. She found Lara's bulletins irksome.

"Do you know what a peninsula is?" Lara asked the next day. "It's a land that's surrounded by water."

"Surrounded by water on *three sides*," Dominique said.

"*Borr-ring!*" Kristine complained.

In April, Lara came home from school to talk about wants and needs. "You might *want* an iPad. But you *need* food and water."

Rosalie stared at her phone and said, "*Tssss.*" Manila had been swept by a rumor that Filipinos no longer needed visas to come to the States; thrilled, Rosalie had started making plans to bring Tita and Emet for a visit. The rumor had caused so much chaos in Manila the American embassy had just issued a statement knocking it down. "It's not true," Rosalie said with a sigh.

In May, Lara learned new idioms, which appealed to her sense of humor. "Turning over a new leaf" did not require a rake. "I've got a bone to pick with you" did not involve surgery. Letting something "go in one ear and out the other" was not a magic trick but a good way to deal with your parents. "That's what I always do to Mom. She says, 'Hurry up, finish your rice, take your bath!' I let that go out the other ear!"

Lara started the year in the lowest reading group, four months below grade level. She finished in the top group, two months ahead. She no longer sat as if she had rigor mortis but as third graders sit—with hands tapping, legs kicking, conspiring with friends.

"Bye, Lara!" her friend shouted.

"Bye, Audrey—I'll see you again!"

Their affection drew scorn from a boy at their table. "They love each other! Pretty freakin' nasty."

Earlier, Lara might have wilted. Instead, she laughed. "You like her too! *You* hold hands!"

When the class learned "walking on air," Lara's practice sentence wrote itself: "When I was at school, I was *walking on air*."

———

KRISTINE WASN'T WALKING ON AIR. She was running in and out of Ms. Fabian's room, grabbing hard candies and wondering where she fit in. In the middle of the year, her English teacher, Ms. Sherrod, pulled her aside to say her behavior was disrupting the class. Kristine's earnestness impressed her. "I understand and I'll try to do better," Kristine said. Her homework improved.

Then the science teacher, Mr. Matthews, found an eraser on which someone had written the word "bitch." He recognized the eraser as Kristine's and told Ms. Fabian, who bought Kristine's explanation. "She said it was supposed to be 'birth,'" Ms. Fabian said. "Mr. Matthews said she's becoming very Americanized, but I felt like she was being honest."

Ms. Fabian made Kristine feel special. "Hi, Doll!" she said one day.

"I'm not a doll—I'm a human," said Kristine.

"It's an idiom, Kristine," Ms. Sherrod said. "It shows affection."

Kristine lit up. "Hi, Doll! Hi, Doll!" she sang for a week.

For her spring project, the family mobilized. Kristine had to read a novel, summarize it on a poster, and give an oral presentation. Rosalie was wary of the novel, but making a poster was something she could do. The Villanuevas spent the weekend cutting and pasting, while Kristine texted Ms. Fabian with questions for Ms. Sherrod: Does "character" come before "setting"? Was "tone and mood" one question or two? The result was a yellow triptych, creative with contractions, light on punctuation, and hard to follow for anyone who didn't know the story. But it looked terrific. It was the work of someone who cared.

Giddy, Rosalie made Kristine practice for the judge.

"Hi, I'm Kristine Villanueva, and I'm presenting the book *Ivy + Bean*."

"By Annie Barrows," Rosalie said. "Don't forget to tell that one."

"By Annie Barrows," Kristine said. "You can see the main elements. There's character plus setting—"

"Plus tones and moods!" Rosalie said.

"Plus tones and moods—"

"Take it slow," said Rosalie. "Don't say, 'Um, um, um'!"

"Hi, um, I'm Kristine Villanueva. . . ."

"Just be natural! Relax! Breathe!"

Kristine stopped. "Mommy, I'm scared."

The book report scared her, but so did the STAAR test. If she didn't pass, she couldn't go on to sixth grade. The test, a few weeks away, had the whole school in its grip. The teachers convened "Staary, Staary Night," a parents' meeting on how to prepare.

A hundred book posters lined the halls as Rosalie arrived, and she was proud to see that Kristine's looked as good as any. With so many parents on hand, Ms. Sherrod decided to announce the winner. A woman shouted from the back of the room.

"Oh my God, I'm her mom!" Rosalie said.

Kristine smiled. Rosalie cried. Chris stood in the hall, to avoid talking to the teacher in English. "My first time winning in America!" Kristine said. Perhaps another girl would have experienced a jolt of pre-test confidence. To her Girlie Girl, Mean Girl grab bag of identities, she could add another: Smart Girl. But Kristine didn't want to raise expectations, including her own. "I feel happy, not smart."

STAAR, STAAR, STAAR—it loomed over everything. The principal halved history class, to steal more time to prepare. Ms. Sherrod found an English-Tagalog dictionary for Kristine to use during the test. Ms. Fabian made plans to read the math problems aloud.

"I'm scared," Kristine told the principal.

"I'm scared," she told her friends.

"What if I don't, like, understand the questions? I won't pass fifth grade."

The teachers had as much at stake as the kids, possibly more. They ended the day before the test with a STAAR pep rally.

"Do not eat doughnuts and cinnamon rolls for breakfast!" one warned.

"You'll crash and burn," said another.

"Don't drink too much—Mr. Bladder is going to be acting up!"

The warnings kept coming. "You need to get eight hours of sleep."

"*Ten* hours of sleep."

"No video games tonight!"

"If you beat the scores from last year, we'll go to the Pleasure Pier!"

"Wait, it gets better—we'll buy you lunch!"

A hundred fifth graders sang a reworked pop hit, with lyrics about No. 2 pencils:

> *STAAR Testers Reach the Sky-yy*
> *Scantrons and Pencils Hi-igh.*

"I'm still scared," Kristine said.

The morning began with bad news. Ms. Fabian couldn't read the math questions aloud as planned. Someone had neglected to file the paperwork. To keep Kristine from getting upset, Ms. Fabian lied: she told her she no longer needed the help. Kristine worked hard but felt certain she had failed. English, the next day, left her equally pessimistic.

At least it was over. She returned to the Fashion Fashionistas. Now fully assimilated in the new country, Stacy was too busy with prom dates and shopping to keep up with school. "Hu, hu," she sobbed to the principal. "I didn't do my homework because my dog died." The principal asked why she heard the dog barking over the phone. "Um—we have three dogs!" Stacy said.

On the night before the scores' release, Ms. Fabian learned they could be found online one student at a time and searched them out until midnight. Nearly two-thirds of her fifth graders passed. Kristine failed by a single question. Permission to read her the problems aloud would have made a difference. Kristine teared up, but her defeat was softened by a surprise: with the Tagalog dictionary that Ms. Sherrod had tracked down, she passed the English test.

A letter warned of summer school, but Ms. Fabian redoubled her after-school tutoring, and Kristine passed a retest. She was on to sixth grade. There's plenty to fault in the nation's emphasis on standardized testing, but in Kristine's case it brought a struggling student the extra attention she needed.

With the STAAR test over, everyone slacked off. Teachers filled class time with videos, and the girls slipped each other elaborately folded "push notes" that foretold who would kiss her crush. Kristine gave me a tour of her locker—a mound of Americanization awaiting excavation. The artifacts included a Statue of Liberty magnet, a Filipino flag, a note to Mama Wena ("I know that you love me"), a Do Now about wanting to meet Benjamin Franklin, and a carpet of notes from friends that read like scripts for Stacy Fashionista's adventures in the new country.

"I feel left out."

"You're starting to change."

"That's so MEAN!"

"Do you want us in your life or not?"

A short boy with glasses walked by and told her she smelled like strawberries. "It smells nice!" he said.

Kristine signed yearbooks under the name "shoppingal" and saved a big place for Ms. Fabian to sign hers. "To my sweet and smart Kristine," she wrote. "I adore the time we spent in tutoring and in class. You've made so many accomplishments this year and I can't wait to see many more."

Kristine added a note of her own: "It was the greatest year ever."

FIFTEEN

Cruise Ship Calamity

Part of what drew me to Rosalie's story was the gratification of seeing striving rewarded: born poor, she ventured abroad and beat the slum girl odds. But migrants don't always find happy endings. They suffocate in the backs of trucks or come home to damaged families. When a Filipino says, "I'm going to try my luck," he knows the luck can turn bad.

One of my favorite couples in the clan was Rosalie's cousin Ariane and her husband, Manu, cruise ship workers who brought home tales of exotic destinations. Seafarers take migration to an extreme: they migrate every day. The Philippines supplies up to a quarter of the world's maritime labor and is known as the "ship-manning capital of the world." If you've taken a cruise, chances are it was partly staffed by Filipinos.

Ariane and Manu were the family romantics. They had met on a gangplank in Barcelona and dated in ports from Saint-Tropez to Bora-Bora. If overseas work strained some marriages, it kindled theirs. Whenever the ship returned to Barcelona, Manu decorated Ariane's pillow with a rose. With cover girl looks and matching ambition, Ariane was all diligence and plans, while Manu made his happy-go-lucky way with a smile.

Ariane and Manu sailed the world together for four years, but after Ariane took time off with their second child, she got hired on a different ship. Once inseparable but now oceans apart, they texted half a dozen times a day and met every six months or so for vacations in the compound, where Ariane's parents raised the kids.

Every overseas worker dreams of building a house; Ariane and Manu dreamed in style. In a family of DIY builders, they bought a lot in a subdivision and hired an architect. Manu had a vision he called "modern Zen," with sleek lines, big windows, and open interiors. They hoped to pay down enough of the mortgage for Ariane to quit and move in with the kids, while Manu supported them from sea. Home on vacation during one of my visits, Manu gave me a tour. The design was modern, but the foundation was old-school: to the concrete, he had mixed in chicken blood to ward off evil, coins to attract prosperity, a comb to sweep away trouble, and cotton to cushion life's blows.

Good vacations make hard departures. Upset to be leaving the kids, he spent his last week at home having their names tattooed on his chest: Ren Travis and Zoe Amber. Then he flew to Istanbul to meet the ship.

A few months later, Rosalie called me with a family news flash: Manu was within a few hours of dying.

IF THE PHILIPPINES is the ship-manning capital of the world, Antique is the ship-manning capital of the Philippines—a small island province three hundred miles from Manila known for its seafaring schools. Emmanuel Navarette—Manu—grew up there with his mother and four siblings while his father was away in the army. Military pay was modest; the family lived in a thatched hut until Manu's early teens. But seafarers came home to big houses and big TVs. Glimpses of *Baywatch* through his seafaring uncle's window stoked Manu's curiosity. "There were cars, trains, white girls—you'd dream of going big."

A middling student at a middling school, Manu graduated with uncertain prospects but an eagerness to see the world. He moved to Manila, lived with an aunt, and did office work for free at a manning agency, in the hopes of getting a break. Four months later when a German cruise ship needed kitchen aides, Manu got the nod. He flew to Genoa and turned twenty-two on board, crying from loneliness.

The homesickness passed. Ship life was rich in discoveries, like the verve of cold weather and the smell of bacon. Onshore, he saw "this big cave where the cars go inside—what do you call that one? A tunnel?" The pay was low, about $2.50 an hour, with no days off. But Mykonos mesmerized, and the women along the Copacabana were "bodacious." After his second cruise, he brought home his girlfriend, the French maître d', and set the village a-chatter.

On Manu's fourth cruise, the ship stopped in Barcelona. As he got off, a housekeeper asked him for help with the pay phone. She was three days into her first voyage and so homesick she sobbed through the call. Manu admonished her not to worry her family and walked her around the pedestrian mall. She called him *kuya*—big brother—and asked to be port pals at the next stop. At twenty-two, she looked so young the crew joked she had run away. It was only when she stopped crying that Manu noticed how pretty she was. His port pal was bodacious.

Ariane Salazar is the twenty-third of Rosalie's forty-one first cousins on Tita's side. Her mother, Peachy, is Tita's sister. When I lived in Leveriza, I slept on the floor beside Ariane's father, Weny, who was there to study at a Manila technical school. Peachy urged him to go to Saudi—"a good provider is one who leaves"—and he didn't return for good until Ariane was grown. Weny's earnings built a house and sent Ariane to college, but his extramarital affair, and the child it produced, nearly destroyed his marriage. Ariane never fully forgave him. Even as a child, she understood that overseas work carried risks.

Nine years younger than Rosalie, Ariane had the same striver's streak. She graduated cum laude with a hospitality degree and apprenticed at two high-end hotels, with her eye on the ultimate prize: a job as a cruise ship maid. It's the odd career ladder that requires four years of school and careful ticket punching for the chance to clean cabins at sea. But a cruise ship maid can earn $2,000 a month with tips—three or four times what a doctor makes.

After their first cruise, Manu visited Ariane in the family compound, amazed at how freely her relatives wandered through each other's homes. Even by Philippine standards, their closeness was intense. After the second, she visited Antique, where Manu's father offered him pithy advice: "Marry that girl." A few cruises later, he did.

If Ariane resented using her cum laude talent as a maid, she didn't show it. "Even though you're cleaning toilets, you're earning dollars," she said. She had worried she might encounter men with "hot eyes," but among the aging guests incontinence was a greater threat. Ariane sent her brother to high school, her sister to college, and her mother to graduate school. That the clan boasts its first doctorate—Dr. Mercelita "Peachy" Portagana Salazar, school principal—is because Ariane cleaned bathrooms at sea until her fingers bled.

After half a dozen cruises together, Ariane and Manu had the kids in quick succession. For a seafaring couple, children changed everything. Manu moved to a cargo ship, which offered more chances to advance. But cargo work, with minuscule crews and weeks away from port, was too isolating. He returned to cruise ships as a deckhand on the Silversea *Silver Spirit*, where rooms went for as much as $500 a day. Out of sync with Manu's schedule, Ariane settled for a different cruise line. Calling each other "Mommy" and "Daddy," they posted gushy Facebook posts and swapped texts about their future with the kids in the "Dream Hauz."

When the house was almost finished, they flew home for a long vacation—three months of family time. They painted the walls, picked out furniture, bought a dog, and drew close to the kids. After Ariane left, Travis, now four, turned *malambing*—clingy. He wouldn't let any-one but Manu feed or bathe him, and when he saw his father packing, he grabbed his own suitcase and announced he was going to work on the ship.

"I don't want that for you," Manu said. "It's much better if you can be with your kids."

At thirty-three, Manu was *malambing*, too. He inked the kids' names on his chest, not his arm, "so I can have them by my heart all the time." A seafarer learns to finesse departures. But Travis's howls left Manu upset all the way to Turkey, where he boarded the *Silver Spirit*.

IN A WORLD of blurred borders, seafaring shows globalization at an extreme. As scholars often note, ships can be built in one country, owned in another, managed in a third, flagged in a fourth, and staffed from everywhere. About two-thirds of cargo vessels and virtually all cruise ships operate through open registries, or "flags of convenience," which offer light regulation, low taxes, and access to cheap labor, in exchange for remunerative fees. (Panama, the Bahamas, and Liberia register more than half the world's ships.) A ship flying an American flag has to hire American workers at American wages. A foreign-flagged ship can hire from anywhere.

Many hire Filipinos. Seafaring was once a Westerner's job, but the oil shock of the 1970s sent prices rising and owners racing to cut costs. Filipinos spoke English and worked for a fifth of Western wages. The government markets seafarers and requires that 80 percent of their pay be sent to a Philippine bank, which swells remittances by $6 billion a year.

Filipinos are especially prominent on cruise ships, whose rise is one of the great tales of modern business. Jet travel doomed the stately old tradition of transatlantic crossings with orchestras and furs. By the 1960s, the industry seemed slated for extinction when a few swashbuckling entrepreneurs started circling the Caribbean on rust buckets based in Miami. Ted Arison launched his company with a decrepit ship whose maiden voyage ran aground. The company, Carnival Cruise Lines, made him a billionaire.

Two features distinguish the modern cruise. It is no longer a means of travel but a destination itself, and it is no longer mostly for the rich. The industry thrives by selling escapist fun at prices the middle class can afford. The mega-ships circling the Caribbean are essentially floating American hotels, freed by foreign flagging from American labor laws. Filipinos work seventy hours a week at less than the minimum wage to bring Americans the blessings of cheap mai tais.

As a rich, lightly regulated, offshore industry, cruise lines have a reputation for roguish behavior that appears well earned. Lining the anti-industry shelf are such titles as *Sweatships*, *Cruise Ship Blues*, and *Devils on the Deep Blue Sea*. When Manu was still in maritime school, an investigation by *The New York Times* found cruise lines illegally dumping wastes, concealing shipboard crimes, providing passengers with substandard medical care, abusing port communities, and paying virtually no income taxes. But in the Philippines, cruise jobs are coveted. With two cruise ship incomes, an up-from-nothing couple like Ariane and Manu could outearn nine of ten households.

It takes a special person to work on a ship. He—often she—faces long hours, close quarters, family separations, and hazards as varied as fires, falls, and chemical spills. One study found that seafarers die on the job twenty-one times as often as workers in general. To consult the literature of maritime torts is to be reminded how terribly awry a day on deck can go. A Filipino named Lito Asignacion was docked on a ship in New Orleans when an overflowing tank in the engine room scalded a third of his body, including his stomach and genitals. Potenciano Aggarao Jr. was approaching the Port of Baltimore when he got caught in a deck-lifting machine that crushed his spine, bowels, and spleen. A federal judge who considered his tort claim noted, "Due to his severe financial constraints . . . he has been forced at times to reuse colostomy bags."

Two of Manu's duties caused him to worry. One was reloading small boats called tenders, which required him to stand in bobbing seas and grasp an overhead hook. Another was docking the ship, a ritual performed in hard hats with a safety officer. A swaying vessel can snap the lines and turn them to deadly whips. "The WHOLE MOORING DECK is a DANGER AREA," a Maersk safety manual warned. The Coast Guard counted nine mooring accidents over two years in the Houston Ship Channel alone, two fatal. A maritime insurer reminded clients "how horrific some of these injuries can become."

Historically, foreign sailors who worked from American ports had ready access to American courts, regardless of their ship's flag, on the theory that they were especially vulnerable—far from home, confined to ships—and especially valuable to commerce. "Generally poor and friendless," is how Justice Joseph Story described them in 1823, in an opinion that shaped nearly two centuries of law. "Every court should watch with jealousy an encroachment upon the rights of seamen. . . . They are emphatically the wards of the admiralty."

But as the number of foreign seafarers grew in the 1970s and 1980s, so did the number of injured foreigners filing lawsuits. One Louisiana attorney, Richard J. Dodson, represented so many Filipinos hurt on the Mississippi River that he opened an office in Manila. He estimated their awards over twenty-five years totaled $100 million. In Florida, the suits often involved cruise ships.

Ship owners and insurers fought back. At their urging, the Philippine government imposed a contract on Filipino seafarers that barred them from seeking damages in foreign courts beyond those specified in their contracts. A detailed schedule specifies the compensation for 142 injuries. A severed half ear is worth $1,870; "total loss of penis," $20,900. While American verdicts had reached millions, the Philippine limits, first imposed in 2000, capped the awards at $60,000, even for death.

Seafarers challenged the contract, but the Philippine Supreme Court bought the government's argument that jobs (and remittances) were at risk: if Filipinos filed too many suits, ships would hire elsewhere. "Our seafarers were perceived as 'Filipinos who complain too much,'" the court ruled.

U.S. judges weren't obliged to honor the Philippine contractual constraints: the tradition, back to Justice Story, had been to ensure that foreign seafarers injured in the States (or on ships operating from the States) had access to American courts. But in 2000 a seaman named Ernesto Francisco fell on a tanker in the Mississippi River and smashed his eye socket. When he sued, a federal judge ruled that his contract required him to pursue arbitration in the Philippines, and the conservative Fifth Circuit Court of Appeals upheld the decision.

Then, in 2003, an explosion rocked a cruise ship in Miami, killing eight seafarers and seriously injuring ten, mostly Filipino. This wasn't just a tragedy but a crime: Norwegian Cruise Line had known for years that the SS *Norway* was unsafe and pleaded guilty to operating the ship "in a grossly negligent manner that endangered the lives, limbs and property of the persons on board." The seafarers' case seemed so strong that a lawyer representing ten of them spurned a settlement offer of $11 million. Then a federal judge threw out their case and sent the victims to arbitration in the Philippines. Another appeals court affirmed.

The concerns of American justice had shifted. The seafarers were no longer "wards of the admiralty." They were "Filipinos who complain too much."

MANU BOARDED THE SHIP in Istanbul and settled for the top bunk. Having circled the Med fifty times, he headed for Greece like a trucker down I-95—all business and no anticipation. To save money, he stayed off-line for four days, then took shore duty in Santorini for the free

Wi-Fi. Ariane had written from Estonia, complimenting the pictures he had posted of the kids.

"Zoe looks so chubby!"

"I love you, Mommy," he wrote.

One week bled into the next: the Aegean, the Adriatic, the Black Sea. The only excitement was a crew bus to Jerusalem, where he bought five rosaries.

When the weather cooled, the *Silver Spirit* crossed the Atlantic and began running Caribbean cruises from Fort Lauderdale. Manu had docking duty in St. Martin when a mooring line snapped and whipped across the deck. No one made a fuss. "If you're complaining too much, you could be the one not hired," Manu said.

The Caribbean sparkled, but Zoe's third birthday was the third he had missed. Travis was the only preschooler with neither parent at Family Day. Christmas at sea always felt cheerless. "Mommy, I feel so lonely," Manu wrote. "Being so far from the kids makes me cry."

"Just hang in there," Ariane replied. It's for the kids.

Soon after, Manu awoke at 4:30 a.m. to wash the decks, then reported for mooring duty. The *Silver Spirit* was back in St. Martin. It took six crewmen, plus two safety officers, to send the heavy ropes to the pier and tighten them with motorized winches. The crew usually followed a routine: two spring lines in front, two breast lines to the side, two stern lines to the rear. But an officer called for a third breast line before the stern was set. Manu figured he was positioning the gangway, but a third breast line was dangerous: it forced Manu to stand in the snapback zone, between other ropes, as the ship heaved and swayed.

The line snapped.

The severed rope traveled at bullwhip speed and hit him behind the knee, knocking him to the deck. "I can't move my leg!" he screamed.

When they got him to the onboard clinic, the report was reassuring: an X-ray found the leg wasn't broken. Just to check, the ship doctor sent

Manu to the island hospital twice. It confirmed the results both times: no break. But despite a day of ice and rest, Manu's leg swelled and turned numb. The ship sailed at 11:00 p.m., and the pain worsened overnight.

At an Antigua clinic the following morning, an MRI revealed the problem: a clotted artery behind Manu's knee. He needed immediate surgery to keep blood flowing to his lower leg. Silversea would pay the medical bill and fly him home, but a curtailed trip meant lost earnings, and an injury could make it hard to get rehired. The ship left his gear and sailed away while Manu underwent surgery alone. He came to in better spirits. At least his leg would be OK.

The next day, Monday, the numbness returned. The nurse said vaguely, "Let's just see how it goes." On Tuesday, the doctor said the leg was infected. If the poison spread, it could be fatal. "We might have to amputate."

The words hit him like another snapped line. Feverish, alone, Manu panicked. The doctor agreed to wait another day. A nurse urged him to get to the States, but Miami was thirteen hundred miles away, and he couldn't even make a call. His phone only sent texts. He borrowed the nurse's and reached his brother in Manila, who tried to get the staffing agency to help. But the manager had left the office and refused to return. The delay cost Manu twelve hours.

On Wednesday morning, the surgeon was firm: the leg had to go. The infection could kill him in hours. Manu refused. Armed with nothing but two texting thumbs, he launched a frantic bedridden campaign to get himself off the island.

"They will cut if off," he wrote to a friend on the ship.

"Don't let them cut it off, bro," Julius wrote back.

"I have requested an airlift to America," Manu wrote. "They have specialists there. Please tell the nurses to go to the captain now."

"We're going," Julius wrote.

"Don't check out, please," Manu wrote. "I want to save my legs for the future."

An air ambulance could cost tens of thousands of dollars. Manu figured that only the captain or the bosses in Monaco could approve.

"Get me out of here," Manu pleaded.

"Stand by, bro," Julius wrote. "Keep praying."

When Silversea approved the ambulance, Manu wept. But more time
slipped away. Finally, he learned the plane would reach Antigua at midnight.

Ariane was cleaning cabins in Mumbai. Manu had shielded her from
the worsening news, perhaps to shield himself. Once he told her, the
family bulletin spread, and Rosalie called me. I knew a doctor who had
worked at Jackson Memorial Hospital in Miami, where Manu was
going. He alerted the emergency room.

The flight took four hours. Manu had willed himself off the island
by refusing to contemplate anything but success. He landed at 4:00 a.m.
My phone rang and a thin voice said, "I'm here in the hospital, *kuya*,
but they say it's too late—they have to amputate." Manu had made me
his medical surrogate, and the doctor asked my permission. When I
asked what the options were, he said there were none. "I would classify
this as urgent."

TRAUMA CENTERS TAKE WHAT they get—gunshots, car wrecks,
floods of sorrow—and do their best. When I arrived the next day, a
guard stood outside Manu's room, watching the prisoner next door, and
a delusional man slept in the hall, where the understaffed nurses could
see him. Manu had drawn a Haitian roommate who played evangelical
radio at volumes sufficient to reach Port-au-Prince. A week's scruff covered Manu's face, his soft eyes were bloodshot, and tubes curled from
his stump. He looked as if he'd been trampled by horses.

He was terrified that Ariane would leave him. After surgery, Manu
had asked me to call her. "I don't know how to tell her myself that I
don't have legs." At first I heard "legs," plural, as a quirk of Filipino

English but came to regard it as a measure of the loss he felt: everything was gone. "If I don't have legs, how can I have work? What about the house we built, the dreams we had?" When I walked in, he was on the phone with Ariane, who assured him their marriage wouldn't change.

"She's *strong*," Manu said.

So was he. Medical students filed in to gape, and a truculent nurse withheld the painkiller as the nerves in his stump rioted. But two words I never heard him utter were "Why me?"

I had contacted a New York advocacy group that helps seafarers. Doug Stevenson, a lawyer with the group (the Seamen's Church Institute), happened to be in Miami and stopped in. He cautioned Manu that he probably wouldn't be able to sue. In signing the standard contract, a condition of getting the job, Manu had unwittingly agreed to arbitration. The damages were capped and low. Like most seafarers, he had never read the fine print and wouldn't have understood it if he had. The good news was the cruise line had to pay the hospital bills and fly in a relative for a visit. Nothing felt more pressing than seeing Ariane.

Stevenson complimented Silversea: in his view, most shipowners wouldn't have sent an ambulance. Company officials had brought Manu an iPad and a cell phone, and Manu said they had told him he could stay in Miami to finish his recovery. But it was clear that the hospital staff distrusted cruise lines. Before I even arrived, a social worker warned me by phone that the company would try to send Manu home before he was medically ready. "They always do," she said.

Manu's surgeon, Edward Lineen, stopped in. The rope had hit the popliteal artery, which supplies blood to the lower leg. The ship's doctor had missed the diagnosis, he said, and the surgeon in Antigua had botched the operation: the blood vessel had to be replaced, not repaired, to avoid re-clotting. An American ER would have caught it. "You probably should have been transferred immediately."

More danger remained: some of the surviving tissue was damaged, and "we might have to sacrifice the knee," which would make walking

much harder. Manu would need extensive training to use a prosthesis—
"that's going to take months!" Dr. Lineen warned—and the insurance
company had already called. While he hadn't called back, "it wouldn't
be the first time an insurance company wants to discharge a patient
before we think it's done."

Sacrifice the knee. Manu listened so stoically that I wondered if he
understood. But when the doctor left, his voice broke. "They're going to
cut my leg again!"

Two days later, Manu lost his knee.

When I returned the next week, Manu looked great. The pink had
returned to his face, and he proved spry with a walker. He had stopped
reading messages from well-wishers to protect himself from their pity.
"No point in crying over spilled milk," he said.

"Why should I be depressed? I still have my wife, still have my kids."

Manu was so upbeat in subsequent days the psychologist feared he
wasn't grieving. Manu googled high-end prosthetics and watched men
with $80,000 limbs ride trail bikes. He joined a therapy group led by a
double amputee skilled at salsa dancing. When anyone asked how he
stayed positive, the answer was the same: Ariane was on her way. "I feel
blessed, loved. She said nothing's going to change."

Ariane flew home from the ship and waited ten days for an appointment at the U.S. embassy. To visit, she needed a visa. As a cruise ship
worker, she'd gotten visas a dozen times to enter the States. But when
the officer learned she had quit her job, he denied her application. Being
jobless, she might overstay. The logic was perfectly circular: to see
Manu, she had to quit, but if she quit, she couldn't see Manu. As a maid,
she was welcome. As a wife, she was banned. She called Manu from the
street, crying. She faced the worst of all worlds: no income and no visit.

Soon there was more bad news: one of the staff warned Manu he had
a discharge date. The insurer planned to send him home in eight days,
without a prosthesis. If he had to fight for one in the Philippines, he
feared he would never get it. Suddenly the Silversea officials refused to

answer his calls. Dr. Lineen put a note in the file opposing the discharge and told Manu to get a lawyer. I helped find one, who rushed into court to argue that Manu would face "irreparable harm" if removed over his doctor's objections. It took an order from a federal judge, but for the moment Manu was safe.

The staff was surprised to see him. "Oh, you're still here!" the rehab doc said.

MANU HAD BEEN a reluctant litigant, but now he was stuck in a foreign country with twin legal fights—one for monetary damages and one for a leg. The money was a long shot. His lawyer, Michael Winkleman, took the case for a contingency fee in the hopes of getting around the arbitration clause. A decade earlier, he said, a seafarer who lost a leg could expect a settlement of $3 million or $4 million. Manu's contract offered $39,180—barely enough to replace a prosthetic limb, which would give out in a few years. But the courts were hostile, and the process would be slow.

Medical care was different: Silversea had an obligation to provide it. It didn't necessarily have to do so in the States, but the judge's order leaving Manu in place seemed to settle the issue. The hospital requested a computerized limb that cost $55,000. The insurer didn't respond. Then the hospital requested one at half the price, which would be easier for Manu to maintain. Again, no answer. It had been seven weeks since the amputation. Concerned that the delay was slowing Manu's progress, the prosthetist, Stephen Dsida, built a temporary leg with spare parts. "I wanted to get him out of bed."

After all the videos of athletic amputees, Manu imagined he would slip on the socket and go. But he spent a day just standing still, learning to shift his weight. Then a physical therapist held him with a belt and timed his stumbling strides with a metronome. Manu overdid it and was sidelined for a week. Calcium deposits idled him again. "I feel like I'm not progressing."

A month later, Manu was the star of the rehab room. "He's doing so well he's teaching us things," said Seema Khurana, the rehab doctor. He shed his crutches and practiced his balance by serving demitasses of Cuban coffee. He did yoga poses. Soon he could swat tennis balls.

His cheer charmed the staff. Manu took to the disability world as he had taken to ships—visiting the lab and admiring metal femurs as he had admired bollards and bitts. He spoke up so often in group therapy that another patient asked him to start a support group. A hospital volunteer named Goofy Manny (he passed out $2 bills stamped with the Disney character) took him out for dinners. A Filipino church adopted him from twenty miles away; every Sunday a parishioner named Joel came to fetch him. "The way they live their faith, it's really extraordinary," Manu said. "Who am I to them?"

But three months after the accident, the insurer still hadn't approved a leg. What had once seemed like red tape now looked like resistance— an effort to stall until the judge sent Manu home. Manu's lawyers sent a letter accusing Silversea of "willfully and deliberately delaying" his recovery. The cruise line responded not with a leg but with a litigator, to depose the rehab doctor. Jeffrey Foreman, who specialized in defending cruise ships, once explained his strategy for discrediting plaintiffs:

> There's a saying that pigs get slaughtered. If you make them look like they're greedy . . . that usually has a negative impact. So we tried to paint them as greedy, exaggerating, malingering.

The deposition was long and turned combative when Foreman implied it could be illegal to send Manu home with an artificial leg. "Is it legal to export the prosthesis to the Philippines?" he asked.

"I don't know," Dr. Khurana said, adding, "I don't export prostheses." She wasn't used to thinking of legs as contraband.

Foreman asked again. "Was that something that was considered?"

The doctor seemed exasperated. "I'm not sure what you're saying, they are not allowed to wear their leg?"

"So you don't know that, do you?" Foreman said.

This wasn't justice; it was farce. (Is it illegal to travel with false teeth? Pacemakers?) Silversea was adding months to Manu's hospital stay and racking up legal fees—wouldn't it be cheaper just to buy the leg? Dsida, the prosthetist, explained that insurers often pay capped rates for hospital stays, while prosthetics are extra. Perhaps by the logic of cost containment, someone thought the battle made sense. (Silversea declined to comment.)

If the process was meant to wear Manu down, it did. The psychologist who once feared that he wasn't grieving now warned that the insurance fight was "overwhelming his coping resources."

"What if I don't get my leg?" Manu said. "What will happen to me?"

Sure enough, Silversea returned to court without approving the leg and asked the judge to send Manu home, arguing that prosthetic care was just as good there. This was doubtful. It was also beside the point: nothing in the Silversea filing explicity promised to provide him a leg, even in the Philippines. Manu had seen friends sent home with assurances of care that never materialized. In a written statement to the court he said flatly, "Silverseas [sic] lied to me about giving me a new leg."

Perhaps the cruise line had a change of heart. Or perhaps the judge signaled his impatience: it's hard to make a one-legged sailor look like a pig. The day after Manu submitted his statement, the insurer sent a late-night note: "The prosthesis . . . is approved."

The device was magical. The old limb (with a pin and lock) felt like wearing a leg. The new limb (with a vacuum grip) felt like having one. "It's like part of my body!" He could walk on a treadmill.

While American health care helped him heal, so did American

attitudes. In the Philippines, the disabled are shunned. "People will look away; they won't want to talk to you." In the States, he saw life could go on. One day he led an outing to a restaurant nine rail stops away. A parade of wheelchairs followed him down the block, up the elevator, onto the platform, and into the car, where he was trying not to feel self-conscious when a guy plopped down beside him and said, "Awesome leg!"

"American exceptionalism!" Manu enthused one day. It wasn't a phrase that I imagined he would know, but he heard it on TV and immediately grasped the idea. "You can't go to China and become Chinese, but you can go to America and become American." That's what he'd done—assimilated to the equal-opportunity ideals of an American rehab ward. Had he been able to stay in the States, he could have launched a productive life in any number of disability-related fields—as a prosthetist or social worker or medical device rep. In the Philippines, his work life was almost certainly over.

I thought I had understood the godlike powers that passports exert, but I hadn't glimpsed them through the disability lens. In the United States, Manu epitomized man's power over adversity. Back home, he would become another reminder of adversity's power over man.

WITH HER SAVINGS DEPLETED after five months at home, Ariane was returning to the ship. Manu hadn't seen her in a year, and by the time he got home, she'd be gone. Now that she had a contract, I suggested she reapply for a visa. Humiliated by the earlier rejection, Ariane was reluctant to spend time and money on what seemed a lost cause.

Her doubts proved justified. The embassy gave her an appointment in five weeks; by then, she'd be back at sea. Her request for an expedited date was denied. Only the help of an embassy official I knew got her an appointment in time. "I got it!" she announced on Facebook. "I can visit Daddy!" If she hurried, she'd have three days in Miami.

Manu lurched between euphoria and fear; what if she recoiled from the limb? He shaved his hospital Fu Manchu, swapping an outcast's image for the look of a guy with a date. The physical therapists tittered like big sisters and planned a party.

Ariane flew for twenty-five hours. The therapists gave Manu a bouquet. Goofy Manny supplied a teddy bear, and Church Joel drove him to the airport. It wasn't awkward, as he had feared, but only when Ariane fed him dinner in bed, with her hand on his stump, did Manu finally feel at ease. "I felt really loved."

The next day brought the rehab-room party. Poor Ariane. After a bad night's sleep in a shared hospital bed, she struggled through jet lag to make small talk in her second language in a roomful of strangers. Not for nothing was she a cum laude hospitality grad. She charmed the room through bloodshot eyes as everyone toasted Manu.

"He's been so eager to learn!"

"He's extremely positive!"

"Your husband has an amazing talent for getting people to like him."

Invitations poured in: dinner Saturday night, church Sunday morning. Despite how little time they had, Ariane insisted they accept to show their gratitude. When I called to say good-bye, they were lying in bed giggling. Manu was teasing Ariane about her English, which had weakened with fatigue, and she was marveling that he'd made so many friends. "I'm not expecting so many people will gonna be amazed by him!"

Manu had gotten better, not bitter, but there was no sugarcoating the future. Though Silversea had operated from an American port, with mostly American passengers, he was unlikely to get access to an American court. The sum he was due in the Philippines, about three years' earnings, would have to last the rest of his life. When his leg gave out in a few years, he would have no way to buy another. The *Silver Spirit* was back at sea, and there was no shortage of Filipinos eager to take his place. He and Ariane would stay together, but only by being apart. She alone was now the good provider.

Church Joel arrived at 2:45 a.m. to take Ariane to her flight. Manu went downstairs in a wheelchair to say good-bye, but Joel insisted he come to the airport—he didn't mind driving him back. Manu climbed in without his prosthesis and said farewell in boxers as he leaned against the car. None of the travelers rushing past seemed to notice the one-legged man whose wife made him feel almost whole again.

A few weeks later, the judge granted Silversea's request to dismiss the case and left Manu to arbitration in the Philippines. Either Silversea or its insurer splurged and flew him home in a first-class seat.

SIXTEEN

The Filipino Cul-de-Sac

The Villanuevas set off to find America, with a stop for Filipino food at the Houston Jollibee. The San Antonio SeaWorld was four hours away. Fortified by *halo-halo*, they drove late, slept in, and barely caught the dolphin show, then left for a Filipino restaurant on the other side of town. Roller coasters screamed through the SeaWorld skies; orcas lurked. But Chris took a nap, and by the time they returned and grabbed a quick swim the park was nearly closed. They had dinner at a Filipino buffet. When it rained the next day, they skipped the park for spring rolls at an Asian café. The five-hundred-mile trip brought three hours of theme park fun and four encounters with Filipino cuisine.

Rosalie was elated. It was just the family life she had hoped for in the States. "Relaxing, eating, swimming, resting—happy day!"

Rosalie's third summer in America was the summer of her content. She had spent the first summer homesick and the second overwhelmed. Now the kids were settled, Chris had a job, and she was about to finish her contract and get a big raise. At her low point, Rosalie had cried, "I don't know where to find my happiness." Now she knew—on I-10, with the kids in the backseat eating junk food. When she told me, "I'm happy," I did a double take.

A migration that once seemed as if it might never work had become a success—and by historical standards, a rapid one. The uprooted had become the transplanted. Rosalie had overcome her disappointment, earned plaudits from her patients, provided for her parents, become a better mother, and kept inverted gender roles from ruining her marriage—and at the end of the summer, she returned to SeaWorld and bought a season's pass. "Straight-line assimilation" in its classic form had taken half a century or more. In three years, Rosalie achieved what used to take three generations.

Part of what made Rosalie happy was a deepening friendship with another Filipino nurse. Marilen Garcia was as shy as Rosalie, and since they worked on different wards, they had been slow to connect. Rosalie called Marilen modest, loyal, and generous—"simple," as she tried to be. "I am nice, but she is more nicer. I am good to people, but she is more good." Marilen's husband, Kim, also a nurse, liked fighting cocks almost as much as Chris did, and their daughter, an only child, saw the Villanueva kids as the siblings she lacked. In child-care jams, the Garcias would step in. Far from home, needing support, the couples became fictive kin.

On the Fourth of July, they made plans to meet by the Galveston seawall and watch the parade. But Chris detoured to check a pumping station that he'd been summoned to fix earlier in the day. The ground bubbled with goo. "Pretty much stinky!" Lara enthused. "Is that like a spa?" By the time they found the Garcias, the parade had passed. But the fireworks dazzled, and Rosalie considered any group outing a success, even with a sewage inspection.

It was 11:00 p.m. when they got home—morning in the Philippines. The phone rang. Rowena asked about the parade and said she felt forgotten. "Mama, I didn't forgot you," Kristine said, but the call dropped, and she got caught up in *The Suite Life of Zack & Cody* instead of call-ing back. Chris's mother called. Chris's father was dying, twenty years after his immobilizing stroke. The faith healer said the only thing keep-ing him alive was an amulet he had swallowed in his youth. Chris's mom had decided to let him go in peace, with a potion to dissolve the charm. She tried to lure Dominique to the phone by singing, but a Taga-log serenade was no match for *Zack & Cody*. He ignored her, and Lara politely stepped in to ask her grandmother how she'd been sleeping.

The next day Chris and Kim took a trip to a rooster farm. The owner, Kuya Benjie, was a figure of local renown, having successfully competed in the World Slasher Cup, a Manila event billed as the "Olym-pics of Cockfighting." He was a hulking man with rooster tattoos and pecking scars on his hands. For two minor-league breeders, a stroll across his field was a trip to Fenway Park.

Chris and Kim were shopping for birds to ship home and breed in the Philippines. Touting his White Clarets, Roundheads, and Speeder Brown Reds, Kuya Benjie sounded like a rooster sommelier. One cock was so mean he had killed a rat. "You can see it—he's still mad!" Kuya Benjie said, stroking the bird. Such regal bloodlines came at a cost, but Rosalie didn't complain. Chris's friendship with Kim abetted hers with Marilen.

The potion worked. Chris's father "passed away"—Lara's phrase, because "it sounds rude to say he died." Chris flew home and at his mother's request brought Dominique. But after nearly two years away, the seven-year-old could no longer speak Tagalog. He was crying when he called Rosalie. "I miss the United States," he said.

As they finished their contracts, the foreign nurses could move anywhere. But for all their initial gripes about Galveston, most decided to stay. Permanent jobs and big pay raises sparked a real estate rush. Rosalie started looking, too, but was still paying for a house in the

Philippines where no one had ever lived. She vowed to avoid rash decisions.

Rosalie and realtors were not a natural match. Nervous energy thickened her accent and tangled her syntax. She introduced herself to one agent by saying, "I'm from Philippines, nurse who works in Middle East—here now as immigrant—how many years in Abu Dhabi?"

"Coming from nights," she yawned to another. "Like that, like that."

I tagged along to a cheerless old house listed on the internet for $150,000. It had a cracked driveway and a 1960s bath. "This one old already," Rosalie complained. "The *sala*, it doesn't fit my *soofa*."

"Do you have a price range?" the agent asked.

"One thirty, like that," said Chris.

"Maybe for ninety, like that," said Rosalie.

"That's a little tough, the price range you're in."

One agent got so frustrated at Rosalie's lack of price range she drove away. Rosalie fumed at the snub.

Three Filipino nurses bought neighboring lots in Texas City, a suburb halfway to Houston, where homes were popping up in a pasture with the suddenness of a wildflower bloom. Rainsong, the subdivision, promised GE appliances, free credit repair, and "open concept living"— airy kitchens and two-story living rooms. You could stand at the sink and watch the kids play in the loft. The young agent, Andrew, seemed fresh from salesmen's school, but having sold three houses to Filipino nurses, he didn't mind Rosalie's accent.

"I'm going to take care of you—trust me," he said, sniffing through a summer cold.

Kim had come, too. They found adjoining lots on a cul-de-sac, each slated for a four-bedroom home.

Rosalie's eyes widened as she toured the model. "Is the furniture included?"

Andrew reached for a tissue. "We don't furnish homes."

The model refrigerator gleamed. "No *ref*?" asked Rosalie.

"We want *ref*," Chris demanded.

Andrew stood firm: "Microwave, dishwasher, and stove."

Casual interest deepened. They ping-ponged between the show house and the lots. "You could go crazy with all the options and still stay under $200,000," Andrew said. He touted the schools and mumbled something about the Fed and interest rates. Then he left the room and returned to announce his manager had approved a deal: if they bought within two days, they could pick their exterior colors and brick. After that, "even if you come back to me and say, '*Please, please*, Andrew,' I'm going to have to say no."

They broke for lunch. Kim summoned Marilen, who'd been asleep after working all night. She was as excited as Rosalie.

"Now is a great time to buy," Andrew said.

"You never know who's going to walk in tomorrow."

"You make too much money not to buy a home."

They agreed to reconvene the next day.

By morning, the deal was dead. Chris wouldn't promise to help pay the mortgage. Rosalie feared she'd get stuck with the bill and accused of extravagance. She was working herself into high dudgeon when I slipped out for an hour. When I returned, both couples were buying. They'd be next-door neighbors.

As she returned to Rainsong to pick her bricks, Rosalie, battling doubts, tallied the pros and cons. The cons were numerous. She didn't have an agent, she hadn't priced comps, she wasn't sure she could afford the payment, and she didn't know the builder or the schools. The house was twenty miles from work, and she still couldn't drive. It would triple her shelter costs, and Chris might not help pay.

The pros were fewer but more persuasive: Filipinos. Other nurses were moving in, and Marilen would live next door. Rosalie could reinvent the compound. A Filipino cul-de-sac offered an ingenious solution to her biggest problem in the States, the absence of family. With six months of construction ahead, they could back out later without losing anything more than the $1,000 deposit. When Chris said the backyard would be good for raising roosters, I couldn't tell if he was kidding.

"This is the start of my American Dream!" Rosalie gushed on the way home. As if on cue, Labor Day fireworks exploded over Galveston Bay.

FOR LARA, fourth grade was . . . *wel-lll, prr-retty great.* She discovered a delightfully absurd poem about a crocodile who ate his dentist. Lara had never heard of the author, Shel Silverstein, but was charmed by his weird humor. Another of his sweet, strange poems described a puddly snowman on a quest to see July. "The moral is you should live your dreams," Lara wrote.

She was living hers. "I'm not so shy anymore!" she said, as if startled by the news. Having once seen herself as a nurse, Lara said, "I think I want to be a pediatrician." She cited sloth, not ambition: "Mom said nurses have to carry heavy patients, and I don't like carrying stuff." But in a world where snowmen see July, anything's possible.

Lara again won the teacher lottery. Courtney Hailey, the young instructor, grasped what made her tick: the search for moral instruction. "With her, school is news you can use," Ms. Hailey said. For a project on fairy tales, Ms. Hailey listed the lessons the stories conveyed, like "hard work pays off" and "honesty is the best policy." For Lara, it was ice cream for breakfast. She read about Harriet Tubman again ("she saved people, *even though they weren't her relatives!*"), learned more idioms, and made the straight-A honor roll.

"WOOH!" Lara wrote.

What made Kristine tick was her peers—a desire for their approval. Heading into sixth grade, she was no longer a Girlie Girl. "I'm mostly a Crazy Girl," she said. Crazy Girls act silly to win popularity. While Lara's new word was "onomatopoeia," Kristine's was "stuffy-fluffy." Her English teacher groused that she was acting ditzy to fit in. "You know that look: Airhead, Cutesy-Pootsie. She's moving into that stage of Americanization. She wants to be part of the group." Perhaps the academic disengagement helped her manage her frustration. Though she had passed the STAAR test, she still lagged her grade level in reading and math.

In fifth grade, Ms. Fabian had seen her gifts, but Ms. Fabian didn't teach sixth grade. Kristine's social studies teacher called Brussels a city in England and Dublin a country nearby. Unfortunately, she also taught Kristine math. The science teacher was caring but new. The English teacher was experienced but tired. Somehow the school put Kristine in Chinese. Rosalie didn't return the withdrawal form, consigning Kristine to a year of Mandarin even as she shored up her English. A smart girl lurked behind the Crazy Girl facade. But given the luck of the teacher draw, there was no one who could reach her.

ALMOST AS SOON AS she bought the house, Rosalie had doubts. "Oh, headache!" she said the next week. "It's too much, this signing of the house! I couldn't sleep. I'm not yet driving. I don't know if Chris will really gonna help. Maybe I just got—what's the word?—*nabibigla*." Overwhelmed. "How can I carry this one for fifteen years? My body is already aching."

Then she urged her friend Estrella to buy across the street. Rainsong had its sixth Filipino nurse—the cul-de-sac had its third—and Rosalie would have another ride to work. "I'm not sorry I bought it—just scared. I'm just continuously praying, 'God help me to pay for it.'"

After forty-one hundred hours on the job, Rosalie finished her contract. The night nurses staged a mock commencement, and she walked out humming "Pomp and Circumstance." The promotion to core staff brought a 40 percent raise to a base salary of $78,000. It sounded even better in Philippine pesos: 3.4 million. "I feel rich!"

Forced to wait for a new orientation, Rosalie got a three-week break.

She used it on a burst of domesticity of the sort the night shift didn't allow. She scheduled overdue dentist appointments, sold cookie dough for the school, and succumbed to Kristine's pleas for puppies—dachshunds named Marshmallow and M&M. "Been busy Mom today with visit to the vet!" Rosalie texted me. She hardly needed more creatures to care for, but Kristine glowed.

The next week the puppies pooped on the floor, ran out the door, and peed in the hall as the manager walked by. Dominique retrieved them but stepped in their mess and tracked it across the living room. Rosalie yelled, and the manager raised the rent. Kristine cried and said puppies need hugs, not scolding. "I know how to love them. I get a lot of licks."

The real estate rush sparked a nurses' competition. Immigrants measure their progress against other immigrants. Who had the premium brick facade? The bigger backyard? Chelita, Rosalie's Filipino boss, had seen it coming. "Filipinos like to gossip: 'OK, you got a Mercedes—I've got to have a Mercedes.'" Several nurses had bought cheaper homes on the island and suggested that Rosalie back out of Rainsong and join them. Their overtures fanned her doubts.

But once the house was under roof, it looked . . . so big! "And also the kids—they are so excited!" Rosalie was embarrassed to show Tita pictures, much less confide the price. "She would be shocked." Humility kept her quiet—only God's grace could explain why she had so much more than the rest of the family—but so did self-defense. "They will think I'm rich; they will expect more of me."

HOME BUYING HAD AN unexpected effect on unit 7B: patient satisfaction scores plunged. Rosalie's ward once boasted the hospital's highest marks. But with mortgages to pay, the nurses extended their average workweek to fifty-six hours—50 percent more than the hospital as a whole. "They're working, working all the time—they're sick, they're tired," Chelita said. "You're going to be irritated when patients call you. It's going to get to you."

The Filipino and American nurses started to quarrel. Foreign nurses had opened the unit, and Chelita had wanted to add more, but the hospital decided they were too expensive. (They were the opposite of cheap labor.) As vacancies arose, she mixed in local hires, mostly recent grads. While there hadn't been enough experienced local nurses to open the whole ward—which is why the hospital had recruited abroad—it was safe to blend the recent grads with more seasoned foreign staff. Rosalie's night shift of four Filipinos began transferring patients back and forth with a day shift of four Americans.

The Americans spoke slang; the Filipinos stared blankly. The Americans rushed to leave; the Filipinos chatted and delayed them. What really annoyed the Americans was Tagalog. While there was no formal policy against it, the Americans considered it impolite. The Filipinos rarely spoke it in front of patients, but they had Tagalog break-room chats, told Tagalog stories at staff parties, and swapped Tagalog asides at the nurses' station. Speaking Tagalog felt so natural the Filipinos scarcely knew they did it. Even the most fluent joked that too much English made their noses bleed.

The Americans suspected the Filipinos were talking about *them*. At a party in the conference room, the Filipinos were so segregated in a Tagalog huddle that Chelita chided them. "Look, you're not in the Philippines!" The tensions weren't unique. A hospital near Bakersfield, California, paid a group of nurses nearly $1 million after trying to enforce an English-only policy. The Filipinos who sued said they had been mocked for their accents and barred from speaking Tagalog in the cafeteria.

One night, the chief of nursing paid 7B a surprise visit. The Filipinos rushed to clean the staff refrigerator and dumped what seemed like old food but turned out to be the Americans' lunches. When the Americans retaliated, a fridge war was on. "It just catapulted," said Jennifer

Nelson, a supervisor. A Filipino with child-care problems was known for last-minute arrivals. When she came early one night, an American nurse offered a mocking ovation. The Filipinos seethed. "It started having a not-good relationship with the white people," Rosalie said.

A patient died near the end of the day shift. An American nurse completed a form for the morgue, but the Filipino who replaced her thought it needed a different signature and sought another opinion, in Tagalog. The American nurse spun around and announced she was filing a complaint. A few days later, Rosalie and the other Filipinos were summoned to the conference room, where two stern managers handed them each a form to read aloud and sign. It was a pledge not to speak Tagalog. The Filipinos felt humiliated, hauled before scowling overseers and handed a linguistic loyalty oath. Not even the Saudis had treated them like that. "We don't deserve this," Rosalie said. "We are really working hard. We felt like we're kind of—what you call it?—racial discriminated."

But Americans were equally indignant, including Jennifer Nelson, the supervisor. In addition to risking medical errors, talking "Tagalah" at the nurses' station struck her as plain wrong. "It's just offensive to me not to do it in our language. It makes it feel like you're hiding stuff, or that our language is beneath you. . . . I've had one of them tell me one time that English makes her *nose bleed*. . . . Like what does that mean? You don't like English?" Plus she was tired of being told to try Filipino food! "They're like, 'What do you mean you're not hungry—let's eat!' . . . It's like a huge culture clash."

I thought she was saying it had been a mistake to hire foreign nurses. But she wasn't. "I was very excited about bringing them all aboard . . . and I still am." The hospital needed "fresh blood." Are they good nurses? "A lot of them are excellent!" What about Rosalie? "Patients love her; I've always had them say she's very caring." (Since Nelson monitored patient satisfaction, she would know.) Does her English get in the way? "There's a listening face, and then there's a fake listening face. She has that listening face." She added, "I would have her take care of me."

Chelita hadn't known that the supervisors beneath her would demand the language oaths, which she considered heavy-handed. As the Filipino American boss of squabbling Filipinos and Americans, she saw both sides: she was annoyed that the Filipinos kept speaking Tagalog and annoyed that the Americans got so upset.

"This is America," she told the Filipinos. Speak English.

"This is America," she told the Americans. It's a melting pot.

The hospital did a round of sensitivity training; then the Filipinos returned to speaking Tagalog and the Americans fumed. But when Rosalie was upset by a patient's death, no one was more helpful than Jennifer. "She really supported me."

ONE SURPRISE OF Rosalie's move to the States was how little she talked to her Abu Dhabi friends. For eight years, she and Mylene had worked together, prayed together, gone into credit card debt together, and talked up their future lives in the States. But Rosalie had been too embarrassed by her letdowns in Texas to stay in close touch. Three years later, Mylene and her family moved to Dallas.

She was miserable in all the same ways: Texas was expensive, the malls were far, there weren't enough Filipinos, American English was hard to understand. "I got a nose bleed!" she complained on Facebook.

Rosalie assured her that she would adjust, and the Villanuevas made the five-hour drive to Dallas with $100 worth of homesickness cure—takeout from Jollibee.

Eager to see Rosalie as a sage hand counseling a greenhorn, I went along. But by the time Rosalie arrived, Mylene was feeling better, and the rescue became a reunion. Because Mylene is an extrovert, she had always struck me as the tougher of the two, but she said she couldn't have come to America alone, as Rosalie did. "I'm just talkative; *she's* very strong."

Other nurses from Abu Dhabi lived nearby, and the reunion grew.

Nostalgic for the old shopping, the group trekked to the outlet mall. Having once led each other to the precipice of financial ruin, Rosalie and Mylene vowed caution, then disappeared into the Coach store. They emerged with arms full, laughing like tipplers at closing time. As Saint Augustine might have said had antiquity been blessed with outlet malls: Lord, make me pure but not yet.

Mylene seemed so nostalgic for Abu Dhabi that I asked why she had come to the States. The answer wasn't just money. Like Rosalie, she talked of "opportunity" in a more expansive way. The Emirates was like a fling, fun but insecure. "In America, you can settle. Your children can have a future."

"This is the land of opportunity," Rosalie agreed. "But it's hard work. You have to sweat a lot."

Talk turned to the Philippines, where forty-four members of an elite police group had been slaughtered in a botched antiterrorism raid.

"Nothing will change in the Philippines," Mylene said.

"It's the OFWs"—Overseas Filipino Workers—"that is really helping the economy," another nurse said.

"They are saying we are 'New Heroes,'" Rosalie said.

"We *are* the heroes," said Mylene.

The talk of home led Rosalie to warn the girls: no American boyfriends. "I want only Filipino."

In an instant, a generation gap appeared, with the girls on the American side. "That's *racist*, Mommy!" Lara said.

Kristine frowned. "What about Mexicans? It's the same thing."

"No, I don't want—only Filipino," said Rosalie. "So he can go home to visit the Philippines with us."

But even at eleven and nine the girls weren't having it. "As long as he's kind, Mommy," Lara said.

"It doesn't have to be Filipino," Kristine said.

"I want him to be caring," Lara said. "Anything else doesn't matter."

By the end of the school year, Kristine and Lara had each become a high-concentrate version of herself, with Lara piling up grade-school accolades and Kristine evermore dazzled by middle school intrigue. She attended her first unchaperoned movie, with her friend "Baby Jo-Gi," and reeled from the thrill. "We saw *tons* of people that we knew. We were *shaking* because we were so excited and stuff." Baby Jo-Gi was a *"crazy animal."*

On our last ride to school, she previewed a sixth-grade social order so coded and complex it cried out for Margaret Mead. Her fifteen or so closest friends were arrayed in a fluid hierarchy, with "sisters" at the top, followed by "best friends for life," then "baes for life" and "ride or dies." "Your ride or dies are like your best friends but not your *best-est friends.*"

"I think there's going to be a drama today," Kristine enthused.

Actually, two. Baby Jo-Gi's boyfriend was mad because she wouldn't kiss him. Also Gabrielle was going to the dance with Franco after breaking up with Stevie, who didn't know he'd been dumped until Brittany sent him a text. "I don't want to get in their dramas anymore," Kristine said. "It's kind of fun."

In English, the class was passing time by doing PowerPoint presentations about the states. One student wrote, "Louisiana has a relatively constant semi-tropical environment." Kristine's began, "California's bird is a quail, and they have a pointy thing that looks like a chicken thing."

The teacher arched an eyebrow.

"It's something we say," Kristine said with a shrug. "It's a thingy."

Her English teacher blamed "Americanization." Her science teacher said she "wants to be one of the popular girls. . . . I don't want to say airhead-ish, but sometimes they act like they don't have a clue." The

Chinese teacher didn't care if she gave up on Chinese, as long as she didn't give up on school. "This happens with people in this age-group." The point wasn't that Kristine was doing worse than her American peers, only that her eagerness to imitate them kept her from doing as well as she could.

If there was good news in the teachers' reports, it was the agreement that the Crazy Girl was only a pose. "Trust me, she's supersmart," the Chinese teacher said. "She can learn anything." Of the "Cutesy Pootsie" posture, her English teacher said, "I don't think that's really her." A crumpled essay in her backpack indulged her earnest side:

> If someone gave me a Million dollars I would give 20,000 dollars to the Philippines because of the people who need help from the flood and disaster of the super typhoon. Then I would give $50,000 to my parents . . . . I will go home to the philippines and donate $5,000 to the church and schools.

And, she added, "I would go shopping all over the world."

LARA SPENT OUR LAST RIDE to school talking about the difference between mean, median, mode, and range. When she heard that Ms. Hailey was giving a quiz, she pumped her fist and said, "Yes!" Ms. Hailey had run a yearlong reading contest. The bulletin board announced that Lara had won.

Ms. Hailey did have one bit of surprising news: Lara had sassed her. When Ms. Hailey asked if she had pushed someone, Lara said, "*Yeah?*"—as in, *Yeah, what about it?* "I was shocked!" Ms. Hailey said, laughing. "Not my sweet Lara!" Lara quickly apologized and returned to her hyper-obedient self, but perhaps a seed of adolescence was growing.

"She's really become a writer," Ms. Hailey said. As an English learner in the second grade, Lara had written that "snitices" studied "elens"—scientists studied aliens. Two and a half years later she wrote,

> If I could magically turn myself into any age, it would be 22. . . . I think that 22 would be the most astonishing age. . . . When I'm 22, I would move to Florida. . . . The sun makes my eyes sparkle like the stars. . . . It will be so majestic!

Ms. Hailey was teaching the class to defend opinions—just the kind of exercise in independent thinking that made Rosalie nervous about the States. The day's question put Lara on the spot: Should parents be allowed to spy on their kids? The American in her agreed with the class—no way!—but her inner Filipino was loath to challenge parental authority. Lara found common ground: she'd let parents spy, but on American grounds of efficiency. "This way I won't have to explain everything. They'll already know!"

"That's a cool way to think about it," Ms. Hailey said.

After school, we picked up Kristine, who said matter-of-factly, "My friends are cutting themselves." She meant with razors. Over issues with boys. Talk of it had dominated the day's field trip.

"Did *you* cut yourself?" Lara asked.

"Me? No!"

Kristine made light of the situation but seemed disturbed. Girls in the Philippines "haven't even *heard* of cutting themselves."

She returned from school the following day with reports of more drama: the fallout from her friends' jilted romance had landed them in the principal's office. "I cried—oh my God!" she told Rosalie.

"Why did you cry?" Rosalie asked.

"Because they're my *friends*, Mommy, and somebody told on them."

"It's 'told,'" said Lara, trying to be helpful.

"Shut up, Lars," Kristine said.

"Do you have boyfriend also?" Rosalie's tone turned sharp, despite Kristine's truthful denials. Demanding Kristine's phone, she found a text that said, "He was putting his hands all over you!" Kristine had written it about someone else, but Rosalie couldn't follow whose hands were on whom.

"What's 'putting his hands to you'!" she screamed. Warnings about kidnapping and gang rape followed.

Boyfriends, breakups, razor blades. "Some crazy stuff," Lara said. "I'm not supposed to be hearing about that, because I'm only a kid."

I had offered her a trip to the toy store for making straight As, but Lara chose Office Depot and stocked up on pads and pens. Then she wrote her first book—an enigmatic study of a girl who likes to ask questions, with a hint of Shel Silverstein. To understand the first line, it helps to know that Chris had teased her for swallowing a bug in her sleep.

Why Would I?
By Lara

Why would I swallow a fly? Why? Why? Why? I can't figure
   out why!
Can you answer my question?
Why would I wanna be a Puppy? Can you answer it please?
Why would I be excited for a TEST? Just why?! . . .
Why would I be sad if I live in a Cave? Is it because I'm not a
   caveman?
Why would I be sad if my Ballon fly's away?
Why do I have emotions just why—please tell me? Would you?
Why am I so curiouse, just why?

I secured an interview with the author, who explained that she wondered about being a puppy out of guilt: she felt bad that she loved the dachshunds more than her goldfish. She wondered about the balloons out of sheepishness: she liked them more than she thought a fourth grader should. But mostly she just wondered about wonder. "Because I'm curious!"

FROM THE MOMENT ROSALIE had agreed to buy the house, the deal had been shadowed by doubt. She might change her mind or fail to get a mortgage; her Abu Dhabi debts, still unpaid, could resurface on a credit report. Construction delays lengthened her wait, and she put off the loan paperwork. By the time she applied, Marilen and Estrella had already moved in. Finally, she got a closing date. I came to watch the big day.

At the last minute, the lender canceled. Rosalie thought she had paid off her U.S. credit card, but a $22 balance had accumulated penalties for months. "I mis-look it," she said. For the want of a nail, a mortgage was lost: the error left her credit score too low for a conventional loan. She'd have to find another mortgage or lose the house and deposit. "Headache!" she said. We stopped by the empty home, which basked in the sunset like Shangri-La. Rosalie was surprisingly serene. "I love the house. I hope I can close it. Leave it to God."

She had another concern: the next day's Manny Pacquiao fight. She had been praying about it for months.

It's hard for a non-Filipino to grasp what Manny Pacquiao means to the Philippines. Only a historically marginalized people can find such meaning in a boxer's rise. A street urchin from the provinces, Pacquiao stood a towering five five but boasted world titles in eight weight classes, with each bloodied opponent a vindication of Filipino might. "He's a symbol of hope and victory for the Filipino people," Rosalie said, as if reciting a catechism. He was everything Filipinos admire—a devout Christian, a politician (soon Senator Manny Pacquiao), and a crooner of karaoke songs.

The fight with Floyd Mayweather was five years in the making, with negotiations to rival the Treaty of Versailles. Athletically, it paired the two greatest boxers of their generation. Metaphorically, it pitted good against evil. Pacquiao was a man of faith known for charity. Mayweather was a domestic abuser who posed in bed with stacks of $100 bills. Pacquiao's fans touted his humility. Mayweather's touted his arrogance. They would split $300 million, the biggest purse in boxing history.

"Everything's in favor of Mayweather," Rosalie complained. The fight was in his adopted hometown (Las Vegas), and he got 60 percent of the pot, win or lose. Rosalie even knew that Mayweather had challenged Pacquiao's gloves. She was clearly following the fight more closely than mortgage documents. "I'm like Mommy Dionisia"—Pacquiao's mother—"when he gets hit I feel the pain."

The kids had limited interest. "I don't want to pick sides. I don't like racism," Kristine said. When Pacquiao appeared on TV, Dominique noticed only that "his English is bad."

On fight night, everyone gathered at Estrella's, across the street from Rosalie's would-be home. The serving table groaned with holiday fare—spring rolls on silver serving dishes and a roast pig. Between feast and fight, there was time to tour the neighboring nurses' homes, each furnished with a plush new living room suite. One bragged that "this is the price"—she meant the reward—"of wiping poo."

Even on a night of ethnic pride, assimilation was impossible to miss. Two nurses brought American boyfriends. Estrella's son skipped the fight for his high school prom. The daughter of the lone Muslim couple talked up her season in high school soccer; she had just made the National Honor Society. The group sang along to both national anthems, Philippine and American, with special oomph at "home of the brave." If this was ethnic chauvinism, it carried dual passports.

Pacquiao entered in a T-shirt that said, "Jesus Is the Name of the Lord." Mayweather wore python skin. Pacquiao smiled and took a selfie with his trainer. Mayweather scowled. Mayweather, the favorite, was taller and heavier—a disciplined, defensive fighter who had never lost a pro fight. Pacquiao was faster and more aggressive, with more wins but five defeats. He'd have to score early or Mayweather would dance away.

"I want one punch in the face of Mayweather—one punch!" Rosalie said.

The bell rang. For sixty seconds, neither man hit much. Then Mayweather slipped a jackhammer past Pacquiao's gloves and into his head. Rosalie winced. "I can't watch," she said. In the second round, Pacquiao lunged, but Mayweather countered, scored, and clinched. Rosalie inched closer to the TV and complained that Mayweather wouldn't stand still. "He's cheating!"

The fourth frame brought Filipino joy. Pacquiao knocked Mayweather in the head, pinned him to the ropes, and beat him like a rug. The Filipinos high-fived and hugged. But Mayweather took the fifth. And the seventh and the eighth. He ducked and dodged and mouthed "nope" to declare himself immune to Pacquiao's blows. Pacquiao chased. Mayweather preened.

"Sometimes Darth Vader wins," *The New York Times* wrote. The trash-talking, woman-beating, money-worshipping American beat the humble incarnation of Filipino values.

"Boo, boo," Rosalie sulked. "Not fair."

FOR A FEW WEEKS after the fight, Rosalie's patient load turned heavy. She rushed an amputee with an infected stump to the ICU and consoled a bipolar woman who couldn't stop crying. When the patient saw a rosary wrapped around Rosalie's badge she asked if they could pray together, which Rosalie was happy to do.

The mortgage broker demanded a larger down payment and found Rosalie a loan. She took out the mortgage alone but added Chris's name to the deed so he wouldn't feel overshadowed. Rosalie worked the night before the closing, then spent an hour signing papers she didn't understand. A home in the suburbs was hers.

Three weeks later, Donald Trump stood before a wall of flags in his Manhattan skyscraper and launched his presidential campaign with an attack on immigration. "The U.S. has become a dumping ground for everybody else's problems," he said. "When Mexico sends its people, they're not sending their best. . . . They're bringing drugs. They're bringing crime. They're rapists. And some, I assume, are good people."

At the time, it hardly seemed a sideshow, not a turn in immigration history; few people imagined the campaign going anywhere. Trump subsequently pledged to ban Muslims, accelerate deportations, abolish birthright citizenship, cut refugees, punish sanctuary cities, reduce legal immigration, and seize remittances from unauthorized workers. He led his electrified crowds in chants of "Build the wall!" He branded immigrants as criminals, terrorists, welfare cheats, people who "want Sharia law," and a danger to "jobs, wages, housing, schools, tax bills and general living conditions." It was a song in the key of grievance. "We will not be taken advantage of anymore." One of Trump's most popular routines was the recital of an old poem called "The Snake," which he repurposed as a parable about immigrants' treachery. It's the tale of a kind woman who takes in a serpent and is repaid with a venomous bite. Picture the crowd in MAGA hats as their leader reads on:

> *"I saved you," cried that woman*
> *"And you've bitten me even, why?*
> *You know your bite is poisonous and now I'm going to die"*
> *"Oh shut up, silly woman," said the reptile with a grin*
> *"You knew damn well I was a snake before you took me in."*

"U.S.A.! U.S.A.!" the audiences cheered.

"Who likes 'The Snake'?" Trump would ask, preening. "Should I do it again?"

Rosalie said little about Trump—"I cannot judge what's in his heart"—but her life was an eloquent retort to the case he made. She didn't take from Galveston; she gave to it. She was a nurse, not a snake. In standard cost-benefit terms, Rosalie's experience was a triple win: good for her, good for America, and good for her family in the Philippines. But cost-benefit analysis alone doesn't do the story justice.

Rosalie's escape from Leveriza is a minor miracle. Migration was her vehicle of salvation. It delivered her from the living conditions of the nineteenth century. It respected her talent, rewarded her sweat, and enlarged her capacity for giving. It made her life deeper, fuller, and more filled with hope. It's great that migration helped her help others. It's also great that it helped her help herself. That her quest ended in Texas is something for Americans to cheer. It's good for your country to be the place where people go to make dreams come true.

The new house had what Rosalie wanted: laminate wood floors, a double-door fridge, premium cabinets, and a big tub where a nurse could soak her legs. The garage alone was larger than the house in Leveriza. Each of the kids had a separate room, but they were scared to sleep alone in a house so big. For months they curled up beside Rosalie and Chris, Filipino-style.

When I asked Rosalie how the house compared with the hovel where we met—with the leaks, rats, heat, crowds, and stench—she couldn't find the words. I couldn't either. "Omigod," she told the kids. "Big difference. Mommy didn't have like this. Mommy grew up in a shanty."

"What's a shanty?" Kristine asked.

Complete

D onald Trump didn't assimilate.

To rationalize the support of the candidate reciting "The Snake," Republicans sometimes assured themselves that Trump would "pivot" after the election and become "more presidential." "I'm going to be so presidential that you people will be so bored," Trump said. But high office did not dispel low bigotry: having run as a nativist, Trump governed as one, shattering American norms.

No element of immigration escaped attack. He cut refugee admissions by three-quarters, to the lowest level since the program began. He issued his long-promised "Muslim ban"—three bans, actually, until one passed constitutional muster. He engineered the longest government shutdown in American history in an attempt to get Congress to finance a wall for which he had insisted Mexico would pay. When he failed, he declared a national emergency. A defining moment of Trump's policy was the separation of parents and children at the border, mostly Central Americans seeking asylum. Though illegal crossings were experiencing a spike, they have generally been on the wane; in 2017, apprehensions fell to a forty-six-year low. Authorities seized thousands of children, including infants and toddlers, and sent them to distant foster homes as their frantic jailed parents tried to figure out where they were. Thirteen Republican senators called the policy an affront "to ordinary human decency." Laura Bush called it "cruel" and "immoral." Trump suspended the policy a few days before a federal judge ordered the children reunited. The chaotic reunion effort took months, and hundreds of migrants were deported without their kids.

Americans are usually advised to measure politicians less by what they say than by what they do. The adage doesn't wholly apply to Trump, because his words do such harm, to ethnic relations at home and America's stature abroad. He said Haitians coming to the States "all have AIDS," *The New York Times* reported, and Nigerians would never "go back to their huts." His gripe that America attracted "all these people from shithole countries" was a slur heard around the world. (An editorial in the *Times* said plainly, "The president of the United States is a racist.") More subtle assaults on American traditions are equally telling. Under Trump, the U.S. Citizenship and Immigration Services quietly revised its mission statement to excise the phrase "Nation of Immigrants."

Despite Trump's ascent, Americans tell pollsters they support immigrants. In the culture wars, of which immigration is now part, fervent factions often triumph over placid majorities. Gallup regularly asks whether immigration is "a good thing or bad thing." In 2018, "good thing" hit 75 percent—a record high. (Paradoxically, public opinion is more supportive now, in an age of backlash, than it was a generation ago, when policy turned so expansive.) Even as restrictionists gain strength, the United States has integrated more people more successfully than anyone in 1965 could have guessed had they known the changes to be wrought by LBJ's pen. As for immigrants from shithole countries, the *Houston Chronicle* was happy to have them. "We hereby raise a Sunday morning toast to 'shithole city,'" it editorialized. "To our city. To Houston, the most diverse city in America."

Trump did all he could to make the midterm elections in 2018 a rejection of immigration. But Democrats captured the House with a slate of candidates noted for their remarkable diversity. The previous Congress already included immigrants from eight countries and children of immigrants from twenty-six others. To their ranks came two Muslim women, an Ecuadorian-born university administrator, and a son of Eritrean refugees. That *sounds* like a Nation of Immigrants.

Outside the United States, migration toppled Europe's most powerful leader, Germany's Angela Merkel, and propelled the United Kingdom's vote to leave the European Union.

Merkel's problem was refugees. With the Syrian civil war ablaze in 2015, hundreds of thousands of desperate people took to the Med in waves of floundering rafts and ships. Victims of other conflicts—Afghans, Iraqis, and Eritreans—swelled their ranks. More than thirty-seven hundred people drowned. By July, fifteen hundred or more a day washed ashore on overwhelmed Greek islands.

EU law requires asylum seekers to file their cases in the country where they land. But most migrants wanted to press on to Germany, which had more jobs and a larger safety net. Tens of thousands marched through the western Balkans and into Hungary, determined to reach the German border. Humanitarian principle was at stake and so was the cause of open internal borders at the heart of the EU. "*Wir schaffen das*," Merkel said. *We can do it.*

Initially, the mood was euphoric. Germans crowded train stations and cheered as refugees rode in shouting "Merkel" and "Germany." But a million people arrived in 2015. It proved hard to distinguish victims of war from the economic migrants among them. Other EU states reneged on a plan to resettle 160,000 people. On New Year's Eve, scores of young men, mostly asylum seekers from North Africa, shocked the country with a rampage of sexual assault and robbery in Cologne.

Merkel's popularity plunged to 45 percent, from 75 percent a year earlier, and a far-right anti-immigrant party, Alternative for Germany, or AfD, dealt her a humiliating defeat in state elections in her home state. A few months later, in December 2016, a failed Tunisian asylum seeker drove a truck through a Berlin Christmas market and killed a dozen people.

Merkel never recovered from the refugee issue. Arrivals rapidly fell to pre-2015 levels, largely because she pushed through an EU deal—much criticized by human rights groups—that gave repressive Turkey billions to keep them away. She hung on to win a fourth term as chancellor in 2017, but the margin was thin, and AfD became the first far-right party in the Bundestag in six decades. As political support continued to erode, Merkel announced in late 2018 she was stepping down as party leader and would not seek reelection as chancellor at the end of her four-year term. *Wir schaffen das* did her in.

Migration was also the main issue in Britain's decision to leave the EU. By Europe's standards, its migration challenges were not especially pronounced. Its foreign born were more skilled than those elsewhere in Europe and paid significantly more in taxes than they collected in benefits. Far from the Mediterranean, Britain shouldered little of the refugee burden that fell on Germany, Italy, or Greece.

But unlike most of the EU, Britain did open its job market to citizens of the eight central and eastern European states that joined the EU in 2004. Prime Minister Tony Blair, a Labour Party supporter of enlargement, was eager to integrate the new states, and the job market was strong. But Britain attracted twenty times as many migrants as it expected, perhaps because so few other countries let them in. As the Polish plumber and Lithuanian nanny became stock figures in British life, strains registered in housing, health care, and schools. Resentments festered, especially outside London. By 2013, three-quarters of Britons said they wanted immigration reduced, and 56 percent wanted it reduced a lot.

David Cameron, a Tory, was elected prime minister in 2010 with a pledge to cut annual net immigration to the tens of thousands. It was a rash pledge, impossible to keep, especially within an EU framework of open internal movement. Within five years, the numbers surged to a record 330,000. Under pressure from some Tories and the far-right U.K. Independence Party—which he once called "a bunch of fruitcakes, loonies, and closet racists"—Cameron kept a promise to hold a referendum on leaving the EU. Migration wasn't the only issue, but it was the most salient, especially as the debate occurred in the wake of the German refugee crisis.

The campaign was ugly and tense. The Independence Party leader, Nigel Farage, framed his closing message with a poster of nonwhite refugees on the march (shot in distant Croatia) and the headline "Take Back Control of Our Borders." The day of its release, a mentally disturbed man shouted "Britain First" and murdered Jo Cox, a member of Parliament known for her support of refugees. Was the anti-immigrant rhetoric to blame? What the journalist Alex Massie wrote in *The Spectator* offers a warning beyond Britain:

> If you spend days, weeks, months, years telling people that they are under threat, that their country has been stolen from them, that they have been betrayed and sold down the river . . . that their problem is they're not sufficiently mad as hell, then at some point, in some place something or someone is going to snap.

Brexit passed with 52 percent of the vote. Cameron resigned, and Farage, leader of the "loonies," flew off to Mississippi to campaign with Trump.

TRUMP'S RISE, MERKEL'S FALL, BREXIT—is there a lesson for supporters of immigration? Perhaps several, starting with the recognition of its sheer explosive potential. "Potential" is a key word. There's nothing inevitable about a blowback. Ireland and Spain have lots of immigrants with little backlash; Hungary has few and backlash aplenty. While the issue is ripe for demagogues, their success is not guaranteed. Still, liberals have to take seriously the risk that migration can fuel illiberal politics.

One way to do that is to be wary of seeing the issue in absolutist terms. Immigration is generally good for America. But that doesn't mean it's good at every level and in all varieties. America's absorptive capacity is great but not unlimited, and not every migrant is as easily absorbed as Rosalie. There's a place for principled compromise. Legal status for the Dreamers is crucial; the diversity lottery is not. The framing of immigration as a civil rights issue has been a great help in promoting assimilation, but it's a problem if it encourages liberals to see every immigration issue as a matter of racial justice. There is no magic number of immigrants, just as there is no perfect mix of high-skilled, low-skilled, relatives, and refugees. What is essential is that America welcome those who are here and remain receptive to the gifts others can bring, whether they come with distinguished degrees or calloused hands.

Migration supporters also need to keep in mind that the issue is caught up in larger class and cultural divides, between the beneficiaries of globalization and those who feel themselves overlooked and left behind. Immigration's benefits don't flow exclusively to "elites," but they do flow disproportionately to them. Its supporters should be mindful of those who suffer the costs, whether in job competition or neighborhood change. And they should highlight the ways in which the benefits of immigration are shared: Rosalie's patients are largely poor and working-class people in decidedly non-cosmopolitan Galveston. The foreign-born share of the American population is the highest in more than a century; not everyone discomfited by the change is a bigot, though they may vote for one if they feel no one else is listening. The more the issue becomes part of the culture wars, like guns and abortion, the more supporters of migration have to lose.

The politics of immigration is in part a contest of narratives. While the empirical data is mostly positive, the story of one crime can over-whelm ten studies of low crime rates. Trump has been deft in framing his narrative: immigrants are predatory invaders. One counter-narrative is this: no one is more quintessentially American than a new American, and no country has grown stronger, richer, or more vibrant from wel-coming immigrants than the United States. The story of immigrant an-cestors is a story that Americans have always loved to tell. Someday Rosalie's descendants will tell it about her.

ROSALIE MADE HER HOUSE in Texas City a home. A reclining sofa the size of an aircraft carrier filled the living room, in front of a booming Texas-sized TV. On the freshly painted wall she stenciled a six-foot crucifix that proclaims Jesus the "Redeemer" and "King of Kings." She fashioned an altar to Mary and added a nurse's prayer for a "compas-sionate heart" that she passes in the hall as she leaves for work. She hasn't learned to drive, but the Filipino nurses nearby are generous with rides. She's been at the hospital for nearly seven years.

Among her housewarming gifts to herself was a $6,000 cookware set sold door-to-door by a Filipino salesman who said it would lower the risks of cancer. It was an indulgence, but it didn't go to waste because Chris dirties every pan for frequent house parties. A man of routines, he remains on the wastewater crew, but he did upend expectations on Mother's Day: he bought Rosalie roses.

It turned out Chris wasn't kidding when he talked of raising roosters in the backyard. He keeps them until they're old enough to crow, then takes them to Kuya Benjie's farm. The neighbors haven't complained, but the dachshunds slipped out one day and left a grisly tableau of poultry-cide.

The kids transferred to a new school district where Kristine, now in high school, is no longer a Girlie Girl or a Crazy Girl. Compared with her middle school self, she is much calmer—sufficiently comfortable that she is no longer looking for a label. She's the makeup artist for the theater group, which lets her feel part of something big and exciting without the worry of flubbing her lines. I got a text one day that said, matter-of-factly, "My current grades":

History: 91
Chemistry: 99
Geometry: 100
English: 100

Two texts quickly followed:

"Yes!"
"Yesssss!"

The new district put Lara in the fifth-grade gifted and talented class. She did fine but found the accelerated pace took the fun out of learning and switched out the following year. Between the move and the way the new district was organized, she wound up in four schools in four years, feeling as though she were always starting over. Her grades were solid, As and Bs, but she lost some of the excitement she felt in the Galveston elementary school. The start of eighth grade (without switching schools) brought new signs of spark. Dominique got into the middle school STEM program, where he is building robots and designing solar cars and making straight As. By the time he turned twelve, he had a red belt in karate, one level below black belt.

They are Filipino American, yes, but with the emphasis evermore on the latter.

ROSALIE WAITED FOUR YEARS before she returned to the Philippines. In the summer of 2016, Emet had a stroke, and Tita urged her children to come home. Rosalie flew in with Chris and the kids, and her brothers arrived from the Persian Gulf. It was the first time in memory that she and her siblings were all together. Emet survived, though greatly weakened, and a three-week reunion ensued. I joined them.

The kids and their cousins instantly meshed. Rosalie's children could no longer speak Tagalog (though they could understand it), and their English gave their relatives nosebleeds. But body language filled the gaps as they grinned, hugged, shadowboxed, and chased the other kids around. The compound had riches the cul-de-sac lacked: older cousins, younger cousins, fresh coconut and *guyabano*, a motorcycle, and a newborn baby—Tita's first great-grandchild. Kristine assumed duties as a proud god-mom. Rosalie, so protective in the States, let the girls take helmetless rides to buy fish balls and purple yam ice cream.

Tita, almost seventy, beamed. Her house was alive again with chaos and kids. *"Kain na, Kain na!"* she shouted half the day. *Come eat!* What could be happier than a family so large they had to visit the table in shifts? Tita tried not to condescend, but she felt bad for the world's non-Filipinos. "Happy family! Only in the Philippines!"

Four years earlier, she had worried her grandchildren would forget Tagalog. Now she just marveled instead at how well they spoke English, "the number one language in the world!" Dominique had such an American accent his request for a blanket stumped the whole room.

"What is 'blank it'?" said Peachy.

"I did not understand the 'blank it,'" Tita said.

"Blink-blink?" another relative tried.

"Electric fan?" Tita said.

"*Kumot,*" someone said. *Blanket!*

"Amazing, amazing changes," Tita said.

Tita noticed Rosalie was more comfortable as a mother and said Lara had changed the most. "When she left, she is very shy. And now, very talkative—smart, alert, confident." She leaned in as though sharing a confidence: "I like very much Lara." Kristine and Rowena had a happy reunion, sleeping together on pink sheets and Hello Kitty pillows beneath a mosquito net.

The pictures of Rosalie's house had sparked much speculation about her salary. Some of the family thought it could be as high as $50,000 a year, though such a sum was hard to imagine. When Tita finally asked, Rosalie said it was secret but promised to keep paying Emet's medical bills. Rosalie bought new curtains, though she already had a set in the States, and Tita tried not to find fault with the extravagance. "When I see their house, I said you have so many things, decorations. But I'm not against her, because she deserves to be happy. That was her dream. She worked hard and did not give up."

I CAUGHT UP WITH MANU, who was nearby in the Dream Hauz. His legal case had followed a winding path. After arbitration in the Philippines, his lawyer went back to the U.S. courts to argue the award was so low that it violated American public policy—a condition for invalidating arbitration awards. Since that argument formed a "case of first impression" (the first to reach the Eleventh Circuit Court of Appeals), the stakes were high. A victory could open the way for a flood of suits. Probably with an eye to eliminating that risk, Silversea offered a settlement, which Manu is not allowed to disclose. It didn't appear life altering. Ariane was still away, cleaning cabins at sea, and the socket on his prosthesis was cracked and digging into his flesh. He had patched it with duct tape.

Silversea was in the news. The U.S. Olympic men's basketball team was staying on one of its ships—a coup for the luxury brand. "I could have been there!" Manu said, more envious than angry. Later, a sale of a two-thirds stake in the firm netted the Monaco-based owner $1 billion.

Manu walked the kids to school and pointed out three seafarers' homes, one with a Norwegian Cruise Line towel drying on the line. As he feared, there weren't any jobs nearby for a man with one leg and no disability community to speak of. After a life of crowded ships and ports, he seemed lonely. He said he was trying to enjoy the time with the kids and looking for a business project, like building a storefront to rent. Since coming home, he'd gotten two more tattoos, each part of his search for peace. His shoulder quoted the Bible: "I can do all things through Christ." His wrist quoted the Beatles: "Let It Be."

TESS IS NO LONGER The Best Paid Nanny in Abu Dhabi. She's a receptionist at Vince Gordon's law firm, at two and a half times her nanny salary. As stories of Persian Gulf guest workers go, she's a staggering success. She misses the Gordon kids, but she feels as if she is growing again—wearing nice clothes and sitting in an office tower around lawyers and businessmen. She bought a parcel of land outside the family compound in the Philippines, hoping to build some apartments, and at forty-six she has gone back to school part time to get a business degree. "I believe you should never stop learning."

She's also no longer a Facebook Mom, at least not to her eldest child. Marielle moved to Abu Dhabi. She is working as a nurse and living in a small apartment with Tess, who gets up at four thirty to cook her breakfast and wash her uniforms. "I am a nanny again—nanny for a twenty-five-year-old woman!" Tess laughs. "After twenty years, I'm finally fulfilling my role as a mom." Noreene is finishing college in the Philippines, and with her mother and sister in the Emirates it's easy to guess where she hopes to go next. For Christmas, Tess brought her parents to

Abu Dhabi, and their three-week visit filled her with a special pride. "That was always part of my dream, to take my mom and dad to another part of the world. It's not too late to reach your dreams."

WHEN I FIRST VISITED the compound three decades ago, it was mostly still a farm rather than a collection of remittance-built homes; it felt remote and time-bound, frozen in a previous century. But now a globalizing world was encroaching. A Taiwanese firm was raising chickens on one flank. A Korean church was buying up land on another, to house Koreans coming to study English. A couple of Tita's siblings still farmed in the back, but the old life was dying. At sixty, her brother Fering took me to his muddy plot, hacked open two coconuts for us to drink, then showed me how to choose the best sow to inseminate. (Fat feet.) But his son is a chemical engineer in Abu Dhabi; he has no interest in pregnant pigs.

Perhaps no one in his generation does. Immigrants a century ago revisited their villages and rued the backwardness, but the worlds of the compound and the cul-de-sac are converging, at least culturally. Rosalie's brother had gotten Emet a new cable package, with American sports, so Tita's shouts of "Come eat!" competed with the latest news on Colin Kaepernick. When the kids and their cousins went to the mall, they watched *The Secret Life of Pets* and ate at Pizza Hut. Just as they would have in Texas.

Rosalie took advantage of the time in the Philippines to schedule the kids' First Communion. Dinner at a restaurant followed, with a table for twenty-four. Tita held Emet's hand, and Rosalie's blessing of the meal clocked in at eleven minutes as she prayed for Emet's health and thanked God for bringing together five siblings from four countries. After dinner, she sat down beside me and choked up. "It's a miracle," she said. I thought she meant the reunion, but she was talking about something even bigger—the whole improbable arc of her life. "I was able to finish my studies, to help my family members, to have a good job. . . . Now everything is complete. . . . It's more than happiness. It's joy."

It dawned on me that there was a reason she had waited so long to go back, a reason beyond vacation time and money. She had waited until everything was "complete"—until she had recaptured her children, strengthened her marriage, built her home, and anchored her career. Then she went back whole, fulfilled. She nodded. "Part of me wanted to focus on our life in the U.S.—settling us there first." She just hadn't imagined she would succeed so well.

Twenty-four hours later it was time to leave. Emet sat in a wheelchair, his face streaked with tears. The stroke had reduced his speech to a whisper. Rosalie leaned in and held his shaking hand.

"Maybe I won't see you again," he said.

"We will meet again," Rosalie reassured him. "God is good. Just be sure you pray."

"Too much time apart," he said.

"Don't cry," she said. "It will make me sad." Then she cried a little herself. She promised to send money. She promised to return. "I worry about you."

It took half a dozen false starts and repeated farewells to load everyone into the car, which rumbled out of the compound at midnight for an early flight. While Rosalie was trying not to admit it to herself, there was a good chance that Emet was right: they might not see each other again. I thought she was in for a mournful ride after a wrenching goodbye. But the kids were giggling, and her voice brightened.

"I feel like I'm going to my home," she said. "The U.S. is my home."

ACKNOWLEDGMENTS

When Filipinos want to express deep appreciation, they say they have an *utang na loob*—a debt of gratitude. After three decades of reporting this story, my *utangs* are many. They start with my debt to Tita and Emet Comodas for offering me a place in their home and a treasured friendship. I've valued it more than I know how to say, in English or Tagalog. No one is more central to this book than their daughter Rosalie; at its heart is her remarkable journey from a Manila shantytown to a Houston suburb. For her honesty in sharing it with me, and her courage in letting me share it with others, she has my gratitude and respect. My *utangs* extend to Chris Villanueva for years of gracious welcomes and kind assistance; to Kristine, Precious Lara, and Dominique Villanueva for so enthusiastically making me part of their Galveston lives and letting me see America through their eyes; and to Tess Aliscad, Manu Navarette, and Ariane Salazar-Navarette—three brave and incisive observers of the migrant experience. Every reporter who sets off across the borders of class and culture should find such kind, candid, and wise guides.

The idea for this book began at *The New York Times*, where I've had the good luck to spend most of my career. In late 2006, *The New York Times Magazine* sent me to the Philippines to write about Tita, Emet, Rosalie, and the culture of migration. Gerry Marzorati and Alex Star skillfully guided the article, which appeared in 2007, and gave it the title: "A Good Provider Is One Who Leaves." Bill Keller, then the executive editor, let me pursue my interest in global migration, and Rebecca Corbett and Dean Baquet expertly edited my stories. Dean, now executive editor, generously granted a book leave (and even more generously extended it), and Elisabeth Bumiller and Bill Hamilton were supportive beyond the cause in letting me finish. I am grateful as well to Arthur Ochs Sulzberger Jr. and A. G. Sulzberger for their devotion to *The New York Times*. In an age of news retrenchment, I am fortunate to work in a newsroom of such talent and ambition.

My work wouldn't have been possible without generous and patient philanthropic support. I was especially fortunate to have been an Emerson Fellow at New America's Fellows Program, an essential haven for journalists seeking to write books. At New America, I enjoyed the help of Steve Coll, Anne-Marie Slaughter, Andrés Martinez, Peter Bergen, Becky Schafer, and Awista Ayub. Most of my New America fellowship was underwritten by the Emerson Collective, which offered much and demanded nothing. For their extraordinary patience and generosity, I thank Laurene Powell Jobs, Anne Marie Burgoyne, and Amy Low.

I first went to the Philippines in 1986 on a fellowship from the Henry Luce Foundation. Helene Redell, Tom and Kris Stoever, and Abby Young enhanced the unique opportunity I enjoyed as a Luce Scholar. Three health care foundations with an interest in nursing provided grants for the book, which allowed me time with Rosalie on the ward. My thanks go to Drew Altman at the Henry J. Kaiser Family Foundation, Robin Hogen and Susan Hassmiller at the Robert Wood Johnson Foundation, and Peter Long at Blue Shield of California Foundation. At the Smith Richardson Foundation, Mark Steinmeyer was an early and generous supporter. (Drew Altman and Mark Steinmeyer also supported my previous book, *American Dream*; with them, I have double *utangs*.) At The Pew Charitable Trusts, I appreciate the support of Rebecca Rimel, Sonia Chessen, Susan Urahn, and Melissa Skolfield. I also benefited from the help of the Russell Sage Foundation, which has a longstanding commitment to immigration research and contributed both financial and intellectual support. My thanks to Sheldon Danziger, Eric Wanner, Aixa Cintrón-Veléz, David Haproff, and Suzanne Nichols. For help with fundraising, I am grateful to Phil

Bennett, Gregg Easterbrook, James Fallows, David Johnson, and Donna Shalala.

Among the *utangs* I cannot repay are those to a group of friends and scholars who repeatedly took time from their demanding lives to offer encouragement and ideas. Ann Hulbert has been an especially steadfast friend. Her letter of support helped me get to Manila three decades ago, and her gifts as sounding board guided the reporting toward its narrative logic. To Philip Kasinitz of the City University of New York, I am grateful both for the breadth of his knowledge and his willingness to share it over many hours of patient tutelage. Charlie Peters published my first story on Leveriza in *The Washington Monthly* in 1987 and encouraged me to return and pursue the migration theme—I owe him on both accounts. Mark Greenberg was an abiding source of encouragement, insight, and smart questions. Others especially helpful as I took an interest in migration include Jeanne Batalova, Nancy Foner, Susan Martin, Mark Miller, Michelle Mittelstadt, Kathleen Newland, Dilip Ratha, and Dan Tichenor.

Every writer needs early readers, especially candid ones. James Gibney, Mark Greenberg, Ann Hulbert, Noah Lanard, Susan Martin, Charlie Peters, and Mary Waters all read full drafts; Patricia Pittman, Julia Preston, Doug Stevenson, and Dan Tichenor generously reviewed individual chapters. Their frank feedback saved me from many errors. I also enjoyed the help of some gifted research assistants, none more so than Valerie Cardenas Diment, who traveled with me to the Philippines and Texas, juggled Tagalog and English with nary a nosebleed, and took great notes. Lory Hough sleuthed out articles and books, as she did on *American Dream*; Raine Bunag transcribed Tagalog tapes with care, enthusiasm, and speed; and Dan Spinelli was a meticulous fact-checker. For research and translation, I also appreciate the help of Kitty Bennett, Vanessa Cardenas, Claire Cororaton, Janess Ellao, and Jon Melegrito. For computer support, I owe Ron Skarzenski. Several friends coaxed the project along with their insight and encouragement: I am grateful to Henry Brinton, Tim Golden, Stuart Jones, and the late Jack Rosenthal. No list of my editorial debts is complete without a special word of thanks to Jane Isay, who signed on as a freelance editor and helped me find the story lines. She was a light when I wasn't yet at the end of the tunnel.

The size of Filipino clans offers new meaning to the phrase "extended family," and the Portaganas are extended indeed. Their hospitality has enriched my visits and my understanding of migration. I owe a special thanks to Rosalie's siblings: Rolando, Rowena, Roldan, and Bhoyet Comodas. I am also grateful to Fortz Portagana, Sheryl Portagana, Sheralyn Portagana, Fering Portagana, Cora Portagana, Jackson Portagana, Gloria Aliscad, Nonong Aliscad, Michael Aliscad, Belinda Aliscad, Myra Merto, Rodel Merto, Marielle Reyes, Noreene Reyes, the late Bandoy Portagana, Aurora Portagana, Peachy Salazar, Weny Salazar, Ivy Salazar, John Forrell Salazar, Pablito Portagana, Enyang Aviles, Chang Idhay Alcantara, Jonvic Alcantara, Marie Comodas, Danilo Malicdan, Merly Sepulveda, and Brigida Comodas Osorio. On Chris's side of the family, my thanks to Zenia Villanueva, Nanette Villanueva, the late Amorfina Oca Rebong, Pinky Trinidad, Vince Trinidad, Prospero Gonzales, and Glenda Gonzales.

For facilitating my stay in Leveriza, I appreciate the help of the late Sister Christine Tan. Among those who offered their hospitality there are Pen Apostol, Manny Apostol, Jovita Arevalo, Fely Balce, Benjie Barbosa, Beng Co, Baby Delgado, Mutya Diangson, the late Viring Diangson, Fe Espellegar, Conchita Fenequito, Rosita Herediano, Baby Herediano, Rosita Jaranilla, Imelda Nineda, Nilda Nineda, Butch Santos, and the late Angeles Serrano. For his spirited visit, I am grateful to E. J. Flynn. In researching Leveriza and Manila slum life, I received guidance from Lito Atienza, Rose Nartates, and Mary Racelis.

My understanding of the Philippine migration program was enhanced by conversations with the people who helped run it. Among them were five labor secretaries: Rosalinda Baldoz, Arturo Brion, Nieves Confessor, Marianito Roque, and Patricia Sto. Tomas. Other current or former officials of the Department of Labor and Employment to whom I owe thanks include Venus Abad, Carlos Cao Jr., Hans Cacdac, Libby Casco, Cynthia Cruz, Carmelita Dimzon, Nicon Fameronag, Rene Ofreneo, Minda Padilla, Reynaldo Parungao, Jo Sanchez, the late Roy Señeres, Emma Sinclair, Teng Torres, Ma. Celeste M. Valderrama, Benito Valeriano, Willy Villarama, and Lites Viloria. Outside the department, I appreciate the help of Rica Arevalo, Marla Asis, Walden Bello, Ditsi Carolino, Carlos Conde, Kara David, Roberto Delgado,

William Gois, Doris Magsaysay Ho, Carmelita Nuqui, Jeremiah Opiniano, Susan Ople, Manny Palo, Steve Peregino, Rory Quintos, Patricia Riingen, Ellene Sana, Ching Uranza, Manny Villar, and Baby Ruth Villarama.

In Abu Dhabi, Vince Gordon and Christina Aboyoun, Tess's employers, extended a warm welcome, as did Grace Princesa, the Philippine ambassador. My thanks there as well to Dante Bolisay, Adelio Cruz, Hassan Fattah, Mylene Gonzales, Zuriel Gonzales, and Alejandro Pabiano.

In Galveston, I benefited greatly from being able to accompany Rosalie to work and the kids to school. The University of Texas Medical Branch and the Galveston Independent School District have my gratitude. At UTMB, David Marshall and Chelita Thomas generously offered me a close-up view of nursing. The other nurses on Rosalie's shift—Rosario Mendoza, Lori Nepomuceno, and Veronica Serona—made me part of the overnight crew. At Oppe Elementary School, principal Helena Aucoin opened her doors, and teachers Courtney Hailey, Karen Jobe, and Margaretanne Morgan shared their classrooms and insights. At Scott Collegiate Academy, principal Debra Owens was equally accommodating, as were teachers Ashley Conner, Melody Fabian, Cory Mallory, John Matthews, Georgia Sherrod, and Susan Voigt. Other school officials who offered their help include Johnston Farrow, Gabriel Flores, Jeff Liwag, Karen Liwag, and Selah Tacconi.

Many people in Galveston took time to talk, often at length. While not all appear by name in the text, their insights deepened my understanding of local life for natives and immigrants alike. They include Eli Abad, Agnes Allego, James Allego, Judy Austaisuain, Joni Bareo, Jacinto Belen, Daphne Belen, Yasmin Bulagas, Ray Burdeos, Rene Capulong, Sabrina Capulong, Sam Capulong, Steve Christmas, Rose Cinco, Ruby Dayasan, Kim Garcia, Marilen Garcia, Mike Garza, Betty Gounah, Meredith Herzog, Dionne Hickling, Alicia Kaba, Sheldon Lawrence, Becky Major, Ruth Ann Marr, Ivy Martinez, Duane Mendoza, Irene Mendoza, Kevin Mendoza, Delia Mercado, Ben Mopia, Kevin Moran, Jennifer Nelson, Mike Nepomuceno, Miles Nepomuceno, Victoria Nepomuceno, Estrella Orfilla, Teddy Paz, Arlene Rayos, Gary Rayos, Raul Reyes, Jun Rivera, Frank Ross, Rosalie Run, Benjie Sagullo, Mercy Santos, Larry Santos, Bong Serona, Heber Taylor, Michelle Times, Donna Torres, and Vivencio Villano.

To write about a nurse I tried to learn about nursing. Patricia Pittman was an especially helpful guide to the field. I am grateful as well to James Buchan, Peter Buerhaus, Sinead Carberry, Catherine Davis, Julie Fairman, Philip Kelly, Michele Kilkenny, Shannon Lederer, Bruce Morrison, Joe O'Grady, Lusine Poghosyan, Susan Reverby, Marla Salmon, Franklin Shaffer, Joanne Spetz, Barbra Mann Wall, and Margaret Walton-Roberts. For background on seafarers, I drew on help from Richard Dodson, Ross Klein, Ralph Mellusi, Matthew Nickson, Karen Parsons, Doug Stevenson, William Terry, David Villarreal, and Michael Winkleman. For help in Miami, my thanks go to Rick Boxer, Stephen Dsida, Caroline Galindo, Cathy Herring, Edward Lineen, Joel Lleto, Manny Offen, and Gayle Steiner. As president of the University of Miami, a partner with Jackson Memorial Hospital, Donna Shalala (now a member of Congress) went out of her way to help Manu.

Others who generously shared their time and insights include Manolo Abella, Michael Abramowitz, Richard Alba, Dovelyn Agunias, Joaquín Arango, Pallavi Banerjee, Natalia Banulescu-Bogdan, Roy Beck, David Blight, Caroline Brettell, Rebecca Callahan, Kurt Campbell, Randy Capps, Kevin Carey, Jørgen Carling, Joseph Chamie, Michael Clemens, Patricia Cortes, Ian Coxhead, Reid Cramer, Maurice Crul, Katharine Donato, Gretchen Donehower, Paul Donnelly, Joanna Dreby, Dorothy Duncan, Greg Duncan, Peter Eisner, Paula Fass, Michael Fix, Gary Freeman, Patricia Gándara, Herbert Gans, Sheba George, David Gerber, Terri Givens, Carl Haub, Robert Hauser, Hal Hill, Jim Hollifield, Sarah Hooker, Bela Hovy, Paul Hutchcroft, Tamar Jacoby, Michael Jones-Correa, Kirin Kalia, Lori Kaplan, Lawrence Katz, Mickey Kaus, Peter Kivisto, Stephen Klineberg, Rey Koslowski, Mark Krikorian, Aprodicio Laquian, Michael Lind, Vivian Louie, Mirca Madianou, Froilan Malit, Gregory Maniatis, Phil Martin, Douglas Massey, Adam McKeown, Cecilia Menjívar, Anthony Messina, Joel Millman, Jeffrey Mirel, Cecelia Muñoz, Richard Murnane, Victor Nee, Manuel Orozco, Çağlar Özden, Demetri Papademetriou, Rhacel Parreñas, Alejandro Portes, Lant Pritchett, Steven Raphael, David Reimers, Neil Ruiz, Rubén Rumbaut, Martin Schain, Maurice Schiff, Amy Ellen Schwartz, Eric Schwartz, Frank Sharry, Michael Shear, Audrey Singer, Ron Skeldon, Sandra Susan Smith, Will Somerville, Barbara Span, Sara Staedicke, Carola Suárez-Orozco, Don Terry, Aaron

Terrazas, James Traub, Nisha Varia, Roger Waldinger, Sarah Leah Whitson, Jeffrey Williamson, Jamie Winders, Minky Worden, Dean Yang, Hania Zlotnik, and the late Ari Zolberg.

This is the second book I've done with Wendy Wolf, my editor at Viking, and I relied on her even more heavily than I did for the first. A narrative that tracks three generations across multiple countries needs an air traffic controller. Wendy saw the flight paths and landed the planes. For her patience, focus, and judgment, she has my deep thanks. Her assistant, Terezia Cicel, read an early draft and offered insightful comments, especially regarding the experiences of Kristine and Lara. Ingrid Sterner, my copy editor, and Gabriel Levinson, the production editor, expertly made a manuscript a book. Others at Viking to whom I owe debts include Maya Baran, Meighan Cavanaugh, Clare Ferraro, Linda Friedner, Brooke Halsted, Julia Rickard, Andrea Schulz, Brian Tart, Matthew Varga, and Jessica White. My agent, Chuck Verrill, and his partner Liz Darhansoff, were quick to help when needed.

Book writing is solitary work but also a family affair and sometimes a family intrusion. More perhaps than my family knows, I drew on their support. My mother, Joan DeParle, traveled with me to Galveston to visit the Villanuevas and took a special interest in Rosalie's story (perhaps because she, too, was an unsung working woman). She died before the book reached print, but her interest and encouragement helped sustain me. My sons, Nicholas and Zachary, were middle schoolers when the project began. They grew up not entirely sure about what their father was doing or why it took so long. Now that one is in college, and the other will be soon, I only hope they find work that brings them as much gratification. The last time I thanked my wife, Nancy-Ann, for enduring the tribulations of being a book writer's spouse, I kept it simple, noting only that she was the best thing that had ever happened to me. She still is.

A NOTE ON SOURCES
AND METHODS

This is a work of journalism, but with a gestation period that journalism rarely affords. When I met Tita Comodas in 1987, neither of us imagined I'd be taking notes on her children and grandchildren three decades later. Some of my reporting over the years has taken the form of standard interviews, but my perspective has been greatly enriched by the long periods of free time I've had with the extended family. We've washed dishes, watched movies, gone to church, gone swimming, shopped for groceries, played UNO, clicked selfies, and toured rooster farms from Southeast Asia to East Texas. Many of the events described in the book are those I witnessed firsthand. Where I have reconstructed scenes, I have checked them multiple times and, where possible, confirmed them with multiple sources or contemporaneous evidence. I drew on the subjects' memories but also on their records: Rosalie and her family shared letters, diaries, passports, bank statements, tax returns, text messages, report cards, and other private materials. Tess and Marielle generously shared their mother-daughter Facebook chats. Most of our conversations have occurred in English, but I have sometimes used Tagalog interpreters to add nuance and detail.

I met Tita in January 1987 and lived with her family, off and on, until September. We kept in touch, but we didn't see each other again until 2006, when I returned on assignment for *The New York Times Magazine*. Periodic visits followed with Tita and Emet in the Philippines and with Rosalie and Chris in Abu Dhabi. I had just committed to write the book in 2012 when Rosalie got the job in Texas, and its focus shifted from guest work in the Persian Gulf to assimilation in the States. I spent three years following Rosalie, Chris, and the kids, through near-daily calls and frequent visits. After Manu was injured in January 2014, I visited him often in Miami. Rosalie's bosses generously allowed me to follow her on her shifts, and the kids' teachers offered me a classroom perch. In Galveston, I stayed with the Villanuevas and joined in family life. This is immersion journalism; I immersed.

Our relationship defies easy categorization; it's part author-subject, part old friends. I am *kuya* (big brother) to Rosalie and Chris (and Tess and Manu) and *tito* (uncle) to the kids. At times my presence shaped events, but I don't think it altered them greatly. While I helped Rosalie from time to time, the determination that propelled her from the slums to the States is hers alone.

This is not a book about one family. Their experiences across three generations can only be understood as part of a broader epoch of migration that is transforming much of the world. I have been fortunate to have intermittently covered that story for *The New York Times*. My reporting on the government's migration program drew on interviews with dozens of officials as well as visits to the library of the Department of Labor and Employment in Manila, where a haphazard collection of old memos and reports awaits its archivist. (*Philippine Labor*, the department's newspaper, is another helpful source.) Beyond the Philippines, I reported on migration from ten other countries, both rich (Canada, Spain) and poor (Haiti, Bangladesh). Those stories were not about the main characters in this book—but in a sense they were.

Reporting on migrants across four continents helped me better understand Rosalie.

Immigration has inspired a vast literature. I've drawn on history, social science, journalism, fiction, and film and benefited from running conversations with a number of migration scholars. There isn't nearly enough space to list the works that have enriched my understanding, but a few have gotten especially dog-eared. For an analysis of contemporary immigration in the States, two volumes from the National Academy of Sciences stand out—*The Integration of Immigrants into American Society* (edited by Mary C. Waters and Marisa Gerstein Pineau) and *The Economic and Fiscal Consequences of Immigration* (edited by Francine D. Blau and Christopher Mackie). For a historical perspective on American immigration politics, Daniel J. Tichenor's *Dividing Lines* is incisive and detailed. Two works are especially helpful in thinking about the children of immigrants: *Legacies*, by Alejandro Portes and Rubén G. Rumbaut, and *Inheriting the City*, by Philip Kasinitz, John H. Mollenkopf, Mary C. Waters, and Jennifer Holdaway. For calls to reduce immigration, see works by Roy Beck and Mark Krikorian titled, respectively, *The Case Against Immigration* and *The New Case Against Immigration*. Few migration trends, in the United States or abroad, escape the notice of the Migration Policy Institute, whose website is a data trove.

As a work of nonfiction, the book relies on real people in real places. I have not created composite characters or altered scenes. To protect medical privacy, I use pseudonyms for Rosalie's patients in the hospital, though nothing about their conditions or comments has been changed. (Jeanette Dotson, the former patient who approached Rosalie in the grocery store, is not a pseudonym.) Likewise, to protect the privacy of Kristine's and Lara's classmates, I did not use their actual names in my passing references to them. No other names have been altered.

With growing polarization comes sharp dispute over what to call migrants who lack legal status. Illegal? Undocumented? Unauthorized? Supporters of immigration hear "illegal" as pejorative; opponents hear the alternatives as euphemistic. Even *The New York Times* stylebook seems flummoxed; it advises reporters to avoid "taking sides." Lacking a neutral alternative, I've varied my usage in the hopes of keeping the attention on people rather than nomenclature. Too often in debates about immigration, the immigrants get lost.

NOTES

Abbreviations
HC: *Houston Chronicle*
IOM: International Organization for Migration
MPI: Migration Policy Institute
MPI-DH: Migration Policy Institute Data Hub
NYT: *New York Times*
LAT: *Los Angeles Times*
PL: *Philippine Labor*
UN: United Nations
POEA: Philippine Overseas Employment Administration
WP: *Washington Post*

PROLOGUE: FINDING JESUS IN THE SLUMS

1 **"I hate their deceitfulness":** Sister Christine Tan, interview by Charles Krause, *Mac-Neil/Lehrer NewsHour*, PBS, Sept. 16, 1985.
2 **Sunk into a mudflat near Manila Bay:** For conditions in Leveriza, it is useful to consult three World Bank reports about the Third Urban Redevelopment Project, a slum renewal effort of which Leveriza was a part. See "Philippines Third Urban Development Project, Staff Appraisal Report," Report No. 2703a-PH, WB, Feb. 26, 1980; "Report and Recommendation of the President of the International Bank for Reconstruction and Redevelopment to the Executive Directors on a Proposed Loan to the Republic of the Philippines for a Third Urban Development Project," Report No. P-2734-PH, WB, March 5, 1980; "Project Completion Report, Philippines, Third Urban Development Project (Loan 1821-PH)," Report 7897, WB, June 30, 1989. The Philippine National Housing Authority also prepared reports on the project, including "Leveriza Develop-

ment Program: First Technical Report, June 1981–June 1982," National Housing Authority, Manila. For an academic study of Leveriza conditions, see Jaime C. Laya, Remedios C. Balbin, and Romulo N. Neri, "An Economic Survey of a Manila Squatter Community, Agno-Leveriza Area, 1970," *Philippine Economic Journal* 12, no. 23 (1973). In addition, I wrote an account after my stay there in 1987. Jason DeParle, *Washington Monthly*, Dec. 1987, 32.

5 **next four countries combined:** The next four are Saudi Arabia (12.2 million), Germany (12.2 million), Russia (11.6 million), and the United Kingdom (8.8 million). UN Population Division, UN Migrant Stock, 2017 Revision.

5 **Nearly 90 percent come from:** In 2016, 53 percent of the immigrant population was from the Americas, 31 percent was Asian, 11 percent was European, and 5 percent was African. "Regions of Birth for Immigrants in the United States, 1960–Present," MPI-DH.

5 **Non-Hispanic whites, 83 percent:** Mary C. Waters and Marisa Gerstein Pineau, eds., *The Integration of Immigrants into American Society* (Washington, DC: National Academies Press, 2015), 27.

5 **about a quarter, who are here illegally:** Jeffrey S. Passel and D'Vera Cohn, "U.S. Unauthorized Immigrant Total Dips to Lowest Level in a Decade," Pew Research Center, Nov. 27, 2018. They estimate that in 2016 there were 10.7 million unauthorized migrants out of a foreign-born population of 45.1 million—23.7 percent. MPI-DH cites 11.3 million unauthorized, out of 43.7 million immigrants, or 25.9 percent.

5 **With one in four children:** "Children in U.S. Immigrant Families," MPI-DH. The figure for 2017 was 26 percent.

5 **Immigrants brought a hundred languages:** The website for the Des Moines Public Schools, English Language Learners page.

5 **the foreign-born population of Greater Atlanta:** The number of immigrants in Greater Atlanta grew from 47,800 in 1980 to 613,000 in 2005. Audrey Singer, Susan W. Hardwick, and Caroline Brettell, eds., *Twenty-first Century Gateways: Immigrant Incorporation in Suburban America* (Washington, DC: Brookings Institution Press, 2008), 26.

6 **About 258 million migrants are scattered:** UN, *International Migrant Stock: The 2017 Revision*, UN Population Division, New York, Dec. 2017.

6 **grown nearly 50 percent:** UN, *International Migrant Stock: The 2017 Revision*.

6 **Ireland elected its first African-born mayor:** Jason DeParle, NYT, Feb. 25, 2008.

6 **"I went to bed in one country":** Roddy Doyle, *The Deportees, and Other Stories* (New York: Viking, 2008), xi.

6 **A few decades ago, migration:** Martin A. Schain, "The Comparative Politics of Immigration," *Comparative Politics* 44, no. 4 (July 2012): 481–97.

6 **Mexico earns more from remittances:** Holly K. Sonneland, "Weekly Chart: Oil and Remittances in Mexico's GDP," Americas Society/Council of the Americas, Aug. 30, 2017, www.as-coa.org/articles/weekly-chart-oil-and-remittances-mexicos-gdp.

6 **Sri Lanka earns more from remittances:** Peter Reeves, ed., *Encyclopedia of the Sri Lankan Diaspora* (Singapore: Didier Millet, 2013), 99.

6 **About $477 billion a year:** Remittances to the developing world rose from $75 billion in 2000 to $477 billion in 2017 (more than three times as much as the $155 billion distributed in 2017 in foreign aid). Author communication with Dilip Ratha, WB.

7 his counterpart today: Lant Pritchett, *Let Their People Come: Breaking the Gridlock on Labor Mobility* (Washington, DC: Center for Global Development, 2006), 19.

7 More than two million Filipinos depart: The Philippine government reported 2.6 million departures in 2016. Website of the POEA, "OFW Statistics."

7 one Filipino worker in seven: Jason DeParle, *NYT Magazine*, April 22, 2007.

7 the $32 billion that Filipinos send home: Website of the WB, "Migration and Remittances Data."

7 10 percent of the GDP: WB, "Personal Remittances, Received (% of GDP)," data .worldbank.org/indicator/BX.TRF.PWKR.DT.GD.ZS.

8 "Remittances Seen to Set New Record": DeParle, *NYT Magazine*, April 22, 2007.

9 cut refugee admissions: "U.S. Annual Refugee Resettlement Ceilings and Number of Refugees Admitted, 1980–Present," MPI-DH.

10 erased the words "Nation of Immigrants": Miriam Jordan, *NYT*, Feb. 23, 2018.

10 more Asians: Waters and Pineau, *Integration of Immigrants into American Society*, 24.

CHAPTER ONE: MASSES, HUDDLED

14 nearly fifty million Europeans crossed: Douglas S. Massey et al., *Worlds in Motion: Understanding International Migration at the End of the Millennium* (Oxford: Clarendon, 2008), 1.

14 In the decade after World War II: From 1946 to 1955, annual admissions averaged 195,000 a year, compared to 1.01 million per year from 1905 to 1914. "Legal Immigration to the United States, 1820–Present," MPI-DH.

14 "He is economically little more than a serf": Michael P. McIntyre, "Leyte and Samar: A Geographical Analysis of the Rural Economies of the Eastern Visayans" (PhD thesis, Ohio State University, 1951), 181.

15 "the Pearl of the Orient": Richard Connaughton, John Pimlott, and Duncan Anderson, *The Battle for Manila* (Novato, Calif.: Presidio Press, 1995), 16.

15 Japanese occupation: Citing the "promiscuous cruelty" of the Japanese soldiers, Stanley Karnow writes, "They increasingly beheaded innocent victims and displayed their bodies as an example." Stanley Karnow, *In Our Image: America's Empire in the Philippines* (New York: Random House, 1989), 309.

15 A hundred thousand Filipinos died: Connaughton, Pimlott, and Anderson, *Battle for Manila*, 15.

15 Japanese soldiers massacred scores of civilians: Connaughton, Pimlott, and Anderson, *Battle for Manila*, 130, 144, 151. Footage of the stadium battle can be found on YouTube: www.youtube.com/watch?v=4wmGMbJ8yVw.

15 "The living conditions are extremely bad": Laya, Balbin, and Neri, "Economic Survey of a Manila Squatter Community, Agno-Leveriza Area, 1970."

16 the Philippines's future seemed bright: Arsenio M. Balisacan and Hal Hill, eds., *The Philippine Economy: Development, Policies, and Challenges* (Oxford: Oxford University Press, 2003), 3. See also Paul D. Hutchcroft, *Booty Capitalism: The Politics of Banking in the Philippines* (Ithaca, N.Y.: Cornell University Press, 1998).

18 It tripled and quadrupled: UN, *World Population Prospects: Key Findings & Advance Tables: The 2015 Revision* (New York: UN, 2015), 18. Bangladesh grew from 37 million in 1950 to 160 million in 2015; Mexico, from 28 million to 127 million. See also

John Bongaarts, "Human Population Growth and Demographic Transition," *Philosophical Transactions of the Royal Society* 364, no. 1352 (2009): 2985–90.

18 **It was demography that propelled:** Stephen Castles, Hein de Haas, and Mark J. Miller, *The Age of Migration: International Population Movements in the Modern World,* 5th ed. (New York: Guilford Press, 2014).

19 **tens of millions of migrants:** Douglas Massey estimates that forty-eight million people left Europe from 1846 to 1924, approximately 12 percent of the continent's population in 1900. British emigration equaled 41 percent of its 1900 population. About 60 percent of the European migrants went to the United States. Douglas S. Massey, "Economic Development and International Migration in Comparative Perspective," *Population and Development Review* 14, no. 3 (1988): 385–86.

19 **life expectancy in low-income countries:** UN, *World Population Prospects: The 2010 Revision,* vol. 1, *Comprehensive Tables* (New York: UN, 2010), 324.

19 **roughly a dozen years each:** UN, *The World at Six Billion* (New York: UN, 1999), 5.

19 **Philippines grew especially fast:** The population of the Philippines rose from 19 million in 1950 to 101 million in 2015. UN, *World Population Prospects 2015.*

19 **urban population of the developing world:** Ronald Skeldon, "Interlinkages Between Internal and International Migration and Development in the Asian Region," *Population, Space, and Place* 12, no. 1 (2006): 16.

19 **a megacity of nearly twelve million:** UN Population Division, World Urbanization Prospects, 2018 Revision, File 15. Metro Manila grew from 1.5 million in 1950 to 11.9 million in 2010.

19 **Tagalog developed multiple words:** UN, *The Challenge of Slums: Global Report on Human Settlements* (New York: UN, 2003), 10.

19 **about a third of Manila's residents:** The UN report *Survey of Slums and Squatter Settlements* (Dublin: Tycooly International, 1982), 25, found 35 percent of Manila lived in slums or squatter zones and said the two were hard to distinguish. WB, "Philippines Third Urban Development Project, Staff Appraisal Report," 2, says more than 30 percent "live in squatter or slum settlements without secure tenure and lacking safe water supply, drainage, human waste disposal, and clean access."

20 **cholera:** M. C. Lim-Quizon et al., "Cholera in Metropolitan Manila: Foodborne Transmission via Street Vendors," *Bulletin of the World Health Organization* 72, no. 5 (1994): 745–49.

20 **Malnutrition was prevalent:** WB, "Philippines Third Urban Development Project, Staff Appraisal Report," 1; DeParle, *Washington Monthly,* Dec. 1987, 34.

20 **Leveriza was nearly 40 percent more dense:** Tondo had a density of 1,240 people per hectare (UN, *Survey of Slums and Squatter Settlements,* 66). Leveriza's density was more than 1,700 people per hectare (WB, "Philippines Third Urban Development Project, Staff Appraisal Report," 7).

20 **about 40 percent of Metro Manila residents:** WB, "Philippines Third Urban Development Project, Staff Appraisal Report," 6.

21 **Wrecking crews descended:** Aprodicio A. Laquian, *The City in Nation Building: Politics and Administration in Metropolitan Manila* (Manila: School of Public Administration, University of the Philippines, 1966), 151–69.

22 **remains a minor classic:** F. Landa Jocano, *Slum as a Way of Life: A Study of Coping Behavior in an Urban Environment* (Quezon City, Philippines: New Day, 1975).

22 **Hong Kong, Singapore, Taiwan, and Korea:** Balisacan and Hill, *Philippine Economy,* 4.

22 Thailand: Balisacan and Hill, *Philippine Economy*, 4.

22 They bought banks, factories, utilities: Hutchcroft, *Booty Capitalism*.

22 inequality *grew*: Reporting in 1974, an international team of economists led by Gustav Yanis of Yale found that "the distribution of income in the Philippines, which was already highly unequal, has become increasingly so during the last two decades." In rural areas, the share of income going to the poorest fifth of families fell from 7 percent to 4.4 percent. International Labour Office, "Sharing in Development: A Programme of Employment, Equity, and Growth for the Philippines" (Geneva: International Labour Office, 1974), 9–10.

23 in exchange for economic favors: Benedict Anderson, "Cacique Democracy in the Philippines: Origins and Dreams," *New Left Review* 169 (May–June 1988).

23 The Election Day death count: Mark R. Thompson, *The Anti-Marcos Struggle: Personalistic Rule and Democratic Transition in the Philippines* (New Haven, Conn.: Yale University Press, 1995), 42.

23 "cruised around town in a bulletproof limousine": Karnow, *In Our Image*, 364.

23 They *were* the politicians: For Osmeña and Lopez, see Alfred W. McCoy, ed., *An Anarchy of Families: State and Family in the Philippines* (Madison: University of Wisconsin Press, 1993), 311, 506. For Cojuangco, see Anderson, "Cacique Democracy," 4.

23 committee members: Anderson, "*Cacique Democracy*," 28.

23 overturn his conviction for murdering: Karnow, *In Our Image*, 368.

23 he stole as much as $10 billion: Karnow, *In Our Image*, 378, 385.

23 Marcos spent so much: Thompson, *Anti-Marcos Struggle*, 35. See also Lela Garner Noble, "Politics in the Marcos Era," in *Crisis in the Philippines: The Marcos Era and Beyond*, ed. John Bresnan (Princeton, N.J.: Princeton University Press, 1986), 80.

23 a civic beautifier: In the mid-seventies, Ferdinand Marcos appointed his wife both the governor of Metro Manila and Minister of Human Settlements, giving her power to order slum demolitions, which she often did in advance of visits from prominent international guests. When the World Bank and International Monetary Fund met in Manila in 1976, she bulldozed shanties and put up whitewashed walls to keep slum areas out of the bankers' sight. *Time*, Oct. 18, 1976; Bernard Wideman, *WP*, Oct. 6, 1976.

25 martial law: Karnow, *In Our Image*. Abolished Congress, 387; seized businesses, 359, 382; closed newspapers, jailed opponents, 359.

25 "your adherence to democratic principles": Raul S. Manglapus, *NYT*, July 10, 1981.

26 In a 1974 May Day speech: Ferdinand E. Marcos, "Labor—Our Greatest Weapon," May 1, 1974, published in *PL*, May 15, 1974, 5.

26 Korea: Most placements in Korea were handled by the Korean Overseas Development Corporation, a state-owned company. The Philippine system was initially meant to emulate the Korean model, but the lucrative business of placing workers came to rest with a scandal-ridden private sector. Manolo I. Abella and K. J. Lönnroth, "Orderly International Migration of Workers and Incentives to Stay—Options for Emigration Countries," International Labour Office, 1995, 9.

27 Two-thirds of the Saudis were illiterate: Nana Oishi, *Women in Motion: Globalization, State Policies, and Labor Migration in Asia* (Stanford, Calif.: Stanford University Press, 2005), 44–45.

27 departures had risen to 434,000: IOM, *Country Migration Report: The Philippines 2013*, 59. By 2016, the figure was nearly 2.6 million. Website of the POEA, "OFW Statistics."

27 **capped the amount:** Placement agencies are now allowed to charge workers a month's salary, although domestic workers and seafarers are supposed to be exempt from placement fees.

27 **lowest level in Southeast Asia:** Thompson, *Anti-Marcos Struggle*, 57.

27 **incomes of unskilled urban workers:** In 1980, the World Bank reported that the average unskilled worker in Manila made about 12 pesos a day, or $1.60, down by a third from 1970. At the stadium, Emet made 18 pesos a day, or $2.40. WB, Third Urban Development Project, Staff Appraisal Report, March 5, 1980, 1.

28 **salary would rise tenfold:** Increases of such magnitude were common. Describing the post-1973 migration to the Middle East, the political scientists Stephen Castles and Mark J. Miller wrote, "The big attraction for workers was the wages: often ten times as much as could be earned at home." Stephen Castles and Mark J. Miller, *The Age of Migration: International Population Movements in the Modern World*, 1st ed. (New York: Guilford Press, 1993), 158.

CHAPTER TWO: MIGRATION FEVER

30 **Some hung posters of dollar bills:** Arnel F. de Guzman, "'Katas Ng Saudi': The Work and Life Situation of the Filipino Contract Worker in Saudi Arabia," *Philippine Social Sciences Review* 51, no. 1–4 (Jan.–Dec. 1993): 49, 38.

30 **a recording of his pig:** Fe R. Arcinas, Cynthia B. Bautista, and Randolf S. David, *The Odyssey of the Filipino Migrant Workers to the Gulf Region* (Quezon City: Department of Sociology, College of Social Science and Philosophy, University of the Philippines, 1987), 66.

31 **"symbols of hope to neighbors":** Arcinas, Bautista, and David, *Odyssey of the Filipino Migrant Workers to the Gulf Region*, 82; stereos and TVs: 84; meat: 86.

32 **More than three-quarters of Filipino wives:** Stella P. Go and Leticia T. Postrado, "Filipino Overseas Contract Workers: Their Families and Communities," in *Asian Labor Migration: Pipeline to the Middle East,* ed. Fred Arnold and Nasra M. Shah (Boulder, Colo.: Westview Press, 1986), 129.

32 **Women as far away as Egypt and India:** Ian J. Seccombe, "International Labor Migration to the Middle East: A Review of Literature and Research, 1974–84," *International Migration Review* 19, no. 2 (1985): 335–52.

32 **the world's migrant population doubled:** It rose from 76 million in 1960 to 154 million in 1990. UN, Department of Social and Economic Affairs, *World Economic and Social Survey 2004: International Migration*, viii.

33 **Nearly half a million West Indians:** The website for the National Archives, United Kingdom, "Bound for Britain: Experiences of Immigration to the UK," www.national archives.gov.uk/education/resources/bound-for-britain/.

33 **1.5 million colonial migrants:** Gary P. Freeman, *Immigrant Labor and Racial Conflict in Industrial Societies: The French and British Experience, 1945–75* (Princeton, N.J.: Princeton University Press, 1979), 21. Despite skeptical public opinion, there was a left-right convergence among political elites in favor of immigration from former colonies. The pro-colonial right supported it as a reminder of the colonial past, while the anti-colonial left supported it for reasons from "commitment to internationalism to guilt for past colonial sins" (41–42).

33 **Germany hosted 600,000 "temporary" Turkish workers:** Nermin Abadan-Unat, "Turkish Migration to Europe," in *The Cambridge Survey of World Migration*, ed. Robin Cohen (Cambridge, UK: Cambridge University Press, 1995), 279.

33 **more than half a million Turkish dependents:** Mark J. Miller, "The Problem of Foreign Worker Participation and Representation in France, Switzerland, and the Federal Republic of Germany" (PhD diss., University of Wisconsin–Madison, 1978), 93.

34 **7 percent in Germany:** Miller, "Problem of Foreign Worker Participation," 87.

34 **"We wanted workers":** Max Frisch, foreword to *Siamo Italiani: Die Italiener: Gespräche mit italienischen Arbeitern in der Schweiz* (Zurich: EVZ-Verlag, 1965), 7.

34 **Some called the mayhem "nigger hunting":** Mark Olden, *Independent*, Aug. 29, 2008.

34 **a Tory MP named Enoch Powell:** Anthony M. Messina, *Race and Party Competition in Britain* (Oxford: Clarendon Press, 1989), 40, 105.

34 **"murdered foreign laborers":** Miller, "Problem of Foreign Worker Participation," 277–80.

35 **10 percent of Western Europe's labor force:** Michael J. Piore, *Birds of Passage: Migrant Labor and Industrial Societies* (Cambridge, UK: Cambridge University Press, 1979), 1. Piore notes that different societies have different definitions of low-status work. "In Europe, for example, assembly-line jobs, particularly in automobiles, are considered low status and generally unacceptable among the native population, and these jobs are heavy employers of immigrants. In the United States automobile assembly-line jobs have remained attractive to the native population" (18).

35 **"The last thing I worry about":** *NYT*, July 7, 1977, cited in Miller, "Problem of Foreign Worker Participation," 95.

35 **three-quarters of them from the developing world:** David M. Reimers, *Still the Golden Door: The Third World Comes to America* (New York: Columbia University Press, 1985), 92.

35 **rich countries added 380 million:** UN Population Division, *World Population Prospects: The 2010 Revision*, vol. 1, *Comprehensive Tables*, 146.

35 **by 2000, it was thirty-six times as great:** Website of the WB, "GDP Per Capita."

35 **Soaring numbers of refugees:** By 1990, the United States had 737,000 Cubans and 543,000 Vietnamese, both clear examples of the impact of Cold War politics on immigration policy. "Countries of Birth for U.S. Immigrants, 1960 to present," MPI-DH.

35 **public opinion generally opposed:** The skepticism toward late twentieth-century migration largely sets it apart from the mass movements of the nineteenth century. As Douglas Massey and his colleagues write, "Whereas officials in destination countries of the past saw immigration as necessary for industrialization and a vital part of nation building, today's political leaders view immigrants as a social and political problem to be managed" (Massey et al., *Worlds in Motion*, 6).

35 **Migrant-friendly courts were one constraint:** One example is the 1982 ruling by the U.S. Supreme Court in *Plyler v. Doe*, which found that children in the United States illegally have the right to attend public schools.

36 **7 percent of the workforce:** European numbers are for 1978 and come from Miller, "Problem of Foreign Worker Participation," 90. United States is for 1980 and comes from MPI: "Immigrant Share of the U.S. Population and Civilian Labor Force, 1980–Present," MPI-DH. Persian Gulf is for 1980–81 and comes from J. S. Birks, I. J. Seccombe, and C. A. Sinclair, "Migrant Workers in the Arab Gulf: The Impact of

Declining Oil Revenues," *International Migration Review* 20, no. 4 (Winter 1986): 799–814.

36 **an Arab workforce:** J. S. Birks and C. A. Sinclair, *International Migration and Development in the Arab Region* (Geneva: International Labour Office, 1980).

36 **nearly two-thirds of the Gulf's foreign workers:** Myron Weiner, *The Global Migration Crisis: Challenge to States and to Human Rights* (New York: Harper Collins, 1985), 81.

36 **up from 20 percent:** Birks and Sinclair, *International Migration and Development in the Arab Region*, 133.

36 **Remittances rose sevenfold:** The IOM, relying on data from the Philippine Central Bank, reports that remittances rose from $103 million in 1975 to $694 million in 1985. *Country Migration Report*, 114. The World Bank reports they were $626 million in 1980, $1.5 billion in 1990, $7 billion in 2000, $21.6 billion in 2010, and $32.2 billion in 2017. Website of the WB, "Migration and Remittances data."

37 **"our feeling and thinking process":** *PL*, Jan. 1, 1979.

37 **"Department of Social Conscience":** *PL*, May 1, 1979.

37 **not one Filipina, but three:** Patricia Sto. Tomas, interview with author. Sto. Tomas then headed the Philippines Overseas Employment Administration; the story was conveyed to her by the subordinate who received the visiting official's request. She later became secretary of labor.

37 **praised as "Dollar Earners" those who took them:** "Dollar Earners: Construction Industry Yields New Heroes," *PL*, May 1, 1979.

37 **"Armed with slide shows":** *Wingtips* was the magazine of Philippine Airlines, which was then government owned. The article was reprinted in *PL* on August 17, 1977.

37 **Fluor Daniel, the giant construction firm:** Interview with Marianito Roque, former secretary of labor.

37 **the board counted placements in 108 countries:** Overseas Employment Development Board, Annual Report, 1981, 2. In 1980, 84 percent of deployments were to the Middle East. Edita A. Tan and Dante B. Canlas, "Migrant's Saving Remittance and Labour Supply Behaviour: The Philippines Case," in *To the Gulf and Back: Studies on the Economic Impact of Asian Labour Migration*, ed. Rashid Amjad (New Delhi: International Labour Organization Asian Employment Programme, 1989), 224.

37 **"mettle, versatility, and temperament":** Overseas Employment Development Board, Annual Report, 1977, 10.

37 **"friendly and cooperative guest":** "Lure of Overseas Jobs," *PL*, Dec. 8, 1978.

37 **"Filipinos don't pose the problems":** *Wingtips* article cited in *PL*, Aug. 17, 1977, 3.

38 **phaseout went the other way:** The OEDB was abolished in 1982. Its successor, the Philippine Overseas Employment Administration, continued to place workers with foreign governments, but the lucrative business of recruiting for private-sector jobs was left to the country's growing ranks of job-placement firms.

38 **Shady labor agents were nothing new:** After a visit to the United States in 1842, Charles Dickens discovered some of the passengers on the ship back to Europe had been victimized by crooked recruiters at home. Agents "are constantly travelling about those districts where poverty and discontent are rife, and tempting the credulous into more misery, by holding out monstrous inducements to emigration which can never be realized." Charles Dickens, *American Notes for General Circulation* (1842; New York: Penguin Books, 2000), 245.

38 **phony maids' jobs in Italy:** *PL*, March 14, 1997.

38 **"thousands upon thousands of unsuspecting"**: Ferdinand Marcos, Presidential Decree No. 1693, May 1, 1980.

38 **A 1981 raid at the Labor Department**: Interviews with Marianito Roque and Patricia Sto. Tomas, both former secretaries of labor.

39 **"Are you hardheaded?"**: Patricia Sto. Tomas, interview by author.

39 **a new agency**: The POEA was created in 1982 and took over the functions of three predecessor agencies: the Overseas Employment Development Board, which marketed workers; the Bureau of Employment Services, which regulated recruiters; and the National Seaman's Board, which licensed maritime staffing agencies.

39 **"Pitifully inadequate" is how Ople described**: "Filipino 'Labor Force Explosion' Abroad Cited," *PL*, March 14, 1977, 1.

39 **reports of misfortune poured in**: For a while, the Department of Labor and Employment compiled a monthly volume called *The Labor Attaché Reports*, some of which remain in the department's library in Manila: Iraq, Nov. 1981; Bahrain, May 1980; Ontario, Sept. 1979; Greece, Sept. 1982.

39 **The Labor Department's Tokyo rep**: "Ray Maraan: Filipino Workers Knock on His Door in Tokyo," *PL*, Nov. 22, 1976, 3.

39 **The Labor Department improvised**: Marianito Roque (Kuwait), Reynaldo Parungao (Jeddah), and Roy Seneres (Abu Dhabi), interviews by author.

40 **staff of nearly six hundred**: Dovelyn Rannveig Agunias and Neil G. Ruiz, "Protecting Overseas Workers: Lessons and Cautions from the Philippines" (Washington, DC: MPI, 2007), 9–10.

40 **thirty thousand Filipino workers**: Agunias and Ruiz, "Protecting Overseas Workers," 7.

40 **the agency's logo depicts the sun**: The website of the Overseas Workers Welfare Administration explains that "the sun and rain symbolize the gains and pains of OFWs." www.owwa.gov.ph/?q=content/owwa.

40 **even the least fortunate doubled his wage**: The pay raises the family enjoyed varied greatly. Rosalie's brother Rolando raised his pay 2.5 times when he first left Manila for Saudi Arabia. Rosalie raised hers 3.3 times. Emet's grew tenfold. Rosalie's uncles—Bandoy, Fering, and Fortz—saw their respective earnings rise nine times, fifteen times, and twenty times. Those are just the initial pay increases: sometimes their overseas pay continued to climb, as it did for Rosalie. Though the figures are not adjusted for inflation or cost of living, Rosalie's base salary in Texas ($78,000) is fifty-six times greater than what it was ($1,380) when she left the Philippines two decades earlier.

40 **asked Tita to raise the child**: Tita suffered the collateral damage from Fortz's affair twice—first when he asked her to take on the expense and effort of raising Sheralyn, and again when Sheralyn's mother took her back. In surrendering the nine year old, Tita felt as if she were losing a child of her own: "It really felt like my heart was breaking." Sheralyn, too, became an overseas worker, in Dubai and on a cruise ship.

42 **an Amnesty International campaign**: The arrested worker was Oswaldo Magdangal. Amnesty International issued an alert on December 22, 1992, amid reports that he would be beheaded on Christmas.

43 **Marcos warned him through Imelda**: Karnow, *In Our Image*, 402.

43 **"a human sea" flooded the streets**: Karnow, *In Our Image*, 418.

43 **1,060 pairs of shoes**: Seth Mydans, *NYT*, Feb. 9, 1987. The figure was originally reported as 3,000.

44 **Annual departures rose:** Departures increased from 377,000 in 1986 to 686,000 in 1992; remittances rose from $696 million to $2.2 billion. IOM, *Country Migration Report*, 59, 114.

CHAPTER THREE: GIRL GETS GRIT

45 **When I reached Manila:** I arrived in September 1986 on a yearlong fellowship from the Henry Luce Foundation through its Luce Scholars program.

47 **Tita's curiosity:** I was surprised that Tita and her neighbors didn't have more class anger, given all they had to be angry about. Sister Christine sent them to visit a giant hacienda, where a tour of the family museum included big-game trophies, tennis awards, and a note from the patriarch that advised, "Live simply. Expect little. Give much." As I stopped to write it down, Tita agreed, without irony, it was a beautiful thought. The only time I saw her angry at a slight was when anti-Aquino protesters sang, "Cory is a washwoman." "There's nothing wrong with being a washwoman," Tita fumed. Rosalie seemed to have class conflict in mind when she wrote an Alay Kapwa play about a scheme by Imelda to evict the squatters, but it ended with a rich friend of Imelda's defecting to help the poor. Emet, on the other hand, did blame the rich when an Alay Kapwa donor abandoned a plan to help him start a business.

49 **World Bank project:** Under the program, called the Third Urban Development Project, the World Bank loaned the Philippine government $72 million to finance improved drainage, sanitation, water, and streets. In addition, the project "reblocked" the homes (paving and widening crooked alleyways for better firefighting access and demolishing some homes in the way) and sold the lots to the residents. The program served 350,000 people at thirty-one sites but was plagued by "endemic petty graft" and low repayment rates on the mortgages. Emet's house cost about $910, plus a $120 bribe to a city clerk. He paid it off almost immediately, with his savings from Saudi Arabia. Leveriza's central location made it a good investment: twenty-eight years later, he sold it for nearly $28,000. WB, "Project Completion Report, Philippines, Third Urban Development Project."

50 **the first Philippine nursing school:** Catherine Ceniza Choy, *Empire of Care: Nursing and Migration in Filipino American History* (Durham, N.C.: Duke University Press, 2003), 23.

50 **suited to work in the United States:** While the United States barred most Asian immigration in 1917, when it created the Asiatic Barred Zone, the law exempted the Philippines, which was still a colony. The exemption ended in 1934 with the Tydings-McDuffie Act, which established a process for independence.

50 **Their numbers soared:** As opportunities rose to move to the States, so did the demand for nursing education. The number of nursing schools in the Philippines grew eight-fold, from seventeen in 1950 to 140 in 1970. Yen Le Espiritu, *Home Bound: Filipino American Lives Across Cultures, Communities, and Countries* (Berkeley: University of California Press, 2003), 33.

50 **more than eleven thousand Filipino:** Choy, *Empire of Care*, 65.

51 **But nursing school was a stretch:** Overseas work is the Philippines's substitute for a system of financial aid. But given Emet's modest and irregular pay, I'm not sure whether Rosalie could have finished nursing school had I not been able to help.

54 **a lauded book:** John Berger and Jean Mohr, *A Seventh Man: A Book of Images and Words About the Experience of Migrant Workers in Europe* (New York: Penguin

Books, 1975). My attention was directed to this work by Mirjana Morokvasic, "Birds of Passage Are Also Women," *International Migration Review* 18, no. 4 (Winter 1984): 886–907.

54 **nearly half the world's migrants were women:** While scholars broadly agree that modern migration has feminized, a lack of reliable data makes measurement difficult. The United Nations estimated that the female share of the world's migrant population grew only modestly, from 46.7 percent in 1960 to 49.6 percent in 2005; scholars Katherine M. Donato and Donna Gabaccia have argued the rise may have been even smaller. But more women now migrate as autonomous workers, rather than as dependents, as the Philippine data show. What is often called the "feminization of migration" is to a significant degree the feminization of the breadwinning role. It is all the more notable because some countries have constrained the emigration of women, including at various times India, Bangladesh, and Pakistan. Katherine M. Donato and Donna Gabaccia, *Gender and International Migration* (New York: Russell Sage Foundation, 2015); Oishi, *Women in Motion.*

54 **more than half in the United States:** In 1990, there were 119 immigrant men for every 100 women, while a century later there were 100 women for every 99 men. Waters and Pineau, *Integration of Immigrants into American Society*, 34.

54 **from 12 percent in 1975 to 72 percent:** Twelve percent in 1975 is from Maruja Milagros B. Asis, Shirlena Huang, and Brenda S. A. Yeoh, "When the Light of the Home is Abroad: Unskilled Female Migration and the Filipino Family," *Singapore Journal of Topical Geography* 25, no. 2 (2004): 203. Seventy-two percent in 2005, which excludes seafarers, is from the website of the POEA, "OFW Global Presence: A Compendium of Overseas Employment Statistics," 2005.

54 **nearly two-thirds of American women:** Barbara Ehrenreich and Arlie Russell Hochschild, introduction to *Global Woman: Nannies, Maids, and Sex Workers in the New Economy*, ed. Barbara Ehrenreich and Arlie Russell Hochschild (New York: Henry Holt, 2002), 8.

54 **many needed domestic help:** In the United States, African Americans, denied other jobs, had historically provided a large share of domestic labor. But after the civil rights movement, they were more likely than immigrants to see it as stigmatized.

54 **number of Filipina maids rose tenfold:** Joaquin L. Gonzalez III, *Philippine Labour Migration: Critical Dimensions of Public Policy* (Singapore: Institute of Southeast Asia Studies, 1998), 3.

55 **"a new phase in the history":** Saskia Sassen-Koob, "Notes on the Incorporation of Third World Women into Wage-Labor Through Immigration and Off-Shore Production," *International Migration Review* 18, no. 4 (Winter 1984): 1144–67.

55 **increased their power within their marriages:** Among Filipina maids in Rome, 70 percent said they had left to escape abusive or irresponsible husbands. Rhacel Salazar Parreñas, *Servants of Globalization: Women, Migration, and Domestic Work* (Stanford, Calif.: Stanford University Press), 66.

55 **"I found myself stunned by the extent":** Oishi, *Women in Motion*, xi.

55 **Aquino banned domestic workers:** The ban began in early 1988 and covered domestic workers younger than thirty-five. Two Filipinas were caught trying to smuggle themselves out of the Philippines in an airplane vent. Pennie S. Azarcon, United Press International, Aug. 26, 1988.

55 **"heroes of our country's economy":** Seth Mydans, *NYT*, May 12, 1988.

55 **"housemaids and janitors"**: Fidel V. Ramos, "State of the Nation Address," July 27, 1992.

55 **"a pillar"**: Fidel V. Ramos, "Overseas Employment Program: An Indispensable Program," *Overseas Employment Info Series 5*, no. 2 (Dec. 1992): 6–12.

55 **Sarah Balabagan**: She went to work in the Emirates at fourteen with fake papers that said she was twenty-eight and stabbed her employer more than thirty times in what she described as self-defense. An Emirati court found she had been raped, but a retrial concluded she hadn't and sentenced her to die. Balabagan variously described her employer's attack as rape and attempted rape. A Filipino businessman paid $40,000 to the slain man's family, and Balabagan was released after being lashed one hundred times. (Uli Schmetzer, *Chicago Tribune*, March 12, 1997; Jim Gomez, Associated Press, Jan. 18, 2009.)

56 **Flor Contemplacion**: For an overview of the case, see Harvey Simon, "Philippine President Fidel Ramos and the Flor Contemplacion Crisis" (Kennedy School of Government Case Program, C18-95-1305.0, 1995).

56 **funeral dirges**: Philip Shenon, *NYT*, March 18, 1995.

56 **"She is a symbol of millions"**: Philip Shenon, *NYT*, March 28, 1995.

56 **Hailing her as a "heroine"**: Philip Shenon, *NYT*, March 19, 1995.

57 **But it defined "protected" so weakly**: Countries merely had to take "positive concrete measures" to protect workers. That language was tightened in 2010 with a new law, RA10022, which specified three criteria a country had to meet to show "positive concrete measures." Still all six members of the Gulf Cooperation Council have been deemed in compliance. The Philippine government sometimes bans deployments to counties it has deemed compliant, as it did with workers to Kuwait in 2018 after a Filipino nanny, Joanna Demafelis, was found dismembered and hidden there in her employers' freezer. But the bans have generally been short-lived and ineffective. Workers eager for the jobs often find ways to travel to banned destinations anyway. Author communication with Ellene Sana, Center for Migrant Advocacy, Manila.

57 **central assertion was plainly untrue**: While the "Magna Carta" says "the State does not promote overseas employment as a means to sustain economic growth," Ramos himself had said, "My Administration has defined overseas employment as a key component of our national employment plan." Ramos, "Overseas Employment Program."

57 **female domestic workers rose**: Deployments of female domestic workers rose from 62,167 in 1995 to 81,725 a decade later. Website of the POEA, "OFW statistics."

57 **duties ranged from table-side flirting**: Sociologist Rhacel Parreñas worked as a bar girl in Tokyo for her book *Illicit Flirtations* and argues that prostitution is less common than perceived. She describes the typical interaction as a form of "commercial flirtation" that occupies a "middle zone between human trafficking and labor migration." Rhacel Salazar Parreñas, *Illicit Flirtations: Labor, Migration, and Sex Trafficking in Tokyo* (Stanford, Calif.: Stanford University Press, 2011), 5, 7.

57 **scantily clad women**: The number of overseas performing artists rose from seventeen thousand in 1996 to more than seventy thousand in 2004. DeParle, *NYT Magazine*, April 22, 2007.

57 **I once asked Marianito Roque**: DeParle, *NYT Magazine*, April 22, 2007.

62 **She could take a different test**: The first test Rosalie took was called the CGFNS, for Commission on Graduates of Foreign Nursing Schools, the group that administers it. The NCLEX is administered by the National Council of State Boards of Nursing.

CHAPTER FOUR: THE GUEST WORKER STATE

64 **Emirates Palace was no ordinary hotel:** Susan d'Arcy, *Sunday Times*, Feb. 27, 2005; "Emirates Palace Facts and Figures," fact sheet distributed by the Emirates Palace hotel.

64 **88 percent of the population:** UN, *International Migration Report 2017* (New York: UN Department of Economic and Social Affairs, 2017), 28. The next two countries with the highest share of migrants relative to their population were also in the Gulf: Kuwait (76 percent) and Qatar (65 percent).

64 **Canada, France, Australia, or Spain:** The Emirates has 8.3 million migrants, more than Canada (7.9 million), France (7.9 million), Australia (7.0 million), and Spain (5.9 million). UN, "Trends in International Migrant Stock," 2017 Revisions, www.un.org /en/development/desa/population/migration/data/estimates2/estimates17.shtml.

65 **Just over a million Emiratis:** Philip L. Martin and Froilan Malit, "A New Era for Labor Migration in the GCC?," *Migration Letters* 14, no. 1 (Jan. 2017): 113–26.

65 **thousands walked off the job:** Jason DeParle, *NYT*, Aug. 6, 2007.

65 **Human Rights Watch reported that the workers:** "Building Towers, Cheating Workers: Exploitation of Migrant Construction Workers in the United Arab Emirates," *Human Rights Watch* 18, no. 8(E) (Nov. 2006).

65 **A trade magazine counted 880 construction deaths:** The magazine is *Construction Week*, cited in "Building Towers, Cheating Workers," *Human Rights Watch* 40.

65 **"indentured servitude":** Ariel Kaminer and Sean O'Driscoll, *NYT*, May 19, 2014.

65 **few countries offer foreigners more jobs:** Only the United States (44.5 million), Germany (12.2 million), Russia (11.7 million), and Saudi Arabia (12.2 million) have larger foreign-born populations. All figures but that for the United States are from the UN, "Trends in International Migrant Stock," 2017 Revisions. The U.S. figures are from the Census Bureau.

65 **send home more than $19 billion:** WB, *Migration and Remittances Factbook 2016* (Washington, DC: WB, 2016).

65 **remittances India receives from the Gulf:** From 2012 to 2017, India received $215.4 billion in remittances from the Persian Gulf and $215.3 billion in private investment worldwide. Author communication with Dilip Ratha, World Bank.

66 **$100 billion richer:** Pritchett, *Let Their People Come*, 3. Pritchett's calculations were based on data from the early 2000s; the increase would be greater than $100 billion now.

66 **I took a trip with Pritchett:** DeParle, *NYT Magazine*, June 10, 2007.

70 **the number of credit cards in the Emirates quintupled:** Jason DeParle, *NYT*, Aug. 20, 2011.

70 **soon had a shop of his own:** As a foreigner, Roldan could not open a business on his own, but had to pay an Emirati to do business under his license; for Emiratis these arrangements are a lucrative income stream.

71 **Next came Rosalie's cousin Tess:** Tess's mother, Gloria, is Tita's sister. Rosalie's old boyfriend, Ariel, is Tess's cousin on her father's side.

73 **Ratha suspected the sums were substantial:** Jason DeParle, *NYT*, March 17, 2008.

73 **in 2003, when Ratha first published:** WB, "Analysis and Statistical Appendix," in *Global Development Finance: Striving for Stability in Development Finance*, 2003, 157–170. The remittance figures are for 2001.

73 **projected to exceed** *half a trillion* **dollars:** The World Bank's estimate for 2018 is $528 billion. Author communication with Dilip Ratha, WB.

73 **a tenth of the GDP:** Website of the WB, "Migration and Remittance Data," figures as of December 2018.

74 **No large country relies on remittances:** There are roughly thirty countries where remittances are a greater share of the GDP than they are in the Philippines, but most of them are small. While remittances in Tajikistan are 32 percent of the GDP, the population is only nine million, less than a tenth of the Philippines. Only India ($69 billion) and China ($64 billion), countries with ten times the Philippines's population, receive more money. Website of the WB, "Migration and Remittance Data," figures as of December 2018.

74 **"They send home more than":** See DeParle, *NYT Magazine*, April 22, 2007.

74 **a cottage industry arose:** Dovelyn Rannveig Agunias, "Remittances and Development: Trends, Impacts, and Policy Options" (Washington, DC: MPI, 2006), 58.

74 **researchers found Mexicans in the States:** Dean Yang, "Migrant Remittances," *Journal of Economic Perspectives* 25, no. 3 (Summer 2011): 135.

74 **Latin Americans in the States still send:** Roberto Suro, "A Survey of Remittance Senders and Receivers," in *Beyond Small Change: Making Migrant Remittances Count*, ed. Donald F. Terry and Steven R. Wilson (Washington, DC: Inter-American Development Bank, 2005), 23.

74 **It's also countercyclical:** Increased remittances have helped offset losses from hurricanes in Haiti, crop failures in El Salvador, earthquakes in Pakistan, and the 2004 tsunami in Indonesia and Sri Lanka. UN Development Programme, Human Development Report, 2009. *Overcoming Barriers: Human Mobility and Development* (New York: UN Development Programme, 2009), 72. Some researchers also argue that remittances may be better targeted than foreign aid; a migrant may direct more aid to the diligent relative than to the wasteful one.

74 **"Remittances, in fact, do reduce poverty":** *Global Economic Prospects: Economic Implications of Remittances and Migration* (Washington, DC: WB, 2006), 118.

75 **seventy-one poor countries:** Richard H. Adams Jr. and John Page, "Do International Migration and Remittances Reduce Poverty in Developing Countries?," *World Development* 33, no. 10 (2005): 1645–69. Among migrant households in the Philippines in the 1990s, remittances supplied 37 percent of their income and reduced poverty for nonmigrant households through spillover effects (Dean Yang and Claudia A. Martinez, "Remittances and Poverty in Migrants' Home Areas: Evidence from the Philippines," in *International Migration, Remittances, and the Brain Drain*, ed. Caglar Ozden and Maurice Schiff [Washington, DC: WB, 2006], 81–121). Other researchers have found that migrant households enjoy better nutrition and lower levels of infant mortality.

75 **To analyze spending priorities:** Dean Yang, "International Migration, Remittances, and Household Investment: Evidence from Philippine Migrants' Exchange Rate Shocks," *Economic Journal* 118, no. 528 (April 2008): 591–630. Another Philippine study compared two groups of otherwise similar households; one group got a chance to send a worker to Korea, and the other didn't. Among the families with an overseas worker, the share of kids in private school rose 41 percentage points. Michael Clemens and Erwin Tiongson, "Split Decisions: Family Finance When a Policy Discontinuity Allocates Overseas Work" (working paper 324, Center for Global Development, Washington, DC, 2013), 19.

75 **In Pakistan, where household spending:** Ghazala Mansuri, "Migration, Sex Bias, and Child Growth in Rural Pakistan," WB Policy Research Group Working Paper, 3946, June 2006.

75 **Concerns about migration once focused:** The exodus of African health professionals is the classic example. It's not quite true, as alleged, that there are more Malawian doctors in Manchester than there are in Malawi. But of the first 250 graduates of Malawi's first medical school, 40 percent did go abroad. Sometimes conditions at home are so rudimentary that medical professionals have limited impact even when they stay. Charlotte McDonald, "Malawian Doctors—Are There More in Manchester Than Malawi?," BBC News, Jan. 15, 2012, www.bbc.com/news/magazine-16545526.

75 **With twelve million skilled migrants:** Slesh Anand Shrestha, "Essays on the Empirical Study of Migration, Intrahousehold Trade-Offs, and Infrastructure Investments" (PhD diss., University of Michigan, 2012), 1.

75 **As many as half of skilled migrants:** U.N. Development Programme, "Human Development Report, 2009," 77.

75 **Brain gain boosted:** AnnaLee Saxenian, *The New Argonauts: Regional Advantage in a Global Economy* (Cambridge, Mass: Harvard University Press, 2006).

76 **often raises his salary at least three or four times:** A WB survey of 485 returning workers from Saudi Arabia in 2016 found an average wage gain of 4.5 times (from $113 a month in the Philippines to $506 in Saudi Arabia). Author communication with Manolo Abella, WB Knomad Working Group on Labor Migration. Three researchers estimated the wage gains Filipino men experience by immigrating to the United States. After adjusting for cost of living, wages rise 3.3 times for men with 13-plus years of schooling; 4.5 times for those with 9 to 12 years; and 6.4 times for those with 5 to 8 years. Michael A. Clemens, Claudio Montenegro, and Lant Pritchett, "The Place Premium: Bounding the Price Equivalent of Migration Barriers," *The Review of Economics and Statistics*, published ahead of print, Nov. 2, 2018.

76 **"There are two possible ways":** Pritchett, *Let Their People Come*, 87.

76 **I returned to write about them:** DeParle, *NYT Magazine*, April 22, 2007.

81 **But there weren't any visas:** Foreign nurses generally enter the United States on an employment visa called an EB-3, which admits them and their immediate families as permanent residents. The numbers are capped at forty thousand including dependents, with additional limits by country. During the late-1990s tech boom, many firms hired engineers on temporary H-1B visas, which expire after six years. Soon, tens of thousands of engineers wanted to convert to the permanent EB-3 visas, creating long waits for the whole pool, which included nurses. In 2005, Congress created fifty thousand nursing visas to relieve the backlog. Had Rosalie passed her English test earlier, she would not have faced a wait. But once those visas were used up by early 2007, long waits returned. Author communication with attorney Bruce Morrison.

81 **Their arrival left a dozen people:** The apartment held the five members of Rosalie's immediate family, three siblings, Tita Nanette and her two relatives, and Rosalie's aunt Chang Idhay—plus the occasional visitor.

CHAPTER FIVE: THE FACEBOOK MOM

84 **mothers who were sisters and best friends:** Tess's mother, Gloria, is the oldest of Tita's sisters. Tita and Emet are Tess's godparents, and Rosalie is the godmother of Tess's

eldest child, Marielle. It was Tess's cousin on her father's side, Ariel, whom Rosalie almost married.

84 **a course in midwifery:** While Tess could have retaken the college entrance test, it cost money, and she doubted her father could pay for nursing school even if she passed.

87 **"Once the realm of science fiction":** John Biggs, *NYT,* Aug. 23, 2007.

88 **her sons received life sentences:** *Philippine Daily Inquirer,* March 9, 2011.

88 **"The loss of their mothers' nurturing":** UN, *A Passage to Hope: Women and International Migration* (New York: UN Population Fund, 2006), 33.

88 **nationwide study of kids with a parent abroad:** The study examined 1,443 children between the ages of ten and twelve. The children of migrants had slightly higher grades, received more awards, and were more likely to participate in extracurricular activities; they were less likely to repeat a grade. They were taller and heavier than nonmigrant kids and suffered from fewer diseases. *Hearts Apart: Migration in the Eyes of Filipino Children* (Manila: Episcopal Commission for the Pastoral Care of Migrants and Itinerant People-CBCP, Scalabrini Migration Center, and Overseas Workers Welfare Administration, 2004).

89 **Asis did another study:** Maruja M. B. Asis and Cecelia Ruiz-Marave, "In the Wake of Parental Migration: Health and Well-Being Impacts on Filipino Children, Child Health, and Migrant Parents in South-East Asia, Highlights from CHAMPSEA-Philippines" (Manila: CHAMPSEA and the Scalabrini Migration Center, 2011). Asis did the fieldwork for the first study, *Hearts Apart,* in 2003, and gathered data for the second study from 2008 to 2009.

89 **Filipinos with cell phones tripled:** Mirca Madianou and Daniel Miller, *Migration and New Media: Transnational Families and Polymedia* (London: Routledge, 2012), 26.

90 **landlines had long been prohibitively expensive:** The high cost dates back to the 1960s, when Marcos awarded a monopoly to Ramon Cojuangco, *Asia Week,* Nov. 20, 1998. The Philippine Supreme Court later ruled that Cojuangco was secretly holding $530 million in shares for Marcos himself. Philip M. Lustre Jr., *Rappler,* Feb. 25, 2016.

90 **Tech culture and migrant culture were instantly intertwined:** Costs fell 99 percent: Madianou and Miller, *Migration and New Media,* 26; Smart ad: 105; pen and paper: 66–68; cesarean: 51; ambivalent or negative: 87; birthday party: 77; feel like a mother: 13.

91 **Marielle was sixteen:** Until recently, Filipinos entered high school after sixth grade and graduated at sixteen. A 2013 law added seventh and eighth grades.

93 **"communion . . . in which ties of union":** Bronislaw Malinowski, "The Problem of Meaning in Primitive Languages," in *The Meaning of Meaning: A Study of the Influence of Language upon Thought and of the Science of Symbolism,* ed. C. G. Ogden and I. A. Richards (New York: Harcourt, Brace & World, 1923), 315.

95 **mutual links in the global care chain:** Arlie Hochschild, "The Nanny Chain," *American Prospect,* Dec. 19, 2001.

CHAPTER SIX: THE VISA

104 **global migrants surged:** When Emet went abroad in the early 1980s, there were about 100 million global migrants; the number rose to 173 million in 2000, 220 million in 2010, and 258 million in 2017. As a share of the world's population, migrants were 2.8 percent in 2000, 3.2 percent in 2010, and 3.4 percent in 2017. Rosalie lived in Abu

Dhabi from 2004 to 2012. Khalid Koser, *International Migration: A Very Short Introduction* (Oxford: Oxford University Press, 2007), 5; UN, *International Migrant Stock: The 2017 Revision.*

104 **more consequential than ever:** Castles, de Haas, and Miller, *The Age of Migration*, 1.

104 **José becomes the most popular name:** Website of the Social Security Administration.

105 **One in seven Korean births:** Stephen Castles and Mark J. Miller, *The Age of Migration: International Population Movements in the Modern World*, 4th ed. (New York: Guilford Press, 2009), 134.

105 **Captivated by migration's reach:** My articles in the *NYT* include: Cape Verde, June 23, 2007; Ireland, Feb. 24, 2008; the Dominican Republic, Dec. 26, 2007; Dilip Ratha, March 17, 2008.

106 **sixty Irish towns:** Anthony M. Messina and Abigail Fisher Williamson, "Dimensions of Variation in Newly Diverse Transatlantic Destinations," in *The Politics of New Immigrant Destinations: Transatlantic Perspectives*, ed. Stephanie Chambers et al. (Philadelphia: Temple University Press, 2017), 9.

108 **French were expected to "crossbreed":** Mabel Berezin, *Illiberal Politics in Neoliberal Times: Culture, Security, and Populism in the New Europe* (Cambridge, UK: Cambridge University Press, 2009), 130.

108 **"Monsieur Ebola could fix this":** Nele Obermueller and Angela Waters, *USA Today*, Oct. 31, 2014.

109 **Geert Wilders . . . said Islam was "not a religion":** Trip Gabriel, *NYT*, Jan. 16, 2019.

109 **"Radical-right parties are successful":** Cas Mudde, "The Relationship Between Immigration and Nativism in Europe and North America," MPI, May 2012, 31.

109 **calling immigrants "Moroccan scum":** Alisa J. Rubin, *NYT*, Feb. 28, 2017.

111 **bad debt as a crime:** Jason DeParle, *NYT*, Aug. 21, 2011.

CHAPTER SEVEN: IMMIGRANTS, AGAIN

121 **lowest level on record:** Most demographers think the foreign-born share of the population in 1970 (4.7 percent) was the lowest ever, but Census Bureau data only go back to 1850.

121 **highest in more than a hundred years:** The immigrant share of the population reached its peak of 14.8 percent in 1890. Its modern growth (from 4.7 percent in 1970 to 13.7 percent in 2017) feels even more dramatic than the numbers suggest because many immigrants in the 1970s were elderly and therefore inconspicuous in daily life.

121 **with a majority in suburbs:** Waters and Pineau, *Integration of Immigrants into American Society*, 212.

121 **slightly more women than men:** Waters and Pineau, *Integration of Immigrants into American Society*, 34.

122 **Asians have quietly outnumbered Latinos:** Waters and Pineau, *Integration of Immigrants into American Society*, 24.

122 **college-educated Asian woman:** In 2017, 31 percent of immigrants had college educations, compared with 20.3 percent in 1990. Author communication with Jeanne Batalova of the MPI, who analyzed data from the U.S. Census Bureau.

122 **"millions of immigrants":** Ronald Reagan, "Address Accepting the Republican Presidential Nomination at the Republican National Convention in Detroit," July 17, 1980.

123 **Nearly a quarter of the Houston area's seven million people:** Randy Capps and Ariel
   G. Ruiz Soto, "A Profile of Houston's Diverse Immigrant Population in a Rapidly
   Changing Policy Landscape," MPI, 2018, 1–2.

123 **America's most diverse:** Michael Emerson, Jenifer Bratter, and Junia Howell, "Houston Region Grows More Racially / Ethnically Diverse, with Small Declines in Segrega-
   tion," Kinder Institute for Urban Research and Hobby Center for the Study of Texas,
   Rice University, 2012.

123 **"open-arms approach has worked":** *HC*, Aug. 7, 2016.

123 **more than double the pace:** From 1905 to 1914 (the start of World War I), an average
   of 1.01 million immigrants a year arrived in the United States, up from 369,000 in the
   1890s. MPI-DH.

123 **Relative to the population:** From 1900 to 1910, the United States added 6.9 immigrants
   for every 1,000 residents, compared with 3.2 immigrants per thousand in 2012, when
   Rosalie arrived. Francine D. Blau and Christopher Mackie, eds., *The Economic and
   Fiscal Consequences of Immigration* (Washington, DC: National Academies Press,
   2017), 48.

123 **immigrants and their children filled three-quarters:** Website of the Library of Congress, "Teachers, Classroom Materials, Progressive Era to New Era, 1900–1929."

123 **Seventy percent of the "New Immigrants":** Select Commission on Immigration and
   Refugee Policy, *U.S. Immigration Policy and the National Interest* (Washington, DC:
   Government Printing Office, 1981), 70.

123 **"beaten men from beaten races":** Francis A. Walker, "Restriction of Immigration,"
   Atlantic Monthly, June 1896.

124 **"Germanize us instead":** Daniel J. Tichenor, *Dividing Lines: The Politics of Immigration in America* (Princeton, N.J.: Princeton University Press, 2002), 50.

124 **the Know-Nothings in 1854:** Susan F. Martin, *A Nation of Immigrants* (New York:
   Cambridge University Press, 2011), 98.

124 **"In every face, there was something":** Tichenor, *Dividing Lines*, 144.

124 **"impulsive" Italians:** Reports of the Immigration Commission, *Dictionary of Races or
   Peoples* (Washington, DC: Government Printing Office, 1911), 82.

124 **problem of "the Jewish nose":** Tichenor, *Dividing Lines*, 131.

124 **an "insatiable drive" for workers:** Martin, *Nation of Immigrants*, 112–13.

124 **Reed-Johnson Act of 1924:** Congress passed a less restrictive law in 1921. It gave each
   national origin group an annual quota of 3 percent of their numbers in the 1910 census. The 1924 law cut the quota to 2 percent of the 1890 census, when there were fewer
   Italians, Jews, Russians, and Poles. Under the first law, southern and eastern Europeans had 45 percent of the quota. The second law cut their share to 15 percent. Tichenor,
   Dividing Lines, 145.

124 **Immigration fell by more than half:** The United States received 707,000 immigrants in
   1924 and 294,000 in 1925. MPI-DH.

124 **the arrival of Italians and Poles:** Aristide R. Zolberg, *A Nation by Design: Immigration Policy in the Fashioning of America* (New York: Russell Sage Foundation; Cambridge, Mass.: Harvard University Press, 2006), 243–44.

125 **"When we want you, we'll call you":** Zolberg, *Nation by Design*, 258.

125 **the public favored low immigration:** A Gallup poll taken in 1946 found that 51 percent
   of Americans preferred less or no immigration, 32 percent favored the status quo, and
   just 5 percent supported an increase. Most college-educated respondents favored the

same or higher immigration levels, while those with a high school education or less—the majority—"overwhelmingly favored decreased immigration or closed borders." Tichenor, *Dividing Lines*, 182.

125 **labor's opposition eased and concerns:** The American Federation of Labor, which represented skilled workers, had favored the restrictions, while the Congress of Industrial Organizations opposed them. Many of its own members were from southern and eastern European backgrounds. After their merger in 1955, labor began adopting a more permissive attitude toward immigration. Tichenor, *Dividing Lines*, 163, 203.

125 **which denounced the quotas as "an indefensible racial preference":** John F. Kennedy, *A Nation of Immigrants* (New York: Harper Perennial, 1964), 45.

126 **"What can you do for our country?":** Lyndon B. Johnson, State of the Union, Jan. 8, 1964.

126 **Johnson got Eastland to cede control:** Eastland was chairman of both the Senate Judiciary Committee and its subcommittee on immigration. His decision to step aside is one of the story's oddest twists. An unbending opponent of civil rights, Eastland would have fought any law he thought would threaten whites' numerical superiority. But he was hesitant to oppose legislation meant as a tribute to his party's slain president, and he struck up an unlikely friendship with Ted Kennedy, who was decades younger and courted him over long drinking sessions. He also got his way with a federal judgeship in exchange for letting the bill proceed. Perhaps he thought Johnson was likely to win anyway. Tom Gjelten, *A Nation of Nations: A Great American Immigration Story* (New York: Simon & Schuster, 2015), 107–33.

126 **"The ethnic mix of this country":** Gjelten, *Nation of Nations*, 121.

126 **"immigration from that source would":** Reimers, *Still the Golden Door*, 74.

126 **at least 90 percent of the newcomers:** Gjelten, *Nation of Nations*, 122.

126 **three-quarters of the visas to people:** Gjelten, *Nation of Nations*, 125.

127 **arrivals would remain "substantially the same":** Craig A. Horowitz, *The Legislative Legacy of Edward M. Kennedy: Eleven Milestones in Pursuit of Social Justice, 1965–2007* (Jefferson, N.C.: McFarland, 2014), 23.

127 **more than tripled:** In the decade before the law (1955–64), legal admissions averaged 282,000 a year. Subsequent ten-year averages are 425,000 (1970s), 624,000 (1980s), 965,000 (1990s), and 1.03 million (first decade of the twenty-first century). MPI-DH.

127 **the Filipino population has risen:** From 1970 to 2016, the number of Filipinos grew from 185,000 to 1.94 million; Mexicans from 760,000 to 11.5 million; and Indians from 51,000 to 2.44 million. MPI-DH.

127 **More than sixty immigrant groups:** In 2017, sixty-three ethnic groups in the States counted at least 100,000 immigrants, and nine had more than 1 million. MPI-DH.

127 **"None of the people involved":** Gjelten, *Nation of Nations*, 137.

128 **even added a "diversity lottery":** The added visas were largely aimed at the Irish, whose ability to migrate had been constrained by the 1965 law since many lacked close relatives or the necessary job skills. Lawmakers of Irish descent pushed for the lottery and extended visas to other groups under the diversity label to gain political support. It was ethnic politics wrapped in multicultural garb. When the Irish economy boomed in the 1990s, Irish interest in emigration fell. By 2017 the leading beneficiaries of the diversity lottery were people from Nepal and the Democratic Republic of Congo. Anna O. Law, "The Irish Roots of the Diversity Visa Lottery," *Politico*, Nov. 1, 2017;

U.S. Department of Homeland Security, "2017 Yearbook of Immigration Statistics," table 10.

128 **in national polls:** The share of Americans who favored increased immigration was 7 percent in 1977, 5 percent in 1981, 4 percent in 1982, 7 percent in 1986, 6 percent in 1988, and 9 percent in 1990. Rita J. Simon and Susan H. Alexander, *The Ambivalent Welcome* (Westport, Conn.: Praeger, 1993), 41.

128 **"The research findings are clear":** Select Commission on Immigration and Refugee Policy, "U.S. Immigration Policy and the National Interest," 6. The commission, led by Father Theodore Hesburgh, the president of Notre Dame, is the quintessential example of bipartisan elites shaping immigration policy. It included the Senate's two leading immigration experts—Democrat Ted Kennedy and Republican Alan Simpson—and helped lay the groundwork for the 1986 legalization and the 1990 increase in legal immigration.

129 **the quest for racial justice:** The influence of the civil rights movement on immigration politics can be seen in the divide within the Democratic Party in the 1970s. Labor allies like Representative Peter Rodino wanted to penalize employers who hired undocumented workers. But the party's civil rights wing argued the penalties could lead businesses to discriminate against Latinos. Cesar Chavez, the iconic leader of the United Farm Workers, once bitterly opposed undocumented workers, whom growers hired as strikebreakers. In 1968, he asked Senator Robert Kennedy "to remove Wetbacks . . . who are being recruited and imported to break our strikes." But influenced by civil rights groups, he later moderated his stance, and the farmworkers union strongly supported the 1986 legalization. Tichenor, *Dividing Lines*, 226.

129 **With only modest debate, a foreign-born:** When Congress raised the ceilings in 1990, *The New York Times* ran a single front-page story, and even that had a civil rights angle. The lead focused on eased restrictions on "Communists, homosexuals, and people with AIDS," rather than the sharp growth in numbers. Philip J. Hilts, *NYT*, Oct. 26, 1990.

129 **nearly a third of today's are college graduates:** In 2017, 17.6 percent of immigrants had bachelor's degrees (compared with 20.1 percent of natives), and another 13.4 percent had graduate degrees (12.1 percent among natives). Unpublished analysis of U.S. Census Bureau data by Jeanne Batalova, MPI.

130 **lack a high school degree:** The share of adults without high school degrees is 27.5 percent among immigrants and 8.7 percent among natives. Unpublished analysis of U.S. Census Bureau data by Jeanne Batalova, MPI.

130 **Monterey Park:** Timothy P. Fong, *The First Suburban Chinatown: The Remaking of Monterey Park, California* (Philadelphia: Temple University Press, 1994).

130 **"We created this nation":** Berkley Hudson, *LAT*, Oct. 9, 1988.

131 **Seadrift:** The Seadrift episode also shows the impact of the civil rights movement on immigrant incorporation. The Southern Poverty Law Center took the Klan to court, where the judge, Gabrielle McDonald, was the first African American on the federal bench in Texas. She ordered the Klan to stop harassing the Vietnamese.

131 **Texans were shell-shocked by defeat:** See Paul Taylor, *WP*, Dec. 26, 1984.

131 **immigration played little role in national politics:** One law that did generate some controversy was the 1986 Immigration Reform and Control Act, which eventually legalized about three million illegal immigrants in exchange for tougher enforcement. But it passed with support from a Democratic House, a Republican Senate, and a Republican president, Ronald Reagan.

132 **few Californians ranked immigration a major concern:** Andrew Wroe, *The Republican Party and Immigration Politics: From Proposition 187 to George W. Bush* (New York: Palgrave Macmillan, 2008), 33.

132 **It passed in a landslide:** Some prominent Republicans opposed the measure, including two former cabinet secretaries, Jack Kemp and William Bennett, who issued a joint statement saying, "Immigrants have become a popular political and social scapegoat." The conservative Heritage Foundation warned that Prop 187 would increase "government intrusion." Opponents of the measure were gaining, but a late rally backfired when protesters were filmed waving Mexican flags. Wroe, *Republican Party and Immigration Politics*, 87–88.

132 **The leading immigration-control group:** The organization was the Federation for American Immigration Reform, or FAIR. Tichenor, *Dividing Lines*, 284.

132 **One reason the restrictionists faltered:** In the mid-1990s, the GOP still had a large libertarian wing, supportive of immigration. "I'm hard-pressed to think of a single problem that would be solved by shutting off the supply of willing and eager new Americans," said Representative Dick Armey, the House majority leader. Wroe, *Republican Party and Immigration Politics*, 150.

133 **an additional 1.3 million Latinos:** Tichenor, *Dividing Lines*, 285.

133 **more than 80 percent voted Democratic:** Wroe, *Republican Party and Immigration Politics*, 159.

133 **"For the first time in 20 years":** Tichenor, *Dividing Lines*, 286–87.

133 **the largest single-decade rise:** The foreign-born population grew by 46 percent in the 1970s, 40 percent in the 1980s, and 57 percent in the 1990s. The record single-decade rise was 84 percent during the 1850s—the decade that produced the Know-Nothings. MPI-DH.

133 **The number of illegal immigrants more than tripled:** It rose from 2.5 million in 1989 to 8.4 million in 2000. Jeffrey S. Passel, "The Size and Characteristics of the Unauthorized Migrant Population in the U.S.," Pew Hispanic Center, Washington, DC, March 7, 2006.

133 **the undocumented peaked in 2007:** The undocumented fell from 12.2 million in 2007 to 10.7 million in 2016. Passel and Cohn, Pew Research Center, Nov. 27, 2018.

133 **two-thirds had settled in five traditional states:** Douglas S. Massey and Chiara Capoferro, "The Geographic Diversification of American Immigration," in *New Faces in New Places: The Changing Geography of American Immigration,* ed. Douglas S. Massey (New York: Russell Sage Foundation, 2008), 35.

133 **foreign-born population rose fourfold:** These state figures, which cover 1990 to 2010, are from an unpublished analysis of U.S. Census Bureau data by Jeanne Batalova, MPI.

134 **Few explosions of diversity:** See Susan Wolcott, "Overlapping Ethnicities and Negotiated Space: Atlanta's Buford Highway," *Journal of Cultural Geography* 20, no. 1 (2009): 51–75, and Mary E. Odem, "Unsettled in the Suburbs: Latino Immigration and Ethnic Diversity in Metro Atlanta," in Singer, Hardwick, and Brettell, *Twenty-first Century Gateways,* 105–36.

134 **"improbable melting pot":** Deborah Scroggins, *Atlanta Journal and Constitution,* Jan. 1, 1992.

134 **"The overall picture still shows":** Charles Hirschman and Douglas S. Massey, "Places and Peoples: The New American Mosaic," in Massey, *New Faces in New Places,* 13, 17.

134 **"Immigration is not a problem"**: The quote is from a speech on June 26, 2000. "George W. Bush on Immigration," On the Issues: Every Political Leader on Every Issue, www .ontheissues.org/celeb/George_W__Bush_Immigration.htm.

134 **governor of Texas with nearly half their votes**: Zolberg, *Nation by Design*, 429.

135 **John Tanton went on to help found**: Jason DeParle, *NYT*, April 17, 2011.

136 **"energetic, ambitious, optimistic people"**: George W. Bush, "Remarks on Immigration Reform," Washington, DC, Jan. 7, 2004.

136 **"until we no longer have to press 1 for English"**: Federal News Service, "Republican Presidential Candidates Debate Sponsored by CNN, WMUR-TV, and the New Hampshire Union Leader," June 5, 2007.

136 **His House caucus attracted more than a hundred**: Michael Sandler, *Congressional Quarterly Today*, Oct. 29, 2007.

136 **Sheriff Joe Arpaio of Maricopa County**: My lone encounter with Arpaio, in 2010, was memorable for its weirdness. I can't recall meeting another politician—or anyone—so openly craving media attention. *"I've got the only female chain gang in the world. . . . I was just up in New Hampshire. . . . People are thinking I'm gonna run for president."* The monologue ensued before I could ask a question and ended with an unsolicited gift: a framed poster of himself. When I declined his first offer to visit the tents, he continued to ask. When I accepted, his assistant expressed disappointment that I hadn't brought a camera. The twenty-five hundred striped men in his tents were props. In 2017, Arpaio was convicted of criminal contempt for disobeying a court order to stop detaining people based solely on suspicions of their immigrant status. President Trump pardoned him a few weeks later.

136 **"Let's give a welcome to *macaca*"**: Tim Craig and Michael Shear, *WP*, Aug. 15, 2006.

136 **need for labor had waned**: Margaret E. Peters, *Trading Barriers: Immigration and the Remaking of Globalization* (Princeton, N.J.: Princeton University Press, 2017).

137 **"We will deport you"**: *All Things Considered*, National Public Radio, June 27, 2006.

137 **In more than a dozen polls**: Waters and Pineau, *Integration of Immigrants into American Society*, 47.

137 **"don't want to do"**: Ron Hutcheson, *Fort Worth Star-Telegram*, May 30, 2007.

137 **The unlikely rise of Barack Obama**: My wife, Nancy-Ann DeParle, served in the first term of the Obama administration, as director of the White House Office of Health Reform and as deputy chief of staff for policy.

137 **executive powers he had suggested he lacked**: In 2011, Obama said, "Sometimes when I talk to immigration advocates they wish I could just bypass Congress and change the law myself. But that's not how a democracy works." Barack Obama, "Remarks by the President on Comprehensive Immigration Reform, in El Paso, Texas," May 10, 2011. In 2014, he tried to extend protections to another five million people—parents of children legally here—but a federal court struck down the measure and the Supreme Court deadlocked, 4–4.

138 **constant clash of opposite traditions**: Rogers M. Smith, "Beyond Tocqueville, Myrdal, and Hartz: The Multiple Traditions in America," *American Political Science Review* 87, no. 3 (Sept. 1993): 549–66.

138 **show-me-your-papers laws**: Arizona passed the first such law in 2010, which made the failure to carry immigration papers a crime and gave police broad authority to stop people they suspected of being in the United States illegally. Critics warned it could lead to racial profiling. The Supreme Court largely upheld it, but Arizona, facing

further litigation, placed some limits on the police checks. Other states passing similar laws include Utah, South Carolina, Georgia, Alabama, and Indiana, though many faced setbacks in court.

138 **immigrant population had grown 500 percent:** The foreign-born population of the Houston metro area rose from 220,000 in 1980 to 1.33 million in 2010. Author communication with Stephen Klineberg, Rice University. As of 2017, it was 1.6 million. Capps and Ruiz Soto, "Profile of Houston's Diverse Immigrant Population," 1.

139 **Nearly half the metro area's kids:** Capps and Ruiz Soto, "Profile of Houston's Diverse Immigrant Population," 2.

139 **English lessons:** Nestor P. Rodriguez, "Economic Restructuring and Latino Growth in Houston," in *In the Barrios: Latinos and the Underclass Debate*, ed. Joan Moore and Raquel Pinderhughes (New York: Russell Sage Foundation, 1993), 120.

139 **as many people in health care:** Jenny Deam and L. M. Sixel, *HC*, Sept. 6, 2015.

139 **A third of the metro area's workforce:** Capps and Ruiz Soto, "Profile of Houston's Diverse Immigrant Population," 2, 20.

139 **"Whether we are talking about":** Testimony by Jeff Moseley, president and CEO, Greater Houston Partnership, before the Senate Judiciary Subcommittee on Immigration, Border Security, and Citizenship, April 30, 2009.

139 **Only about half the area's foreign born:** Capps and Ruiz Soto, "Profile of Houston's Diverse Immigrant Population," 33.

139 **a hundred languages sound:** Monica Rhor, *HC*, March 8, 2015.

139 **a quarter million Muslims:** St. John Barned-Smith, *HC*, Oct. 22, 2016.

139 **Thirty percent of the region's immigrants:** Capps and Ruiz Soto, "Profile of Houston's Diverse Immigrant Population," 2, 7.

139 **More than one in seven kids has a parent in the country illegally:** Capps and Ruiz Soto, "Profile of Houston's Diverse Immigrant Population," 17.

140 **One of the deadliest smuggling incidents:** Simon Romero and David Barboza, *NYT*, May 15, 2003; Simon Romero, *NYT*, May 16, 2003; Kate Zernike, *NYT*, May 21, 2003.

140 **Shipley Do-Nuts:** Karen Chen, *HC*, May 24, 2015; Robert Downen, *HC*, March 5, 2018.

140 **"no matter how the questions are worded":** Stephen L. Klineberg, "The Kinder Houston Area Survey: Thirty-six Years of Measuring Responses to a Changing America," Kinder Institute for Urban Research, Rice University, May 2017.

140 **"a place where the immigrant experience":** Rhor, *HC*, May 8, 2015.

140 **Filipinos in the United States have more education:** Among Filipino immigrants, 50 percent have bachelor's or graduate degrees, compared with 32 percent of native-born Americans. The Filipino poverty rate (5.9 percent) was less than half the native-born average (13.1 percent). Among the ten largest immigrant groups, Filipinos' household income ($90,300) ranked second only to Indians' ($120,100) and far exceeded that of native-born Americans ($60,800). Unpublished analysis of U.S. Census Bureau data by Jeanne Batalova, MPI.

140 **More than 70 percent speak English:** Unpublished analysis of U.S. Census Bureau data by Jeanne Batalova, MPI.

140 **85 percent are present legally:** Sierra Stoney and Jeanne Batalova, "Filipino Immigrants in the United States," MPI, June 5, 2013.

141 **Filipinos are here because we were there:** Espiritu, *Home Bound*, 25.

141 **Filipinos in the U.S. Navy:** Espiritu, *Home Bound*, 29, 227n28. Those who served three years or more were eligible to naturalize.

141 **over two decades more than 100,000 went:** H. Brett Melendy, "Filipinos," in *Harvard Encyclopedia of American Ethnic Groups*, ed. Stephen Thernstrom, Ann Orlov, and Oscar Handlin (Cambridge, Mass.: Harvard University Press, 1980), 357.

141 **Alaskan canneries:** Chris's grandfather, whom he never met, spent seven years as an *Alaskero* and named one of his daughters after an American movie star, Glenda Farrell.

141 **"Positively No Filipinos Allowed":** Espiritu, *Home Bound*, 45.

141 **"ten years removed from a bolo":** E. S. Bogardus, "Anti-Filipino Race Riots: A Report Made to the Ingram Institute of Social Science of San Diego," May 15, 1930, 9.

141 **Four hundred white men rioted:** Ronald Takaki, *In the Heart of Filipino America: Immigrants from the Pacific Isles* (New York: Chelsea House, 1995), 51.

141 **to petition relatives under a system:** Each country is limited to no more than 7 percent of the family visas the United States issues each year. There are so many Filipinos trying to bring relatives that waiting times for some family visas, especially those for siblings, can exceed twenty years.

CHAPTER EIGHT: HARD LANDING

145 **not designed "with habitation in mind":** Paul Burka, "Grande Dame of the Gulf," *Texas Monthly*, Dec. 1983.

145 **95 percent of the state's trade goods:** Gary Cartwright, *Galveston: A History of the Island* (Fort Worth, Tex.: TCU Press, 1991), 117.

145 **eight newspapers, three concert halls, and an opera house:** Cartwright, *Galveston*, 118.

145 **It killed almost a fifth:** Burka, "Grande Dame of the Gulf."

146 **Depression-era speakeasies slowed the decline:** Cartwright, *Galveston*, 211.

146 **Galveston "knows its future can never equal":** Burka, "Grande Dame of the Gulf."

146 **Eighty percent of the homes:** Audrey White, *NYT*, April 26, 2013.

146 **marooned boats:** Mimi Swartz, "Emergency!" *Texas Monthly*, Jan. 2009.

146 **more than $700 million of damage:** *HC*, Oct. 12, 2008.

154 **Rosalie's doubts had ample precedent:** Mark Wyman, *Round-Trip to America: The Immigrants Return to Europe, 1880–1930* (Ithaca, N.Y.: Cornell University Press, 1993). Hungarian, 91; Pole, 90; Irishman, 74; Russian, 73; Lithuanian, 87; Franklin, 4.

154 **"Some of them had been in America":** Dickens, *American Notes for General Circulation*, 242; cited in Wyman, *Round-Trip to America*, 4.

155 **"I was surprised and indignant":** Wyman, *Round-Trip to America*, 117.

155 **"At home, their dream was of America":** Wyman, *Round-Trip to America*, 51. Some of the return migrants, staying put, fell into nostalgia for the place they unhappily left. I noticed the same dynamic among Rosalie's uncles when they talked about Saudi Arabia: it was both the place where they had suffered and where their youthful dreams had shone.

CHAPTER NINE: JUST LIKE A FAMILY

163 **named for a real beauty queen:** Lara was named for Precious Lara Quigaman, who won the Miss International contest in 2005, a few weeks before Lara was born.

164 supporters of public education: Beyond the British, the settler population included sizable groups of German, Dutch, French, and Scots-Irish. Benjamin Rush, a signer of the Declaration of Independence, argued that public schools would make Americans "more homogeneous" and "fit them for uniform and peaceable government." Paula S. Fass, "Immigration and Education in the United States," in *A Companion to American Immigration*, ed. Reed Ueda (West Sussex: Wiley-Blackwell, 2011), 492.

164 Jane Addams denounced: In a 1908 address to the National Education Association, Addams warned that weakened parental authority could lead to more delinquency and urged teachers to respect immigrant culture: "The public school too often separates the child from his parents and widens that old gulf between fathers and sons." Jane Addams, "The Public School and the Immigrant Child," *Journal of Proceedings of the National Education Association* 46 (1908): 99–102.

165 "the great savior": Addams, "Public School and the Immigrant Child."

165 the difference in outcomes is growing: Jason DeParle, *NYT*, Dec. 23, 2012.

165 10 percent of the K–12 population: "English Language Learners in Public Schools," website of the National Center for Education Statistics.

165 About three-quarters are Latino: "ELL Information Center Fact Sheet, No. 3," MPI, 2010.

165 fewer than a third of English-language learners: The federal government hasn't done a study since 2002, when it found 32 percent of ELL students received any bilingual instruction. Given the resistance to dual-language instruction, the figure is probably much lower now. Author communication with Rebecca Callahan, University of Texas.

165 some recent evidence: See, for instance, a large study of the Portland, Oregon, public schools by the Rand Corporation and the American Councils for International Education, which found children who started bilingual instruction in kindergarten were about nine months ahead of their peers on reading tests by eighth grade. Jennifer L. Steele et al., "Effects of Dual-Language Immersion Programs on Student Achievement: Evidence from Lottery Data," *American Educational Research Journal* 54, no. 1, suppl (April 2017): 282S–306S.

165 most non-English speakers are in weak schools: "The problem of English learners' underachievement, like that of other Latino students, is more likely related to the quality of education that these students receive, regardless of the language of instruction." Patricia Gándara and Frances Contreras, *The Latino Education Crisis: The Consequence of Failed Social Policies* (Cambridge, Mass.: Harvard University Press, 2009), 145. Starting in the late 1990s, a team of sociologists followed 407 newly arrived immigrants in fifty-one schools in Boston and San Francisco. They found the schools "toxic sinkholes . . . ugly, hostile, and dangerous. . . . Paradoxically, many families migrate to seek a better education for their children, only to find their children mired in the worst schools in the United States." Carola Suárez-Orozco, Marcelo M. Suárez-Orozco, and Irina Todorova, *Learning a New Land: Immigrant Students in American Society* (Cambridge, Mass.: Belknap Press, 2008), 266.

165 about twice the average rate: Rebecca M. Callahan, "The English Learner Dropout Dilemma: Multiple Risks and Multiple Resources," California Dropout Research Project Report No. 19, 2013.

166 "a listing ship": Dolph Tillotson, *Galveston Daily News*, May 16, 2010.

166 The program for English-language learners: Galveston's program for English-language learners earned a rare investigation from state officials and a scathing

report. The investigators found the district failed to identify limited-English students, failed to track their progress, "lacked a curriculum," suffered a shortage of teachers and materials, and made Spanish-speaking parents feel unwelcome. In a high school with 120 limited-English students, there was a single Spanish-language textbook for both biology and algebra I. Texas Education Agency, "Bilingual Education/English as a Second Language: Preliminary On-Site Findings Report 084-902," attached in correspondence from Laura Taylor, associate commissioner, to Lynne Cleveland, superintendent, Galveston Independent School District, Oct. 30, 2009.

166 Only 19 percent: Rhiannon Meyers, *Galveston Daily News*, Feb. 6, 2008.

CHAPTER TEN: THE GOOD NURSE

179 "The notion that we would have": Barack Obama, "Remarks and Discussion at the Closing Session of the White House Forum on Health Reform," March 5, 2009.

179 more than 90 percent of nurses are women: Website of the Kaiser Family Foundation, "Total Number of Professional Active Nurses by Gender."

179 most first-wave feminists regarded: Between the early 1970s and the late 1990s, the share of young women with an interest in nursing declined about 40 percent. Douglas O. Staiger, David I. Auerbach, and Peter I. Buerhaus, "Expanding Career Opportunities for Women and the Declining Interest in Nursing as a Career," *Nursing Economic$* 18, no. 5 (Oct. 2000): 234.

179 about a third of the workforce growth: Linda H. Aiken, "U.S. Nurse Labor Market Dynamics Are Key to Global Nurse Sufficiency," *HSR: Health Services Research* 42, no. 3, pt. 2 (June 2007): 1299–320.

180 "a permanent feature of the nursing workforce": Barbara L. Nichols, Catherine R. Davis, and Donna R. Richardson, "International Models of Nursing," in *The Future of Nursing: Leading Change, Advancing Health*, Institute of Medicine (Washington, DC: National Academies Press, 2011), app. J, 631.

180 In the first six or seven years of the twenty-first century: Organization for Economic Cooperation and Development, "International Migration of Health Workers: Improving International Co-operation to Address the Global Health Workforce Crisis" (Policy Brief, Feb. 2010), 3. The figures cover 2001 to 2007 or 2008, depending on the country.

180 group of about twenty mostly rich countries: The countries include Australia, Canada, France, Italy, Switzerland, and the United Kingdom. Data for 2015 are from the OECD, available online at www.oecd-ilibrary.org/.

180 A quarter of the nurses in London: Linda H. Aiken et al., "Trends in International Nurse Migration," *Health Affairs* 23, no. 3 (2004): 73.

180 "The Philippines must be half-empty": *Independent*, Feb. 21, 2013.

180 Ireland, a classic nurse supplier: By 2008, 47 percent of the nurses in Ireland were trained abroad. OECD, "International Migration of Health Workers," 3.

180 Jamaica sends nurses to the United States: Marla E. Salmon et al., "Managed Migration: The Caribbean Approach to Addressing Nursing Services Capacity," *HSR: Health Services Research* 42, no. 3, pt. 2 (June 2007): 1354–72.

180 about 8 percent of registered nurses: The figure counts those born and trained abroad, like Rosalie. Others immigrated as children and became nurses in the States. Aiken, "U.S. Nurse Labor Market Dynamics Are Key to Global Nurse Sufficiency," 1299.

180 **a fifth of the workforce:** In 2010, the share of the nursing workforce born and trained abroad ranged from 30 percent in the District of Columbia and 26 percent in California to less than 1 percent in West Virginia, North Dakota, and Wyoming. Patricia Cortés and Jessica Pan, "The Relative Quality of Foreign Nurses in the United States" (working paper, June 2012), table A1.

180 **more than a third are Filipino:** Aiken, "U.S. Nurse Labor Market Dynamics Are Key to Global Nurse Sufficiency," 1306.

180 **displace natives or depress their wages:** Dozens of studies have examined the impact of immigration on the employment and wages of natives in general, and most find the impact, if any, is small. Only a few have specifically examined nurses. The economists Robert Kaestner and Neeraj Kaushal found only "weak" evidence for the theory that nurse importation hurts domestic nurses. They found that a 10 percent increase in the foreign-nurse supply reduced the earnings of U.S. nurses by 1 to 4 percent but had no effect on their wages. They said the inconsistency in the findings "is not easily explained" and suggests that if nurse importation has a negative effect, it is modest. Robert Kaestner and Neeraj Kaushal, "Effect of Immigrant Nurses on Labor Market Outcomes of U.S. Nurses," *Journal of Urban Economics* 71, no. 2 (March 2012): 219–29. Likewise, Patricia Cortés and Jessica Pan found "little evidence of wage declines in response to the influx of foreign nurses." But they did find "large displacement effects—over a ten-year period, for every foreign nurse that migrates to a city, between 1 and 2 fewer native nurses are employed." They speculated that a rise in foreign nurses may make the workplace less appealing to natives. Patricia Cortés and Jessica Pan, "Foreign Nurse Importation and the Supply of Native Nurses," *Journal of Health Economics* 37 (2014): 164–80. Edward J. Schumacher found foreign nurses typically earn about 10 percent less than natives when they first arrive but catch up within four years and have "little to no wage effects" on natives. Edward J. Schumacher, "Foreign-Born Nurses in the U.S. Labor Market," *Health Economics* 20 (2011): 362–78.

181 **foreign nurses, who have more education:** The economists Patricia Cortés and Jessica Pan found "the majority of foreign nurses have at least a bachelor's degree, whereas a larger fraction of natives have an associate's degree." The Filipino nurses were paid 8 percent more in 2000 and 4 percent more in 2010. Patricia Cortés and Jessica Pan, "The Relative Quality of Foreign-Educated Nurses in the United States," *Journal of Human Resources* 5, no. 4 (2015): 1009–50.

181 **$60 an hour for the foreign nurses:** Of the $60 an hour, the nurses got half for the duration of the contracts—generally about two years. After that, the hospital hired them directly, at about $37 to $39 an hour, depending on their training and experience. Author communication with Chelita Thomas.

181 **praise their attitudes and skills:** Interviewing ten managers of foreign nurses, Rose O. Sherman and Terry Eggenberger found them "overwhelmingly positive about their experiences with international nurses. They commented frequently that the nurses were smart, willing to learn, loyal, and hard-working." Rose O. Sherman and Terry Eggenberger, "Transitioning Internationally Recruited Nurses into Clinical Settings," *Journal of Continuing Education in Nursing* 39, no. 12 (Dec. 2008): 535–44. Citing research by the Commission on Graduates of Foreign Nursing Schools, two other researchers write that "the majority of nurse executives view the hiring of international nurses as positive," although they caution that the "transition into U.S. practice can be

challenging." Patricia A. Edwards and Catherine R. Davis, "Internationally Educated Nurses' Perceptions of Their Clinical Competence," *Journal of Continuing Education in Nursing* 37, no. 6 (Nov./Dec. 2006): 265–69.

181 **premium "reflects actual quality differences":** Cortés and Pan, "Relative Quality of Foreign-Educated Nurses in the United States," 1011. Elsewhere the same authors wrote, "We provide strong evidence that foreign nurses, in particular Filipinos, are on average more productive than native nurses." Cortés and Pan, "Foreign Nurse Importation and the Supply of Native Nurses," 165.

181 **foreign staffing could be detrimental:** The percentage of foreign nurses had no effect on patient outcomes in hospitals with better-than-average nurse-patient ratios. But in hospitals with average or poor staffing ratios, those with a high percentage of foreign nurses (25 percent or more) had higher mortality rates. It's not clear whether that's because the foreign nurses were less skilled or whether the hospitals where they were concentrated had other problems, which might have hampered their ability to attract natives. Donna Felber Neff et al., "Utilization of Non-US Educated Nurses in US Hospitals: Implications for Hospital Mortality," *International Journal for Quality in Health Care* 25, no. 4 (2013): 366–72. A related study found that hospitals with high shares of foreign-educated nurses had modestly lower patient satisfaction scores. In hospitals where foreign nurses were less than 14.3 percent of the staff, 61 percent of patients gave the hospital the highest rating (a 9 or 10 on a 1-to-10 scale). In hospitals where foreign nurses were 14.3 percent or more of the staff, 57 percent of patients gave the highest rating. The authors said the lower satisfaction could reflect lower productivity among foreign nurses, communication problems, or workplace discrimination. Hayley D. Germack et al., "U.S. Hospital Employment of Foreign-Educated Nurses and Patient Experience: A Cross-Sectional Study," *Journal of Nursing Regulation* 8, no. 3 (Oct. 2017): 26–35.

181 **about 70 percent of migrant nurses:** Cortés and Pan, "Foreign Nurse Importation and the Supply of Native Nurses," 166.

181 **more education generally improves patient outcomes:** Linda H. Aiken writes, "There is ample evidence, however, that a more educated nurse workforce is associated with better patient outcomes." Aiken, "U.S. Nurse Labor Market Dynamics," 1314.

181 **Research also shows that numbers matter:** "Higher patient loads have been associated with more medical errors, longer hospitalization, lower patient satisfaction, and increases in the mortality rate." Cortés and Pan, "Foreign Nurse Importation and the Supply of Native Nurses," 164.

189 **A landmark study published in 2000:** Linda T. Kohn, Janet M. Corrigan, and Molla S. Donaldson, *To Err Is Human: Building a Safer Health System* (Washington, DC: National Academies Press, 2000).

192 **as many as 40 percent:** Linda H. Aiken et al., "Hospital Nurse Staffing and Patient Mortality, Nurse Burnout, and Job Dissatisfaction," *JAMA* 288, no. 16 (2002): 1987–93.

CHAPTER ELEVEN: RUFFLED FEATHERS

201 **"When the two are working":** Patricia Pessar, "The Role of Gender in Dominican Settlement in the United States," in *Women and Change in Latin America*, ed. June Nash and Helen Safa (South Hadley, Mass.: Bergin and Garvey, 1986), 273.

201 **Sheba George's study:** Sheba Mariam George, *When Women Come First: Gender and Class in Transnational Migration* (Berkeley: University of California Press, 2005), 68, 92, 132. Another study of Indian immigrants compared the husbands of nurses with the wives of engineers. In each case, spouses who followed their partners to the States lost earnings and status. But the women could fall back on traditional identities as wives and mothers, while "men merely suffer humiliation." Pallavi Bannerjee, "Constructing Dependence: Visa Regimes and Gendered Migration in Families of Indian Professional Workers, " PhD diss., (University of Illinois, Chicago, 2012), 131.

202 **poor Salvadorans in San Francisco:** Cecilia Menjívar, *Fragmented Ties: Salvadoran Immigrant Networks in America* (Berkeley: University of California Press, 2000), 169.

202 **middle-class Koreans in New York:** Pyong Gap Min, *Changes and Conflicts: Korean Immigrant Families in New York* (Boston: Allyn & Bacon, 1998), 51–55.

202 **Dominican men in New York:** Sherri Grasmuck and Patricia R. Pessar, *Between Two Islands: Dominican International Migration* (Berkeley: University of California Press, 1991), 156.

203 **"Here, the woman is the king":** Nazli Kibria, *Family Tightrope: The Changing Lives of Vietnamese Americans* (Princeton, N.J.: Princeton University Press, 1993), 108, 146.

203 **Gender relations weren't on my mind:** These assertions of masculinity, I came to realize, had been part of local Filipino life since the first nurses arrived in the 1960s. It took little—often, nothing—to prompt men of this generation to boast of their sexual conquests. One past leader of the local Filipino association told me he had outearned his wife as a mechanic and demonstrated his independence by cheating on her. Another volunteered the story of impregnating, and ditching, an American woman. A Filipino doctor, unable to practice medicine in the States, told me he became an alcoholic and was gripped by "extreme possessiveness" toward his breadwinning wife. "In the U.S. it's easy to get a man," he said. "If she's gone, I cannot do anything at all."

205 **The most famous scholar to explore cockfighting:** Clifford Geertz, "Deep Play: Notes on the Balinese Cockfight," in *The Cockfight: A Casebook*, ed. Alan Dundes (Madison: University of Wisconsin Press, 1994), 94–132.

212 **why workers in Sussex County, Delaware:** Timothy J. Dunn, Ana Maria Aragones, and George Shivers, "Recent Mexican Migration in the Rural Delmarva Peninsula: Human Rights Versus Citizenship Rights in a Local Context," in *New Destinations: Mexican Immigration in the United States,* ed. Víctor Zúñiga and Rubén Hernández-León (New York: Russell Sage Foundation, 2005), 162.

212 **persistence of ethnic connections:** I'm grateful to Professor Philip Kasinitz of the CUNY Graduate Center for the insight on how migrant networks defy modern assumptions about social organization.

212 **Manhattan cafeteria:** Mary C. Waters, *Black Identities: West Indian Immigrant Dreams and American Realities* (New York: Russell Sage Foundation, 1999), 105.

213 **"They bring in their friend":** Philip Kasinitz and Jan Rosenberg, "Missing the Connection: Social Isolation and Employment on the Brooklyn Waterfront," *Social Problems* 43, no. 2 (May 1996): 188.

213 **"personable and easy":** Sandra Susan Smith, "A Test of Sincerity: How Black and Latino Service Workers Make Decisions About Making Referrals," *Annals of the American Academy of Political and Social Science* 629, no. 1 (May 2010): 37.

214 **"physical assault and riot"**: Victor Greene, *For God and Country: The Rise of Polish and Lithuanian Ethnic Consciousness in America* (Madison: State Historical Society of Wisconsin, 1975), 68.

214 **"overly romanticized notions of immigrant unity"**: Menjívar, *Fragmented Ties*, 241.

CHAPTER TWELVE: INFERRING AMERICA

221 **recent immigrants in San Francisco and Boston:** Suárez-Orozco, Suárez-Orozco, and Todorova, *Learning a New Land*, 35.

CHAPTER THIRTEEN: MORAL HAZARDS

233 **exercise in "myth-manufacturing":** Peter Brimelow, *Alien Nation: Common Sense About America's Immigration Disaster* (New York: Random House, 1995), 15.

233 **the statue's French promoters:** For accounts of the statue's origins, see Peter Skerry, "Mother of Invention," *Wilson Quarterly* (Summer 2006): 44, and John Higham, "The Transformation of the Statue of Liberty," in *Send These to Me: Immigrants in Urban America*, rev. ed. (Baltimore: Johns Hopkins University Press, 1984).

234 **"the rule of law" or to "stay and fight":** Roy Beck, *The Case Against Immigration: The Moral, Economic, Social, and Environmental Reasons for Reducing U.S. Immigration Back to Traditional Levels* (New York: W. W. Norton, 1996), 61.

234 **"That poem that you're referring to":** Peter Baker, *NYT*, Aug. 3, 2017.

234 **"poor brown people":** Ann Coulter, *¡Adios, America! The Left's Plan to Turn Our Country into a Third World Hellhole* (Washington, DC: Regnery, 2015), 27.

234 **Barbara Jordan:** The U.S. Commission on Immigration Reform (or "Jordan Commission") would have reduced legal immigration to 550,000, from a baseline of 725,000, after a period of increased admissions to reduce backlogs. It called immigration a source of economic strength, cultural richness, and global leadership but also warned immigrants may compete with low-wage workers, impose fiscal costs, or stir ethnic tensions. U.S. Commission on Immigration Reform, *Legal Immigration: Setting Priorities* (Washington, DC: Government Printing Office, 1995).

235 **there's no objectively right amount:** I thank the journalist James Traub for making that point in a helpful conversation.

235 **helped the American economy:** The National Academy concluded "immigration is integral to the nation's economic growth." It has helped the United States avoid the demographic problems of aging societies like Japan, and high-skilled immigration has "boosted the nation's capacity for innovation, entrepreneurship, and technological change." In addition, immigrant labor benefits consumers by reducing the prices of goods and services in areas that include "child care, food preparation, house-cleaning and repair, and construction." Blau and Mackie, *The Economic and Fiscal Consequences of Immigration*, 6.

235 **Many are doubly disadvantaged:** Nearly half the unauthorized twenty-five-year-olds or older lack a high school degree. Julia Gelatt and Jie Zong, "Settling In: A Profile of the Unauthorized Population in the United States," MPI, Nov. 2018, 5.

235 **They are raising about five million children:** Gelatt and Zong, "Settling In," 4.

235 **About 7 percent of all children:** Randy Capps, Michael Fix, and Jie Zong, "A Profile of U.S. Children with Unauthorized Immigrant Parents," MPI, Jan. 2016, 3.

236 **the so-called Dreamers:** About 700,000 of the so-called Dreamers are covered under Deferred Action for Childhood Arrivals, or DACA, the 2012 program President Obama created by executive order. But many undocumented immigrants who arrived as children did not qualify. Estimates of the total population have reached as high as two million. Author communication with Randy Capps, MPI.

236 **"Every illegal alien must understand":** Mark Krikorian, *The New Case Against Immigration: Both Legal and Illegal* (New York: Sentinel, 2008), 219.

236 **"You should be uncomfortable":** The official was Thomas D. Homan, the acting director of U.S. Immigration and Customs Enforcement, in 2017 testimony to Congress. Randy Capps et al., *Revving Up the Deportation Machinery: Enforcement and Pushback Under Trump*, MPI, May 2018, 1.

236 **children of a woman deported to Honduras:** Sarah Stillman and Micah Hauser, "Parenting While Deported," *Politics and More* (podcast), Sept. 10, 2018.

236 **UCLA researchers surveyed:** Patricia Gándara and Jongyeon Ee, "U.S. Immigration and Enforcement Policy and Its Impact on Teaching and Learning in the Nation's Schools," Feb. 28, 2018.

237 **"Immigrants don't bother learning English":** Coulter, *¡Adios, America!*, 147.

237 **"Today's immigrants are actually learning English faster":** Waters and Pineau, *Integration of Immigrants into American Society*, 313.

237 **arrive already knowing English:** Waters and Pineau, *Integration of Immigrants into American Society*, 314.

237 **children of immigrants in New York City:** Philip Kasinitz et al., *Inheriting the City: The Children of Immigrants Come of Age* (New York: Russell Sage Foundation, 2008), 243, 256.

237 **"linguistically isolated":** Among children of immigrants, about 22 percent live in households where no adult speaks English very well. Waters and Pineau, *Integration of Immigrants into American Society*, 310.

237 **"Immigrants and their descendants are learning":** Waters and Pineau, *Integration of Immigrants into American Society*, 332.

238 **"most insidious costs":** Beck, *Case Against Immigration*, 215.

238 **"inconclusive":** Krikorian, *New Case Against Immigration*, 83–84.

238 **"*less likely* than natives":** Waters and Pineau, *Integration of Immigrants into American Society*, 330, 326.

238 **"The *reconquista* of Alta California":** Patrick J. Buchanan, *State of Emergency: The Third World Invasion and Conquest of America* (New York: Thomas Dunne Books/ St. Martin's Press, 2006), 12.

238 **"demographic *reconquista*":** Samuel P. Huntington, *Who Are We? The Challenges to America's National Identity* (New York: Simon & Schuster, 2004), 221.

239 **"no reason for Republicans to legalize":** Coulter, *¡Adios, America!*, 6.

239 **"Many demographers believe Texas will turn blue":** Jon Feere, "CPAC 2016 Event on Immigration Rhetoric," Center for Immigration Studies, March 3, 2016.

239 **"The ceaseless importation of Third World foreigners":** Publius Decius Mus, "The Flight 93 Election," *Claremont Review of Books*, Sept. 5, 2016.

239 **"Every hour sees the black man"**: Beck, *Case Against Immigration*, 159. Beck devotes
two of his ten chapters to arguing that immigration harms blacks.

239 **Douglass later became a vocal supporter**: Douglass's views changed after the Civil
War, when he became more hopeful about the cause of racial equality. He opposed
efforts to exclude the Chinese, spoke of migration as a human right, and celebrated
ethnic diversity as an American strength, in terms that anticipated the imagery of the
melting pot. In an 1869 speech called "Our Composite Nationality," Douglass said, "I
have a great respect for the blue eyed and light haired races of America. . . . But I reject
the arrogant and scornful theory by which they would limit migratory rights, and any
other essential human rights to themselves, and which would make them the owners
of this great continent to the exclusion of all other races of men. . . . We shall mold
them all, each after his kind, into Americans; Indian and Celt; negro and Saxon;
Latin and Teuton; Mongolian and Caucasian; Jew and Gentile; all shall here bow to
the same law, speak the same language, support the same Government, enjoy the same
liberty, vibrate with the same national enthusiasm, and seek the same national ends."
Frederick Douglass, "Our Composite Nationality," in *The Speeches of Frederick
Douglass*, ed. John R. McKivigan, Julie Husband, and Heather L. Kaufman (New
Haven, Conn.: Yale University Press, 2018), 278; author communication with David
Blight, Yale University; see also Ilya Somin, *WP*, April 10, 2014.

239 **"For European-American society and culture"**: DeParle, *NYT*, April 17, 2011.

239 **"when you enter the INS waiting rooms"**: Brimelow, *Alien Nation*, 28.

240 **"People notice when their little girls are raped"**: Coulter, *¡Adios, America!*, 28.

240 **Do immigrants threaten jobs**: I thank Professor Lawrence Katz of Harvard for taking
time to discuss the labor market impacts of immigration.

241 **High school dropouts**: Dropouts, though the most vulnerable workers, are a declining
share of the native-born workforce. From 1980 to 2000, the share of native workers
without a high school degree fell from 24 percent to 9 percent among men and from 19
percent to 7 percent among women. George J. Borjas and Lawrence F. Katz, "The
Evolution of the Mexican Born Workforce in the United States," National Bureau of
Economic Research, April 2005, 54.

241 **"a wage reduction of at least three percent:"** George J. Borjas, *We Wanted Workers:
Unraveling the Immigration Narrative* (New York: W. W. Norton & Co., 2016), 149.
Borjas's estimate of a wage reduction of at least 3 percent assumes a 10 percent increase in immigrants with the same skills as low-skilled natives. Under rare circumstances, he argues, the wage reduction could be as high as 10 percent. His estimates are
higher than those of most other economists.

241 **fiscal costs**: In addition to varying by generation, fiscal costs vary by the skills of the
immigrants and the level of state spending. Estimates also depend greatly on the treatment of "public goods," like the cost of national defense. (Each new immigrant doesn't
increase defense spending, but assigning him a share of the defense budget makes immigration seem more expensive.) Under the strictest assumptions (sharing the costs of
public goods), the National Academy estimates that immigrants cost state governments $1,600 a year, but their grown children save states $1,700 a year. Blau and
Mackie, *Economic and Fiscal Consequences of Immigration*, 541.

241 **newcomers' level of education**: With the education levels of immigrants rising, the
Academy found that on average new immigrants produce a net fiscal benefit, over

seventy-five years, of $259,000. Blau and Mackie, *Economic and Fiscal Consequences of Immigration*, 430.

242 **"Productivity growth has steadily eroded":** McKinsey Global Institute, "The Future of Japan: Reigniting Productivity and Growth," Executive Summary, March 2015.

242 **the fear that assimilation is failing:** People concerned about assimilation correctly note that the last great wave of arrivals (1880 to 1921) was followed by a four-decade hiatus that allowed both sides to adjust: assimilation is harder when it occurs in a context of replenishment, as it does today.

242 **"The important thing" about earlier immigrants:** Lawrence Auster, *The Path to National Suicide: An Essay on Immigration and Multiculturalism* (Monterey, Va.: American Immigration Control Foundation, 1990), 46.

242 **"premodern habits":** Krikorian, *New Case Against Immigration*, 41, 39.

243 **"Those who chose to cross the Atlantic":** Huntington, *Who Are We?*, 189.

243 **"There is no room in this country":** Teddy Roosevelt's speech to the Knights of Columbus remains much quoted, but the educator John Dewey got the better end of the argument a year later in noting that ethnicity can serve as a bridge, rather than a barrier: "The point is to see to it that the hyphen connects instead of separates." J. Christopher Eisele, "John Dewey and the Immigrants," *History of Education Quarterly* 15, no. 1 (Spring 1975): 67–85.

243 **Coercive forms of assimilation:** For a discussion of how diversity helps facilitate assimilation, see Richard D. Alba and Victor Nee, *Remaking the American Mainstream: Assimilation and Contemporary Immigration* (Cambridge, Mass.: Harvard University Press, 2003).

243 **"We were becoming Americans by learning":** Kasinitz et al., *Inheriting the City*, 10.

244 **"Schools today are failing utterly":** Krikorian, *New Case Against Immigration*, 31.

244 **"two languages, two homes, and possibly":** Huntington, *Who Are We?*, 207.

244 **"The billions of dollars that ampersands":** Huntington, *Who Are We?*, 213.

245 **more than half lack high school educations:** Waters and Pineau, *Integration of Immigrants into American Society*, 250. About half of Mexicans are unauthorized. Author's communication with Randy Capps, MPI, who estimates the share is 47 percent.

245 **warned of an ethnic underclass:** One conservative concerned about an ethnic underclass is Reihan Salam of *National Review*. He has proposed a large amnesty in exchange for new rules on legal immigration that prioritize the highly skilled. "My greatest fear is that a decade or two from now, we will find that today's poor kids, and particularly the many millions of them with immigrant parents, will conclude that America has failed them. . . . our already threadbare social fabric might come undone." Reihan Salam, *Melting Pot or Civil War? A Son of Immigrants Makes the Case Against Open Borders* (New York: Sentinel, 2018), 177.

245 **Herbert J. Gans warned that the children:** "Second-Generation Decline: Scenarios for the Economic and Ethnic Futures of the Post-1965 American Immigrants," *Ethnic and Racial Studies* 15, no. 2 (1992): 182–83.

245 **"rainbow underclass":** Alejandro Portes and Rubén G. Rumbaut, *Legacies: The Story of the Immigrant Second Generation* (Berkeley: University of California Press, 2001), 45.

245 **"the new second generation seems to be achieving":** Portes and Rumbaut, *Legacies*, 268; intact families, 38; grades, 237.

245 **"In every case, the second generation":** Kasinitz et al., *Inheriting the City*, 16. Although the children of immigrants outperformed peers of the same race, they did not
close the gap with native-born whites; some critics have argued that comparing immigrants with disadvantaged minorities is not a reassuring gauge of success.

245 **Average schooling:** Waters and Pineau, *Integration of Immigrants into American Society*, 250. Among Central American men, the gain is even greater: average schooling
rise from 9.8 years among immigrants to 13.4 years among their children.

245 **College completion rates nearly triple:** From the first to the second generation, the
share of Mexicans without high school degrees falls from 55.2 percent to 15.2 percent,
while the share with college degrees climbs from 5.4 percent to 14.9 percent (Waters
and Pineau, *Integration of Immigrants into American Society*).

245 **down about 12 percent:** Passel and Cohn, "U.S. Unauthorized Immigrant Total Dips
to Lowest Level in a Decade," Nov. 28, 2018.

246 **"Parents' undocumented status":** Waters and Pineau, *Integration of Immigrants into
American Society*, 149.

246 **a Salvadoran suburb of Washington, DC:** Jason DeParle, *NYT*, April 18, 2009.

CHAPTER FOURTEEN:
SECOND-GENERATION AMPERSANDS

250 **straight-line assimilation:** For a classic version of straight-line assimilation, see
W. Lloyd Warner and Leo Srole, *The Social Systems of American Ethnic Groups*
(New Haven, Conn.: Yale University Press, 1945).

250 **"God Bless America" and "White Christmas":** Kasinitz et al., *Inheriting the City*, 355.

251 **"the blight of assimilationist ideology":** The 1970 quotation is from the historian Ru-
dolph Vecoli. Matthew Frye Jacobson, *Roots Too: White Ethnic Revival in Post–Civil
Rights America* (Cambridge, Mass.: Harvard University Press, 2006), 38.

251 **celebrated ethnic struggle:** As Matthew Frye Jacobson notes, the embrace of ethnic
identity offered a "haven of authenticity" in a soulless, homogenized world. But it also
had political uses, especially among conservative working-class whites who were re-
sisting black demands for busing and affirmative action. By embracing the struggles of
their immigrant ancestors, they could claim to be victims, too. "I'm not white, I'm
Italian"—so the slogan went (Jacobson, *Roots Too*, 23, 1).

251 **Statue of Liberty did a metaphorical about-face:** Richard Alba, *Ethnic Identity* (New
Haven, Conn.: Yale University Press, 1990), 1.

251 **"Symbolic ethnicity":** Herbert J. Gans, "Symbolic Ethnicity: The Future of Ethnic
Groups and Cultures in America," *Ethnic and Racial Studies* 2, no. 1 (1979): 1–20.

251 **"ethnic options":** Mary C. Waters, *Ethnic Options: Choosing Identities in America*
(Berkeley: University of California Press, 1990).

251 **"bumpy line":** Herbert J. Gans, "Ethnic Invention and Acculturation: A Bumpy-Line
Approach," *Journal of American Ethnic History* 12, no. 1 (Fall 1992): 42–52.

251 **assimilation prevailed:** "The word may be dead, the concept may be disreputable, but
the reality continues to flourish," wrote the sociologist Nathan Glazer in 1993. Nathan Glazer, "Is Assimilation Dead?," in *Incorporating Diversity: Rethinking Assimilation in a Multicultural Age*, ed. Peter Kivisto (New York: Routledge, 2016), 4, 125.

252 **"undesirable outcomes":** Portes and Rumbaut, *Legacies*, 59. Alejandro Portes is the
scholar more closely associated with the theory of "segmented assimilation," meaning

different segments of the immigrant population integrate into American society in sharply contrasting ways. While the privileged thrive, Portes fears the most disadvantaged may assimilate downward into an underclass.

252 **smoke, grow obese, or commit crimes:** Sabrina Tavernise, *NYT*, May 18, 2013; Waters and Pineau, *Integration of Immigrants into American Society*, 329.

252 **"combine the best of both worlds":** Kasinitz et al., *Inheriting the City*, 21.

252 **"can be highly conducive to success":** Kasinitz et al., *Inheriting the City*, 354.

252 **the two camps have warred:** They aired their differences in a three-part exchange in an academic journal. The optimists (Richard Alba, Philip Kasinitz, and Mary C. Waters) titled their article "The Kids Are (Mostly) Alright." The pessimists (William Haller, Alejandro Portes, and Scott M. Lynch), responded with "On the Dangers of Rosy Lenses." See *Social Forces* 89, no 3 (March 2011): 733–81.

252 **think about a different daughter:** I write less about Dominique because, arriving at a younger age, he was less able to express his thoughts and felt less of a conflict between his lives in the Philippines and the United States.

253 **an immigrant's belief in opportunity:** Kasinitz et al., *Inheriting the City*, 360.

254 **"Innovation . . . occurs":** Kasinitz et al., *Inheriting the City*, 355.

CHAPTER FIFTEEN: CRUISE SHIP CALAMITY

263 **up to a quarter of the world's maritime labor:** The IOM estimates Filipinos account for 20 to 25 percent of all international crews and cites a survey that found them 29 percent of cruise ship workers. *IOM Country Migration Report*, 71–72.

265 **Manu graduated with uncertain prospects:** Because there are so many schools, many seafaring graduates, like their counterparts in nursing, never find jobs.

266 **three or four times what a doctor makes:** The Philippine Department of Labor reports that salaries for general practitioners range from about $380 to $600 a month. www .ble.dole.gov.ph/index.php/doctor-general-practitioner.

267 **built in one country, owned in another:** Christine Chin, *Cruising in the Global Economy: Profits, Pleasure, and Work at Sea* (Burlington, Vt.: Ashgate, 2008), 32; see also Helen Sampson, "Transnational Drifters or Hyperspace Dwellers: An Exploration of the Lives of Filipino Seafarers Aboard and Ashore," *Ethnic and Racial Studies* 26, no. 2 (2003): 259.

267 **About two-thirds of cargo vessels:** Elizabeth R. DeSombre, *Flagging Standards: Globalization and Environmental, Safety, and Labor Regulations at Sea* (Cambridge, Mass.: MIT Press, 2006), 3.

267 **virtually all cruise ships:** Author communication with Doug Stevenson.

267 **Panama, the Bahamas, and Liberia:** Chin, *Cruising in the Global Economy*, 8.

267 **which swells remittances by $6 billion a year:** The Philippine Central Bank reports that in 2017 Filipino seafarers sent home $5.9 billion. www.bsp.gov.ph/statistics/efs _ext3.asp.

267 **a few swashbuckling entrepreneurs:** Kristoffer A. Garin, *Devils on the Deep Blue Sea: The Dreams, Schemes, and Showdowns That Built America's Cruise Ship Empires* (New York: Viking, 2005).

268 **investigation by *The New York Times*:** Douglas Frantz's reporting included stories that ran on Nov. 16, 1998 (shipboard crime); Jan. 3, 1999 (dumping waste); Feb. 19, 1999 (income tax); Oct. 31, 1999 (medical care); and Nov. 29, 1999 (port communities).

268 **two cruise ship incomes:** Both Ariane and Manu worked seven days a week. He made $1,450 a month (about $5.20 an hour) and she made about $2,000 with tips. Though they typically worked only eight or nine months, that still meant an annual income of $30,000 or more, when median family income is less than $6,000. See the Philippine Statistics Authority, Oct. 24, 2016, psa.gov.ph/content/average-family-income-2015 -estimated-22-thousand-pesos-monthly-results-2015-family-income.

268 **seafarers die on the job:** S. E. Roberts et al., "Fatal Accidents and Injuries Among Merchant Seafarers Worldwide," *Occupational Medicine* 64, no. 4 (2014).

268 **Lito Asignacion:** *Asignacion v. Rickmers Genoa Schiffahrtgesellschaft MBH & CIE* (U.S. Court of Appeals, Fifth Circuit, April 16, 2015).

268 **Potenciano Aggarao Jr.:** U.S. District Judge Catherine C. Blake, *Potenciano L. Aggarao Jr. v. MOL Ship Management Co. Ltd. et al.*, Aug. 7, 2014, 10.

269 **a Maersk safety manual warned:** Dutch Maritime Authority, "AP Moeller: Accident to Seafarer," Marine Accident report, Dec. 19, 2009.

269 **Houston Ship Channel:** U.S. Coast Guard, "Marine Safety Alert, Sector Houston-Galveston," May 26, 2011.

269 **"how horrific":** "Understanding Mooring Incidents," *LP News*, Jan. 2009.

269 **ready access to American courts:** Two Supreme Court cases, *Lauritzen v. Larsen* (1953) and *Hellenic Lines v. Rhoditis* (1970), cite eight principles to be considered in deciding whether U.S. courts should apply American law to a foreign seafarer's claim, including the nationalities of the owner and seafarers, the place of the injury, and the overall connection between the ship's enterprise and the United States. Writing for the Court in the latter case, Justice William O. Douglas warned against letting "the façade of the operation"—like foreign flagging—obscure the "actual operational contacts that the ship and owner have with the United States."

269 **"Generally poor and friendless":** *Harden v. Gordon*, "11F. Cas. 480, D. Maine, 1823."

270 **jobs (and remittances) were at risk:** Whether the jobs were really at risk is debatable: hiring had risen 20 percent in five years.

270 **"Our seafarers were perceived as":** *Linsangan v. Laguesma*, www.chanrobles.com /scresolutions/resolutions/2001/september/9-10%20143476.php.

270 **Fifth Circuit Court of Appeals upheld:** *Francisco v. Stolt Achievement MT* (U.S. Court of Appeals, Fifth Circuit, June 4, 2002).

270 **killing eight seafarers and seriously injuring ten:** National Transportation Safety Board, Marine Accident Brief, Accident No. DCA-03-MM-032.

270 **"pleaded guilty":** Jay Weaver and Curtis Morgan, *The Miami Herald*, May 3, 2008. The National Transportation Safety Board found the cruise line knew the boilers were faulty. Five years before the accident, an NCL port engineer warned a company vice president, "We must realize that we have reached a point where the operation of the vessel is not safe." NTSB Marine Accident Brief.

270 **offer of $11 million:** Jay Weaver, *The Miami Herald*, May 23, 2004.

270 **sent victims to arbitration:** Jay Weaver, *The Miami Herald*, Oct. 15, 2003.

270 **Another appeals court affirmed:** *Bautista v. Star Cruise Lines* (U.S. Court of Appeals, Eleventh Circuit, January 18, 2005). While the arguments are couched in legalese, the effect was a simple transfer of wealth from labor to capital. Colin Veitch, the CEO of NCL, said the decision saved the company $100 million. Patrick Danner, *The Miami Herald*, May 23, 2004.

273 **I knew a doctor:** I am grateful for the help of Dr. Richard Boxer.

275 **more bad news:** While the Philippine government boasts of its services for overseas works, it did nothing to help Manu with either his medical care or Ariane's visa, even with me pushing on his behalf. Many of the bureaucrats I had met over the years had seemed hardworking and caring. Perhaps with so many Filipinos abroad they were simply overwhelmed.

275 **no income and no visit:** While Ariane had no income after leaving the ship, Manu continued to get paid for several months.

276 **Dr. Lineen put a note in the file:** Dr. Lineen was uncertain whether Silversea or its insurer was in charge. After speaking with a Silversea doctor, he had the impression the cruise line was willing to let him stay and get his prosthesis in Miami. But he said the doctor told him the insurance firm was making the decisions.

276 **Manu would face "irreparable harm":** *Emmanuel Navarette v. Silversea Cruises, Ltd.*, Verified Seaman's Complaint for Maintenance and Cure, Feb. 17, 2014.

276 **reluctant litigant:** Manu feared that if he sued, the company might resist its obligation to buy Ariane a plane ticket; seeing her was his top priority.

276 **the process would be slow:** Manu's best hope was to argue that the award was so low that it violated the American public policy of protecting seafarers. Such "public policy defenses" could void arbitration agreements—parties can't surrender their fundamental rights—but first the case had to run its course in the Philippines. Manu would have to sue in Miami, where a judge would refuse to hear the case, and then ask the American judge to reconsider on the grounds that he had gotten a pittance. But the process could take years, and in the meantime Manu wouldn't see a cent.

277 **"pigs get slaughtered":** Jordan Weissman, *National Law Journal*, June 22, 2009.

277 **The deposition:** *Emmanuel Navarette v. Silversea Cruises, Ltd.* (U.S. District Court, Southern District of Florida), deposition of Dr. Seema Khurana, April 21, 2014.

279 **she'd have three days in Miami:** Though Manu's contract gave him the right to a plane ticket, there seemed little prospect of getting one in time from Silversea with Manu suing the company. I paid for it. This was another way in which the Philippine government's protections meant little in practice.

CHAPTER SIXTEEN: THE FILIPINO CUL-DE-SAC

283 **The uprooted had become the transplanted:** Oscar Handlin's classic immigration history, *The Uprooted*, emphasized the dislocation the European immigrants experienced, while John Bodnar's retort, a generation later, emphasized their ability to adapt. Oscar Handlin, *The Uprooted: The Epic Story of the Great Migrations That Made the American People* (Boston: Little, Brown, 1951); John Bodnar, *The Transplanted: A History of Immigrants in Urban America* (Bloomington: Indiana University Press, 1985).

284 **most decided to stay:** Of the nineteen foreign nurses hired, seventeen finished their contracts and fourteen stayed at the hospital as permanent employees. Three others left town, including the Filipino nurse who had vowed to leave Galveston and "move to the United States."

289 **average workweek:** Author communication with David Marshall, chief of nursing.

290 **hospital near Bakersfield:** Delano Medical Center. Anh Do, *LAT*, Sept. 18, 2012.

293 **botched antiterrorism raid:** Floyd Whaley, *NYT*, Feb. 7, 2015.

300 **"Sometimes Darth Vader wins":** Michael Powell, *NYT*, May 4, 2015.

301 **"U.S. has become a dumping ground":** "Here's Donald Trump's Presidential An-
nouncement Speech," *Time*, June 16, 2015. http://time.com/3923128/donald-trump
-announcement-speech/.

301 **Sharia law:** Maggie Haberman, *NYT*, March 22, 2016.

301 **"jobs, wages, housing, schools":** "Transcript of Donald Trump's Immigration Speech,"
NYT, Sept. 1, 2016.

301 **"We will not be taken advantage of":** Trump campaign, "Immigration Reform That
Will Make America Great Again," 2015.

301 **an old poem called "The Snake":** Eli Rosenberg, *WP*, Feb. 24, 2018.

EPILOGUE: COMPLETE

303 **"I'm going to be so presidential":** Wesley Morris, *NYT Magazine*, May 22, 2016.

303 **forty-six-year low:** Website of the Department of Homeland Security, https://www
.cbp.gov/sites/default/files/assets/documents/2019-Mar/bp-total-apps-fy1925-fy2018
.pdf.

303 **Authorities seized thousands of children:** The administration reported that it separated nearly 2,737 children under the "zero tolerance" policy that began in the spring
of 2018, but the inspector general of the Department of Health and Human Services
found that thousands more might have been separated in actions dating back to the
previous year. Miriam Jordan, *NYT*, Jan. 18, 2019.

304 **deported without their kids:** Kirk Semple and Miriam Jordan, *NYT*, Sept. 2, 2018.

304 **Haitians coming to the States "all have AIDS":** Julie Hirshfeld Davis and Michael
Shear, *NYT*, Dec. 23, 2017. The White House denied the story, which was based on
two anonymous sources, though Trump used similar language soon after in complaining about immigrants' "shithole countries."

304 **"shithole countries:"** Josh Dawsey, *WP*, Jan. 12, 2018. Trump waited several days before weakly disputing he had used that precise phrase, though two senators, Democrat
Richard Durbin of Illinois and Republican Lindsey Graham of South Carolina, confirmed he did. Thomas Kaplan, Noah Weiland, and Michael D. Shear, *NYT*, Jan. 15,
2018.

304 **"The president of the United States is a racist":** "So Much for the Beacon of Hope,"
Editorial Board, *NYT*, Jan. 13, 2018.

304 **excise the phrase "Nation of Immigrants":** Miriam Jordan, *NYT*, Feb. 27, 2018.

304 **"good thing" hit 75 percent:** Megan Brenan, "Record-High 75% of Americans Say Immigration Is Good Thing," Gallup, June 21, 2018. Gallup notes that support has run
strong even among Republicans. In 2018, 85 percent of Democrats and 65 percent of
Republicans considered immigration a good thing. "In all but one year since Gallup
started asking this question in 2001, majorities of Americans across party lines have
viewed immigration as a positive for the U.S."

304 **"We hereby raise a Sunday morning toast":** *HC*, Jan. 14, 2018.

305 **The previous Congress already included:** Katherine Schaeffer and Drew DeSilver,
"Immigrants or Children of Immigrants Make Up at Least 12% of Congress," Pew
Research Center, Aug. 21, 2018. While immigrants and their children make up 12
percent of Congress, they are about 26 percent of the population.

305 **To their ranks came two Muslim women:** The two Muslim women were Rashida
Tlaib of Michigan, whose parents are Palestinian immigrants, and Ilhan Omar of

Minnesota, a Somali American who arrived as a child refugee. The Ecuadorian-born woman is Debbie Murcasel-Powell of Florida. The son of Eritrean refugees is Joe Neguse of Colorado.

305 **More than thirty-seven hundred people drowned:** Jonathan Clayton and Hereward Hollard, "Over One Million Sea Arrivals Reach Europe in 2015," UN High Commissioner for Refugees, Dec. 30, 2015.

305 **fifteen hundred or more a day:** Suzanne Daley, *NYT*, Aug. 5, 2015.

305 **shouting "Merkel" and "Germany":** "Two Weeks in September: The Makings of Merkel's Decision to Accept Refugees," *Der Spiegel Online*, Aug. 24, 2016.

305 **a million people arrived in 2015:** Anna Sauerbray, *NYT*, Jan. 9, 2016.

305 **On New Year's Eve, scores of young men:** Alison Smale, *NYT*, April 28, 2016.

306 **Merkel's popularity:** Reuters, Aug. 5, 2016; Noah Barkin, Reuters, Sept. 10, 2017.

306 **Its foreign born were more skilled:** Simon Tilford, "Britain, Immigration, and Brexit," *CER Bulletin*, no. 105 (Dec. 2015–Jan. 2016).

306 **Britain attracted twenty times as many migrants:** Erica Consterdine, "The Huge Political Cost of Blair's Decision to Allow Eastern European Migrants Unfettered Access to Britain," *Conversation*, Nov. 16, 2016.

306 **By 2013, three-quarters of Britons:** Amanda Taub, *NYT*, June 21, 2016.

307 **"If you spend days, weeks":** Alex Massie, "A Day of Infamy," *Spectator*, June 26, 2016.

313 **a sale of a two-thirds stake:** "Royal Caribbean to Take Majority Stake in Luxury Line Silversea Cruises," *USA Today*, June 14, 2018.

314 **five siblings from four countries:** Rosalie was in the States; Roldan was in Abu Dhabi; Bhoyet was in Qatar; and Rolando and Rowena were in the Philippine compound.

INDEX